Wacker

SOCIAL CONFLICT

AND

SOCIAL MOVEMENTS

ANTHONY OBERSCHALL

Yale University

PRENTICE-HALL, INC.

Englewood Cliffs, New Jersey

Library of Congress Cataloging in Publication Data

OBERSCHALL, ANTHONY.
    Social conflict and social movements.

    Bibliography:
    1. Social conflict.   2. Social movements.
3. Social control.   I. Title.   [DNLM: 1. Conflict
(Psychology).   2. Social Problems.   HM 136 012s 1973]
HM136.02   301.6'3   72–6320
ISBN 0–13–815761–8

Prentice-Hall Series in Sociology, NEIL J. SMELSER, Editor

© 1973 by Prentice-Hall, Inc.
Englewood Cliffs, New Jersey

Printed in the United States of America

10   9   8   7   6   5   4   3

Prentice-Hall International, Inc., *London*
Prentice-Hall of Australia, Pty. Ltd., *Sydney*
Prentice-Hall of Canada, Ltd., *Toronto*
Prentice-Hall of India Private Limited, *New Delhi*
Prentice-Hall of Japan, Inc., *Tokyo*

Dedicated
to

JUAN LINZ

CONTENTS

PREFACE

This book is addressed to the general reader who, like the author, has lived through a decade of social conflict that might have left him in turn puzzled, hopeful, saddened, and perhaps also apprehensive about the future. But my intention is to provide more than reactions to and ad hoc commentaries on contemporary events—it is to bring to bear on the topic the systematic and disciplined thinking of social scientists and historians. Indeed, one of the pleasures of writing on social conflict is that one is able to carry on an intellectual dialogue with leading thinkers in many disciplines, for social conflict is a topic that resists efforts to confine and compartmentalize it. Those who are familiar with the works of Crane Brinton and George Rudé, Barrington Moore and Eric Wolf, Ralf Dahrendorf and Lewis Coser, Seymour Lipset and Samuel Hunting-ton, Charles Tilly and Ralph Turner, will realize how much of what is written here rests on their contributions.

The material covers many aspects of the topic: the causes of social conflict; the formation of conflict groups and social movements; partici-pation in opposition movements; the role of leaders and activists; the formulation and spread of ideologies; confrontation; the mechanisms of social control, and the processes of conflict regulation. Much has been written about the causes of social conflict and the sources of discontent. Because of this, my intention is to cover mainly those aspects of the topic that have received somewhat less attention, namely, the theory of mobilization and the process of confrontation, social control, and conflict regulation. I have tried to avoid polemics, because they belong more properly in the periodical literature than in a work of synthesis. The single exception is the theory of mass society, which offers an alternative approach to mobilization that I felt had to be met head on.

A word about theory. A theory in the usual sense is made up of hypotheses than can be empirically confirmed or disconfirmed, that are systematically linked in order to provide explanations for a large body of observations bearing on the same topic and that can be used to predict future events. Single hypotheses that repeatedly have been confirmed are best thought of as empirical generalizations. Conceptual schemes, typological elaborations, semantic analyses of concepts and terminological controversies cannot be empirically verified and are not theories; rather, they are approaches to a topic preparatory to the formulation of theory. Sociology has reached the stage where these preparatory activities need no longer hold center stage, as they have for so long. Many statements in this book are hypotheses and empirical generalizations, and some have been loosely linked into a partial system of explanation. But these pages do not provide a systematic and comprehensive theory of social conflict. For many reasons such an undertaking would be premature.

Instead, I have tried to make a plausible case for the hypotheses and generalizations that I advance in three ways: (1) by appealing to the common fund of experience and knowledge shared by the reader and myself; (2) by citing the views and positions expressed by other writers and theorists; and (3) by providing illustrative case materials from historical sources and contemporary events. Many of the illustrations are drawn from recent United States and African history, because I am most familiar with these events as participant-observer, citizen, and scholar. This diversity has one advantage: it shows that the approach and hypotheses offered here are not tailor-made to fit special situations but have a wide range of application. The reader may be unfamiliar with the substance and details of some case materials. To overcome this difficulty I have treated some cases extensively: the origins of the Nigerian civil war, the mobilization and confrontation processes during the Hungarian revolution of 1956, and the civil rights and black power movement in the United States. I only hope that my summaries of complex events and large bodies of observation are clear and have caught the essence of the conflicts and processes discussed.

Although I have tried to remain objective and dispassionate toward the topics and illustrations discussed, I have not attempted to eliminate my own personal opinions or bias altogether, an enterprise that would be doomed to failure in any case. I have no particular political and ideological ax to grind, and I am not writing to curry favor with or to discredit any particular group or constituency.

My intention to write a book about social movements and social conflict from the political sociology perspective originated in the mid-1960s when I started lecturing on these topics. None of the existing texts was entirely satisfactory for purposes of instruction, and the excellent textbook *Social Movements* (1951), written by Rudolf Heberle after the war, contained much that was dated. Much of the research for this volume was carried out from 1964 to 1968, and about one-half of the first draft was completed by the end of 1969. Two years of study and research in Africa, first in Uganda in 1965–1966 and later in Zambia in 1970–1971, interrupted the project, which was finally completed during the summer of 1971. Since then, I have added an introductory, historical chapter. Readers not interested in the history of sociological ideas might wish to start with chapter 2.

Some parts of the book have benefited from valuable criticism by students, friends, and colleagues, for which I am grateful. I owe an intellectual debt most of all to Juan Linz, with whom I first studied political sociology. I wish to thank the Society for the Study of Social Problems for permission to include portions of my paper "The Los Angeles Riot of August 1965," *Social Problems*, Vol. 15, No. 3 (1968), in the section entitled "The Behavior of Hostile Crowds"; Frank Cass and Co. Ltd. for permission to include portions of my paper "Rising Expectations and Political Turmoil," *Journal of Development Studies*, Vol. 6, No. 1 (October 1969), in the section entitled "Crises of National Unity in New States"; and the Law and Society Association for permission to reprint portions of my paper "Group Violence: Some Hypotheses and Empirical Uniformities," *Law and Society Review*, Vol. 5, No. 1 (August 1970), in several sections. I also wish to thank Mrs. Mary Moore for typing the manuscript and Mrs. Ruth Bush for compiling the index.

Chapter *I*

THE SOCIOLOGICAL STUDY OF CONFLICT, SOCIAL MOVEMENTS, AND COLLECTIVE BEHAVIOR

INTRODUCTION

Until well into the nineteenth century, theories of social conflict at the macrosocietal level were part and parcel of the basic writings of political theorists, political economists, and philosophers on society, the social order, and social change. To write about the antecedents of macrotheories of social conflict and social movements would be tantamount to writing the history of sociological thinking itself, starting with Marx and Tocqueville. This has been done interestingly and capably by a number of writers (Aron, 1968; Coser, 1965; Dahrendorf, 1959; Nisbet, 1966; Parsons, 1949) and need not be repeated here. The works of the classical theorists are now routinely taught at both the undergraduate and graduate levels of instruction. None of the great classical theorists, however, with the exception of Simmel, dealt systematically with middle-range and microlevel aspects of conflict (i.e., the group bases of social conflict and its psychological and social psychological foundations, including such topics as public opinion, crowds, sects, riots, and social movements).

The foundations of present-day theories of group conflict, collective behavior, and social movements were laid by the eighteenth-century *philosophes* and moral philosophers, by the late nineteenth-century French social scientists, social Darwinists, and historians who specialized in the French Revolution and in the history of the socialist and labor movements.

1

At the University of Chicago in the 1920s and 1930s, Robert Ezra Park formulated a sociological synthesis of these diverse traditions. More recently, Neil Smelser endeavored to do the same within the framework of Parsonian macrosociology and Freudian psychology. Political sociologists such as Lewis Coser, Barrington Moore, and Ralf Dahrendorf built on the classical theorists and the historians. Students in the Chicago tradition, especially Ralph Turner, Lewis Killian, and Joseph Gusfield, then combined the older Park approach with advances in social psychology and experimental psychology and also provided collective behavior theory with a wider and more accurate empirical foundation.

Most recently, Tilly and others succeeded in incorporating the work of contemporary European historians and of the political sociologists with existing sociological contributions in the collective behavior tradition, all within the framework of a sophisticated theory of social change. Tilly is also the first sociologist in this field whose theoretical work is based on constant interaction with a large body of data on civil disorders and group conflict, which he and his collaborators painstakingly assembled. Meanwhile, as a result of, first, the numerous studies and government commission reports based on the civil rights, black power, antiwar, and student movements in the 1960s; second, the many studies of nationalist movements in the former colonies and postindependence civil strife in the new states; and third, the impressive work by historians on popular movements, the empirical foundations of the study of group conflict and collective behavior have once and for all been firmly established.

Although closer collaboration and interchange between theorists and empirical workers, and among historians, political scientists, and sociologists have benefited all concerned, sociologists, with the exception of James Coleman (1966), have continued to neglect the very important contributions of economists to the study of conflict and collective action. This is a real loss, for economics has a firmer theoretical foundation and a more sophisticated methodology than the other social sciences. In particular, the distinctions between basic assumptions and hypotheses that ought to be tested; the difference between static and dynamic analysis; rigorous systems analysis based on sets of difference and differential equations; the link between macro- and microlevel theorizing; and an awareness of the possible contributions other social science disciplines might make to economic theory are more clearly articulated in economics than in the other social science disciplines. Therefore, it is fortunate that precisely at the three weakest points of sociological theories of conflict and collective behavior economists have done important work and produced useful results that can be exploited by sociologists.

The first point of weakness is the failure of sociologists to analyze microlevel and group processes from a dynamic rather than static perspective, a promising procedure even when a dynamic system cannot be fully specified. Game theory and the contributions of Boulding (1962) have been largely overlooked by sociologists. The second point of weakness is the lack of a theory of group formation and of mobilization and the filling of this gap with mass society theory and ad hoc applications of psychologistic concepts such as alienation and relative deprivation, even though the empirical evidence keeps accumulating against them. Olson's theory of collective action (1968) has shown a way out of this difficulty. The third point has to do with incorporating motivational assumptions into theory, specifically, what relative weights to give to rationality and nonrationality in social action—and to interests as opposed to beliefs and ideologies. Economists have succeeded in going a long way with a commonsense psychology that emphasizes rationality and self-interest. They have made important contributions to sociopolitical analysis from this perspective, as the works of Joseph Schumpeter, Anthony Downs, Mancur Olson, and Charles Lindblom attest. Might it not be that Parsons's reaction in the 1930s to the utilitarian component in neoclassical economic theory, which led him to emphasize the importance of values and of socialization in social action, useful as it was for a time, has actually become an obstacle to the further progress of sociological theory? I believe that the assumption of enlightened self-interest and the application of commonsense psychology (when it comes to *motivation*, but not to *perception*)—the legacies of the Scottish moralists—can be employed advantageously in theories of group conflict and collective behavior. This volume builds on the sociological foundations mentioned earlier and attempts to bridge the three gaps by borrowing from economics, with suitable modifications.

THE EIGHTEENTH-CENTURY BACKGROUND [*]

When one reads the writings of eighteenth-century moral philosophers, he cannot help but notice the frequent references to non-European peoples and their customs—Egyptians, Persians, Chinese, Turks, Arabs, Thais, American Indians—as well as to the deaf, dumb, and blind, wild boys found in the forest, orangutans and other apes, and the social animals such as ants and bees. What insights and knowledge did the *philosophes* hope to gain from discussing these topics at such length? The answer is, in contemporary language, that they were seeking among other things to lay the empirical foundations for theories of motivation and perception,

[*] This summary draws heavily on Cassirer (1955), Hazard (1935), Bryson (1945), Barth (1945), Lazarsfeld (1961), and my own earlier work on the history of social research (Lecuyer and Oberschall, 1968).

of norm formation and group processes that might explain the origins
and persistence of groups and larger social units such as nations and societies. The religious view of human nature, the medieval view of the social
order, the divine right theory of kings, had by then been largely discredited. More scientific explanations were sought to take their place.
By the first half of the eighteenth century the metaphysical doctrine of
innate ideas and of reason, entrenched in Cartesian philosophy, was being undermined by Locke and his followers. Not only reason but also
sentiments and nonrational beliefs (superstitions, religious fanaticism),
were being subjected to critical scrutiny. Shaftesbury inveighed against
"enthusiasm"—the misdirected, emotional, fanatical religiosity of sects.
Pierre Bayle, Anthony Collins, and other freethinkers challenged super-
stitious beliefs about miracles and comets from the Newtonian perspective and that of common sense. For them, only the Church profited from
continued fear, hysteria, and superstition about such matters. Enlightenment, the formation of an educated, literate public, provided the way out
of an age of fanaticism, ignorance, intolerance, religious sectarianism, and
bellicosity, and of arbitrary, authoritarian forms of government.

The basic observational data which supplied the raw materials for
epistemological and moral reconstruction were obtained from two sources.
The description by European missionaries, explorers, travelers, diplomats
and commercial agents of the societies and customs of non-European
peoples (on which a voluminous popular literature was also based), combined with a few rare instances of "noble savages" and oriental ambassa-
dors produced in the flesh at the royal courts, gave the occasion for
innumerable treatises on the history of humanity and civil society, on the
state of nature, on the origin of inequality and of ranks, on the constant
and variable elements in human nature, institutions, and customs. The
concurrent fascination with children, deaf and dumb people, foundlings
and wild boys discovered in forests, with pygmies and apes, ants and bees
were the other means, also based on observation, for deriving knowledge
about man's intellectual and moral faculties and for studying the relationship between the various senses, cognition, emotions, and instincts.

From all this information several conclusions were inescapable to
most of the moral philosophers and scientists of the eighteenth century.
The tremendous diversity of peoples, cultures, and institutions stood out
for all to behold and marvel. Happiness and sorrow, virtue and vice,
beauty and ugliness, the sublime and ridiculous, were relative and variable matters. What aroused intense passions in some nations were matters of indifference to others. Simple people or "savages" were possessed
of a moral sense, different as its content might be from Christian morality.
They possessed a faculty for rationality and common sense that enabled
them to adapt to their environment. The laws and institutions of distant
kings and civilizations were remarkably enlightened and tolerant—more

so than those of some European monarchies. The wisdom of Confucius and Buddha largely paralleled the fundamental moral teachings of Christianity, even if their religious doctrines and beliefs were so different from those of Europeans.

Behind these differences and variations there was, nevertheless, an underlying common thread. Some societies were, to be sure, at an earlier stage of societal development—owing to their isolation, harsh environment, or the effects of unenlightened rulers and priestly oligarchies—but potentially all peoples had the same capacity to develop and to progress. Writing before the age of imperialism, social Darwinism, and racism, the Enlightenment thinkers had, on the whole, favorable stereotypes of non-Western peoples: the American Indian was virtuous and generous; the Egyptian was wise; the Turk, though cruel, was witty and clever; the Thai, pious and enlightened; the Persian, refined, civilized, and tolerant; the Arabs had preserved ancient Greek thought through the Dark Ages. In France, the institutions of the *ancien régime* and the Church measured up poorly in comparison with institutions of non-European peoples. The Great Chain of Being linked humans to the animal world in incremental steps and gradations. Human beings everywhere had similar capacities, both intellectual and moral. Differences in physical environment and institutions had kept these capacities from being fully and comparably developed.

Despite their optimism about the perfectibility of human society and the power of education in advancing toward it, moral philosophers reached different conclusions on many questions that furnished the basic assumptions and methodological foundations of nineteenth-century social science disciplines. The Scottish moralists articulated a variant of eighteenth-century thinking that became the foundation for political economy and economics. Among Continental thinkers there were two conflicting orientations, never successfully reconciled to this day, that are associated with Rousseau on the one hand and with Condorcet on the other. Diderot was to be found somewhere in the middle, fully aware of the complexity and ambiguity of the Enlightenment's intellectual accomplishments. Sociology today is the heir to both the Continental and the Scottish moralist traditions with the Rousseauian variant predominating. But all the classical theorists, especially those who like Marx, Weber, and Pareto were schooled in economics, drew from all these diverse sources.

THE SCOTTISH MORALISTS

The Scottish moralists, also known as the school of common sense and of whom Adam Smith is best known, were much influenced by Locke in their basic methodological position (Bryson, 1945). Simple commonsense empiricism, an analysis of one's daily experience, thoughts, feelings, emotions, sentiments, introspection as a form of observation for gaining knowledge, and knowledge of non-Western peoples and primitive peoples would reveal the motivational and moral foundations of society. They found 'that they themselves, and men everywhere, were moved by a mixture of selfish and unselfish dispositions. Sentiments operated more universally and predictably than did reason. Judgment and choice in human action depended on a moral sense and the ability to project oneself and adopt another's point of view. This they called sympathy—a human faculty for communicating and grasping the inclinations and sentiments of our fellow human beings even when these differ from ours. Man was a social animal, living in groups and communities from the earliest of times. In his moral sense man possessed a keen sociological radar; he was aware of and responsive to his fellows' approval and disapproval. Although each man pursued his own happiness based on a calculus of pleasure and pain, his drives and dispositions were very much circumscribed by his moral sense and by sympathy, which, combined with rationality, led to enlightened self-interest. Thus, man did not pursue his ends ruthlessly and unmindful of the selfish interests of others—he understood and took into account the motives of others, the probable outcome of their activities, and their power to sanction him. Law and the authorities backed up the moral sense with sanctions to make sure that self-interest stayed enlightened. The concept of interaction, of exchange theory in present-day sociology, is very closely related to the Scottish moralists' thinking.

We owe several other useful insights to them. One of these is a point of view about what today are called socialization and social influence. The Scottish moralists held that the opinions, habits, and pursuits of men are a product of their upbringing and social milieu, of group life and not of innate ideas and faculties or of unconscious drives and instincts. Rights and duties are relative to each other and are to be explained with reference to the mutual relations among men. The self and moral sense are developed and formed through interaction with members of the group. Referring to the pitiable condition of man brought up in isolation, Adam Smith wrote that

> bring him into society, and he is immediately provided with the mirror which he wanted [lacked] before. It is placed in the countenance and behavior of those he lives with. . . . This is the only looking glass by which he can, in some measure, with the eyes of other people, scrutinize the propriety of his own conduct. (Quoted in Bryson, 1945:160)

The theories of moral sense and sympathy had a profound impact, by way of turn-of-the-century social psychologists like McDougall, on Cooley and later sociologists associated with the symbolic interactionist school.

For the sake of historical accuracy it should also be pointed out that Hegel's theory of the consciousness of self resulting from interaction with others, the dialectic of master and servant (*Herr und Knecht*) described in chapter 4 of the *Phenomenology of the Mind,* also played a part in this intellectual tradition, especially insofar as it has come down to us in the methodological writings of Max Weber, particularly in his notion of *verstehen* (Abel, 1948–1949). Hegel had written that

> self consciousness has before it another self consciousness . . . [it] sees its own self in the other . . . each sees the other do the same as itself, each itself does what it demands on the part of the other . . . action from one side only would be useless, because what is to happen can only be brought about by means of both. (Hegel, 1953:399–400)

But in this German philosophic tradition these concepts had a quite different connotation than did the concept of sympathy for the Scots, since the link between social control, socialization, and enlightened self-interest was not emphasized.

Although the Scottish thinkers had a keen sense for stratification and incorporated conflicts of interest into their basic model of interaction and group life, they never developed theories of the state and authority corresponding to their analysis of the division of labor and of the economy. Nor did they provide us with theories of group conflict and ideology. They tended to blame social problems, human misery, and economic backwardness on imperfect institutions, the shortcomings of selfish rulers and unwise laws that interfered with the natural propensity of group life to ensure the happiness of its members. Adam Smith's "invisible hand" was an expression of this belief.

Continental thinkers were more sensitive to conflict processes, to authority, and to the nonrational side of human affairs. More than the Scottish moralists they were the intellectual heirs of Hobbes, even when they were bent on refuting him. To Rousseau, the state of nature was not Hobbesian. Man became selfish, brutish, and "artificial" as a result of civilization—of group life in the urbane, civil, refined, learned environment of Paris. For him, the logic of feelings, natural sexuality, and equality have become suppressed precisely through those institutions that some of his contemporaries associated with the heights of human progress. Not only property, but the division of labor itself, that precondition of all group life, contained the seeds of corruption, alienation, and unhappiness. Even Diderot, who ridiculed the state of nature as a utopian figment of Rousseau's mind, was sceptical and ambivalent about the real gains that civilization had made in providing for the happiness of its members compared to the condition of men living in more primitive communities. In

Le Neveu de Rameau, Diderot expressed the malaise of the freefloating intellectual, which became a pervasive concern in subsequent Continental and Russian thought, in philosophy (Nietzsche), letters (Baudelaire, Dostoevsky), and religion (Kierkegaard). In other essays he expressed scepticism about the benefits that European contact might bring to primitive peoples. More than anything else this Continental legacy, especially after the reaction to the events of the French Revolution, became the starting point for the late nineteenth-century theorists of collective behavior and group phenomena like Le Bon and Tarde, which then influenced modern sociological thinking on collective behavior.

MATHEMATICAL MODELS

A final accomplishment of the Enlightenment has to be mentioned, one that to our detriment we have too long ignored. I am referring to the application of mathematical thinking and, especially, of probability models to group processes, which was already implicit in the work of the political arithmeticians and became an articulated scientific program with Condorcet's (1808) *mathematique sociale* (social mathematics) and later with Quetelet's *physique sociale* (social physics). Here again, economics has profited by incorporating this approach into its mainstream, by way of intermediaries like Edgeworth (1881). Condorcet, a friend of the great French mathematicians d'Alembert, Monge and Laplace, was not a great creative mathematician himself, but made his most important contribution in what is today referred to as "applied mathematics" (Granger, 1956). Mindful of Bernouilli's application of probability theory to gambling problems, to demographic questions such as the sex ratio at birth, and to the desirability of vaccination against smallpox, Condorcet sought to apply probability models to the field of collective decisionmaking: juries in criminal cases, and more important, assemblies such as legislatures and committees, under various rules for aggregating individual choices into a collective decision. The sociological interest is in his double approach to these questions. In the first approach Condorcet assumed that each decisionmaker makes a choice independent of other group members only on the basis of information he possesses, which might be "correct" or "mistaken" to varying degrees. This led him to probability models in which the usual multiplication rule for independent events was appropriate. Despite his rationalistic bent, Condorcet was mindful of social influence in group processes, of "opinion" in eighteenth-century language; therefore, he created other models that did not assume independent choice and that led him to conditional probability models. This opened the way to introducing the ideas of the Scottish moralists on sympathy, moral sense, and social control in a mathematical manner into the analysis of group processes.

The occasion for Condorcet's work was a practical problem, that of analyzing concrete alternatives should the French absolutist monarchy be forced to adopt the English form of constitutional government by means of elected assemblies and should the French system of justice be reformed. In the early nineteenth century the mathematician Poisson refined Condorcet's work and tested some of the jury models against data on convictions in criminal cases, which were routinely available in the 1830s. At this time in France a number of scientists, physical, medical, and social, were actively developing a new field of investigation they called moral statistics and in which Adolphe Quetelet became the leading figure. In lieu of the political arithmetic of the seventeenth century, of the moral arithmetic of Buffon in the 1750s, statistics now became the rage or, as some have said, an era of statistical enthusiasm came into full swing. As more and more quantitative information about populations, activities, and institutions became available, there was hardly an area of social life that was left unexamined by means of inductive statistical techniques in order to discover the laws that governed it. There was a statistics of crime, as there was a statistics of virtue (whose quantitative indicators, or "symptoms" in the terminology then prevailing, were data on charities and savings deposits); there was a medical statistics, as there was a statistics of religious dispositions (measured with reference to the per capita incidence of priests and seminarians in a region and the financial contribution of the faithful); there was a statistics of education and of literature (newspapers, libraries per population, and so on); of suicide, of mental illness, of the military spirit (voluntary enlistments in the army, mutilations to escape the draft); of marriage and divorce, of social cohesion (litigations, civil suits, conciliation), of pretty much everything. Education and the lack of it measured the degree of enlightenment and of ignorance in different parts of France. Economic indicators measured the "general movement of industry and of civilization."

Many researchers were investigating the association between these several variables, in particular the effects of physical, demographic, and economic variables upon moral, medical, criminal, religious, intellectual, and social variables. Quetelet (1848) especially was optimistic about the scientific payoffs of these investigations. In the preface of a short programmatic volume entitled *On the Social System and on the Laws which Govern it,* he wrote that

> social facts, influenced by free will, manifest even greater regularity than events subject to physical causes. . . . Up to now, there has been vague talk about moral forces that direct men and determine their actions; I

have sought to demonstrate that these forces can be analyzed and their effects resolved in the manner of physical forces; that for most of the laws of mechanics one can find analogies if one moves from the physical to the moral world.

This was the program. The common thread informing it, sometimes lost in the statistical forest, was the conception of a social system analogous to a mechanical system and the relevance of mathematical techniques to sociological analysis and moral philosophy. The belief in quantitative social and demographic regularities and laws that provide the foundations for social life had its seventeenth- and eighteenth-century predecessors— John Arbuthnot, the Scottish physician, satirist, and mathematician; the Reverend William Derham; the physician Süssmilch, and others—when it was still anchored in natural religion and efforts to demonstrate "divine providence" from demographic and societal phenomena manifesting empirical regularities. Gradually, these ideas became secularized from "divine providence" through the "invisible hand" to the "social system." How many needless and fruitless polemics and arguments about functionalism might have been spared modern sociologists had the mechanical-Newtonian conception of system been adopted in American sociology as the basic scheme for systems analysis rather than the biological-Darwinian conception, which is a confusing and overdetermined one—i.e., it is static and structural instead of dynamic and process oriented, and it leads to the proliferation of variables and concepts rather than to a parsimonious set of difference or differential equations. As with so many other aspects of previous intellectual accomplishments, the Social Darwinist revolution in popular and scientific thought managed to obscure and mislead rather than to clarify and enlighten subsequent scientific progress. The fact that political economy and economics, in all its variants—British, Continental, and Marxist—succeeded in insulating itself from the Social Darwinist onslaught most successfully of all the emerging social science disciplines gave it a considerable scientific edge in the twentieth century.

For the theory of group conflict and collective behavior these several legacies of the Enlightenment lead to divergent points of view. In Britain, a theory of public opinion is developed that closely adheres to the conception of man as motivated by enlightened self-interest. Opinion, the influence exercised by men upon each other's ideas, judgments and decisions, is seen as a normal, necessary, and, on the whole, desirable fact of public life that produces beneficial aggregate consequences so long as the carriers of opinion are educated and enlightened. On the Continent, it is the irrational and negative consequences of social influence and group processes that are stressed. In Marx's work, the Rousseauian legacy leads to a theory of alienation and the British-Scottish legacy to a theory of ideology. But Marx owed more to the political economists than to Rousseau. As he himself stated (1959:45),

> I was led by my studies to the conclusion that legal relations as well as forms of the state could be neither understood nor explained by the so-called general progress of the human mind, but that they are rooted in the material conditions of life, which are summed up by Hegel after the fashion of the English and the French of the eighteenth century under the name of "civil society."

And for Marx, Quetelet's laws were not the eternal laws of the social system, but those of "bourgeois" society, as for instance the association between age and crime (1959:488) that the moral statisticians had observed in many countries.

Other French thinkers denied a collective rationality to all groups in which men exercise influence upon each other, whether they be crowds, juries, parliamentary assemblies, or the electorate. Under the influence of racialist conceptions, some writers categorically denied any capacity for rational thinking to even individual representatives of non-Western peoples, the lower classes, and various ethnic groups who happened not to be of Nordic and Anglo-Saxon origin. The conservative reaction to the events and excesses of the French Revolution played its part in this as much as the general scientific acceptance of phrenology, criminal anthropology, and of theories about the inferior mentality of primitive peoples.

GUSTAVE LE BON

Burke's *Reflections on the Revolution in France,* written before the terror, already sets the tone. There are the inaccurate, exaggerated descriptions of the Parisian "mob" on their march to Versailles in October 1789 to bring the royal family from Versailles to Paris. (Burke, 1955: p. 82. For an accurate description of these events, see Rude, 1967, chapter 5, especially pp. 76–78.) The National Assembly is described as follows:

> There a majority, sometimes real, sometimes pretended, captive itself, compels the king to issue as royal edicts, at third hand, the polluted nonsense of their most licentious and giddy coffee houses. . . . It is beyond doubt that under the terror of the bayonet and the lamp post and the torch of their houses, they are obliged to adopt all the crude and desperate measures suggested by clubs composed of a monstrous medley of all conditions, tongues, and nations. . . . They act like the comedians of a fair before a riotous audience. They have a power given to them . . . to subvert and destroy, but none to construct. (Burke, 1955:77–78)

The imagery in Burke is still that of an assembly captive of the Parisian mob. For later writers, the assembly itself is little different from a mob in its collective intellectual capacity. In *Psychologie des Foules* (1895), Gustave Le Bon characterizes the present age as that of the crowd. In a crowd, the rational faculties of the individual, his moral judgment and conscious personality, come under the sway of contagion and suggestion frequently originating with a leader. These produce a "mental unity" or uniformity. The characteristic mark of crowds is credulity, mobility, exaggeration of both noble and base sentiments, and suggestibility. The law of the mental unity of crowds applies not only to the "criminal" crowd, e.g., the type of crowd that stormed the Bastille, but to crowds that possess a sense of responsibility, e.g., juries, the electorate, and parliamentary assemblies. Juries have a weak aptitude for rational judgment, they are swayed by suggestion, oratory, and unconscious sentiments. The electorate lacks critical faculties (*l'esprit critique*), is simplistic and credulous and lionizes strong men. Parliamentary assemblies are equated with the Jacobin Clubs. In the *Psychologie des Foules* only anecdotal data and superficial descriptions are provided as evidence. In his subsequent *La Révolution Française et La Psychologie des Révolutions* (1918), there are more complete descriptions, usually based on the historian Taine and others sharing a negative view of the Jacobins. The conclusions are the same (1918:93):

> When he is the member of a jury or a parliament, collective man renders verdicts or votes for laws which he certainly would not have approved of in an isolated state.

Revolutionary crowds are drawn from the rootless, disorganized, mentally disturbed, criminal classes of big cities. And so it goes.

Though he differed in many respects from Le Bon, Gabriel Tarde arrives at similar conclusions and quotes some of the same passages from Taine's account of the psychology of the Jacobins. He too denies a collective rationality to the group and to the crowd. All groups can be classified along a continuum from crowds to corporate groups like the workshop, monastic order, and political club. In all group life the influence of leaders is dominant. Parliamentary assemblies are placed closer to the crowd end than the corporation end of his classificatory scheme. Writing in the influential *Reveu des Deux Mondes,* Tarde stated that

> an assembly or an association, a crowd or a sect has no other idea than that which it is exposed to; and this idea, this indication more or less intelligent of a goal to pursue, of a means to employ, may well be propagated from the brain of one man to the brain of the others, it remains the same. The prompter is therefore responsible for these direct effects. But

emotion, joined to this idea, spreads with it, and does not remain the same as it spreads. Emotion becomes intensified in the manner of a mathematical progression, and what was the moderate desire or uncertain opinion of the originator of this spreading wave becomes forthwith passion and conviction, hate and fanaticism in the mass. (1893:353)

To be sure, Tarde also developed a theory of publics and of imitation, what we would nowadays refer to as a theory of social influence, communication, and diffusion processes (Clark, 1969:14–53). But the main thrust of the turn-of-the-century crowd and group theorists is very much the same. Trotter, in *Instincts of the Herd in Peace and War* (1916), reiterates the conventional wisdom when he states that "irrational belief forms a large bulk of the furniture of the mind and is undistinguishable by the subject from rational verifiable knowledge." Sigmund Freud (1940) in his long monograph *Massenpsychologie und Ich-Analyse* takes it for granted that the descriptions and observations of crowd behavior and group processes reported by these writers were accurate. He introduced into mass psychology his concepts of the unconscious and the conflict between ego and id. Mass consciousness (*Massenseele*) for Freud bears similarities to the psychic life of primitives and of children. Like the other writers in this group, Freud applies his approach not just to crowds, but to social relationships, group processes, and institutions: the army, the church, two lovers, and the "primitive herd."

We have come a long way from the Scottish moralists and Condorcet. The theories of sympathy, the moral sense, and the social radar that provide a foundation for the conception of man as pursuing his selfish interests in an enlightened manner become the group or herd man, swayed by a leader, caught in the grip of contagion, and engaged in irrational behavior producing negative social consequences. In Freud, even the individual becomes a victim of his unconscious and of the conflict between the ego and the id. Nisbet (1966:7–18) refers to the broader intellectual current in which these reactions against the French Revolution and the Enlightenment developed as "The Revolt Against Individualism." It was also a revolt against the concepts of rationality and the rational individual, even in the mild version of the Scottish thinkers of the eighteenth century.

British thinking at this time never went to the Le Bon and Freud extreme on some of these issues. The conception of a "tribunal of public opinion" put forward by Bentham, of the free expression of public opinion as the chief safeguard against arbitrary government and misrule, and which, together with a press free of censorship, is part of the institutions of liberal government, survived the Social Darwinist and eugenics era, at least in the writing of some theorists of public opinion (Palmer, 1953: 3–13). Unlike the law of mental unity of crowds postulated by the Continental theorists, for the British theorists public opinion is not uniform but divided. It is based on interests, not only on emotions. It might even be amenable to measurement, as Thurstone and other psychologists subsequently did demonstrate. Thus, the theory of public opinion develops in the twentieth century in a broader, more interdisciplinary manner, with a firm empirical foundation, in contrast to mass psychology and collective behavior theory. To be sure, the emotional, nonrational component in public opinion is stressed by those who focus on propaganda and its effects. But the public opinion and the collective behavior approaches increasingly diverged.

THE CHICAGO SCHOOL
AND COLLECTIVE BEHAVIOR

In the 1920s Robert Park at the University of Chicago was the last sociologist to encompass and integrate both diverging approaches within the single framework of collective behavior. His German doctoral dissertation, *Masse und Publikum* (1904), already indicates this concern. One of his most popular courses was "The Crowd and the Public" (Faris, 1967: 101). Park guided and influenced several dissertations and research projects undertaken by his students on various manifestations of collective behavior, from strikes and religious sects to social movements, riots, and revolution. Through Herbert Blumer and latter-day Chicago sociologists like Turner, Killian, the Langs, and Gusfield, the collective behavior tradition was kept alive in American sociology. Important contributions were made and texts were written. Although Park accepted the accuracy of Le Bon's mistaken description of crowd behavior (Turner, 1967: Introduction), he was also mindful of Gabriel Tarde's conception of the public and the tradition of rational public opinion formation kept alive among British writers. The fact that he himself had been a newspaperman and had a good commonsense grasp of the issues compensated for the lack of research on these topics. More importantly, for Park collective behavior was an integral part of the normal operation of society and was an expression of broader processes of social change (Turner, 1967).

Fortunately, these basic truths were never forgotten in the best subsequent scholarly treatment of collective behavior. One of the most influential introductory sociology texts of the 1950s and 1960s includes in its chapter on collective behavior discussions not only of crowds, mobs, riots, panics, fads, crazes, rumors, and social movements, but also of publics and public opinion (Broom and Selznick, 1958: chapter 8). It defines collective behavior as "the study of relatively *unstructured* social situations and their products such as crowds, riots, rumors, public opinion, fads and social movements." Collective behavior is characterized by "behavior which is not fully controlled by cultural norms and ordered social relations." It is important because "spontaneous activities may give rise to new norms and values," and because it "*reflects* . . . underlying changes, but in responding to them it *creates* new perspectives, new lines of action, and new institutions." The text also states that "collective behavior is part of the everyday life of a society though it does not always take dramatic form." Thus, the most useful elements of Park's approach have been preserved: the emphasis on the relationship between social change and collective behavior, and its normal, everyday aspect.

To be sure, elements of the Le Bon tradition are also present. There is a section on emotional contagion, on shared emotional expression, on spontaneity, on the fact that collective behavior does not result from "consciously conducted activity." But the foundations for a linkup between the Park-Chicago approach to collective behavior and the political sociology approach to group processes, change, and social movements are firmly laid. Killian (1964:428) states that the "social movement is one of the most important ways through which social change is manifest and cultural change produced." Furthermore, he calls attention to the "interaction of conscious, striving human beings as part of an emerging collectivity which is the social movement" (1964:427), in contrast to the overdetermined conception of man as "creatures rather than creators of social change" that has become the conventional wisdom among sociologists. Gusfield (1968:445) defines social movements as "socially shared demands for change in some aspect of the social order," which puts the emphasis on "the part played by social movements in the development of social change." Moreover, "it has the character of an explicit and conscious indictment of whole or part of the social order, with a conscious demand for change." And Turner, the foremost American theorist of collective behavior, integrated the findings of social psychologists, psychoanalysts, and experimental psychologists with sociological theory and findings. He stresses the continuities between normal, institutionalized processes and collective behavior:

> . . . the stress on spontaneity and the discontinuity from conventional norms and social structures . . . seems less clear when the complexity of normal social structure and social norms is recognized . . . it is necessary to recognize a collective behavior component in such otherwise institutional phenomena as fashion, financial cycles, organizational morale, and intraorganizational power play. (Turner, 1965:383)

He also writes that

> it is altogether possible that all of the traditioal dynamic distinctions be-
> tween collective behavior and organizational behavior [will ultimately be
> undermined] and . . . that no special set of principles is required to deal
> with this subject matter. (p. 384)

This is the program of my book as well. But my effort was equally influenced by another major intellectual and empirical tradition in sociology,
that of the sociological study of decisionmaking developed by Lazarsfeld
and his students.

THE EMPIRICAL ANALYSIS OF ACTION

There is no necessity to describe in detail the personal, historical, and
intellectual origins of the empirical analysis of action (Lazarsfeld and
Oberschall, 1965). After World War I, a young Viennese mathematician
was exposed to the ideas of the Austrian psychologists Karl and Charlotte
Bühler and undertook with their support a number of empirical studies
of choice and decisionmaking, in particular choice of occupation among
youth. At the same time, Lazarsfeld was personally troubled by contemporary political issues: why was it that working-class Austrians did not
support and vote for the socialist party in greater numbers than they did?
His intention of studying empirically the question of political choice—of
voting—utilizing the techniques and information already developed in
the study of other choice situations, was not to be realized until a decade
and a half later in the United States. He has produced, with the collaboration of other sociologists, such influential works as *The People's Choice*
(1948), *Voting* (1954), and *Personal Influence* (1955). Many techniques
and methodological insights were gained from these studies, including the
idea of panel analysis, impact analysis, process analysis, the accounting
scheme, and the empirical analysis of action as a basic conceptual scheme
for the study of choice and decisionmaking. These techniques were then
applied by many sociologists in a variety of different situations: choice
of marriage partner, divorce, residential mobility, psychoanalysis, the
formation of friendship, buying, and so on. Many of these studies and
the research techniques referred to were published or summarized in *The
Language of Social Research* (Lazarsfeld and Rosenberg, 1955).

There is an underlying thread, theoretical as well as methodological,
in the empirical analysis of action, which Lazarsfeld came closest to
spelling out in the chapter entitled "The Social Psychology of the Voting
Decision" in *Voting* and which his collaborator Berelson also commented
upon in the chapter entitled "Democratic Practice and Democratic Theory." Briefly stated, the unit of sociological investigation is action in the

sense of an individual making a choice or series of choices between several alternatives, all within a group context. Larger societal or group effects are produced by aggregating individual choices. The past history, the preferences, and the values of a particular individual can be empirically measured and are conveniently captured in the notion of "intention" or "predisposition." The group pressures, information, sanctions, and rewards that are pressing in upon the decisionmaker are captured in the concept of "influence." The complex interaction between predispositions and influences then produces the probabilities or rates of alternative outcomes of the choice process, of the action.

How do broader cultural trends, historical traditions, and differences between communities enter the analysis, and what is their impact on the choice process? Here the concepts of climate of opinion and of group context, themselves a result of predispositions and influence processes, have to be invoked. The methodological refinements needed to come to terms with these concepts in an empirical manner are referred to as "contextual analysis." However, the important substantive point is that the influence processes in a collectivity or society are not random processes. Members, including the leadership, of existing groups interact much more frequently with one another than with outsiders. They expose themselves to influences, points of view, and information in a selective fashion. Thus, larger societal trends are filtered through existing group structures and then may have lasting effects because they are repeatedly and selectively reinforced. The different choice patterns of different generations are then accounted for with reference to these selective influence processes. But continuity and stability of the aggregate choices in the short run can also be accounted for in this fashion, or as the authors state:

> Mechanisms discovered in these "microscopic" studies can be linked to macroscopic sociological and historical concerns. (Berelson, Lazarsfeld, and McPhee, 1954:301)

Now in all this there is an interesting paradox. The unit of study is the individual and his choices, but the type of choice situation studied and the aggregate effects achieved are similar to the classical economists' market and to Condorcet's collective decisions in juries and assemblies. Lazarsfeld is aware of this parallel and has himself commented upon it (1959:14–15). In marketlike social structures, the connection between the microlevel behavior of actors and the macrolevel group or societal results can be made by means of simple aggregation techniques. In an earlier time, Quetelet, the moral statisticians, and Durkheim all made use of rates and distributions that are simple aggregates of individual choices or events. The empirical analysis of action uncovered, however, the decisive importance of social influence and group membership in decisionmaking. Thus, an intermediate level of social structure between the individual and the societal outcomes emerges and has to be reckoned with. This discovery complicates the aggregation problem. It is possible, as Condorcet did with juries and assemblies, to express the effects of "opinion" and "influence" in part by means of conditional probabilities, which lead to more complicated mathematical models than the simple aggregation model and to a mode of causal statistical analysis referred to as "contingency" and "specification" (Lazarsfeld and Rosenberg, 1955:115–125), although the basic approach is still based on aggregating individual choices to produce a collective result. However, there is another and ultimately preferable solution to the aggregation problem in nonmarket social structures. It is to start with models of interaction where outcomes are produced through the intersection of individual choices locked in a process of give and take, of mutual influence. Lazarsfeld himself (Berelson, Lazarsfeld, and McPhee, 1954:300) suggests this solution and quite rightly notes that it would lead to a different basic action scheme and mathematical model:

> Two equations might be set down: one would indicate the probability of contact between people having different attitudes, a second would describe the changes in attitudes which might come about as a result of these contacts; such a system of equations would then permit us to predict what attitude distribution would evolve in time for the group as a whole, and it would also permit us to make quite interesting, and not at all obvious, deductions which could themselves be tested.

This is precisely the route taken by economists when they added to classical and neoclassical theory the theory of duopolistic and oligopolistic competition and game theory. Choice situations in nonmarket social structures, precisely those that are typical of group conflict, can be analyzed with this interaction model (Marshak, 1946). Recently, Boulding (1962) has reviewed a number of such economic models and their wider social science applications in conflict analysis. Thus, the application of the empirical analysis of action (not the empirical techniques associated with it, but the basic action model underlying it) leads to difficulties when one deals with choice in nonmarket social structures such as organization behavior and conflict processes. This was not fully realized by Lazarsfeld (1959) in his article on decisionmaking in business. Despite this limitation, the basic approach embodied in the empirical study of action represents a major breakthrough in sociological analysis and the efforts to link micro- and macrolevels in sociological thinking.

The cumulative findings derived from choice studies, especially those from voting studies, also made a contribution to the centuries-long controversy over rationality in human action, and it is this element that Berelson chose to comment upon in the concluding chapter of *Voting* (1954). The "political man" that emerges from these studies is located somewhere between the opposite poles of social man—indifferent to public affairs, flexible and easily influenced, uninterested and uninvolved —and ideological man—absorbed in public affairs, partisan, informed, with strong convictions, inflexible (p. 323). On the one hand,

> the majority of the people vote, but in general they do not give evidence of sustained interest. Many vote without real involvement . . . and even party workers are not typically motivated by ideological concerns or plain civic duty. (p. 307)

On the other hand,

> the voter does have some principles, he does have information and rationality, he does have interest—but he does not have them in the extreme, elaborate, comprehensive, or detailed form in which they were uniformly recommended by political philosophers. (p. 322)

Thus, we have come full circle to the Scottish moralists' view of man as a creature of enlightened self-interest, whose moral sense and "sympathy" lead him to avoid "enthusiasm" and who is quite sensitive to the rewards and sanctions of his fellow group members. The nonrationality of group man postulated by Le Bon and his contemporaries is shown to be mistaken, and so is Condorcet's rational decisionmaker, who does not gain anything from interaction with his fellow citizens. It is interesting that the theorists of social movement and collective behavior starting from the quite different Chicago and Park tradition should end up with roughly the same conception of the individual, the sociological actor, and the degree of rationality in human action.

PARSONS AND SMELSER

To my knowledge, Parsons never specifically wrote about collective behavior and conflict processes. His treatment of these topics is embedded in abstract action theory and social system theory. Its clearest exposition is in the chapters on deviant behavior, social control, and social change in the *Social System* (1951). There are a number of positive elements in Parsons's approach to these topics. For Parsons, the conceptions of conformity and deviance are always in some sense relative (p. 251); normative patterns usually are complex and far from fully integrated (p. 252); deviant behavior is produced in the interaction of two actors or groups and has frequently the character of a vicious circle (pp. 255–56); and lack of consistency, contradictory elements in the societal value system, provides the opportunity for legitimizing patterns of group deviance (p. 291). Parsons writes that

> many of the abstract formulae, such as the desirability of "social justice," of "democracy," of "peace," are shared in common. Who is to say whether one interpretation is more legitimate than the other?

Vested interests block efforts to implement change and the aspirations of negatively privileged social strata (p. 492). Group deviance, legitimized with reference to value inconsistencies, "constitutes one of the principal sources of change in the structure of the social system" (p. 321).

Side by side with these useful conceptions are difficulties and undesirable aspects of the Parsonian approach. First of all, deviant behavior in the sense of crime and delinquency and nonconforming, opposition, and political protest behavior are not conceptually distinguished. Opposition ideas and ideologies in the Western tradition are thought to contain "romantic-utopian" elements, with overtones of fantasy and wish fulfillment. The implementation of these ideas leads to undesirable societal consequences:

> Thus such symbols as freedom and justice may receive interpretations incompatible with the functional needs of the institutional order. But precisely in terms of the approved cultural tradition, it is not possible to stigmatize these interpretations out of hand as illegitimate. (p. 296)

And further:

> Every complex social system is in fact shot through with conflicts and adaptive patterns with respect to whatever value-system it may have . . . It may be suggested that this is one of the points at which the modern liberal-individualistic type of society is most vulnerable to a breakdown of its system of social control. (p. 297)

This curious emphasis of viewing change agents from the point of view of the "trouble" they might make for the established groups who enjoy all the good and desired things in life is just below the surface in Parsons' approach, yet it does not follow logically from the theoretical position he represents. Nothing is to be gained by referring to great religious and political innovators as "utopian deviants." After all, without a dash of "utopian deviance" human societies would be little different from ant colonies or 1984. The winners of historical confrontations and revolutions and their intellectual supporters routinely rewrite history from their own point of view, but sociologists need not follow in their footsteps.

In a subsequent summary of his views on the social system in *Theories of Society* (1961), Parsons reiterates his earlier views on these matters within the context of his discussion of structural change, strain, and discontent:

> . . . strain at this level (of the system of behavioral control) is manifested by a series of symptoms of disturbance showing the psychological marks of irrationality. These will be organized along the major axes of hope and fear, of "wishful thinking" and "anxiety" showing unrealistic trends in *both* respects. . . . There will be fantasies of utopian ideal future states, of idealized past states, of security in a status quo from which sources of disturbance would conveniently be banished. . . . These motivational components are common to all symptoms of disturbance in the institutionalization of social structures. (1961:75)

These views became the starting point for Smelser's *Theory of Collective Behavior* (1963).

If there are several contradictory and incompatible elements in a complex value system, and there usually are (as can be demonstrated empirically from the fact that all groups in a complex society do not agree on what is concretely meant by equality, freedom, justice, and so on), the question of legitimizing collective opposition to entrenched elites and vested interests becomes secondary in the theory of conflict and change. Nor does the theorist have to belabor "fantasy," "wish fulfillment," or "utopian" and "irrational" elements in the motivations and beliefs of the opposition groups, or of entrenched elites. Theoretical interest shifts to mobilization and social control processes, which are sides of the same coin, since a competitive process of assembling resources, both material and ideological, is occurring simultaneously in all the groups locked in conflict, including the incumbents. More than anything else, it is these processes that provide a link between the micro- and macroaspects of theory. It is precisely this level of analysis that was not worked out by Parsons.

Other functionalists have developed this level of analysis more successfully, although more in the context of social change than of conflict theory. The foundations were laid by Merton with the theory of reference groups (1957: chapter 8). Unlike Parsons, Merton clearly distinguishes deviant from nonconforming behavior (pp. 357–68) and links nonconforming behavior to social change. Unlike the deviant who behaves contrary to norms in order to gain a personal advantage but does not challenge the legitimacy of the norms themselves,

> the nonconformist aims to change the norms of the group, to supplant what he takes to be morally illegitimate norms and values with norms having an alternative moral basis. (Merton, 1957:361)

Furthermore,

> the nonconformist . . . can . . . draw upon the latent store of moral indignation. In some measure, his nonconformity appeals either to the moral values of an earlier day which have been lost to view or to moral values of a time which will come to pass. . . . His nonconformity is not a private dereliction, but a thrust towards a new morality. (p. 363)

For Merton, reference group theory and functional sociology deal with different facets of the same subject:

> one centers on the processes through which men relate themselves to groups . . . ; the other centers on the consequences of the processes primarily for social structures. (p. 216)

Reference group theory can serve as the foundation for describing how groups form, grow, and dissolve and how normative and value changes take place through processes of group formation and disintegration. In the theory of collective behavior and social conflict, mobilization deals precisely with these processes, and the insights of reference group theory can be readily exploited to great advantage. Coser (1967) has done just that.

Unfortunately, Smelser's *Theory of Collective Behavior* (1963) emphasizes the negative aspects of the Parsonian approach. Just when collective behavior theorists are coming to see the continuities between everyday behavior and routine social processes, Smelser's emphasis is on discontinuities and differences. When other sociologists are coming to see the rational components in collective behavior, Smelser's emphasis is on the nonrational components; when sociologists emphasize the diversity of beliefs, motives, and perceptions in collective behavior that lead to heterogeneity of crowd behavior and of differential participation in social movements, Smelser emphasizes the homogenizing effects of generalized beliefs, although he never goes to the Le Bon extreme. Already his definition of collective behavior points the way to the subsequent emphasis of his approach, when he writes that collective behavior is

> mobilization on the basis of a belief which redefines social action. . . . Collective behavior is guided by various kinds of beliefs—assessment of the situation, wishes and expectations. These beliefs differ, however, from those which guide many other types of behavior. They involve a belief in the existence of extraordinary forces—threats, conspiracies, etc.—which are at work in the universe. They also involve assessment of the extraordinary consequences which follows if the collective attempt to reconstitute social action is successful. The beliefs on which collective behavior is based (we shall call them *generalized beliefs*) are thus akin to magical beliefs. (Smelser, 1963:8)

Smelser's critics (Skolnick, 1969; Currie and Skolnick, 1970) have taken him to task precisely on these points. In his reply Smelser yields only on points of detail; he is willing to qualify, but not alter, the fundamental assumptions of his approach (Smelser, 1970).

But let us consider the useful aspects of Smelser's approach as well. They consist of the following. Many previous writers have focused on the causes of conflict, whereas Smelser points out how these initial causes, "strain" in his terminology, are mediated and filtered through intervening social structures and processes before they are activated in conflict processes and in episodes of collective behavior. The second contribution he makes is in working out the determinants of collective behavior in a more systematic fashion than earlier theorists and in standardizing the terminology: strain, conduciveness, generalized belief, mobilization, precipitating incidents, and social control. In the language of the empirical analysis of action, these determinants are referred to as an "accounting scheme," without which a social process cannot be satisfactorily studied. Smelser calls it a "value-added" scheme. Smelser's third contribution is his interaction orientation, inasmuch as it is the interaction among the determinants, in particular between strain and conduciveness on the one hand and generalized belief and social control on the other, that shapes the aggregate outcome (Smesler, 1968:100). Finally, as other sociologists also emphasize, collective behavior processes are intimately linked with social change. One does not have to agree with the details of Smelser's contributions to recognize their usefulness.

Nevertheless one would make the following further objections to Smelser. His value-added scheme (1968:97–100), translated into the usual methodological terminology of empirical sociologists, boils down to the use of a static, cross-sectional design in the analysis of social processes. It is not a genuinely dynamic process model. What the value-added approach does is to list certain contingencies under which certain outcomes are more likely to occur than other outcomes (for instance, see 1968:272). A genuinely dynamic approach, however, accounts also for the likelihood of these contingencies themselves. In fact, Smelser's value-added scheme is a very special type of accounting scheme. Smelser's statement that

> each determinant is viewed as a necessary but not sufficient condition for the occurrence of an episode of collective behavior, taken together the necessary conditions constitute the sufficient conditions for its occurrence, (1968:97)

translated into a more familiar statistical terminology means that (1) all the variables have in fact been specified and properly ordered in the accounting scheme; (2) one expects strong interaction effects among the variables; and (3) one expects the variables to explain all of the variation—100 percent of the variance—in the dependent variables. All of these expectations are subject to empirical verification in actual research and should in principle not be stated as assertions, but rather as goals.

A further objection to Smelser is the fact that he does not have a satisfactory theory of mobilization and of social control and does not realize that the interaction between mobilization and control processes generates the dynamic elements of conflict and collective behavior processes. Finally, it is unfortunate that Smelser developed his theory with reference to an inadequate data base, before the findings of historians, political scientists, and sociologists on conflict processes in eighteenth- and nineteenth-century Western Europe, on the post war nationalist movements in the colonies, and on the contemporary minority, student, and protest movements had become widely available. The conception of social change underlying Smelser's position is that of an older generation of social scientists who have not had a chance to familiarize themselves with the findings and more subtle social change theories of other social scientists who have studied social change empirically throughout the world (Tilly, 1969:9–10). It is ironic that Smelser's (1959) own study of changes in the cotton industry and in the family during the English Industrial Revolution has probably misled him, since the British case appears to have been atypical (Morris, 1960; Gusfield, 1967; Bendix, 1967; Geertz, 1963).

THE LEGACY OF THE PAST

What can one learn from all these diverse theories and approaches that is useful for social conflict and collective behavior theory? First, following Merton, the distinction between deviant and nonconforming behavior must be maintained. Precisely in group conflict and social movement situations the discontented group makes a claim to legitimacy for its goals, program, and actions in the name of ideals and values that have some legitimacy. Both sides compete for public support, for third-party support in the contest. The attempt by incumbents to pin the label "criminal" and "deviant" upon their opponents and the corresponding efforts to paint established elites and their agents as corrupt, illegitimate, and unresponsive, are part of the strategy of conflict as all sides seek to mobilize and increase their human, material, and ideological resources at each other's expense. Sociological thinking has passed the point of no return when it comes to the turn-of-the-century conceptions of equating lower-class and political crowds with the criminal classes and the criminal crowd. Contemporary research does not support such simplistic notions.

Second, the continuity between institutionalized, everyday behavior and conflict processes and collective behavior has been empirically demonstrated. Large-scale movements and the periods of conflict and confrontation that result from their contests with established groups opposed to change are made up of a mixture of routine events and episodes of collective behavior, ranging from peaceful demonstrations, spontaneous clashes, and riots to more organized collective efforts taking place in the setting of electoral contests and pressure-group politics. The entire continuum of these processes can be analyzed sociologically with the same concepts, tools, and assumptions.

Third, the rational component in social conflict and collective behavior is present much in the same way as it is present in other choice and decisionmaking situations in everyday life. In group conflict men's choices are invested with political meaning in addition to other meanings, both as they perceive them and as their opponents or uncommitted third parties perceive them. There are emotional and nonrational components in collective behavior, but the same can be said for everyday behavior. This principle applies to the incumbents and the agents of social control as much as to their opponents. Both sides lack full and accurate information about each other; they have misconceptions about each other's strengths and weaknesses; and they respond to concrete problems and choices in complex ways, with a mixture of outrage, anger, puzzlement, and shrewd, informed calculation. The information and conceptions they possess can be found out by means of empirical study and can then be fed back into the model of man, the decisionmaker, whose main features are rationality with respect to means and ends and selfishness with respect to motives in the sense of the Scottish moralists and of the empirical analysis of action. This model has been useful in economic theory, and it seems a good idea to make full use of it for all its explanatory potential. Leader-follower relationships can be analyzed along the lines of this model, as can hostile crowds, panics and other collective behavior phenomena (Brown, 1965: chapter 14). Collective behavior is learned much the same way as other behavior is. In all this men remain the motor force: they make themselves, history, institutions, as well as mistakes. The overdetermined, oversocialized conception of the actor and of social action so common in functional sociology ought to be discarded (Homans, 1964).

Fourth, group conflict and collective behavior combine features of a market structure and of nonmarket processes. The manner of aggregation of individual decisions and behavior into a collective group outcome varies depending on the structure. For theorizing about influence, communications, and diffusion processes in a group situation, the techniques and findings of the empirical study of action can be applied with great profit. In situations of conflict where the aggregate outcome is determined by the intersection of several mutually dependent choices that cannot be treated as independent events, an interaction model of the process in the manner of game theory or of the Richardson equations (Boulding, 1962) is the appropriate model. Brown (1965: chapter 14) has demonstrated the usefulness of such models in the case of collective behavior, and Boulding (1962) has applied them successfully to a much wider class of conflict situations. Another issue can then be resolved in a similar manner. The interaction models are by their very nature dynamic system models describing processes. There is no necessity to adopt a static value-added approach in conflict and collective behavior studies. For purposes of testing theory, one may not have available data over time, and, thus, one may be forced into a static cross-sectional design and mode of causal analysis. But that is another matter altogether from casting a theory in static terms.

Fifth and last, the basic accounting scheme for group conflict and collective behavior processes is the one suggested by Smelser, whether or not one uses the same terminology that he does. But the Smelser determinants, as pointed out earlier, have to be fed into dynamic system analysis rather than into a static analysis. Whether one can do so within the framework of mathematical models or only of a verbal description of system processes depends on substantive theory and not on methodological considerations.

Perhaps the best illustration is Crane Brinton's *Anatomy of Revolution* (1952). Brinton spells out neither the accounting scheme nor the logic of his analysis, yet he applies the systems approach nevertheless. The initial state of the system is called by Brinton "The Old Regime." The variables subsumed under Smelser's strain and their actual magnitudes for old regimes are described in the sections entitled "Structural Weaknesses, Economic and Political," and "Classes and Class Antagonisms." Smelser's conduciveness is covered mainly in the section "Structural Weaknesses . . ."; the growth of generalized beliefs in "The Desertion of the Intellectuals"; precipitating factors in "The Events of the First Stages"; mobilization in "Spontaneity or Planning?"; and social control in "The Role of Force." The outcome of the initial set of confrontations is the fall of the old regime and the rule of the moderates. A new system state is reached; the initial states of the system have changed. Strain has not been reduced; for some groups it has even increased. The issues and ideological positions of the participants have themselves changed (generalized beliefs); the moderates inherit a bankrupt treasury and chaotic administrative apparatus (structural conduciveness) incapable of reversing the economic chaos they also inherit. Meanwhile, the radicals continue mobilization and eventually establish a dual sovereignty structure, pouring all their energies and resources into mobilization for the next round of confrontation, even as the moderates dissipate theirs in trying to reestablish normality, in curbing the counterrevolutionaries, and in checking the radicals (social control). The failure of the moderates leads in the next set of confrontations to the accession of the extremists. The state of the system is now described by Brinton as "Reigns of Terror and Virtue." Again, all the determinants have changed: social control is now terroristic; mobilization is curbed by destroying the moderates, who go underground or flee abroad; the belief system is intolerant; an attempt is made to relieve strain by strong arm techniques of regimentation, forced contributions, price and wage controls, and so on. Civil disturbances multiply under the impact of these extreme measures, and plots and counterplots arise among the radicals themselves. This sets the stage for the next round of confrontations, which moves the system into a new state called "Thermidor."

This dissection of the underlying logic of Brinton's work cannot possibly do justice to the subtlety of his analysis and the range and depth of historical data that he succeeds in capturing and illuminating. The analysis is, however, what I earlier called a dynamic systems approach. The initial conflicts and confrontations are produced from the state of the system itself, and the conflicts change the initial state of the system by changing the magnitudes of the variables used in the description of the system. A new stage or system state is reached, which is again in disequilibrium, and new conflicts are produced that lead to another system state, and so on, until in Thermidor a system state is reached that, for purposes of analysis, can be conceptualized as but a slowly changing state (relative to the earlier, rapid, macrochanges). It is this model, but applied in a more deliberate and studied manner, that can serve as the basic scheme for group conflict and collective behavior theory. Though an appropriate methodology has been found, the theory itself will depend on substantive advances, i.e., the details of the theories and hypotheses about strain, conduciveness, mobilization, and social control that one feeds back into the systems analysis. It is to this issue that I devote the final section of this introductory chapter.

RECENT CONTRIBUTIONS

Within the past few years, a number of sociologists dealing with change and conflict processes have developed an approach that one might refer to as the "resource management" approach. The concept of mobilizing, converting, and transferring resources from one group and one arena of action to other groups and actions is formulated by Coleman (1969) in his discussion of race relations in the United States. A similar conception is very much at the heart of Gamson's (1969) discussion of influence, authority, and power in mobilization and social control processes and of Stinchcombe's (1968: chapter 4) approach to power, social control, and legitimacy. It is explicitly introduced by Tilly (1969, 1970) in his analyses of mobilization, countermobilization, the contention for power, and the conversion of individual resources to collective group goals during group conflict processes. Rather than go into the details of the works of these authors, I will try to summarize the essence of their views and my own and point out the continuity between their approaches and the topics covered in this book.

The basic idea is that of resource. This can be anything from material resources—jobs, income, savings, and the right to material goods and services—to nonmaterial resources—authority, moral commitment, trust, friendship, skills, habits of industry, and so on. In ordinary everyday activity, at work, in family life, and in politics, people manage their resources in complex ways: they exchange some resources for other resources; they make up resource deficits by borrowing resources; they recall their earlier investments. Resources are constantly being created, consumed, transferred, assembled and reallocated, exchanged, and even lost. At any given time some resources are earmarked for group ends and group use, not just individual use. All of these processes can be referred to as "resource management."

Group conflict in its dynamic aspects can be conceptualized from the point of view of resource management. Mobilization refers to the processes by which a discontented group assembles and invests resources for the pursuit of group goals. Social control refers to the same processes, but from the point of view of the incumbents or the group that is being challenged. Groups locked in conflict are in competition for some of the same resources as each seeks to squeeze more resources from initially uncommitted third parties. When one party to the conflict succeeds in obtaining some hitherto unallocated resources, these resources are no longer available to the opposition. The terms mobilization and social control are relative, since both sides seek to mobilize further resources from their supporters and to control resources that are already allocated to their side. But from a societal perspective, from the perspective of conflict and change that result in major shifts of resources from positively privileged to negatively privileged groups, mobilization in the broad sense refers to processes by which an opposition assembles resources for challenging the incumbents, and social control to the processes by which incumbents seek to protect their vested interests. The social system of conflict is an open system, since groups initially outside the conflict, sometimes even foreigners and other countries, may be progressively drawn into the conflict and commit some resources to one or the other side. Demobilization processes can also be analyzed from the resource management perspective, since groups and individuals recall and reallocate to other private or group pursuits the resources they have earlier committed to the conflict and to the pursuit of group ends. In all this the individuals who are faced with resource management decisions make rational choices based on the pursuit of their selfish interests in an enlightened manner. They weigh the rewards and sanctions, costs and benefits, that alternative courses of action represent for them. In conflict situations, as in all other choice situations, their own prior preferences and history, their predispositions, as well as the group structures and influence processes they are caught up in, determine their choices. Indeed, many are bullied and coerced into choices that are contrary to their predispositions. The resource management approach can account for these processes in a routine way.

Although we do not know enough about the precise nature of resource creation, exchange, allocation, consumption, and conversion to be able to express relationships in a quantitative manner, enough is known about them to provide a start for a qualitative analysis of conflict processes, and that is what I have endeavored to do in the following chapters.

Social structures can be analyzed from the point of view of how resources, including leadership, are managed and allocated and the manner in which these resources can be converted to the pursuit of group goals. The theory of mobilization described below rests on such an analysis. The problem that negatively privileged groups have had in assembling their meager resources for the pursuit of their collective goals and the extent to which outside support can make up their resource deficits are described most fully in the chapter dealing with the civil rights and black power movement. How a shared culture, national sentiments, and historical tradition can be rapidly converted into a resource base for conflict, even in the face of an authoritarian regime, is described in greatest detail in the section devoted to the Hungarian revolution of 1956. Participation and leadership in social movements can also be analyzed from the point of view of cost-benefit and resource allocation; so can the ideological component in conflict be viewed as a matter of resources and competition for resources. The strategies of social control utilized by incumbents in the face of growing unrest, in particular also the loosening of social control produced by reform responses, can be usefully viewed from the point of view of the allocation and competition for resources by the conflict groups. How successful my application of the resource management approach has been in the study of social conflict and social movements each reader will have to judge for himself when he compares the insights gained from this approach with those provided by other approaches.

Chapter ***II***

THE SOURCES
OF SOCIAL CONFLICT

DELIMITATION OF THE PROBLEM

Max Weber (1947:132) defined conflict as action, oriented "intentionally to carrying out the actor's own will against the resistance of the other party or parties." In this sense, conflict is an everyday, normal, ongoing, for the most part institutionalized process that is a natural part of social reality. However, the present theory is aimed at a more restricted set of activities and is directed at providing an understanding for what Coser has termed social conflict (1967:232): "Social conflict may be defined as a struggle over values or claims to status, power, and scarce resources, in which the aims of the conflict groups are not only to gain the desired values, but also to neutralize, injure, or eliminate rivals." Coser's definition has the advantage of being more in line with the everyday usage of the word "conflict" than Weber's definition. Nevertheless, a theory of conflict ought also to encompass situations in which divergent interests and disagreements over values can be resolved without necessarily intending or bringing injury and harm to one's opponents. One might modify Coser's definition by stating that "the aims of the conflict groups are to gain the desired values, and the consequence of the struggle is frequently the neutralization, injury, or elimination of the rival group." The theory should also deal with situations involving conflicts of interests—struggles over scarce resources, values, status, and the like—in which both parties can gain by coming to terms, and not only with those situations where one party must gain at the expense of the other.

Any theory of social conflict must address itself to a number of separate aspects of conflict (Dahrendorf, 1962:199–200; Angell, 1965:93).

1. The types of conflict to be distinguished in order to theorize intelligently about the thousands of varieties and forms in which conflict is manifest.
2. The causes of these various types of conflict.
3. How conflict groups come into being—this topic is an aspect of the theory of mobilization.
4. The confrontation process itself: the interaction between the antagonists, the dynamics of the struggle, precipitating factors, polarization, escalation, the factors that account for the dampening or deepening of conflict, the determinants of violence, and so on.
5. Processes of conflict resolution and regulation and the institutionalization of conflict. It is here that a theory of conflict joins up with a theory of social control.
6. What Coser referred to as the "functions of social conflict"—theories about the consequences of conflict for the conflict groups themselves and for the social system.

It would be altogether pretentious and impossible to develop a comprehensive theory covering all six topics for all types of conflict. This work covers the case of substantial group conflict, leaving out at one end interpersonal conflicts and role conflicts, e.g., husband-wife disputes and sibling rivalry, microconflicts between small groups, e.g., gang wars, and intragroup conflicts, e.g., competition between cliques in neighborhoods or college dormitories, and at the other end international conflicts or wars between states. A borderline case would be protracted internal wars or guerrilla wars waged with outside help. Also excluded are institutionalized processes of conflict, such as the competition of political parties in a democratic polity, routine collective bargaining between employers and employees, the competition between firms and organizations for a greater share of the market, and the like. These situations will be limiting cases for the conflict situations that will be discussed. This still leaves the rich and heterogeneous area covering class, racial, and communal conflicts, rebellions, insurrections, revolutions, riots, civil disorders, social disturbances, strikes, banditry, nationalist movements, protest demonstrations, and so on. In all these social conflicts the elements of action and reaction consist of a series of episodes of collective behavior during which groups of people express grievances, voice demands, stage meetings, marches, demonstrations, and sit-ins, occupy property belonging to others, erect barricades, draft petitions, prevent the execution of unpopular orders and laws, interfere with tax collection and the draft, destroy property, assault other individuals or groups, and in turn get dispersed, beaten, gassed, shot at, killed, detained, arrested, imprisoned, and so on. The groups or collectivities that act upon grievances and react to provocations by engaging in collective action will be referred to as opposition groups, negatively privileged groups, protesters, and challengers of the status quo unless they are called by more specific designations such as strikers, demonstrators, squatters, rioters, revolutionaries, and so on. Their immediate opponents will usually be the agents of social control, the rank and file executors of the orders of the authorities, namely, police, troops, militia, national guard, constables, yeomanry, court officials, and the like. The intended targets of the protesters' action usually are not the agents of social control themselves, but the government, the authorities, the monarch, ruling groups, institutional elites, and so on, including third parties who are thought to have influence with the government and the elites and public opinion. Frequently, group conflict takes place not between protesters and the agents of social control but between two or more population groups, for instance, members of different religious communities, employees and employers, or landlords and tenants, during which the agents of social control are called upon to separate the two sides, reestablish peace, protect one party against the assaults of the other, or help one side crush the other. The theory of social conflict deals with these situations as well.

Within this broad range of social conflict many investigators start with a typology of conflict based on the forms it takes and the ultimate outcome, e.g., revolution, rebellion, riot, coup d'etat, or guerrilla war, or classifications based on the social categories of the participants and the social institutions primarily affected, e.g., peasant rebellion, student movement, race riot, labor conflict, political conflict, or economic conflict. From the point of view of a theory of social conflict, these distinctions do not seem very promising, important as they are for historical analysis, case studies, and further refinements of theory. A theory of group conflict ought to have some general applicability regardless of the hundreds of ways in which the participants and the substantive issues can be characterized. Furthermore, all group conflict consists of similar elements of action and reaction, enabling the theorist to utilize a common set of concepts, variables, and propositions in his analysis, regardless of the duration, scale, geographic spread, and ultimate outcome of the confrontation itself. Some riots can expand into a full-scale, successful revolution without anyone's planning, intending, or expecting it. Some intended revolutions never grow beyond the stage of a series of riots easily put down. Therefore, it is preferable to examine the causes of all manner of social conflicts first. Under what circumstances conflict tends to be violent or nonviolent, limited or large-scale, institutionalized or unregulated, will be discussed subsequently within the context of mobilization, confrontation, and social control.

SOCIAL CONFLICT AND THE SOCIAL ORDER

Social conflict arises from the structured arrangement of individuals and groups in a social system—from the very fact of social organization. In every social organization, as Dahrendorf (1962:165–66) has pointed out, some positions are entrusted with a right to exercise control over other positions and to ensure compliance with authority through coercion. In other words, there exists a division of authority such that there are individuals and groups who are subject to authority rather than participants in its exercise. The persistence in time of authority structures gives rise to relations of dominance and subordination and thus provides the occasion for exploitation. At the same time, social organization rests on social differentiation and the division of labor through which the satisfaction of individual wants and the provision of collective goods are pursued. The division of labor creates complex relationships of exchange between different social positions. The combination of the division of labor with super- and subordination makes up the basic configuration of social positions, strata, and classes in the social system.

There is no once-and-for-all solution to the problem of distributing scarce resources among the members of a society thus constituted. At any given moment, there exists a certain distribution of scarce resources and of rewards—the good things desired and sought after by most, such as wealth, power, and prestige—among the individuals, groups, and classes in a society. Some are better off, and others are worse off. Those who are favored have a vested interest in conserving and consolidating their existing share; those who are negatively privileged seek to increase theirs, individually or collectively. Social conflict results from this clash of opposing interests. Duverger (1964:242) expressed it in these words:

> Reduced to its greatest simplicity . . . political conflict opposes those who are more or less satisfied with the existing social order, who want to conserve it, and those for whom this order is unsuitable, who want to change it.

Privileges, the good and desired things in life, and the social positions and relationships that assure their continued enjoyment are not given up without resistance. The very institutions that create the misery and suffering of some contribute to the freedom and security of others (Pettee,

1938:36). Freedom, rights, a greater share of material wealth, are not handed to negatively privileged groups on a silver platter. They have to be gained at considerable risk, sacrifice, and expenditure of time and resources. Trotsky once remarked that society does not change its institutions as need arises the way a mechanic changes his instruments. The tenacity and determination of vested interests in resisting change makes social conflict a fundamental fact of existence.

Nevertheless, not all communities and societies experience the same degree of conflict, nor does a single society experience the same degree of conflict over time. The forms that conflict assumes, nonviolent and violent, institutionalized and uninstitutionalized, vary in time and social space. The locus of conflict shifts from the courts and parliaments into the streets and vice versa. The issues at stake change. The capacity of different institutional arrangements for conflict regulation varies. A theory of social conflict has to address itself to the complexity and variability of conflict.

It is true that there have been and will be periods when negatively privileged groups appear to accept their collective fate passively and without complaint, though as individuals they strive to improve their lot. They may do so because they accept the existing system of stratification, of authority, and of inequality as just and legitimate, or else because they are powerless in the face of superior might and fearful of the consequences of opposition. But the ubiquity of social change and the fact of unrealized ideals ensure that such a state of affairs is but transitory.

Once the hallmark of Western European and North American society, social change has become a worldwide phenomenon in the twentieth century. Schumpeter spoke of capitalism as a process of creative destruction; this is an appropriate characterization of the worldwide process of change as well. Population growth, migration, the growth of cities and of industry, changes in technology, in modes of production, communication, organization, and in the scale of society are everywhere accompanied by changes in the everyday lives and security of ordinary people. Some groups advance while others stand still or decline. Some, threatened with the loss of their livelihood, cling tenaciously to traditional ways; others, advancing and reaping unheard of profits, seek to speed the processes of change and prepare to defend their gains against newer claimants. Others find further progress blocked by the determination of still powerful groups not to yield their inherited privileges. Existing institutions and social arrangements are no longer suited to solve new problems of an altogether different order of magnitude. New ideas that question sacred assumptions and time-honored ways of handling affairs are diffused. Dissatisfaction mounts; impatience, cramp, hatreds accumulate. Reforms lag behind new needs. Eventually, the existing conflicts increase in intensity and new social conflicts erupt. Change and conflict are intimately linked. It is the rising and declining groups and classes formed and transformed during periods of change that usually constitute the core of social movements and organized groups who seek to reform and revolutionize existing institutions or, on the contrary, defend the social order under attack (Moore, 1966:84).

Social conflict is seldom a simple mechanical reaction to grievances and frustrations experienced in the pursuit and defense of material interests. Interests and dissatisfactions are experienced and interpreted by way of moral ideas about right and wrong, justice and injustice of conceptions of the social order as they are expressed in ideals and highly regarded principles. The drive to change existing institutions, whether to reform or revolutionize them, is inspired by unrealized ideals: measured against the ideals that are enshrined in the sacred books, the constitution, and collective myths, reality falls short. The gap may be wide or narrow; its very existence will justify the efforts to close it in the name of legitimate, highly valued, and respected principles (W. Moore, 1963: 18–19).

Every great intellectual and moral tradition contains numerous contradictions that feed the tension between ideal and reality: this is true for liberalism, for socialism and Marxism, for the democratic tradition, and for Christianity. Some people come to realize that certain ideals and principles in their moral tradition have been neglected for other ideals and principles whose institutional implementation has benefited certain social strata disproportionately. They may support a concerted effort to right the balance. Within the American democratic political tradition, which is founded on the ideal of political equality and the principles of popular sovereignty and majority rule, there has existed and still exists—and probably always will exist—tension between elitist (Hamiltonian) and populist (Jeffersonian) orientations. Just how is the people's majority preference to be translated into legislative decisions? Those who distrust the people's wisdom and those who, on the contrary, distrust the motives of the people's elected representatives and desire to minimize the inequalities produced by political differentiation within the citizenry, have preferred different structural arrangements for translating democratic principles into practice. Populists hold that legislators are a necessary evil and ought to be no more than the executors of the people's will. Elitists regard legislators as a useful buffer interposed between popular prejudice and the shaping of public policy. Populists seek frequent and direct elections, party primaries to check the power of party bosses operating in caucuses and conventions, and use of the referendum as a counterweight to the powers of the legislators. Elitists are opposed to these institutional arrangements. An excess of elitism undermines democracy in the direction of oligarchy. Yet an excess of populism may well prepare the way for a dictatorship and the suppression of minority rights by an intolerant majority. The success of the democratic tradition rests in no small part on the contradictions and tensions produced by those two conflicting orientations for it allows democratic institutions to be reformed and restructured from within in response to new circumstances and new social forces.

Human society incorporates fundamental dilemmas that cannot be resolved in a manner satisfactory to all groups once and for all. Both freedom and social justice are highly valued, yet the overemphasis on individual freedom and liberty have led to a waste of human and natural resources, to excessive inequality, to the overcommercialization of social relationships, and to abuses of power by large organized groups. The pursuit of social justice to the complete disregard of freedom, on the other hand, can only lead to sterile uniformity, coerced conformity, and a decline of individual effort. New nations wish to become powerful and develop in an economic sense; at the same time, they seek to diminish the inequality that is associated with past injustices. Yet these two goals are likely to be incompatible, at least in the near future, and it is the short run that counts for most people. To speed development, incentives and steep rewards are needed to encourage production and achievement. The consequence will be increased inequality among the citizenry. Those who seek to eradicate the inequality of rewards and instead rely on ideological and moral appeals may find themselves left in a community of equals living in poverty, or else, disenchanted with the lack of dedication of the masses, will coerce them into doing what is "best for them" within an authoritarian framework.

The dislocations resulting from processes of social change, the resistance to change on the part of those who benefit from the status quo, the entrenchment of new vested interests, the gaps between ideals and reality, the dilemmas of social organization resulting from the inability to achieve simultaneously valued and desired yet contradictory goals, can only be diminished, never eliminated altogether. And thus it is also with social conflict. The structural causes of social conflict require, however, a more concrete and historically specific examination.

ECONOMIC DISCONTENT

The relationship between economic factors, social conflicts, discontent and the outbreak of social disturbances is a complicated one. Tocqueville (1955:175–77) long ago observed that the years preceding the outbreak of the French Revolution witnessed an increase, not a decrease of economic prosperity:

> In 1780, there could no longer be any talk of France's being on the (economic) downgrade; on the contrary, it seemed that no limit could be set to her advance. . . . Twenty years earlier there had been no hope for the future; in 1780, no anxiety was felt about it. . . . It is a singular fact that this increasing prosperity, far from tranquilizing the population, everywhere promoted a spirit of unrest. The general public became more and more hostile to every ancient institution, more and more discontented. . . . Moreover, those parts of France in which the improvement in the standard of living was most pronounced were the centers of the revolutionary movement.

Even Marx, whose views are usually contrasted with those of Tocqueville and who in his theoretical works tended to uphold the misery theory of political upheaval (deepening economic crises, falling profits, lower wages, increased exploitation and misery of the working class, linked to increased revolutionary potential), took a much more flexible and varied approach (Marx, 1959:282–299) in his brilliant case studies and commentaries on contemporary French and European political upheavals. Yet, ever since Marx and Tocqueville there has been a continuous debate by historians and social scientists on just what are the precise links between economic changes and social conflict, in particular revolutionary outbreaks. There is no need to review this long controversy. It is sufficient to recognize that economic changes, broadly viewed, are such a common, perennial, and central component of social change that a discussion of social change, strain and dislocations, grievances and protest, cannot proceed without thorough examination of economic processes. Short- and long-term economic trends, particular sequences of short- and long-term up and down swings, migration patterns, rural-urban demographic shifts, the effects of the introduction of new technologies and novel modes of production and other structural economic changes, changes in the cost of living, of wages, of the cost of basic foods, and a host of other economic facts and processes have received close scrutiny by students of social conflict. Moreover, not only changes in absolute terms, but relative gains and losses have been discussed, and the concepts of relative deprivation, rising expectations, or some other social psychological concepts such as hope and cramp, have been invoked to assess the reactions of various groups and social classes to absolute and relative economic gains and losses. The literature on these topics has grown immense. The conclusion that several diverse patterns of economic change must bear some direct and indirect links to social disturbances, and that this link is mediated by some intervening social psychological processes, is inescapable, but not very helpful. It is worth reviewing the major points in one of the most valuable papers on this topic by an economist and then listing some of the most common patterns of economic change frequently linked to increased protest activity on the part of negatively privileged social strata and social classes.

In an article entitled "Rapid Economic Growth as a Destabilizing Force," Mancur Olson, Jr., (1963:529–52) points out that "economic growth . . . can significantly increase the number of [economic] losers," e.g., increase the absolute number of people whose standard of living has fallen, despite an increase in the average per capita income of the entire population. Especially in the early phases of economic growth, there is a tendency for increased inequality of incomes to come about. Rapid economic growth is frequently associated with new technologies and changes in methods of production, the type of labor and skills demanded, and the geographic configuration of production. While some groups may gain and, indeed, do gain economically in such periods, other groups, living in economically declining regions, working in firms or industries caught with outdated technologies, and having outdated skills, may lose in relative and even absolute terms. Furthermore, consumption levels may decline with economic growth when capital accumulation curbs spending through forced savings, taxation, or some other means. Olson also points out that economic growth as a long-term trend is often associated with short-term downswings, e.g., for particular groups, wages may rise slower than prices, increased unemployment may occur, and, indeed, wages may decline. Although Olson does not neglect the potential for political unrest among economically gaining groups experiencing rising expectations, the chief contribution of his analysis for sociologists is that nothing in economic theory contradicts the possibility of an increase in the number of economic losers during a period of economic growth and that such growth might be associated with changes in the relative economic position of social strata and other population groups. A major conclusion of his paper is that detailed information on the impact of economic changes upon specific groups is needed for understanding the potential for social and political unrest of these groups. Knowledge of aggregate national economic trends alone, or comparative analyses of countries based on aggregate figures, can lead to misleading inferences. Unfortunately, as Lawrence Stone (1965:169 ff.) has pointed out, economic data sufficiently disaggregated and complete are difficult to come by even for present times and locating economic data and data on state-of-mind variables such as relative deprivation, expectations, and aspirations for times gone by presents practically insuperable difficulties.

A brief outline of the kinds of economic changes that commonly produce grievances and frequently result in social disturbances and protest among the lower social strata and classes may be useful. Groups that are economically at the margins of subsistence will react at once to a short-term increase in food prices and/or a diminished food supply. Such shortages and price increases, often localized, occur frequently after a time of crop failures or of war. The protesters' response is typically the food riot, consisting of attacks upon food hoarders and distributors who are holding back their food stocks or selling them at high prices, forced food sales at the preshortage price level, and the prevention of food transfers out of a given locality to meet demands elsewhere. (Rudé, 1964). When such grievances and disturbances coincide with dissatisfaction among other social strata, the lower classes can be mobilized by them beyond the initial limited aims for the provision of cheap food. Writing about the French Revolution, at a time when from 25 percent to 90 percent of the daily wages of urban working people were spent on bread (depending on their trade and skill level) Rudé (1967:200) noted that

> perhaps not surprisingly (an inquiry into the causes of social unrest among the *menu peuple*) reveals that the constant motive of popular insurrection during the Revolution, as in the 18th century as a whole, was the compelling need of the *menu peuple* for the provision of cheap and plentiful bread and other essentials, and the necessary administrative measures to insure it.

An effective response of the authorities in such a situation is to provide food supplies at the usual price, often by means of price controls. The lack of support by the working people of Paris for Robespierre and the Jacobins at the time of their fall in 1794 was due in large part to the inability to assure a stable cost of living by means of wage and price controls (Rudé, 1959: chapter 9).

In the case of rural social strata, one should be careful to distinguish between peasants who are only marginally involved in commercial production for the market and farmers who are independent owner-cultivators producing commercial crops, often for export. Such farmers, especially single-crop farmers producing an export crop, are vulnerable to the fluctuations in the world market prices of their crops and, in particular, to a drop in prices after a period of boom when they may have become excessively dependent for income on one particular crop. Examples of the processes of mobilization among farmers under such circumstances are the Populist movement in the American west in the 1880s and 1890s (Hicks, 1961: chapter 3), right-wing and Nazi vote of farmers in north Germany in 1928 and later (Heberle, 1945), and the positive response of African farmers to nationalist movements in many colonies in the late 1950s and early 1960s after a drop in world market prices for cotton, coffee, cocoa and other export crops following the World War II and post-war boom period.

Peasant disaffection occurs most frequently over the issues of land shortage and attempts by landlords to extract an increased economic surplus by means that violate traditional norms of equity and of distribution (B. Moore, 1966: chapter 9). The occasion for peasant disturbances is provided by demographic pressure and the behavior of the land-lords. Landlords may attempt to increase their income from the peasantry under pressure of indebtedness resulting from conspicuous consumption in cities or the court. Gerschenkron (1964:184) points to the attempt by the French nobility before the French Revolution to revive some rights and claims on land that had not been exercised for a long time and increase the peasants' financial burden. Under such circumstances, peasants are convinced that their grievances are legitimate. Peasant revolts resulting from these issues are extremely common: for instance, Shu-ching Lee (1951:512) reports that in a small border region about the size of Iowa, between Kiangsi and Fukien in China, an investigator found from local records seventy-six instances of peasant revolt, led mostly by tenants, over a period of some 180 years between 1448 and 1627. Another cause of revolt occurs when a landlord class seeks to exploit its estates in a more rational and profitable fashion by consolidating land, evicting tenants, and seizing lands traditionally held in common ownership by the peasant community as occurred at the time of the Mexican Revolution (McNeely, 1966). Furthermore, demographic pressures in rural areas often force peasants to become squatters or otherwise seize the uncultivated lands of neighboring landlords. Of course, a part of the surplus population may migrate to the cities in search of industrial employment, but the alternative may not always be present or may become unattractive during periods of industrial depression and urban unemployment. Putting more land or unused land under cultivation using traditional techniques of production in order to increase or maintain his income is more attractive and realistic for the peasant than using more advanced agricultural technology on his existing holding, since he may lack the required skills and capital. Economic and demographic pressures operating on peasants in Russia before 1905 led to widespread land seizures, illegal grazings, arson of manors, forest destruction, and other forms of peasant disturbances (Gerschenkron, 1964:191).

Land reform is too broad a term to describe an effective response on the part of the authorities to meet peasant land hunger. Tilly (1964a: 196) has shown in the case of the Vendée that the sale of church lands during the French Revolution became an occasion for increased disaffection among the peasantry because the prosperous farmers and small-town bourgeois managed to outbid the small tenants and farmers and grab most of the desirable land that rural people felt was rightfully theirs. Effective land reform means the transfer of available land (not only marginal land) to the peasants themselves. Land reform is likely to be successful if the landlords are foreign nationals: German barons in the Baltic area, Polish aristocrats in Lithuania, Hungarian nobles in Yugoslavia, and Turkisized Bulgars in parts of Rumania, as was the case in the post World War I period in Eastern Europe (Gerschenkron, 1966:94). Nationalization of land and the impressment of tenants and small landholders into collective farms or state farms are usually highly unpopular solutions and will be resisted by peasants, although the state and its agents of social control may be strong enough to put down resistance, as happened in Soviet Russia. Nationalization of land is likely to be more acceptable where the majority of rural working people have been a propertyless, wage-earning, rural proletariat rather than an independent class of smallholders as in Cuba.

Among the urban working class, three major groups have to be distinguished in particular: unskilled, recent, rural migrants, working people in established and growing industries, and "preindustrial" skilled workers and independent artisans and craftsmen who are losing their economic base because of competition from new methods of production. It is the last named group that has been particularly noted for its participation in social and political disturbances, at least in Western Europe. (Rudé, 1967: chapter 13). Starting in the late eighteenth century, as a result of the Industrial Revolution, artisans and craftsmen have been a numerically declining stratum, constantly threatened with being reduced to ordinary wage workers, economically insecure and caught in a spiral of downward social mobility. Long-term economic growth did not benefit them since it occurred mainly in the new manufacturing and industrial sectors. Moreover, reform legislation regulating hours of work, conditions of work, safety, and female and child labor seldom benefited them and, more often than not, represented a further immediate loss of income because of their reliance on family labor. Many of these groups sought a solution to their economic problems in the revival of preindustrial curbs on competition, price and wage controls, and other measures that were inconsistent with the broader social and economic changes taking place and that were therefore not instituted. Because of a tradition of corporate association and collective action, these groups were susceptible to rapid mobilization to defend their interests.

On the other hand, wage workers in new and growing industries did benefit directly from long-term economic growth and labor legislation, but were hurt by unemployment and wage cuts during depressions. These wage earning groups, however, were subject to strain and grievances, most often resulting in strikes, over the reluctance of employers to restore wage levels when prosperity returned, over conditions and hours of work, over the right to form trade unions and engage in collective bargaining (which was itself a result of the workers' conviction that there was no other effective means of protecting their employment security, wage levels, and standard of life), and over the issue of job security when employers tried to hire unskilled workers, often recent migrants, to replace them. Especially explosive outbursts occurred when unskilled strikebreakers, often drawn from an ethnic or racial minority, were introduced after workers had gone on strike against their employer, as was typical of U.S. industrial conflict. An increase in the standard of living of the working class, industrial legislation in the area of hours, child labor, hygiene, and safety, the recognition of the right to collective bargaining, and other reforms instituted during the nineteenth and twentieth centuries, were the appropriate long-term responses that directed labor conflict into increasingly peaceful and institutionalized channels.

As for recent rural migrants with low skills, who are everywhere known to contribute a disproportionate share to all the social pathologies associated with the growing industrial city, a great deal depended on the opportunities they had for temporarily returning to their families in rural areas who provided them with an economic cushion in difficult times. At any rate, this group has not figured as prominently in large-scale collective disturbances, especially of a political sort, as the other groups and has even at certain times been co-opted by the ruling class to fight against other working-class protesters, as was the case with the Mobile Guard in Paris during the 1848 Revolution (Rudé, 1967:173); at other times they have acted as strikebreakers for employers. In effect, recent migrants are so often close to the margins of subsistence that they are very vulnerable to economic pressures, react positively to economic opportunities even when it means breaking the rank of working class solidarity, and are reluctant to take the economic risks that protest activity entails.

Economic grievances also figure among the sources of discontent of economically privileged groups such as merchants, professionals, entrepreneurs, salaried managers, white-collar employees, though perhaps not as prominently as among the causes of discontent of the lower classes. The government and its agencies, although frequently protecting the interests of the relatively affluent groups as a whole in the face of lower-class aspirations and demands, do not and cannot pursue economic policies that are equally beneficial to all middle- and upper-income groups. Much conflict is generated by divisions and conflicts of interest within the upper class and the elites themselves, between the government bureaucracy and the private economic sector. Manufacturers seek low tariffs on grain to keep the price of basic foods and, thus, also, of industrial wages low, while the landed upper class whose life style depends on the inefficient domestic production of grain seeks high tariffs to shut out cheap foreign imports. Industrial entrepreneurs are blocked from the unrestricted economic exploitation of labor by a government controlled by aristocratic groups who insist on a paternalist, welfare-oriented labor policy and who despise the pretensions of the new moneyed classes. Much of Pareto's political sociology is based on an analysis of conflicts within the economic elite between two groups with opposed economic interests, the speculators and the rentiers (Pareto, 1963:§§ 2310–15, §§2233–36).

Speculators do not have fixed incomes. They are the entrepreneurs, businessmen, investment bankers, stockholders, real estate developers, and the lawyers, engineers, technicians, whose livelihood and prosperity depend on the speculators' enterprises. Rentiers are people with fixed incomes—landowners, civil servants, employees of all sorts, and pensioners. Speculators derive profit from a low interest rate and high tariffs and are not hurt by high taxes and prices, since they pass increased costs on to the consumers. Rentiers, on the other hand, prefer a high interest rate, stable prices, low taxes, and free trade. In Pareto's view, these opposing economic interests create alliances across class lines, such as that between entrepreneurs and their employees in favor of tariff protection, or between organized labor and management for action to sustain a wage-price inflationary spiral that hurts primarily the consumers.

Economic conflicts have frequently produced or contributed to lasting cleavages and antagonisms among the positively privileged social strata. They account for the phenomenon of divided elites that many social scientists and historians see as one condition favoring success in revolution. They have played an important part in the histories of many countries, not the least that of Germany (Gerschenkron, 1966), and help explain why economically privileged groups often take the lead in opposing the authorities, as merchants did in colonial America in the latter part of the eighteenth century, or else withhold their support when the government is about to be toppled and is desperately reaching out for support.

POLITICAL DISCONTENT

Political discontent and conflict occur in a bewildering variety of forms and concrete circumstances. No classification or typology can do justice to the richness of historical detail and serve the purposes of all investigators alike. The aim of this section is to discuss and illustrate the most common sources of political grievances and discontent that cause conflicts and that, if left unresolved, are likely to precipitate social disturbances, rebellions, revolts, and revolutions.

A useful way of dividing up the field is to follow Kornhauser's (1964: 142–43) distinction between alien, exclusive, arbitrary, and insufficient authority. Discontent can result from the imposition of an alien, superior, outside authority upon groups or peoples who resent their loss of autonomy; from the demands for greater authority, rights, and recognition by those who are excluded from the polity and from full-citizenship rights; from the illegitimate and arbitrary exercise of authority, and from the ineffective use of authority by the incumbents to solve societal problems. Discontent can also result from the usual, ongoing contest for a greater share of authority by groups and organizations who already have access to power and influence. Political discontents and conflicts of one sort often spill over into other conflicts. At any historical moment, a political crisis can be precipitated by several types of discontent affecting a variety of groups with different intensity.

Discontent and conflicts result from incorporating hitherto autonomous groups or peoples under an external, usually foreign, authority, or from the diminution of the sphere of authority of local and regional groups and notables under a policy of unification and centralization of the national government. The history of imperialism and colonialism testifies to the coercive and violent nature of this process. But the histories of state formation in the "old" states of Western Europe, contemporary problems of nation-building in the "new" states in the postcolonial era, and the long history of conflict over states' rights in the federal structure of the United States indicate that the imposition or extension of external authority, foreign or national, upon regions with a long history of autonomy is a conflict-ridden process. Conflicts over the imposition of external authority need not pit against each other economically negatively and positively privileged groups, but rather different elites, each with its own constituency and following whose support is enlisted during the confrontation. Nevertheless, there are many instances where the economic security and material aspirations, as well as sense of identity and pride, of local and regional populations are closely tied to the autonomy of their existing leaders. New authority is often ambitious and interventionist: it seeks more revenue, labor, and land and a more intensive exploitation of local resources; it intervenes on behalf of some groups and diminishes the power of others; it mobilizes local supporters who abuse their newly won power; alternatively, foreign authority entrenches unpopular elites who might have been ousted. Local ruling groups resent the restriction of their sphere of authority over appointments and patronage, the allocation of revenues, and judicial decisionmaking; they resent their loss of stature and the corresponding increased prestige of officials of the foreign or central government. Ordinary people resent the interference in their accustomed way of life and fear that the new ruling groups will be unjust, inaccessible, lacking in understanding for their concerns and partial to upstart groups who threaten to disturb the existing balance of local interests. Thus, they rally behind their traditional leaders in movements of resistance and opposition to alien authority. If territory coincides with well-defined group boundaries based on community of language, ethnic or tribal membership, religion, or some other ascriptive characteristic, the result may well be secession or civil war threatening the very existence of the state.

Two examples will suffice to illustrate more concretely the processes of discontent and resistance to external authority. In his book on the Vendée counterrevolution of 1793, Tilly (1964a) describes how opposition to the revolutionary government in Paris and its local agents and supporters resulted from its increased demands upon the Vendée population and their interference in local affairs. Military conscription for an unpopular cause was imposed from the outside. Revolutionary reforms, especially the sale of church properties, the Civil Constitution of the Clergy, administrative reorganizations, all diminished the material means and the authority of local notables and of the clergy upon whom the economic security and welfare of many peasants and artisans rested. This resulted in the ascendancy of the small-town bourgeoisie who were opposed to paternalist economic and political relationships at a time of economic depression in the Vendée. These accumulated grievances and provocations resulting from the imposition of external authority sparked the Vendée uprising.

The secessionist crisis in Uganda in 1965–1966 is a typical example of similar conflicts in new states. During the period of British colonial rule in Uganda, the Kingdom of Buganda, the wealthiest and most developed region of Uganda, had enjoyed a favored position in most respects and was resented by most other tribes. The price of Buganda's willingness to join an independent Uganda, rather than seeking independence as a separate state, was a series of political and constitutional compromises over territorial disputes, the respective powers of the president and of the prime minister of Uganda (the presidency was filled by the Kabaka or king of Buganda while Obote, leader of the Uganda People's Congress, became prime minister), and the judicial, fiscal, administrative, and political autonomy of Buganda, which left Buganda still in a favored though not politically dominant position. In the four years following independence in 1962, Ganda expectations of leadership in the new state were disappointed, their veto power in the Uganda National Assembly disappeared as a result of political party realignments and defections, and their ability to withstand the centralizing policies of the UPC government under Obote diminished. As the regional autonomy of Buganda was being whittled away, the Ganda ruling groups, whose security rested upon it, grew apprehensive and defensive. Ganda politicians failed in an attempt to take over the UPC from within and to oust Obote as prime minister on corruption charges. Obote countered by ousting the Kabaka from the presidency, took over this position himself, and proclaimed a new unitary constitution for Uganda. Under the new constitution, Buganda's high court was abolished, the finances of Buganda were brought under close central government supervision, and the lands and voting rights of Ganda chiefs and other court officials in the Buganda Assembly—the Lukiko—were taken away. The Lukiko's power to fill twenty-one Buganda seats in the National Assembly was abolished in favor of direct elections, its right to veto constitutional amendments affecting Buganda's status was eliminated, and the powers of the Buganda public service commission to appoint local officials were weakened (Young, 1966; Hopkins, 1967). In short, the privileged legal, administrative, and constitutional position upon which Buganda's regional autonomy and ruling groups' power and security rested was overturned. Buganda's reaction was the secession attempt of 1966, during which the Ganda citizenry rallied behind their leaders but were unable to withstand the onslaught of the Uganda army.

Discontent and conflicts stemming from exclusive authority result from the efforts of hitherto excluded groups and peoples to achieve full-citizenship status by acquiring greater authority, more or equal rights, and political independence. Those who have enjoyed a monopoly of authority and rights in turn resist the diminution of their favored and exclusive position. Continued denial of political and civil rights, discrimination, denigration of the customs and life styles, and lack of respect and recognition for the achievements, dignity, leaders, and emerging collective pride, of negatively privileged groups becomes intolerable and leads to movements of collective protest and opposition. The well-known movements of the bourgeoisie to abolish the aristocrats' privileges and to achieve political rights, to overturn absolutist monarchies and institute constitutional monarchies or republics; of the working classes for full-citizenship rights; of oppressed religious groups for establishing the principle of toleration; of negatively privileged minorities for civil rights; of colonial peoples for independence, all fall into this broad class of conflicts that have played, and continue to play, such an important part in the histories of most countries, large and small, Western and non-Western.

Closely allied to the conflicts generated by excluded groups' demands to enter the polity are the discontents and conflicts resulting from the illegitimate exercise of power by ruling groups resisting the attempts to crowd them off the center of the historical stage. Lipset (1963:65–66) noted that political stability becomes precarious and a crisis of legitimacy develops when the status of major conservative institutions is threatened during a period of social change. Common ways in which ruling groups seek to block change, and which then become the occasion for organized opposition and social turmoil, are by staging rigged elections, preventing fair elections, cancelling scheduled elections that they expect to lose, preventing constitutionally elected political leaders from assuming office or deposing them after they are in office, withholding or undermining promised reforms and concessions, and in general using a wide range of illegal, coercive methods for staying in power and for consolidating rule. The immediate causes of the Nigerian civil war can be traced to the political turmoil resulting from repeatedly successful attempts by the political arm of the northern Nigerian ruling groups to prevent the victory of their opponents in free and fair elections, rigging elections in favor of their political allies, and ousting from office their most dangerous, constitutionally elected political opponents on dubious charges. The East Pakistani secession started when the military rulers prevented the Awami League leaders, clearcut victors in the elections, from assuming office contrary to their earlier promise of a return to civilian rule. An analysis of military coups in Latin America (Needler, 1966) shows that in the decade 1955 to 1964 a majority of coups resulting in the overthrow of constitutionally elected governments occurred around election time and concludes that their primary purpose was to thwart social change, especially the anticipated diminution in the privileges and power of the upper classes and of the military itself. In all these examples, the incumbents themselves resorted to illegitimate means and prevented the conflict of opposing forces to proceed in established institutional channels. Thus, opponents of these regimes had or may have little choice but to counter coercion with violence.

Political discontent is also engendered by those regimes that have achieved power by illegitimate means, maintain themselves in power by relying on coercion, superior force, and, often, foreign protectors, exercise power arbitrarily and harshly, and do not defend the national interest as the ordinary citizen defines it because they are subservient to a foreign power. Sometimes all of these factors are present in the same situation, as was true of the Rakosi regime in Hungary before the 1956 revolution. As in cases discussed earlier, so also in Hungary, the initial resistance to the arbitrary and coercive regime came from members of the privileged economic strata—the intelligentsia and students who would directly profit from greater intellectual freedom and the members of the free professions and the middle class whose security would be greatly enhanced by reestablishing the rule of law and checking the arbitrary and illegal actions of state bureaucrats, personal cliques of top leaders, and the dictator himself. Since opposition to totalitarian regimes is not possible through peaceful and legal channels, discontented groups will inevitably take to the streets.

Dissatisfaction with inefficient and insufficient authority occurs when the government and ruling groups are incapable of solving pressing societal problems and fulfilling the usual functions of government, such as the protection of territorial integrity and other national interests against foreigners, a fair administration of justice, an effective administration of services for the common good. Corruption, maladministration, nepotism, and officials' remoteness and unresponsiveness to the people may not immediately give rise to major political upheavals, but accumulated frustrations and discontents in time will undermine the regime's legitimacy. The inability to meet threats to national sovereignty or to defend national interests has often become the primary cause of political conflict. In mid-nineteenth-century Tokugawa Japan the previously high ranking samurai, whose political influence and economic position had deteriorated but who remained attached to an aristocratic and military ethos of loyalty and honor, watched with dismay as the Tokugawa rulers were forced into a policy of humiliating concessions by foreign naval and military power. Japan's self-imposed isolation from the outside world crumbled under the aggressive and expansionist commercial imperialism of the United States and European powers. Under the banner of "honor the emperor, expel the barbarians," the samurai of western Japan reasserted themselves, forced the Tokugawa shogun to abdicate, restored the figurehead emperor, and designed a policy of reforms to revolutionize and modernize government and country, in particular to increase industrial and military power (Reischauer, 1965: chapters 8 and 9). Similarly, some recent military coups in Latin America, such as in Peru, were motivated by army officers' dissatisfaction with what they saw as political faintheartedness in standing up to foreign economic interests—large U.S. corporations—and asserted national control over the economy and the exploitation of natural resources.

Discontent and political conflict are also caused by contests for greater power or for maintaining one's share of power by already favorably situated groups and organizations. These contests pit, for example, the state and its agents against business leaders, civilian against military elites, the legislative branch against the executive, officials and officialdom against the articulate public and the press. In a typical case the state restricts the sphere of power of organizations and institutions through legislation, administrative regulations, and enforcement, as the power of big business was restricted in the U.S. through antitrust, labor, and tax legislation during the Progressive and Roosevelt eras. Although

the very stuff of day-to-day institutionalized politics consists of these conflicts, it frequently happens that they spill over into unconstitutional and
illegal channels and lead to major institutional changes. One illustration
is the military coup in Ghana that overthrew Nkrumah in 1966 while he
was on a state visit in Peking. It was precipitated by the top army and
police officers' fear that recent steps taken to reorganize defense and
police affairs in the direction of greater control by the president's office—
e.g., the forcible retirement of General Ankrah, the growth of a Soviet
trained, advised, and armed Presidential Guard Regiment under Nkrumah's personal command, the transfer of security intelligence functions
from police control to the office of the president, Nkrumah's plan to
create a people's militia separate from the army, efforts at political infiltration of the officer corps—would jeopardize their personal safety as
well as diminish their power. The rebels had for some time been dissatisfied with the corruption, mismanagement, inefficient and arbitrary rule,
and economic chaos under the Nkrumah regime, but it was fear for their
personal safety and the weakening position of the army and police as a
whole that occasioned the coup itself. They counted upon widespread
popular dissatisfaction with economic hardship and arbitrary political
rule to ensure the success of the coup and facilitate the consolidation of
military rule (*Africa Report*, 1966: *Venture*, 1966).

Periods of social turmoil and political upheaval almost always result
from combinations of economic and political grievances that are widely
distributed but nevertheless centered in different social strata and groups.
It is this multiplicity that taxes the institutions of conflict regulation to
their breaking point. But quite apart from the substantive issues that produce conflict, a theory of social conflict must examine the dimensions of
the issues themselves, since it is the dimensions as much as the substance
of the conflict that determine the likelihood of successful conflict regulation.

THE DIMENSIONS OF CONFLICT

One of the theoretic gains achieved by game theory is in uncovering the
structure of a great variety of conflict situations without regard to what
the substantive issues are or who the opponents are (Boulding, 1962:
chapter 3; Rapoport, 1965). A similar approach is useful in the theory of
social conflict. After the dimensions of the conflict situation have been
uncovered, the substantive issues, the characteristics of the opponents,
and other similar considerations can be reintroduced to provide further
distinctions and greater concreteness.

One of the most frequently cited generalizations deals with the difference between conflicts over basic principles and values and other kinds of conflicts, for instance, the difference between an application of accepted principles to specific situations or a conflict over the control of material resources (Coser, 1956:73). One would expect conflict over principles to arouse greater enmity, more hostility, to be fought harder and more mercilessly, and to be more difficult to regulate or resolve. According to Simmel and to reformulations of his original insight by Coser, the elimination of the personal element in conflict tends to make conflict sharper and more intense, tends to imbue the participants with self-righteousness and moral fervor that keep being reenforced through group support. In Coser's words (1956:118), "Conflicts in which the participants feel that they are merely the representatives of collectivities and groups, fighting not for self but for ideals of the group they represent, are likely to be more radical and merciless than those that are fought for personal reasons."

For this reason conflicts over symbols tend to be more intense and more difficult to regulate than nonsymbolic conflicts. Symbols are collective representations expressing the moral worth, claim to status, and collective identity of groups and communities. The defense of these symbols is seen as an unselfish action worthy of group support; disrespect for symbols or an attempt to substitute different symbols will be perceived as an attack on the integrity, moral standing, sense of identity, and self-respect of the entire nation or group, threatening the basic consensus and the principles of legitimacy upon which social order is founded. Patriotic concerns over disloyalty and the desecration or ridicule of national symbols are common examples of the type of conflict that arouses intense passions.

Another reason why conflicts over symbols and principles are difficult to settle is that the outcome of the dispute cannot be divided in a way that will partially satisfy both parties. In many conflicts over material interests, the parties can each gain a slice of the pie without either group getting the entire pie. But symbols and principles by their very nature are indivisible goods. One can either have the tricolor flag of the Republic or the Bourbon white, either recite or not recite a prayer in public schools. A principle cannot be compromised and still remain valid to its advocates. The number of national holidays can be increased to satisfy the aspirations of hitherto excluded groups, and national flags, coats of arms, anthems, and other symbols can be created that are a combination of the symbols valued by different groups. Yet, the creation of eclectic symbols usually is feasible only after the conflict has died down and opponents have developed new common values and bonds and no longer share the earlier particularist concerns and mutual antagonism. Various face-saving and compromise arrangements are also possible, for instance, a silent prayer in a public school, or the temporary exit of those not wishing to participate in prayer, or some watered-down prayer that makes only oblique and vague references to the deity or religious beliefs. Yet, such a compromise is likely to be accepted only after the original religious fervor has abated and beliefs are no longer widely held—in other words, only when the basic causes of the conflict no longer operate.

Another formal property of issues that are disputed is their reversibility. One would expect irreversible settlements to be fought over harder than reversible settlements. For instance, assuming a country has scarce resources, the location of a large-scale capital investment project such as a dam, factory, or railroad line is probably going to be fought over intensely, since after it is built in a particular location at great expense it is going to remain there. By contrast, programs and projects that do not require such a large capital outlay and that are annually budgeted and implemented, redistributed, increased and decreased according to demand and pressures, are subject to reversals and renegotiations and will not generate as much heat. In a democratic polity competition for public office is a struggle whose settlement is reversible. A future time table of tests of strength is known in advance and reversal in elections is considered legitimate. While the election of candidate X as opposed to candidate Y has only an indivisible solution (either X or Y will be elected), the conflict is cushioned by the reversible character of the outcome. Since the competition for political power is pursued within the framework of nationwide political parties and a multitude of separate individual competitive struggles for office, under normal circumstances the resolution of the total political conflict will have a distributional aspect, with candidates of each party winning some of the constituencies, districts, localities, and so on, making the outcome divisible. Democratic competition for political office has the double aspect of divisible and repeatedly reversible outcomes built into it institutionally, tending to make conflict less intense and the outcomes more acceptable to the temporary losers.

The difficulty of conflict resolution does not necessarily increase with the number of separate issues over which the conflict takes place. The resolution of a single issue in isolation, such as the location of one factory or the election of a single candidate for office, makes the outcome an indivisible one. However, if many separate issues are fought over simultaneously, as in a national election or the location of several factories, the overall solution becomes distributive and the outcome divisible among the antagonists. However, this property of issues may be a factor making for easier conflict settlement only if the issues are by and large the same or comparable, so that the outcomes of the separate conflicts are comparable and subject to calculable give-and-take exchanges.

The calculability of the costs of various outcomes in a conflict also has a bearing on the ease with which the issues can be resolved or settled.

If the costs are calculable according to a common standard of measurement such as money or number of positions won, it is easier to work out some sort of an equitable outcome within the framework of basic principles. For example, the maxim "to each an equal share" or "to each party according to its contribution or strength" or "to each party according to its size" can be invoked and the outcome adjusted accordingly. If what is fought over is divisible, mutual concessions and gains can be measured and brought into line with a distributive principle established by the conflicting parties. However, if the costs of possible outcomes are difficult to calculate because of the extreme complexity and ramifications of the issues at stake, or if the outcomes to the parties consist of incommensurable factors, an acceptable settlement may be more difficult to reach. What quantity of material goods and what increase in the standard of living can offset the grievances and frustrations of people who have been subjected to foreign rule, who have been humiliated, and whose sense of dignity has been affronted? How can one calculate the costs and consequences of extending the suffrage to a previously disenfranchised group in the population when it is difficult to know what the shifts of political power will be, not to speak of wider secondary consequences that are unknown and impossible to calculate? One would therefore expect conflict over economic goods and over resources and benefits that can be measured to be more amenable to solution than noneconomic conflicts over social status, civil rights, religious freedom, prestige, symbols, morality, and principles.

A final link between the structure of conflict and its potential for resolution rests on the distinction between zero-sum and non–zero-sum games in game theory (Rapoport, 1965). In zero-sum games, the interests of the two parties are diametrically opposed: what one player wins, the other loses. In non–zero-sum or mixed-motive games, the sum of the payoffs of each possible outcome does not necessarily add to zero. The interests of the conflicting parties partially diverge and partially coincide. There are outcomes that both parties would prefer to other outcomes, and there may be outcomes that both parties would prefer to avoid. For instance, if the players are designated by the letters A and B, their choices of action by A_1 and A_2 and B_1 and B_2 respectively, then the payoff matrix for the four possible outcomes might be as follows:

	B_1	B_2
A_1	5, 3	3, 5
A_2	3, 1	-4, -5

[Note: in each cell, A's payoff is written first, followed by B's payoff, thus (3, 1) means that A gains 3 and B gets 1]

The outcome (A_2, B_2) is one that both parties wish to avoid since they would both lose. On the other hand, A would prefer the outcome (A_1, B_1), whereas B would prefer the outcome (A_1, B_2), since they would gain most with these outcomes. Therefore, the disagreement is over whether A should get 5 and B should get 3, or vice versa. Depending on factors extraneous to the logical structure of the game, A and B may well work out a satisfactory settlement of the dispute while studiously avoiding ending up in (A_2, B_2).

The following game, however, is a case of pure conflict: no matter which combination of choices is made, the outcome is such that A

	B_1	B_2
A_1	3, -3	1, -1
A_2	1, -1	-2, 2

gains at B's expense, or vice versa. In this particular instance, the solution is likely to be (A_1, B_2). A knows that B cannot choose B_1 since he would stand to lose no matter what A's choice. Since B is likely to choose B_2, A can opt for A_1 and realize a gain of 1 at B's expense. The hypothesis is that conflict is going to be more bitter, more intense, and more difficult to regulate and settle in situations with outcomes corresponding to zero-sum games than it will be in situations with outcomes corresponding to mixed-motive games. In many instances of group conflict corresponding to mixed-motive games, as Schelling has noted (1963:83), some kind of collaboration and mutual accommodation will be necessary if joint disaster is to be avoided. There will be bargaining, the exchange of concessions, a search for a mutually acceptable distribution of the gains that both can realize. Therefore, a mixed-motive game will exhibit the group-binding functions that Simmel and Coser have described in great detail (Coser, 1956). Zero-sum games or situations of pure conflict, when one party can gain only at the expense of the other, violate all the basic principles of equity, fair exchange, and mutual benefit upon which most social relations are founded. In sum, regardless of the protesters' character (e.g., peasants, workers, students, a religious minority) and the substance of the conflict (e.g., political, economic, religious issues), one would expect conflict situations for which the costs are calculable, the outcomes are divisible and reversible, and the payoff matrix is non-zero sum to be more amenable to regulation and resolution than conflict situations for which the costs are difficult to calculate, the outcomes are indivisible and irreversible, and the payoff matrix is zero-sum. Conflicts over symbols and principles tend to have none of the attributes making for ease of settlement, whereas conflicts over material resources and rewards and the application of accepted principles are more likely to possess the positive attributes. It remains now to apply those ideas to some common forms of social conflict by reintroducing the protesters and target groups, the substance of the dispute, and the institutional realm that is involved.

Let us consider first a conflict over wages between a labor union and a business firm. The conflict is over the relative share of the material output that the owner will realize as profit and the workers as increased wages and other employee benefits. The choice of the employer is to accept the demands of the union or reject them and stick to his initial —or prepare a new, more generous—offer. The union in turn can accept the employer's initial offer, strike, or modify its original demand by entering into bargaining. Bargaining can be fruitful since the outcome consists of divisible goods calculable in money terms. The solution is reversible in time since the labor contract is renegotiated periodically. The payoff structure is non-zero sum: both parties would lose in a prolonged strike, and both parties would gain within a broad range of settlements. The structure of the outcome can be represented visually in a simple two-dimensional space where the vertical axis stands for A's (employer) gain or loss and the horizontal axis for B's (union's) gain or loss. Each point in the space represents a possible outcome of the conflict:

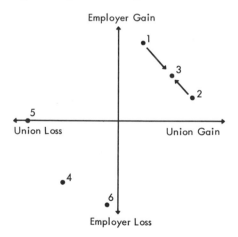

Point *1* might realistically represent the employer's initial offer, point *2* the union's initial demand, and point *3* is the settlement toward which both might be expected to converge by a process of give and take, since it is in their mutual interest to avoid a strike represented by point *4*. If business is slow and the employer plans to curtail production in any event, the employer's bargaining position is stronger, and a strike would then represent little if any loss to him (point *5*). Under these conditions, the settlement is probably going to be a point closer to point *1* than the point *3* indicated in the figure. If business is booming, if there are unfilled orders and high profits to be realized, the union's bargaining strength is stronger. In a strike, the company's loss would be greater (point *6*), and the worker's loss less since some might find other forms of employment in a tight labor market. Under these conditions, the settlement is probably going to be a point closer to point *2* than the point *3* in the figure.

In this illustration contemporary economic conditions and a legal framework for collective bargaining were assumed: the company recognizes the union as bargaining agent for the employees and cannot fire its employees and import strikebreakers, and the economic output is steadily increasing, even if slowly—hence, both sides can realize gains. But what if one assumes conditions not unusual for smaller firms in the nineteenth century during the frequent business depressions, when workers' wages were already close to subsistence level and the employer might have to save his business by cutting the wages? Here the employer's preferred solution is point *1*, a cut in employees' wages to maintain profits, which is a zero-sum

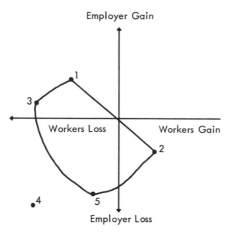

outcome in that the gain of the employer is at the worker's expense. The workers would prefer no cut in wages or increased wages at the employer's expense (point *2*). A prolonged and "successful" strike (point *4*) might well put the firm out of business, a total loss for both parties, whereas a strike during which the employer manages to operate his business with strikebreakers might actually realize some modest gains for the employer and bring great losses to the workers (point *3*). Under these circumstances, the use of coercive tactics to prevent strikebreakers or scabs from working or the destruction of industrial machinery and the use of similar tactics could mean smaller losses to the workers at a great potential loss to the employer (point *5*). Thus, one would expect the conflict to be carried out within the surface *1-2-3-5*, most of which represents outcomes of loss to both parties. Coercive tactics on both sides would tend to make each party's loss smaller at the expense of a greater loss for the other. Under these circumstances, peaceful and orderly negotiations are far less likely to take place than in the earlier illustration.

Let us look at some other kinds of conflict from the point of view of gains and losses for different outcomes, bearing in mind that in this theoretical exercise it will be assumed that group gains and losses can be summarized in one index in such a way that the figures can be used. If a conflict develops over the location of an industry or dam or some other indivisible physical plant generating jobs and economic benefits for a particular region, we have the following situation:

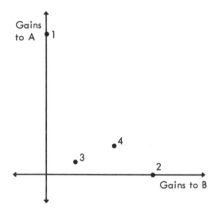

If the facility is located in region *A* (point *1*), group *A* gets all the benefits and group *B* realizes no gain, and vice versa if the facility is located in region *B* (point *2*). Note that locating the facility somewhere on the border between region *A* and region *B* (point *3*) may very well be an uneconomical outcome from the point of view of total benefits, generating a smaller combined gain to both groups than either point *1* or point *2*, even though it does represent a compromise of sorts. The resolution of this kind of conflict is made possible if the original project can be divided into parts enabling a distributive outcome, for instance the location of two factories with *A* getting one and *B* another (point *4*), even though each factory produces less total output and provides fewer total gains than the original one large factory. Therefore, this type of economic conflict is easier to handle provided a country has sufficient resources to undertake several investments. However, there is one fairly common situation that can generate a great deal of conflict. If the existence of a particular local resource (e.g., mines) drawing allied and related investments and projects to a region leads to cumulative irreversible advantages for that region over its neighbor, then the conflict created by the disparity might be heightened further as the population of the deprived region has to undertake labor migration into the favored region, where they become a low-status and exploited minority. However, the noncumulative kind of economic conflict has a high potential for conflict regulation if the total economic output is increasing. Under scarcity conditions when gains for some must be realized from losses to others, conflict will be more intense and violent, as the labor conflict examples illustrate.

Another kind of frequent conflict deals with mobility opportunities, the struggle over civil service and other organizational positions that provide high status and a high standard of living compared to alternative job opportunities. This might happen if members of one group control positions through political patronage and keep out other equally qualified groups, or if members of a hitherto excluded group with fewer qualified individuals demand a share of positions commensurable with their numerical strength or political power. Under conditions assuming a fixed number of positions available, the situation is one of pure conflict, for one group can gain positions only at the expense of the other group's overall mobility chances. But, since the outcome is divisible, the cost calculable, and the process alterable in time, it is possible to work out quota systems based on compensatory or proportionality principles through bargaining. More popular yet would be an expansion of the total number of positions, so that the hitherto excluded group might gain without diminishing the opportunities and benefits available to the incumbents. The struggle for positions is likely to be more intense at the very top of the hierarchy (presidency, cabinet posts, top civil service positions), since the issue of material benefits is very secondary to the struggle for authority and its symbols. In these situations, cabinet members might have to be carefully balanced between various groups, and informal understandings reached about the group affiliation of president, vice-president, prime minister, and other top officials at any given time.

This last example raises the question of the difference between conflict over material resources and benefits and conflicts over authority, social status, moral worth—conflicts involving redistribution and redefinition of mutual rights and obligations, expansion of the sphere of freedom enjoyed by certain groups, entry of hitherto excluded groups into citizenship status, and moral revaluation of groups previously despised and excluded from the "respectable" section of the citizenry (Marshall, 1965). These issues are frequently over principle and have a symbolic aspect transcending the increased material benefits that greater freedom, rights, and authority open up for negatively privileged groups. Outcomes are no longer subject to neat division, costs and consequences of the outcomes are difficult to calculate, gains and losses are usually difficult to reverse in time, and in the short run the excluded group's gains must come at the expense of privileged groups' accustomed rights. The excluded groups have little to offer in compensation for the demands they make and may well be forced to rely on threats to peace and social stability and raising the specter of social disturbances to have their demands considered and acted upon. What positive benefit can an established church with a monopoly of "correct" beliefs and religious practices derive from the establishment of the principle of religious tolerance? What benefits accrue to a group with a monopoly of political power from extending the suffrage to other groups?

The answer to these questions may seem self-evident, but one should not hastily assume that conflicts over rights, authority, moral worth, prestige, and the like are always instances of pure conflict. There may be mutually advantageous outcomes, and outcomes all parties wish to avoid, even though the outcomes cannot be cast into quite as specific, visible, and calculable terms as in the case of conflicts over material benefits and resources. An extension of the suffrage to the negatively privileged group represents definite, tangible gains: they are provided with greater access to the political leaders, they have greater control over decisionmakers, and they have a greater voice in shaping public policy. Conversely, the positively privileged group loses its monopoly over political leadership positions and has less freedom in unilaterally shaping public policy. If the negatively privileged group is a majority, the possibility exists that a major transfer of political power is in the making such that the dominant position of an upper class is threatened outside of the political sphere as well. Thus, from the point of view of the privileged group, a transfer of political power has an open-ended aspect: the ramifications and consequences of the proposed reforms and the limits and total cost of the losses that will be incurred cannot be foreseen, and the newly won rights might enable the hitherto excluded group to mobilize its scattered resources in a direction undermining the entire social system. However, the dominant groups may realize benefits by extending political rights: social control in the long run becomes less costly, and the security of the dominant groups can increase. By creating greater legitimacy for the system, by providing people a stake in working within the polity, by allowing vested interests to grow up within the negatively privileged group that have a stake in the continuation of the system, internal self-policing and loyalty may be increased so that security and domestic peace are enhanced and the costs of coercive control decreased. The problem is that these gains to the privileged class take time, are by no means automatic, and are not as clearly visible as the short-run losses. The conflict tends to have a zero-sum aspect in the short-run.

Many conflicts over civil rights, over the extension of citizenship rights, have a strong pure-conflict element. For blacks, school integration in the United States represents improved education, the assurance that resources for education will be allocated in a more equitable way, and the likelihood of improved academic performance of their children. Whites expect the quality of education to deteriorate, they have fears about the safety of their children in integrated schools, and some groups fear that extended contact with blacks starting at an early age in school will lead to more intimate relationships such as dating and marriage. There are no corresponding gains, or at least not visible and immediate ones, for whites other than those who believe in school integration as a matter of principle. The attraction of the freedom of choice plans is that it shifts the costs of school integration to those who think they will gain by it. In practice that would mean de facto segregation or token integration at best in many parts of the country.

A long-run view of the conflict over civil rights and greater equality demanded by the deprived groups sheds a somewhat different light on the matter. A legitimate system of stratification rests not only on the rights of the superordinate group, but on the obligations that it has for the welfare of the subordinate group. Command rights and exploitative opportunities are limited by custom, beliefs, and institutions frequently of a religious nature, social pressures operating within the superordinate group, and the costs of social control and coercion should an illegitimate extension of exploitation and authority be reciprocated by passive resistance, noncooperation, or open rebellion. The obligations on the superordinate group frequently cover the provision of a minimum economic security, care in old age, jobs, tenancy rights, protection against outsiders, and so on. Over a period of time, and usually as a result of broader economic and demographic changes enabling profits to be realized by a more efficient exploitation of the economic resources of the community, the superordinate group unilaterally divests itself of the traditional obligations that stand in the way of increased profits while still enforcing its command and exploitative rights. If the superordinate group is successful in this endeavor, it realizes a pure gain at the expense of the subordinates, though it has upset the delicate balance of mutual rights and obligations upon which the legitimacy of its rule rested. Usually, no other group, institution, or state authority steps in to defend the rights of the subordinates, nor are alternative institutional mechanisms provided to ensure their security and to protect them from unilateral exploitation. Later, when the subordinates have been able to mobilize their resources and members for a movement demanding rights and a greater share of societal resources, they are in effect seeking to redress the balance of rights and obligations that had been upset earlier. Contemporaries of the conflict, however, do not want to be held responsible and to pay for unilateral gains that a previous generation had realized at the expense of the groups now demanding increased rights. Admitting a group to full-citizenship status is a conflict where, in the short run, a pure gain will be realized by the protest group and where the earlier loss to the protesters is forgotten or judged irrelevant.

Another class of perennial conflict involves disputes over the distribution of authority between a central government and the local governments and other viable communities and associations making up the polity, or between a federal government and its constituent subunits. Such conflict is well known from the history of state formation in Western Europe, which extended well into the nineteenth century in the cases of Germany and Italy, from the history of the extension of colonial rule over non-European peoples, from the problems of administering colonies in which a variety of traditional authorities were recognized by the colonial regimes, and, from events in the contemporary world, the crises of national unity and problems of nation building, not only in new states but in Canada, Ireland, Belgium, and other "developed" countries as well. This type of conflict often shades into the previous case of extending rights to a negatively privileged group. It differs from it in so far as there is either a territorial concentration of the disadvantaged group making secession one of several possible outcomes of the conflict, or as a still viable, legitimate authority is pressured to yield some of its sovereignty to a foreign intruder. Here we touch on the basic principles of legitimacy and of the social contract that binds members of a society to their leaders. Members of a community or the citizens in a state willingly surrender a certain amount of their freedom and willingly accept the state's coercive authority in matters of taxation, justice, and conscription and in the regulation of social interaction, provided that the authorities advance the public welfare through their actions. People are willing to submit to vaccination requirements because the benefit they derive through the eradication of epidemic diseases is worth the nuisance of complying with public health regulations. They accept the coercive aspect of this relationship because they understand the need for universal vaccination. People are willing to be taxed if the government provides public goods, such as education and security, that they would be unable to provide for themselves at the same cost under a system of private initiative and voluntary participation (Olson, 1968). No government or authority can expect to maintain its legitimacy indefinitely if it fails to deliver the public goods that are necessary to keep the system working effectively (Lipset, 1963: chapter 3). The power to limit the freedom of action of the citizens and to coerce them into contributing resources to the authorities will be acceptable if the power is used to provide for the public welfare. However, the government can use its power for the exclusive benefit of certain groups to the detriment of other groups, or for the benefit of certain groups way out of proportion to their contribution or numbers. Here the Janus face of state power is fully revealed (Parsons, 1960: chapters 5 and 6). If particular groups think that they are discriminated against, the outcome may well be a crisis of legitimacy, open revolt, and possibly secession. If foreign rule does not bring in its wake sizable concrete benefits compensating for increased obligations and the loss of autonomous dignity and prestige foreign rule will be experienced as illegitimate.

Because loss of autonomy is a highly symbolic issue, one would expect that an imperialist power would gain greater legitimacy from working through a protectorate or by indirect rule, so that the existing legitimate authorities are continued in office and the imposition of foreign rule is perceived as a contract freely entered into between equals for the mutual benefit of both parties. Outright conquest is both more costly and appears less legitimate. In conflicts between a national government and regional groups having distinct communal characteristics, a decentralized form of government appears more legitimate than a highly centralized form of rule. The benefits deriving from the imposition of foreign rule or the extension of national govenment authority over hitherto largely autonomous units may not be commensurate with the contributions that the new subjects are forced to make. Particularly in colonies, the welfare of the natives may receive low priority. The colony may be administered for the benefit of settlers, concessionaries, investors, and so on, even though it might have been occupied only for strategic reasons in the first place. It is usual for the colonial power to recover the costs of administration and pacification by various methods of taxation and forced labor, to ensure a supply of labor for the administration, settlers, plantations, mines, and industries by similar means, and to enact and enforce a host of regulations and restrictions not benefiting the indigeneous population. The immediate benefits of colonial rule are unlikely to be more than the imposition of domestic peace upon various feuding and warring groups and long-run tangible gains—the provision of education, public health services, transportation, and a higher standard of life through cash crops and employment in the nonsubsistence sector of the economy—are likely to be paid for by the native population. Even in the most favorable cases there will be a time lag between the coercive mobilization of native resources and the delivery of public goods and an increased material standard of life. Similarly, the extension of central government authority over previously autonomous or semiautonomous regions is unlikely to be accompanied by immediate benefits compensating for symbolic and material losses. Usually, the central government does not expand its authority in order to improve the region's welfare, but in order to exploit untapped resources for increasing its own power, to secure a frontier with a foreign country, to extend its taxation and manpower base, to provide more positions in its bureaucracy, to keep its armed forces busy, to prevent the growth of a rival, and so on. Under these circumstances the conflict resulting from the extending central authority is a situation of pure conflict.

Finally, it remains to reflect on the conflicts generated by clashing life styles, standards of behavior and morality, and the denigration or negative evaluation of qualities and attributes such as performing manual labor, being a member of a certain race or religious group, or being on welfare—situations in which particular groups look upon certain beliefs, customs, and behavior as inherently offensive, threatening, degrading, and harmful and, therefore, enforce conformity by social and legal sanctions. Consider for instance the conflict over male youth's right to wear long hair in public schools in the contemporary United States. Certainly, wearing long hair is not intrinsically offensive in the same way as loud noise is physiologically disagreeable. After all, George Washington, Sir Isaac Newton, and all the greater and lesser luminaries and notables of the eighteenth century were able to wear long wigs without adding to anyone's physical discomforts. Nor does it limit the sphere of authority of teachers and school administrators in matters relating to instruction and pupil performance. Rather, wearing long hair is symbolic of many issues that together constitute the conflict of generations as it is expressed today. It symbolizes to many teachers and adults that their right to set and to enforce moral guidelines and standards is being questioned and that their most cherished values and beliefs are being rejected by the youth counterculture. Wearing long hair is but one of many specific manifestations of the youth culture that many adults fear because to them it represents moral decadence, the emergence of a lazy, unproductive, and disorderly generation that threatens stability, the moral foundations of the social order, and the peace and affluence they wish to enjoy. To many, it means that their own children might also be infected by this disease which will in the end bring a great deal of trouble and uncertainty to their own family. In instances where a particular practice that is not harmful to the community and probably not harmful either to the individuals involved, such as smoking marijuana, but which is illegal and around which a social control bureaucracy has grown up, the vested interests of the social control agencies are also endangered by a liberalization of the laws. But, fundamentally, it is the symbolic aspect of the practices and the implied threat to cherished values, social stability, and the moral order that are at stake and at the heart of the conflict. The outcome is thus one that is perceived by many as irreversible, indivisible, open ended in its ramifications, and one they stand to gain nothing from. Therefore, it is a conflict difficult to resolve. Compromise arrangements are not impossible. As long as the deviant behavior is practiced in ecologically segregated and contained areas in contexts of low visibility as is frequently the case with alcoholism, prostitution, homosexuality, and so on, the public is not likely to be offended and, in any case, perceives the problem as a limited one that is well within the capacity of the social control agencies to handle. When the deviants or members of the counterculture make an open, public bid for recognition of their rights and insist on the moral worth and even moral superiority of their way of life, this compromise breaks down.

The problem is to transform a situation of conflict into one where a moral division of labor can take place. It is perfectly possible, and it has happened repeatedly, that two different peoples with a long history of conflict can establish a mutually satisfactory moral division of labor in which their own identity, self-respect, and self-evaluation do not rest on denigration, ridicule, and hostility toward, the other group. A Frenchman can grant that the British have shown throughout history a greater capacity for stable government and a superior ability in the art of politics and of ruling an empire, he can concede to the Germans a superior technical competence and industriousness, and yet feel secure as a Frenchman because of his belief in the magnitude and universal significance of France's contribution to literature and to the arts, to the art of civilized living, and to reason and enlightenment. Similarly, members of different professions, of different scientific and intellectual disciplines, of different specialties within a discipline, can maintain relationships based on mutual respect and reciprocated positive evaluation of each other's differing accomplishments, despite the fact that they may be competing for funds, positions, and other scarce resources. Durkheim long ago noted and commented upon this phenomenon. Just as the division of labor in the economy creates an increased output that can be distributed, so the moral division of labor can create an increased amount of positive evaluations, respect, and recognition available for distribution. Past accomplishments and present performances can serve as the foundation for increasing the total number of qualities that are positively valued. However, it is more difficult to do this in relationships between superiors and subordinates, since the claim to superior status often rests on the possession of valued attributes that the subordinates allegedly do not possess. It is perhaps also difficult to establish a mutually satisfactory moral division of labor when a group of people have few positively valued accomplishments to point to. They will derive their feelings of self-respect and worth from having led an orderly, conformist, and correct life in accordance with the laws and the prevailing moral standards of the community. Groups that challenge these laws and moral standards will be seen as threatening. Those who derive benefits from nonconformity, or those who escape sanctions despite their nonconformity, will be resented. The conflict of generations is set within a framework making it unlikely that a moral division of labor can develop. By challenging the legitimacy of the moral standards from the observance of which many adults derive psychological benefits and a sense of accomplishment and by failing to exhibit qualities and performances that many adults can admire and do value, youths and adults become trapped in a situation exhibiting characteristics of pure conflict. The social and psychological processes involved in the production, distribution, and exchange of moral evaluations are but little understood at the present time. Greater knowledge in this area will increase the conflict management and resolution capabilities of contemporary societies.

INSTITUTIONAL STRENGTHS AND WEAKNESSES

Discontents and conflicts are found in all social systems, yet some conflicts are more likely to arise in and be chronic to societies with particular social and institutional structures and, once they occur, are less likely to be resolved in a peaceable manner in some institutional settings than in others. For this reason, one would not expect simple relationships of cause and effect between the magnitudes and extent of discontents and grievances on the one hand and political instability, social disturbances, and turmoil on the other. Also, a number of accelerating and delaying factors may be present in a conflict situation that exacerbate or dampen conflict, hasten or delay its outbreak, affect the relative strengths of the antagonists, and influence its form and course in other ways.

Institutional and social structural variations can be described, categorized, and specified in many ways. For the purpose of a theory of social conflict, it is useful to focus on the institutional and structural configurations that are expressed in the imprecise, but nevertheless, useful distinctions between homogeneous (uniform) and heterogeneous (plural) societies, advanced and underdeveloped economies, and democratic and authoritarian political systems. It goes without saying that one is dealing not with sharp, discontinuous polar types but with gradations along a continuum.

The historical record will bear out the general observation that societies that are heterogeneous from the point of view of ethnic, racial, religious, linguistic, cultural and similar divisions—plural societies in the anthropological sense (Kuper and Smith, 1971)—are more likely to be the locus of all manner of discontents and conflicts and that these conflicts are more difficult to pursue in a nonviolent and institutionalized manner than in societies that are homogeneous in these characteristics. The imposition of alien rule in its most recent historical forms—imperialism and colonialism—has most frequently been perpetrated upon non-European peoples by those of European origin, and has brought into relations of super- and subordination peoples with a very different material, cultural and religious background. This process has been coercive throughout and could hardly have been other, since the two sides did not share common institutions through which conflict mediation might have been pursued. In a strict sense, it is not even meaningful to speak of the imposition of "alien" rule when referring to a uniform population. If the building of empire was, nevertheless, not accompanied by high casualties compared with civil wars and wars between states, it is probably because the possession of technologically and organizationally superior military force by the colonizing powers when used against small states and peoples resulted in short campaigns and brief periods of overt resistance. Nor can one assign racial differences as such a higher order of violence producing potential than to other differences making for pluralism: one should remember the Boer War and Britain's relations with the Irish over the centuries. Furthermore, the extension of central government authority over regional units is more likely to be resisted and less stable once accomplished if the populations thus linked happen to be heterogeneous or the regional population different from the national ruling groups and the majority in the rest of the country. The problem of nation building in new states, the political instability in these countries, is largely an expression of this fact. Although the unification of Germany and of Italy was a prolonged and conflict-ridden process, involving as it did the diminution of power of ruling groups—always a difficult process —once accomplished, it led to stable national entities precisely because the peoples joined already shared many common cultural and ethnic characteristics and a common historical tradition.

The fundamental principle which guides this line of thought is the following. When two or more different groups of peoples are brought into the same social system, even by coercion, and granted that they have unequal status and authority, their relationships can become based on common interests and mutual, though not necessarily equal, benefit. In this situation one can speak of accommodation. So long as the relationships continue to produce benefits to both sides, they are likely to be tolerated; when they cease to do so, accommodation turns to antagonism and conflict as one or another party seeks to alter the relationships in its favor or break them off altogether. If, on the other hand, the groups develop a dense network of social relationships, such as result from intermarriage, neighborliness, and common memberships in associations and the labor force—a state of affairs called assimilation in the cultural sense and integration in the social sense—then, shared understandings, beliefs, and values will create cohesion and social bonds in addition to common interests, and the sphere of common interests itself will expand. If assimilation and integration have proceeded the full course, a state seldom reached in the real world, one can no longer speak of different groups or peoples since they will have fused into one entity. The greater and the more numerous the differences to begin with, the more difficult it is to proceed from accommodation to assimilation and integration, hence, the less likely it is that problems affecting the groups and their mutual relationships will be approached within a common framework of cooperation rather than on lines of separation and conflict. Shared associations, group memberships and social affiliations, lead to divided loyalties, prevent total commitment to one or the other side, and favor a search for compromise. In plural societies, the relationships of super- and subordination usually extend over all social relationships and institutional realms—the polity, the economy, the social sphere—and mutually reenforce each other. This pattern gives plural societies a castelike structure in which progress from accommodation to assimilation is difficult. Changes in any institution are resisted because they threaten to undermine the system as a whole.

The demand for greater freedom and rights by groups excluded from the polity is more difficult to resolve in plural populations than in homogeneous ones. The experience of African decolonization shows all too clearly that nationalist movements result in a more violent and complicated process of decolonization in white settler colonies—Kenya, Rhodesia, Algeria—than in colonies made up of only African peoples. The issue of full citizenship for nonwhites in South Africa, the continent's most plural society, has not even begun to be seriously considered. Decolonization in Africa since World War II has on the whole been remarkably peaceful as far as major worldwide changes go, but the transition to self-rule has been far more peaceful and smooth in the cases of Australia, Canada, and New Zealand. The conflict over full-citizenship rights for the lower classes is also exacerbated when the lower classes differ from other social strata on noneconomic criteria as well. T. H. Marshall (1965) has shown how the growth of national sentiment in England based on the cultural and ethnic shared characteristics of the population provided a framework within which equal legal and civil rights could be extended to all classes no matter how lowly their social and economic position. In an ethnically and racially more divided country such as the United States, ideologies of racial inferiority can be manipulated to block the orderly entry of deprived groups such as blacks into full citizenship status. Similarly, exploitative economic relationships giving rise to economic and class conflicts are more readily justified and maintained by force if the exploited groups happen to differ from other social strata on cultural and ethnic criteria as well. At best, societal heterogeneity, pluralism in the anthropological sense, plays only a neutral role in the generation and conduct of conflict. However, in most cases it heightens conflict and complicates solutions. Furthermore, as will be shown below in the chapter on mobilization, the conditions for rapid and extensive group formation are likely to be present in the case of unassimilated and unintegrated groups.

What about the conduciveness for conflict generation and regulation of the institutional configurations associated with advanced and underdeveloped economies? Since even advanced economies have pockets of backwardness and lagging sectors and regions, just as underdeveloped economies may have a modern sector and region, one would expect conflicts more typical of underdeveloped economies to persist in some degree even in developed economies, and vice versa. A truly isolated and backward economy in which the ordinary way of making a living still proceeds within the framework of a subsistence economy where market relations have not penetrated, although producing a great deal of misery, insecurity, and unhappiness, is unlikely to have much social conflict. These societies change slowly within the framework of traditional economic relationships that have legitimacy. In many of them extreme differences of wealth do not exist. Once economic isolation breaks down and modernization begins with the more intensive exploitation of economic resources and the reorganization of traditional work roles, one would expect an increase in all manners of conflicts. The initial period of economic change is accompanied by direct and indirect forms of coercion to make labor available for new enterprises. Crafts and village production decline under the impact of imported manufactures, and land for cultivation and grazing may be alienated. New groups with a much higher standard of life than their parents and relatives do not fit readily into the rural society and are not immediately integrated into the emerging modern sector. A floating population of urban unemployed, displaced from the land by population pressures and attracted to towns in the hope of higher incomes and of acquiring a share of the consumer goods associated with modern life, grows restless and disturbed. The linking of the national economy with the world economy, whether or not it takes place within a capitalist framework, exposes the economy to wide fluctuations that depend on world supply and demand and supports a modern high-income sector amidst the hopeful poor piling into the cities. In short, transitional economies experience a growth in inequalities of wealth and standard of life; some groups experience a decline in economic standing and security although the overall aggregate material level of living may be rising; still others benefit disproportionately from these changes, strive to obtain an even greater share, and develop vested interests to protect their gains. Thus, an increase in all manner of economic conflicts can be expected at a time when the new institutions for providing security, welfare, and conflict settlement are yet in their infancy and untried.

Problems resulting from economic growth are heightened because of a lack of institutional fit: the schools feed graduates and school leavers into the labor force and the towns faster than the economy can absorb them at the occupational level and standard of life that they have been led to expect; the commercialization of life, the growth of travel and communications, the aggregation of people in towns and cities with the more visible discrepancies between poverty and wealth invite invidious comparisons and increase material aspirations and feelings of relative deprivation. Political conflicts are also likely to increase in societies caught in the grip of economic transition. Policies designed to foster economic growth usually necessitate more widespread central government penetration into the provinces, which in turn threatens to undermine the standing of regional and local notables and calls forth their opposition; alternately, the notables may manage to take over the administrative and political apparatus through which economic policies are implemented, which in turn gives rise to multiple conflicts. New groups and social strata created through economic change will aspire to political roles commensurate with their importance in running the economy and the administration. The role of the government in allocating scarce resources to different regions, different economic sectors, and, hence, to different groups will be overwhelming, just as the prospects of quick wealth and upward social mobility through patronage, corruption, high government salaries, and control of the government apparatus will be unique. Thus, the contest for political office will be keen and the temptation to exercise political power arbitrarily and illegitimately to maintain oneself in office will be great.

In societies with a developed economy, the dislocating effects of socioeconomic change are cushioned by the institutions of the welfare state. Population pressure on resources is less, and the overall higher level of wealth makes the allocation of economic resources by the government less productive of conflict. The tendency toward extreme inequalities in wealth is checked through taxation, the organized power of trade unions, and the consumer-oriented economy itself, which requires high purchasing power of the many to sustain high sales and corporate profits. Diversification in the economy cushions the impact of economic decline and recession in some sectors. Institutions of conflict regulation between labor and management and between other conflict groups have a long tradition of successful operation. The economic and the political realms are more likely to be insulated from each other. For instance, the relationships between affluence, upward social mobility, and political office is less marked since many nonpolitical avenues for advancement are available. Thus, political and economic conflicts do not so readily spill over and reenforce each other.

A democratic political system is a system in which civil liberties, political freedoms, the rule of law, and universal suffrage are recognized and respected, organized opposition and dissent are tolerated, no official ideology limits and confines the boundaries of political discourse and debate, and political leaders are elected to office in a process of free competition decided by the electorate. Authoritarian political systems lack some or all these attributes in varying degrees. Authoritarian states with a coercive social control apparatus for enforcing ideological orthodoxy and political conformity are usually referred to as totalitarian. As in the earlier contrast between different types of economies, one would not expect to find simple relationships between the number, variety, and intensity of social conflicts and the type of political system. In authoritarian systems, many conflicts fester for years below the surface for the simple reason that the mobilization of discontented groups is a difficult and risky undertaking in the absence of political freedoms and because organized opposition may be suppressed in its early stages. The means of social control are varied and more firmly in the hands of the incumbents, while the strength of the opponents is less than in democratic polities. It is true, as Dahrendorf (1959:314) noted, that even totalitarian systems possess channels for the surfacing of limited dissent and for conflict regulation which provide a safety valve against violent explosions. Nevertheless, social conflict would be expected to erupt less frequently but with greater intensity and destructive potential in authoritarian than in democratic systems.

The major conflicts over entry into the polity and the demand for civil and political rights by negatively privileged groups are already settled in a democracy; they form part of its history. In authoritarian systems these potential conflicts cast a shadow over the future. Democracies do experience crises of participation over full or fuller rights for minorities, youths, and other groups whose needs and aspirations have not yet found an organized political expression—the responsiveness of incumbents varies, the means for expressing grievances may be imperfect, the channels for conveying discontents to the attention of decision makers may be temporarily blocked—but the institutions for entry into the polity have been worked out in the past and are already present, whereas for authoritarian systems the entry problem will require major institutional surgery to be successfully accomplished.

Inefficiency, corruption, maladministration, the illegitimate exercise of authority by incumbents, and conflicts over succession and a greater share of authority exist across all political systems. Yet, the watchdog function of opposition groups and of an independent press for uncovering and checking government abuses and inefficiencies are built into the very structure of democracies, since the opposition gains legitimately at the incumbents' expense. Self-policing systems, whether bureaucracies or authoritarian regimes, are more likely to minimize, ignore, and suppress their shortcomings. Thus, problems become magnified over time. Succession at the top, in particular, is a regularized process in democracies, whereas it is a perennial source of conflict and of instability in authoritarian systems. Numerous crises and conflicts take place because it is impossible to oust the top leaders from office without resorting to illegitimate means. The processes of succession following the death of the leader are unclear and the occasion for a struggle of power by all those who aspire to top office. In democratic systems, the aspirants to top leadership have to work out a formula and compromises with their rivals before the occasion for the transfer of power arises; in authoritarian systems the conflict for top position occurs during the process of transfer itself and is much more complicated as a result. In authoritarian systems, conflict is less likely to remain localized and institutionally isolated. The dominance of political over all other institutions politicizes all manner of conflicts. Where strikes are outlawed and other forms of public opposition prohibited, a strike for higher wages must appear as a political challenge, not simply as a means of gaining economic improvement.

Democracies also have special sources of conflict. The problems of governance in a democracy are more complicated and give rise to discontents and conflicts that an authoritarian system is spared. Widespread popular participation in the polity, if only at the voter level, makes for more unrealistic expectations about the satisfaction of wants and the solution of problems. Competing parties and leaders gain from exaggerating both the magnitude of problems and the ease of solution. Delayed gratification such as is required by belt-tightening policies is more difficult to carry out; the breathing space between the implementation of new policies and the expected benefits more difficult to secure. Many reforms are slow because the power of vested interests has to be overcome by legal and political means. Authoritarian regimes bent on reforms can count on less organized resistance, greater means to overcome them, and a more disciplined population. In democracies, the incentive for the rapid surfacing of dissatisfactions and responsiveness to them are built into the political structure. But the means for implementing changes are often superior in authoritarian systems. Therefore, the incidence of conflict ought to be higher and the time between discontent and conflict shorter in democratic than authoritarian polities, yet democracies are less likely to be shaken by major upheavals of the body politic.

A complicating factor in this discussion of institutional strengths and weaknesses is the confounding of societal pluralism, type of economy, and political system in the real world. Although it is possible to isolate conceptually each of these aspects of the social system and to discuss its impact on social conflict in an isolated fashion, social conflict always takes place in a concrete setting where the social, economic, and political institutions are interrelated in complex ways and at different levels. Economic strengths may compensate up to a point for the structural weaknesses of the polity and of a plural society, homogeneity may compensate for economic weaknesses, and so on. Therefore, to assess the potential for social conflict of concrete social systems is not a simple undertaking.

ACCELERATORS AND DELAYING FACTORS

It has already been argued that the relationships between strain, discontent, and injuries suffered and social conflict are neither simple nor direct. The matter is further complicated by accelerators and delaying factors that affect the timing of the conflict's eruption. Associated with broad, worldwide historical trends transcending the national and subnational levels in which conflicts take place, these factors are largely beyond the immediate control of the antagonists themselves. Conflicts that are delayed usually reappear in an aggravated form later and, consequently, are more difficult to regulate. Acceleration of conflict on the other hand, probably makes for ease of conflict management, since steps can be taken to meet problems before the full intensity of conflict has been reached. Delay favors the opponents of the status quo by creating the likelihood of a big explosion, but delayed victory may have to be gained at a considerable cost of lives and turmoil. An accelerated conflict will find the incumbents in a stronger position to deal with opposition; the temptation to suppress a weak opposition is counterbalanced by the advantages of dealing with problems and regulating conflicts that are of manageable proportion.

The most common delays occur during periods of national crises such as wars or nationalist movements, when the overriding concern with achieving a single objective, victory or independence, pushes all other problems into the background without resolving the underlying causes of conflict. Foreign threats and wars create a temporary support-the-regime syndrome. Incumbents gain legitimacy and opponents are discredited in the name of preserving national unity. Some regimes artificially foster such crises to give them respite from domestic problems and to silence their critics. Haimson (1964) has persuasively shown that the outbreak of World War I in 1914 put a temporary break to the rising crescendo of strikes and industrial unrest in Russia, which was then in the grip of a revolutionary upsurge. Ironically, the Tsarist regime may well have been capable of coping successfully with a peacetime working-class revolution in 1914–1915 since the Bolsheviks and other revolutionaries were disorganized, the peasantry would not have supported urban revolutionaries, and the agents of social control were loyal. Subsequently, in 1917 and 1918, the underlying causes of worker unrest were aggravated by the privations of the war, peasant disaffection had increased, and the agents of social control, especially the army, were demoralized and defected in large numbers to the side of the opponents of Tsarism. The end of wars, especially for losers, provides an occasion for suppressed and delayed conflicts to come to a head and ushers in a period of turmoil (Johnson, 1966:103–4). A quantitative study of violent changes in government in the period 1901 to 1960 found that the sharpest peak in the annual incidence of such events occurred in 1918, i.e., the end of World War I (Calvert, 1970:184).

Nationalist movements in the colonies also tended to relegate into the background a host of problems and conflicts stemming from the ethnic and regional pluralism of these countries, the problems associated with socioeconomic differentiation and the formation of classes. All too often, the political compromises and constitutional settlements with the colonial power were designed to hasten the advent of independence with a minor regard for the new sociopolitical forces. After a brief honeymoon period following independence, the backlog of suppressed problems erupts with added intensity and creates political instability. Similarly, in the United States, an obsession with the Soviet threat after World War II and a singular concern with national security and loyalty problems, even after McCarthy's demise, shifted attention and energies away from dealing with tensions and conflicts resulting from the changing status and aspirations of blacks, the problems of poverty in an affluent society, and the problems of rapid urban growth and population shifts. Subsequently, in the 1960s conflicts resulting from these processes erupted with greater intensity and were more difficult to manage than if they had been dealt with earlier. In England, the curbs on dissent, civil liberties, and organized protest during the French Revolution and the Napoleonic Wars had a delaying effect on the orderly surfacing of working-class discontents and on measures dealing with them and magnified the social tensions and conflicts of the 1830s and the Chartist period.

Accelerators of the pace of social change and of social conflict are also commonplace today. They can be traced to the interconnection of world events resulting from the spread of mass communications, international travel, the interpenetration of national economies within a worldwide economic system, and the increased range and frequency of global political alliances and links. Future political leaders in one country receive their education and political training in another; political ideas and organizational forms developed in one movement are diffused to others; experiences gained in one part of the world are transmitted to another part. The result is that advanced forms of organization, articulate opposition ideas, leadership, and skills spread even to areas where the local sociopolitical structures and opposition forces would have been unable to create them in isolation. This is evident in the case of direct external aid for insurgents, but is also true of national movements occurring within the context of strong interterritorially linked areas, e.g., French West Africa. There the less developed territories profited from the help and experience of the more politically advanced ones and from the support of the leftist parties in metropolitan France (Hargreaves, 1967: chapter 9).

Because of the interconnection of world events, the resolution of conflict in certain countries sets the pattern for a resolution of similar conflicts in related countries and speeds up both the eruption of conflict and its resolution beyond the point and stage one would expect from an analysis of objective conditions and the balance of opposing forces. The independence of Ghana was a model and pacesetter in the rest of British Africa; the Mau Mau uprising in Kenya prepared British public opinion and the government to accept the futility of maintaining the Central Africa Federation against the desires of the vast majority of Africans; France's bitter experience in Algeria made it much less likely that a French government would get boxed into a similar position of suppressing national aspirations in its remaining African colonies, even though it had the military means for doing so.

The diffusion of worldwide standards and expectations about civil and political rights, the material level of living, social justice, and so on increases relative deprivation and magnifies discontents, not so much among the masses themselves as among the potential leaders and activists of opposition movements. This is not to say that the interconnection of world events and the breakdown of isolation have always favored the forces that challenge vested interests and the status quo. Weak, corrupt, unpopular governments can be beefed up by outside military and other aid, as in South Vietnam, and can be encouraged to hold out against challenges with the prospect of success, whereas unaided they would disintegrate rapidly. The success of repression in one part of the world might well encourage repression elsewhere, as happened during the revolutions of 1848 and 1849 in Europe. But in the contemporary world, the forces opposing change have been on balance less favored by accelerators than the forces of change.

REFORM

There remains to examine under what circumstances reforms have a dampening effect on social conflict and a revolutionary upsurge or whether, to use Huntington's (1968:362) felicitous phrase, reform becomes a catalyst instead of a substitute for revolution. This topic has been singularly neglected in theories of social change and social conflict despite its obvious policy implications. In his discussion of the antecedents of the French Revolution, Tocqueville (1955:176–77) observed that

> it is not always when things are going from bad to worse that revolutions break out. On the contrary, it oftener happens that when a people which has put up with an oppressive rule over a long period without protest suddenly finds the government relaxing its pressure, it takes up arms against it. Thus the social order overthrown by a revolution is almost always better than the one immediately preceding it, and experience teaches us that, generally speaking, the most perilous moment for a bad government is one that seeks to mend its ways. Only consummate statecraft can enable a king to save his throne when after a long spell of oppressive rule he sets out to improve the lot of his subjects.

Crane Brinton (1952:40) pointed to a more specific variant of Tocqueville's paradox when he observed in his discussion of the antecedents of the English, American, French and Russian revolutions that

> one of the most evident uniformities we can record is the effort made in each of our societies to reform the machinery of government. Nothing can be more erroneous than the picture of the old regime as an unregenerate tyranny, sweeping to its end in a climax of despotic indifference to the clamor of its abused subjects.

In the contemporary world, this phenomenon has been noted in connection with increased social disturbances and urban racial violence in the U.S. concurrent with and following the most comprehensive social, economic, and political legislation and reforms to improve the condition of blacks since Reconstruction, and the East European anti-Soviet, anti-communist upheavals following shortly upon destalinization and a period of "liberalization" in the Soviet orbit after Stalin's death.

Many theorists stress the importance of the authorities' reaction to social disturbances and the demands of opposition groups as a key variable in shaping the subsequent course of events in the direction of either increased violence and revolutionary potential or, on the contrary, increased regulation of the conflict within the established structures. Hodgkin (1957:187) predicted that in Africa "whether national movements in particular territories employ violent or non-violent, revolutionary or constitutional methods to gain their objects seems likely to depend primarily upon the attitudes of the colonial regimes, the flexibility of their policies, their willingness to make substantial political concessions, and generally upon tactical considerations." Dahrendorf (1959:213) also thinks that when oppressed groups are allowed the right to organize and voice their grievances, the chances of violent conflict are decreased. Coser (1967:106–7) and Heberle (1951:385–87) formulate hypotheses and generalizations along the same lines. Killian (1965a:450) sums up the position appropriately: "Whatever the influence of other variables, the influence of the opposition and of the public reaction to a movement cannot be over-emphasized."

The great merit of all these views is that they do not look upon the values, goals, ideology, and especially the means of conflict used by a protest group as a fixed, constant quantity. Instead, the means used to pursue conflict are the result of a process of interaction between the conflict groups. In particular the reception of the protest groups and the reaction of the authorities and agents of social control are singled out as very important. If the authorities are unresponsive, block channels of communication, do not provide the opportunity for peaceful protest, refuse to make concessions, and so on, the likelihood of violent conflict increases. While the magnitude of discontents, type of strain, and number of grievances account for the increase of conflict and threaten to overload and break down the existing institutions of conflict regulation, the magnitude and forms that conflict is likely to take are explained primarily with reference to the interaction between the antagonists. Still, the above viewpoints must be criticized for their lack of specificity, since responsiveness or unresponsiveness, open or blocked channels of communication and influence, and access or lack of access to decisionmakers are all rather ill-defined, global conceptions of complex social structures and processes. Moreover, the above views assume that if authorities are responsive and act in good faith, they are able to undertake effective reforms to relieve social strain and meet the grievances of the protest group. But what if reforms are ineffective or only partially effective? Concessions and reforms can be "too little, too late." Concessions may whet the appetite of opposition groups and, thus, may become the occasion for expressing more radical demands. Under certain circumstances repression may be an effective means of stopping a protest movement at its start with little violence. How can one sociologically come to terms with the notion of an effective combination of the carrot and the stick for handling social disturbances and for defusing a potentially violent or revolutionary situation? Huntington's (1968: chapter 6) discussion of these issues, the most sophisticated available at the present time, points up the complexities of this topic.

The following discussion will deal only with the question of reform in authoritarian political systems, since the likelihood of major political upheavals and revolution is greater for them than for democratic polities, and, in particular, with the conflicts resulting from demands for civil and political rights, for freedom and constitutional reform. The topic of reform in democratic polities will be covered within the more general context of conflict regulation in a later section. An authoritarian regime can most successfully prevent revolution if it first institutes socioeconomic reform designed to improve the condition of the lower classes, workers and peasants, and, then, only after achieving a measure of success in economic reform, introduces civil and political rights demanded first and foremost by the more privileged economic strata. The opposite strategy of loosening coercive social control with the introduction of civil liberties in the hope of gaining allies for resisting the revolutionary threat from the lower classes, has a higher chance of failing and of generating widespread and continued turmoil during which the ruling groups will be forcefully overthrown.

Attending to the social problems and economic needs of the lower classes first has several advantages: it lowers the general background of unrest within which periods of reform take place and lowers the atmosphere of fear and impending violence that makes piecemeal conflict settlement more difficult. It will moderate the demands and the timetable of change of those aspiring to political rights because they will not be able to rely on the specter of lower-class violence for extracting concessions. And it will create greater confidence and security among the ruling groups, since their chances of continued political influence based on an upper-stratum–lower-class alliance are good. Lastly, many talented individuals from the intelligentsia and the professional classes may be enlisted by the regime into the work of administering and implementing socioeconomic reform, which always requires an expansion of the civil service sector. Successes achieved on the socioeconomic front will also increase the legitimacy of the authoritarian regime with broad sections of the population.

An authoritarian regime that either does not start with socioeconomic reforms or does not implement them effectively will sooner or later be faced by demands for political and civil liberties within the context of growing lower-class unrest and disturbances. Widespread lower-class unrest will encourage other strata to press their political demands in those difficult times. By inaugurating a policy of liberalization, that is, of loosening social control by granting greater freedom of opposition and of organization, the regime provides opposition groups with the means of manipulating economic unrest and of further mobilizing dissatisfied elements in order to gain even wider concessions and political reforms. In other words, the resources gained by the opposition will be used to further mobilization and for undermining the regime instead of generating gratitude, loyalty and support for it. Against a background of growing lower-class unrest, the regime may be less willing to make political concessions and show weakness and more likely to resort to coercive means for remaining in power and suppressing opposition. But by doing so, it will fuel the opposition, unite the disparate elements in it, and forge alliances within it for the purpose of overthrowing the regime altogether, since the regime comes to stand in the way of the fulfillment of the aspirations of all groups. Whether or not the revolutionary movement is successful will depend on many factors, not least of which is the loyalty of the agents of social control. It is also possible for a regime under attack from all quarters to weather a potentially revolutionary onslaught by making far reaching concessions to certain opposition groups that meet their demands fully. Thus, it can hope to split the opposition. But this kind of conflict management requires a great deal of skill and luck.

Authoritarian regimes do not usually undertake major reforms unless they are desperate. Their most likely response to widespread socioeconomic unrest and political demands is erratic reformism and not a well thought-out plan of concessions and of social control. This has been well described by Pettee (1938:94):

> Erratic reformism is the only policy open to a ruling class divided in its attitudes, or strapped by unwieldy institutions . . . in Russia, the utmost repression and occasional barbarism was accompanied by spasmodic reforms in industry and agriculture and politics. The result of such reforms and reaction mixed might well be called the quickest way to make a revolution. The result is to cramp the privileged classes without relieving the exploited. . . . To the cramped, the reforms have an appearance of being forced concessions, and the reactionary measures an appearance of betrayal.

Reform attempts tend to be halfhearted and ineffective because of institutional weakness and deliberate efforts by certain groups to undermine them. A period of liberalization after a long period of oppression allows the surfacing of long-dormant grievances and demands going far beyond those initially voiced and anticipated by the authorities, the mobilization of discontented groups and the anticipation of reforms that cannot be realistically instituted in a short time. The subsequent ineffective attempts to crack down upon the activities of freshly mobilized groups increase and unite opposition and precipitate social disturbances on a wider scale.

The chances of achieving reforms successfully are enhanced by a united, well-organized opposition. The authorities' temptation to initiate a policy of repression leading to a cycle of reprisals is less if the opposition is strong, as is the likelihood of granting substantial reforms rather than minor concessions, and of abiding by promised reforms. The opposition has much to gain from major reforms and, having built up a well-organized machine, a great deal to lose should confrontation lead to successful repression. The conservative tendencies inherent in large organizations and mutual fear and respect based on power increase the likelihood of a peaceful accommodation. But the very opposite conditions are found in authoritarian systems. Since political activity is banned, the opposition cannot develop united leadership, organization, and programs. When social control is loosened, a multitude of groups spring up, united in their common dislike of the regime, but competing with each other for greater support and for greater influence among hitherto unmobilized groups. In this situation, concession by the regime and the new resources gained will be used to expand the mobilization effort and support base of competing groups. Each group is under pressure to increase and radicalize its demands so as not to be outflanked by its competitors. Continued crisis will give splinter groups a chance to recruit followers at the expense of more moderate elements. Thus, political concessions in such a situation are likely to be a catalyst for revolution. Aware of this dynamic, the *ancien régime* becomes less and less attracted to concessions as a way of quelling disturbances and opposition. Also, the regime finds that working out a lasting agreement with a disunited opposition is difficult, since the likelihood of its component elements abiding by it is slim. Repression is the only alternative left: a violent confrontation is the logical outcome.

The trials and tribulations of an authoritarian regime are well illustrated by the response of the Tsarist regime in 1904 and 1905 to increased social unrest and political demands (Harcave, 1964). Russia was faced with an explosive agrarian problem caused by very unequal land distribution, extreme population pressures, peasant indebtedness and hatred of redemption dues, low peasant productivity, fiscal and agrarian policies that benefited the urban population and depressed the level of living of the peasant, all contributing to the peasant risings of 1901 and 1902; an explosive minority problem caused by repressive policies against non-Russians and other minorities such as Finns, Poles, Ukrainians, the Baltic peoples, Jews, Armenians, and Old Believers; an urban working-class problem caused by the hardships always found in the early phases of unchecked industrialization and urbanization; and widespread disaffection among the intelligentsia and the well-to-do, including important segments of the nobility, who favored civil liberties and a constitutional monarchy. The opposition groups at this time were split and fragmented, and the leaders of many revolutionary organizations were in exile or abroad as political refugees. The basic division among them was between liberals and revolutionaries, but each group was further splintered. The liberals had a moderate wing represented by the *zemstvo* movement and a radical wing centered on the Union of Liberation. *Zemstvos* were elected government bodies at the district and provincial levels and, since the days of Alexander II, had been responsible for administering and maintaining schools, public health services, and roads though their power was limited on all sides by the Tsarist bureaucracy. Municipal *dumas* were similar urban institutions. They were an enclave of limited representative institutions within the autocratic Tsarist framework, from which, however, a moderate liberal opposition movement of the nobility and the intelligentsia could be mounted. The revolutionaries were divided into the Marxist social democrats promoting mass action by the working class, the social revolutionaries pinning their hopes to peasant discontent and risings but relying on terrorism in the meanwhile, and the national minority parties—the Jewish Bund, the Polish Socialist Party—seeking to mobilize particular groups.

In 1904, the minister of interior Phleve was supressing all opposition in the autocratic tradition of Tsarist rule. The reverses of the Russo-Japanese war, declining civilian and military morale, economic recession and unrest, and continued political agitation by liberals persuaded the Tsar to inaugurate a "thaw"—to loosen social control—after Phleve was assassinated in July by a terrorist, and to appoint the moderate, compromise-minded Svyatopolk-Mirsky as his new interior minister. Under him harassment of the *zemstvos*, the organizational base of the moderate liberal opposition, was ended. The period of the thaw saw an upsurge of opposition activity in the form of meetings, congresses, assemblies, and banquets not interfered with by the police in which various suggestions and demands for reform were voiced. The Tsar's response was the *ukase* or decree of 12 December granting minor concessions on civil liberties, none at all on the issue of a *Duma* or national legislature and ordering opposition meetings and activities discontinued. No groups were satisfied with these concessions, and social control was once more tightened.

Against a deteriorating war situation in early 1905 and amidst growing industrial unrest, the Putilov Ironworks' strike in St. Petersburg grew into a citywide strike. The strikers' attempt to present a petition directly to the Tsar ended in the massacres of Bloody Sunday when peaceful marchers were fired upon point blank and others cut down by pursuing cossacks. To the ensuing nationwide protest movement and the general state of unrest among many sections of the population, the Tsar responded with a much delayed and inconclusive meeting with a workers' delegation, an aborted commission to investigate the causes of unrest in the capital, the 18 February manifesto promising only to consider plans submitted for an elected Duma, and permitting the right to petition the Tsar directly. These concessions were again too little and too late and completely out of step with the temper of the country, even of the moderate liberal opposition. The conclusion drawn by the opposition was that only continued pressure would force the Tsarist regime into the fundamental constitutional reforms they now saw as necessary to Russia's future.

In the spring and summer of 1905, increased industrial and agrarian unrest and insurrections all over Russia, a spreading strike movement, defeat in the Far East, mutiny in the Navy, and the terror of the Black Hundreds created a chaotic and revolutionary situation in which all semblance of public order broke down, though the rank-and-file soldiers were still obeying orders to put down insurgents. On 6 August the Tsar conceded the so-called Bulygin Duma, which would be no more than an advisory assembly and would be chosen by a limited electorate and indirectly through a tier of electoral colleges. This promised reform might have satisfied some segments of the liberal opposition a year earlier, but now it was completely unsatisfactory and failed to diminish unrest in the country. Only in response to the nationwide October general strike did the Tsar promise, in his October Manifesto, a constitution and civil liberties and schedule elections for a Duma that would have true legislative powers and be elected by a wide suffrage. This satisfied the liberals. Peasant rising, turbulence in the armed forces, and revolutionary activities among workers led by such organizations as the St. Petersburg *soviet* continued and culminated in the December strike movement and the Moscow rising, which was suppressed. Peasant rebellion continued well into 1906. The Tsarist regime weathered the revolution mainly because no opposition groups had established direction over the localized and disjointed peasant insurrections, because the October Manifesto had split the liberals and revolutionaries before the attempted seizure of power in December, because the armed forces, despite some mutinies and refusals to move against insurgents, had remained loyal. This state of affairs would not be repeated in 1917.

The response of Tsarist autocracy to the events of 1904–1905, essentially the granting of unsatisfactory minor concessions under extreme pressure within the context of loosening social control, is an example of erratic reformism that fuels, rather than dampens, the fires of revolution. In the end, in the October Manifesto, the Tsar had to grant more than his most powerful opponents had sought a year earlier, and in the process he very nearly lost his throne as well.

REVOLUTION

There are difficulties with every definition of revolution, just as there are difficulties with every typology of violent conflict. What is meant here by revolution are the great revolutions that have transformed the course of world history—the English, French, Russian, Chinese revolutions—and violent and large-scale upheavals in smaller countries that bear many points of similarity with the great revolutions, such as the Mexican and Cuban revolutions. Kamenka (1967:124) defines revolution as a "sharp, sudden change in the social location of political power expressing itself in the radical transformation of the process of government, of the official foundations of sovereignty and legitimacy and of the conceptions of the social order." Huntington (1968:264) defines it as a "rapid, fundamental and violent domestic change in the dominant values and myths of a society, in its political institutions, social structure, leadership and government activity and policies." In addition to the notion of violent and sudden change, the concept must include as a minimum the replacement of an entire political elite and ruling group and a fundamental transformation of political institutions in an entire country and not just a segment or region within it. Many revolutionary situations do not result in revolutions, some revolutions are unsuccessful as the Russian revolution of 1905 proved to be, and still other revolutions are shortlived and defeated as was the case in Hungary in 1956. For methodological and theoretical reasons one cannot divorce a discussion of revolutionary situations and unsuccessful revolutions from that of successful revolutions. Slower and only intermittently violent social changes that eventually result in the same fundamental restructuring of the social order as during successful revolutions—one thinks of Japan in the second half of the nineteenth century and Egypt after Nasser's seizure of power—are best not classed with revolutions, since the element of sudden and violent change is present only to a limited degree. For these reasons, nationalist movements that gained independence primarily by nonviolent means should also be excluded, although some took place within the context of a revolutionary situation. Where the transition to independence resulted from large-scale violent conflict, as in Algeria, one is more justified in speaking of revolutions, since the points of similarity with the great revolutions are many. At any rate, the analysis developed below does not depend on the precise definition and delimitation of the concept "revolution."

The aim here is to identify that configuration of discontents and grievances, institutional peculiarities and weaknesses, accelerators and delaying factors, that make revolution a likely outcome as contrasted with less turbulent, slower, and more orderly processes of change. The emphasis is on the weaknesses of the *ancien régime*, as the society and polity of the prerevolutionary social system have been designated by students of revolution. Success depends also on the strength of the opposition forces, a topic that will be considered in greater detail below under mobilization.

Revolutions rarely, if ever, take place in democratic political systems. They result from opposition against authoritarian regimes, dictatorships, and autocracies that are oppressive, arbitrary in exercising power, ineffective in getting the business of government accomplished, and unresponsive to the demands of various groups for a share in political authority. Major political conflict results from the demand of groups without political authority and political rights for a greater or a commanding share of political power, which can only be gained in an authoritarian system by way of a fundamental restructuring of political institutions. Since the *ancien régime* is likely to resist the large-scale reforms necessary for restructuring, the opposition will attempt to overthrow the regime by force. No single class or social stratum can make a revolution. Revolutionary situations and revolutions involve the disaffection and active opposition to the regime at the same historical moment of several, large social classes and strata, including those that are not among the most downtrodden and underprivileged, or as Kamenka (1967:129) wrote, "(revolutions) require the support of a significant section of the people not normally given to revolt." Discontent must not be limited to specific, temporary problems and issues but must include dissatisfaction with a wide range of economic and political institutions and practices that are the pillars of the *ancien régime* and that stand in the way of solving its fundamental problems.

The exact nature of the economic problems, grievances, and conflicts in the prerevolutionary society have long been the subject of debate and have not been resolved with any degree of finality. Crane Brinton (1952:264) writes that the old regimes of England, America, France, and Russia "were all societies on the whole on the upgrade economically before the revolution came, and the revolutionary movements seem to originate in the discontents of not unprosperous people who felt restraint, cramp, annoyance, rather than downright crushing oppression." Eckstein (1964:143) notes that many students of revolution believe that "a combination of long term economic improvement and short term setbacks" are typical of an unfolding revolutionary situation. Others more explicitly emphasize the psychological consequences associated with economic up-and-down movements such as frustrated expectations. Although the weight of present evidence rules out the likelihood of revolution in economically stagnant and backward societies, the characteristics of the prerevolutionary economy and of economic changes in it have not been precisely determined. Indeed, it would be surprising if only one clear pattern emerged in all prerevolutionary economies. In all likelihood, the more such societies and revolutions are studied in detail, the greater empirical variance will be found.

Nevertheless, the following observation can be made: in the *ancien régimes,* in addition to frustrated expectations by some because they experience a temporary setback in their previous level of living or because they share unevenly in the benefits of a period of prosperity, there are major structural economic changes taking place which permanently undermine the livelihood and economic security of large numbers of people. Such major structural changes are, for instance, the penetration of market-oriented, capitalist, economic relationships into the countryside and small towns and population pressures on land that cannot be resolved within the existing institutional framework of unequal land distribution, primitive agricultural techniques, and emigration to the cities in search of industrial employment. Structural economic changes also cause crises in public finance and government administration and, thus, increase the likelihood of ineffective government problem solving at a time of great need. Finally, in the period immediately preceding revolutionary outbreaks, the usual economic discontents and conflicts associated with short-run economic setbacks, i.e., unemployment, food shortage, a low standard of living, are present as well. The combination of all these economic processes ensures that the *ancien régime* will have a large reservoir of people with economic grievances susceptible of mobilization into the opposition at a time when a major political crisis breaks out or is already taking place. This combination of economic and political crises and their mutually reenforcing effects is discussed especially well in Labrousse's (1949) account of revolutionary situations in French history.

The presence of widespread disaffection in the *ancien régime* resulting not only from temporary conditions but basic institutional arrangements in itself creates only the prospect of social and political turmoil. The chances that this turmoil will be revolutionary are increased by a number of other institutional characteristics having to do with the ruling groups and the relationships between social classes and the elites and the masses. Students of revolution generally agree that the upper class and important elites are not united in their support of the *ancien régime,* but are in fact internally divided or in opposition, and may even be the principal leaders and organizers of opposition, at least in the early stages of confrontation. This is especially true of the intellectual elite and intelligentsia (Brinton, 1952; Edwards, 1927). These groups produce and diffuse images of a better world and of a more just society, unfavorable comparisons of ideal and future possibilities with contemporary conditions and institutions, that become widely accepted and whose effect is to undermine the legitimacy of the regime and its institutions and to weaken the resolve of other elites and the upper classes for resisting change. In *ancien régimes,* the intellectuals are in opposition. Aside from the intellectuals, important sections of the upper class take an active leadership in organizing opposition and in mobilizing other discontented groups. At the same time other sections of the upper class and within the ruling groups block the successful formulation and implementation of reforms that would diminish social unrest. The relationships between the upper class and other social strata are characterized by bitter class antagonisms and estrangement. Sections of the upper class live in an affluent, segregated world in which they are cut off and isolated from the daily needs and concerns of the lower orders; they often adopt extravagant and foreign styles of life financed by means of their privileges at a time when their qualifications and right to rule are increasingly being questioned and rejected.

The sum total of these developments is that substantial leadership, organizational, and material resources normally brought into play to defend the status quo either pass into the camp of the opponents of the *ancien régime* or are simply not mobilized to support it. The most likely response of an authoritarian regime in the face of mounting social unrest is erratic reformism, which loosens social control without making a dent on the underlying causes of discontent and which speeds the mobilization of radical opposition. If the crisis develops within the context of a lost war, as it often does (Johnson, 1966:103–4), the balance of forces is further tilted against the *ancien régime* since every factor—lack of legitimacy, crisis of loyalty in the armed forces, widespread economic hardship, demoralization and disunity of the ruling groups, and so on—is increased. Whether or not the subsequent revolutionary confrontation will be successful, whether counterrevolution will succeed, which groups among the revolutionaries will prevail in the usual struggle for power between moderates and radicals, depend to a large extent on the leadership and organization of the various opposition groups, the means of violence at their disposal, the extent to which they manage to direct other discontented groups in the population, the splits and alliances among them, and the degree to which the agents of social control—the army, the police, special forces—have come over to their side. These processes will be dealt with under the topics of mobilization, social control, and confrontation.

Chapter III

CRISES OF NATIONAL UNITY
IN NEW STATES:
ORIGINS OF THE
NIGERIAN CIVIL WAR

SOURCES OF CONFLICT

The presence of several types of discontent together with institutional weaknesses, the difficulties of implementing reforms and of resolving conflicts over authority, occur in many new states during the immediate post-independence period and often precipitate a crisis of national unity. With the departure of the colonial power and despite the hasty and patch-work compromises on constitutional matters and a postindependence government worked out with the colonial power just before independence, major issues of legitimacy, social organization, and global alignment arise, and different groups in the society have a vested interest in what appear to be mutually exclusive solutions.

Most newly independent states are faced with the twin problems of forging national unity and advancing material progress. New states enter the contemporary world without having prior cultural unity and a sense of national consciousness among the population. The historical processes that account for the pluralism of the new states are too well known to bear repeating here. Their populations are divided into religious, ethnic, tribal, communal, linguistic, cultural, and other groups whose sense of identity and loyalty is often directed to these collectivities and not to the newly established state.

Nor is there anything unusual or surprising about the existence of "micronationalism" as these sentiments and attitudes have appropriately been called. Mair (1963:113) has aptly stated that "community of language and culture, and association with a common territory, are the sources of the kind of consciousness which is properly called 'national' if the number of people who share it is large, and 'tribal' if the number is small." It is an error to think of these sentiments as an irrational and emotional hangover from the past. Most people in the new states exist within the context of these collectivities, and derive their sense of identity, economic support, and social fellowship from them. Even villagers who have become more or less permanently settled townsmen derive tangible economic, social, and psychic benefits from continued association with their fellows. And this has been the case not only in the new states but for immigrants to the United States and elsewhere. Mutual mistrust, hostility, and fear among members of these groups can often be explained by pointing to memories of antagonism and exploitation, broken promises, and violence in the past, and competition for jobs and other scarce resources in the present. Many of the antagonisms do not have roots in precolonial times, since these groups did not even know of each other's existence. They were often the unintended consequences of economic and administrative policies designed to make the colonies economically viable and governable. Cash crops were introduced and readily accepted, but the economic benefits accrued to those who lived in areas where the soil, temperature, and rainfall were suitable for cultivation. The accident of early missionary activities in certain areas and the location of colonial administrative and commercial centers favored the surrounding population with educational and employment opportunities that resulted in their subsequent monopolization of civil service and clerical positions and was later experienced as blocked opportunity or dominance by other groups. The location of mines and colonial plantations or settlers left these areas with a more highly developed infrastructure of roads, schools, and other services. Even physical differences between groups might give rise to later divisions, since many colonial governments favored taller soldiers and police and, consequently, recruited disproportionately from certain regions where the inhabitants were taller. The consequences of European penetration left a legacy of unequally shared opportunities, development, and modernity.

During the period of the independence movement, these particularist identifications and loyalties recede somewhat into the background for the sake of achieving unity and the common goal of independence. After independence and a brief honeymoon period, they reassert themselves with force as the new state is trying to grapple with some fundamental problems of organization and policy. National symbols such as the flag and holidays have to be agreed upon. The position of traditional chiefs, kings, princes, and other rulers has to be settled. The boundaries of political subunits have to be defined, and the distribution of power between the central government and these subunits determined. The status of the major religions has to be settled. A national language or languages and the languages of instruction at different levels of the school system have to be agreed upon. The status of foreign minorities, who often dominate the business world, and the replacement of European administrators by nationals come up. The position of the new state on the international scene arises and is intimately connected with the necessity of raising capital for economic development. Even at its inception, the territorial integrity of the state may be threatened by a secessionist movement or foreign intervention (Bell, 1967; Mair, 1963).

The settlements or attempts at settlement of each of these issues may accentuate identifications with and loyalties to traditional communites and groups and lead to an articulation and aggregation of interests along lines of cleavage superimposed on each other and threatening to national unity because the same groups face each other as antagonists on all major issues. A secular state may be offensive to the members of the dominant religion, yet the establishment of an official religion unacceptable to other groups who remember past humiliations and injustices suffered at the hands of the majority. The relegation of a traditional ruler to figurehead status may be offensive to a people who see in him a living embodiment of their cherished values, traditions, and collective identity and pride. Yet, continuing the traditional ruler's privileges and authority may be utterly repulsive and unacceptable to those groups who are committed to achieving a centralized structure of authority to a leveling of inequalities and to democratizing the political process. The choice of one over another indigenous language for administration immediately favors some groups' civil service career chances. The replacement of expatriate administrators and army officers by indigenous personnel may favor those groups who for historical reasons have become more highly educated and urbanized and raises fear among the other groups of a government dominated by one particular group. The alternative of staffing posts according to ethnic quotas, rather than according to criteria based on competence and merit, is opposed by the more westernized groups who stand to lose by it and for whom it is ideologically distasteful. And so it goes. As the country initiates social and economic development programs, the competition for the distribution of scarce goods and advantages leads to clashes of interest between previously mobilized groups and to an increase in hostility between them. The very processes of forging a modern state and of economic development heighten ethnic and regional antagonisms and promotes polarization.

According to Lipset's (1963:71 ff.) views on the transition from traditional to modern political institutions, when major issues of societal organization and values are dealt with one by one, with each more or less solved before the next arises, chances of nonviolent and institutionalized conflict regulation are increased. But when major issues pile up unresolved and confront contending groups at the same historical moment, the chances for compromise and tolerance are slim. It is precisely a characteristic of revolutionary and postindependence situations that several major societal issues crop up at the same moment, and that in such an intensely competitive situation, the winners on any single issue look as though they might turn out to be the winners on all issues. Consequently, losing may well mean loss of social, economic, and political power all in one, a situation hardly conducive to compromise.

A second important factor determining the ease of transition, according to Lipset, depends on the major conservative-traditional institutions and groups in the conflict process. If these groups are threatened all at once on all fronts, in their high social status, their economic privileges and standing, and their political supremacy, they are less likely to yield peacefully without a violent struggle. On the other hand, if their political power is whittled away even while their social status and economic position remains secure, they are more likely to compromise and yield under pressure without violent opposition. This second determinant is related to the first, since the piling up of major societal issues usually will affect the global position of ruling social strata in all institutions. Third, the more integrated the society at the time of crisis, the less its major component groups are organized on exclusivist principles with a lack of intergroup ties and the less the likelihood of polarization. However, if a society is already split along class, ethnic, religious, or other lines of cleavage prior to the confrontation phase, no group within each of the major collectivities facing each other has an interest in compromise solutions. The lack of social relations across groups makes for rapid mobilization of loyalties and resources within the groups and the generation of hostility and unfavorable stereotypes across them.

Two more conditions can be added to those mentioned by Lipset. When participation in public affairs in a controversial matter is high and involves previously powerless or apolitical groups who had no voice in the polity, conflict regulation will be more difficult to achieve. But this is precisely the case in major revolutions and the periods of transition from colonial rule to independence, when social control weakens and new social groups surface to make demands not previously articulated. Participation increases when the opposition groups who wish to seize power from the colonial regime or *ancien régime* mobilize the masses. Once activated, these previously quiescent or unorganized peoples do not readily relapse into oblivion, but develop new leaders and new demands not readily fitting into the existing institutional arrangements. Finally, when the stakes are truly high, as in times of revolution when those achieving power often move overnight from prisons to the highest political offices, and when defeat may well mean death, the tendency is for conflict to continue until one or the other party achieves a complete victory. In the same way, the rewards of being a political winner in a new state are very high compared to other nonpolitical means of social ascent, wealth accumulation, and prestige gaining, while the loser in the political struggle finds himself in a situation not much different from that of any other ordinary person. The temptation to remain in office by illegitimate means is high.

NIGERIA

How a crisis of national unity develops under these unfavorable circumstances can be demonstrated with reference to Nigeria. With an area roughly the size of France and Spain, Nigeria was estimated to have about fifty million people in the middle 1960s, living in three distinct regions: The north, with little over half the population, dominated by the Hausa emirates; the west, home of the Yoruba; and the east, where the Ibo constituted the largest single ethnic group. However, about half the Nigerian population does not belong to these three dominant peoples, and within each of the three regions, large areas were inhabited by minorities fearful of falling under the domination of the Hausa, the Yoruba, or the Ibo. At the time of independence in 1960, about three-quarters of the Nigerian labor force worked in agriculture, fishing, and animal husbandry. The government was by far the largest employer of wage labor. Agriculture provided 50 percent of the national product and 80 percent of the exports. In the north, the major resources were groundnuts and mining. Western agricultural prosperity was based on cocoa. The east was a major producer of palm oil, but was otherwise poorly endowed. Since 1960, major oil deposits have been discovered and exploited there, a fact that had a positive impact on the Ibo leaders' decision to secede in 1967. The largely Muslim north was considered to be a backward, undeveloped region compared to southern Nigeria. With half the population, only 2.5 percent of the total secondary school enrollment in Nigeria was in the north. The Christian Ibo had for a long time capitalized on the educational opportunities created by European and missionary penetration. Since the Ibo heartland was agriculturally poor and overpopulated, many Ibos had migrated to towns in the west, to the capital Lagos, and, especially, to the north, where over a million Ibos were employed in the railroads, the post office, transport and motor repair, in retail trade, in white-collar positions and skilled manual work. They filled the man-power vacuum when development in the north created a demand for skilled labor that northerners could not supply.

Nigeria is an extremely plural society. Its three major peoples had a different history, culture, social structure, and colonial experience. The northern emirates resulted from the nineteenth-century Fulani *jihad* and conquest of the Hausa people. The Fulani instituted a system of aristo-cratic rule in which religious and secular authority were fused. The emir was chosen from within a royal dynasty. In this hierarchic social structure, the emir ruled over commoners with the help of a hereditary aristocracy. Tradesmen were regarded as an inferior group, enjoying lower prestige than the farmers who constituted the most numerous social stratum. Islam was the unifying force in northern society. The British policy of indirect rule through native authorities confirmed and even strengthened the traditional authority. When the government ma-chinery was to some extent modernized and reformed and when a north-ern political party, the Northern People's Congress (NPC), was formed in response to the eventual transfer of power from the British to the Ni-gerians, political power in the north remained concentrated in the hands of the ruling class, both in the party and the administration.

The Yorubas had a polity resembling that of a European constitu-tional monarchy. The power of royal dynasties was checked by the rights of other lesser chiefs. While the Yorubas were divided by rivalries and differences between clans and districts, a common ancestry, lan-guage, and culture gave them social cohesion. The Ibos by contrast were not a tribe or people with a centralized authority structure; rather, they were a loose group with a shared culture. They consisted of some seventy clans characterized by a high degree of popular participation in public decisionmaking. They formed an open society in which proven men of talent rose to positions of authority. Ibo national consciousness was a product of modernization, of the adoption of Christianity, the spread of education, the nationalist movement against the British, and the Ni-geriawide Ibo unions and associations that came into being as the Ibos migrated into other parts of Nigeria. These unions enabled Ibos to main-tain ties with their village kinfolk and to seek collective security in the foreign and often hostile environment in which they lived (Amber, 1968).

The Ibos were the first among the Nigerians to take up the cause of nationalism. It is ironic that the Ibo seceded in 1967 to form Biafra, whereas earlier they had been the strongest advocates of an independent Nigeria with a strong central government. As the poorest region, the Ibo heartland in the east stood to gain most from a central government con-trolling Nigeria's resources, and as a highly educated people, the Ibos expected naturally to be in the forefront of Nigerianization of the civil

service when the British departed and to benefit most from a strengthened central government. Living as "strangers" in the north, where their
jobs, their right to lease and buy land, their trading licenses, their civil
rights, in short, their economic and political security, was dependent
upon an alien authority from which they were excluded, the Ibos stood
to gain most if a strong Nigerian central government were to democratize local and regional government and were to undermine the feudal
system in the north. By contrast, the northern ruling circles stood to gain
most from a federal system with strong regional powers that could be
used to shield the vast Northern Region from the rapid pace of social
change in the south.

As it was, the Nigerian federal system gave each region considerable authority in matters of education, welfare, labor relations, industrial
development, and the maintenance of public order. There were vast
discrepancies between north and south. In the south, judges were appointed by a judicial service commission; in the north, appointments were
in the hands of the emirs and the nobility. In the south, the upper
house of the bicameral regional legislature, the House of Chiefs, had
only delaying powers in the manner of the British House of Lords; in the
north, the House of Chiefs had veto powers over bills passed by the
House of Representatives. Moreover, appointments to chieftancy and to
the House of Chiefs were in the hands of councils controlled by the
emirs and their followers. Local government in the north was firmly in the
hands of the ruling class. Even though they ruled through partially
elected councils, the ruling groups controlled the nomination and election
procedures. In addition to controlling the judiciary, the power to assess
taxes collectively upon a village gave the Northern Native Authorities
the means of sanctioning dissident elements. Indeed, local administration in the north was a vast system of patronage, with the local notables
appointing their clients to jobs in the public sector. In a situation where
the majority of wage earners work for local government and public corporations, this sort of patronage represents great power for incumbents,
power to reward one's followers and to deprive one's opponents of the
means of livelihood outside of agriculture. Regional autonomy in Nigeria
meant that the traditional ruling groups in the north remained firmly in
control as independence was nearing.

Reflecting upon Nigeria's diversity, Dr. Azikiwe, the foremost nationalist leader and, subsequently, the first president of Nigeria, had
written in 1945 (quoted in Sklar, 1963:233)

> Nigeria is not a nation. It is a mere geographic expression. There are no
> Nigerians in the same sense as there are English, Welsh, or French. The
> word "Nigerian" is merely a distinctive appelation to distinguish those
> who live within the boundaries of Nigeria from those who do not. There

are various national and ethnic groups. . . . It is a mistake to designate them as tribes. Each of them is a nation by itself with many tribes and clans. There is as much difference between them as there is between Germans, English, Russians, and Turks. The fact that they have a common overlord does not destroy this fundamental difference. The languages differ. The readiest means of communication between them now is English. . . . Their present stages of development vary.

While in the 1950s nationalist sentiments tended to submerge regional differences, the nationalist movement itself had not been really united. People in the south blamed the British and the northerners for delaying independence, keeping the country divided, and hindering development. The north feared that the British and the south were bent on undermining their Islamic society. Thus, it is evident that one of the factors making for a difficult transition to a modern polity, lack of societal integration, was present in Nigeria with particular intensity.

THE POLITICS OF PLURALISM

The political parties that emerged during the colonial period reflected the major divisions within the country. In the east the National Council of Nigerian Citizens (NCNC) led by Dr. Azikiwe controlled the Eastern House of Representatives. The minorities in the Eastern Region were uneasy with Ibo ascendancy both in the region and in the party. Consequently, they were the potential political allies of the other major parties. In the west the Action Group (AG) led by Chief Awolowo was the most popular Yoruba party. It was controlled by a new affluent class of businessmen, lawyers, teachers, and large traders with whom the chiefs had come to terms through co-optation and by sharing the benefits of rule. In that part of the Western Region where non-Yorubas lived and which later became the Mid-West Region, there existed strong local sentiment and, thus, a tendency to support the NCNC against the AG. Because of internal rivalries within the Yoruba polity, some Yoruba chiefs and their followers also supported the NCNC rather than the Action Group. In the Northern Region, the Northern People's Congress (NPC) was firmly in the hands of the northern ruling groups, who successfully enlisted their clients and the Hausa farmers under the banner of Islamic solidarity and traditional loyalty to the emirs. In this they were helped by the extensive patronage in the hands of NPC leaders. Nevertheless, there were centers of opposition to the NPC. In the southern portion of the Northern Region, the so-called Middle Belt, encompassing a third of the region's population, there lived non-Hausa, non-Muslim peoples such as the Tiv, who wished to have the monolithic Northern Region broken up into smaller, locally autonomous states. Their political aspirations were embodied in the United Middle Belt Congress (UMBC), which received the support of Awolowo's Action Group for its stand against the NPC. In some of the former Yoruba areas conquered by the Fulani in their nineteenth-century push to the south, attachment to the Yoruba and, consequently, also to the Action Group was strong. Finally, within Hausaland itself, the negatively privileged artisans, craftsmen, small shopkeepers, and butchers of the towns formed a Hausa opposition party, the Northern Elements Progressive Union (NEPU), which was numerically too weak to challenge the NPC by itself. Yet NEPU was a force to be reckoned with in the Hausa towns. According to Sklar and Whitaker (1964: 606),

> NEPU has sought to interpret the meaning of Western inspired ideas of democracy and egalitarianism in terms of the historic, traditional conflict of interest between the majority of conquered indigenous peoples of the emirates . . . and their overlords, and through the classic social division between *sarakuna* (ruling class) and the *talakawa* (commoner class).

NEPU was the only party that drew its leaders from among the petty traders, shopkeepers and craftsmen, and also rallied many town youths and the rural cultivators who were victims of corruption and maladministration.

The several anti-NPC parties in the north polled as much as 35 percent of the total vote in the north during the federal elections of 1959, demonstrating that the northern electorate was not securely united behind the ruling class. This combined opposition could be expected to increase in the years ahead. The feeling of insecurity this threat produced among NPC leaders is very important in understanding their strategy for courting additional political allies outside the north and has been stressed, especially by Diamond (1967) as the key to postindependence Nigerian politics. They sought to prevent a coalition of the two rival southern parties and of the anti-NPC opposition in the north that would terminate the NPC majority in the federal legislature and seriously challenge NPC control in the Northern Regional Assembly. In the late 1950s rapprochement between AG and NCNC was made difficult by their past electoral rivalries and their bitter competition for supremacy in Lagos. But as a long-term prospect a successful grand coalition that would whittle away the national and even regional power of the northern ruling class was a distinct possibility. Indeed, this was the central issue of the emerging postcolonial Nigerian society: how to accomplish a peaceful and gradual transfer of power from the northern, conservative ruling class based on traditional legitimacy to a more dynamic, development-oriented, progressive elite drawn mainly from the south. The origins of the Nigerian civil war can be traced to this dilemma. In 1965, when the northern ruling groups saw their position weakened, they decided to keep their western political allies in power by fraud and force, and this event in turn initiated a chain of events that led to Biafra's secession.

It would be wrong to exaggerate the contrast between a democratic south and a feudal north. The political leaders of the three major parties almost all belonged to the wealthy upper and upper-middle social strata of their respective regions. In the north, Sklar and Whitaker (1964:617) found that 87 percent of the NPC members in the Northern House of Assembly elected from the emirates belonged to the traditional ruling class, and half the remaining members were lower-ranking employees of the native authorities, i.e., clients of the nobility. In the south, the political leaders included men of new wealth and of high education, professionals, educators, businessmen, and former civil servants. According to Sklar and Whitaker (1964:648),

> in Southern Nigeria the political party has served as an instrument of the political ascendancy of new elites produced by the complimentary process of Western education, urbanization, and commercial development, whereas in Northern Nigeria the political party has served equally well as the instrument of an *ancien régime* that has controlled and limited the political thrust of the "new men."

The gap between the political class and rank-and-file citizens was vast. The income of legislators, ministers, and higher civil servants was from ten to twenty times that of ordinary government-employed wage workers, not counting the opportunities for enrichment that high political office provided. Control of the machinery of economic development through loan boards and finance and development corporations was one of the prizes of being a political winner. Sklar and Whitaker have written that (1966:113)

> these institutions and facilities have given rise to extensive networks of administrative and commercial patronage under the control of the leaders of the major political parties. Top politicians reward their followers with jobs and money. They appoint their lieutenants to manage marketboards and development corporations which control the allocation of trading licenses, contracts, and loans to hopeful businessmen whose interests are thereby linked to the parties in power.

Therefore, the contest for political office was extremely keen and bitter. Elections were the occasion for charges and countercharges, for fraud, intimidation, and violence. The cost of campaigning was high, but the winner expected to recover his "investment." When the material rewards of political victory are high compared to the rewards to be gained by other means, compromise and conciliation are difficult to achieve, and a crisis becomes difficult to settle peacefully. Issues based on ideology and principle become entangled with the personal fortunes of their advocates. The Nigerian political crisis of 1962 to 1966 has to be understood against this backdrop.

The British-supervised federal elections on 12 December 1959, held just prior to independence, resulted in 134 seats for the NPC, all in northern constitutencies, 89 seats for the NCNC-NEPU alliance, and 73 seats for the Action Group. A further sixteen seats were won by minor parties and independent candidates. Over half of the 312 parliamentary seats were located in the Northern Region, in accordance with the estimated population distribution of Nigeria. Because women did not vote in the North, offensive as it would be to Islamic sentiment, the NPC polled only 28 percent of the total popular vote, compared to 36 percent for the NCNC-NEPU alliance and nearly 28 percent for the Action Group. To block the emergence of a north-south split damaging to national unity on the eve of independence, the NPC and the NCNC formed a coalition government. NCNC leader Dr. Azikiwe became the first president of Nigeria, and NPC leader Sir Abubakar Tafawa Balewa became the first prime minister. The opposition in the federal legislature was led by Chief Awolowo, head of the Action Group. Under this arrangement Nigeria started on the road to multiparty parliamentary democracy and capitalist economic development. Although impressive economic gains were made in the years 1960 to 1965, the political compromise of 1959 broke down under the combined strains resulting from the 1962 census and the Action Group crisis of 1962.

THE CRISIS OF UNITY

In a representative system where seats in the legislature are apportioned according to population and where the balance of opposing forces is very close to the fifty-fifty mark, an accurate census leading to reapportionment might tilt the balance against the incumbents and usher in a significant shift of power. The initial results of the 1962 census indicated that the combined population of the two southern regions exceeded the population in the north. NPC leaders, claiming an undercount in the north and an overcount elsewhere, suppressed the census and ordered a new one. In November 1963 the new census showed 30 million people living in the Northern Region, 12 million in the East, 10 million in the West, 2.5 million in the new Mid-West Region, and 700,000 in the federal capital, Lagos. This result gave the north a clear edge over all the other regions combined. The new figures were far out of line with earlier population estimates and the 1962 census, and it was commonly known that the organizers and enumerators had been politically motivated to inflate figures, especially, in favor of the north. In the face of this move to perpetuate NPC domination in Nigera, the NCNC leaders were up in arms and the compromise of 1959 on the verge of breakdown.

The 1962 Action Group crisis was precipitated by rivalries within the AG pitting Chief Awolowo against his deputy party leader Chief Akintola, at the time premier of the Western Region. At stake was the control of patronage in the west. More importantly, Awolowo wanted the Action Group to lead a nationwide people's party whose program would be the eventual democratic overthrow of the ruling groups in the north, and the development of an independent, nonaligned foreign policy and a socialist economic orientation. The Akintola faction sought a live-and-let-live arrangement with NPC leaders, agreeing not to try to mobilize dissatisfied elements in the north, especially the Middle-Belt minorities, in return for a free hand in running the Western Region. An Action Group party congress repudiated the Akintola faction and removed Akintola himself from office. When a series of fights erupted in the Western legislature, the federal government saw an opportunity to come to Akintola's aid. It declared a state of emergency, took over the administration of the Western Region, and appointed a commission of inquiry. The Awolowo group was accused of corruption and mismanagement and of plotting the violent overthrow of the federal government. Awolowo and his lieutenants were charged with treasonable felony, convicted, and imprisoned in what was widely believed to be a political trial (Sklar and Whitaker, 1966:71 ff.). In this manner the NPC leaders put their most dangerous rival out of circulation and their supporter Akintola in firm control of the Western Region. With Awolowo in prison, the resource base of the Western Region out of his reach, the Action Group in disarray, and the 1962 census suppressed, the northern ruling group's position was secure. But the cost of these questionable moves was the final breakdown of the 1959 compromise.

The 1964 federal elections saw the formation of two major party blocs—the United Progressive Grand Alliance (UPGA), or southern bloc, consisting of an alliance between the NCNC, the pro-Awolowo Action Group now out of power in the west, and the anti-NPC parties of the north, and the Nigerian National Alliance (NNA), or northern bloc, consisting of an alliance between the NPC, Akintola's party in the west, the Nigerian National Democratic Party (NNDP), and minority parties in the east opposed to the NCNC and Ibo ascendancy in that region. The central issues were Southern or Northern control of the federal government, Awolowo's release from jail, and, as the campaign progressed, the conduct of the election itself. Countless acts of political violence occurred daily, especially in the final weeks. UPGA candidates were prevented from running in some northern constituencies, yet the UPGA needed some victories in the north to win nationwide. Local government in the north was firmly under NPC control. By invoking prohibition in Moslem law against abusive speech directed at the incumbent politico-religious leaders and by withholding permit requirements for opposition assemblies, freedom of political opposition was curtailed to a degree that ensured a favorable outcome to the NNA in many northern constituencies. Faced with this turn of events, the UPGA called a last minute election boycott. As a result, the NNA won 200 seats altogether and 162 of the 167 seats available in the north, 81 of them unopposed. The UPGA won only fifty-four seats. Many seats, especially in the East, remained unfilled as a result of the boycott. Subsequent elections to fill them boosted the UPGA representation in the federal legislature to over 100 seats, but neither the legislature nor the northern-dominated cabinet reflected accurately the political preferences of the Nigerian electorate. Amidst expectations of the breakup of Nigeria, a last minute Azikiwe-Balewa compromise saved the day, but the long avoided north-south split was now inevitable.

The events leading up to the first army coup of January 1966 were precipitated by the Western Region elections of October 1965, the first major political contest after the disastrous 1964 elections. For Akintola's NNDP and for the northern ruling groups, an NNDP victory in the west would mean a continuation of the north-west political arrangement upon which their mutual security rested, both at the federal and regional levels. A UPGA victory in the west would mean, on the contrary, a reversal of the trend toward northern domination and vindication for Awolowo. The outcome was rigged in favor Akintola, whose party won seventy-one seats to the opposition's nineteen in a result so lopsided and so out of proportion with popular sentiment that civil disturbances broke out throughout the Western Region, which the police were unable to suppress. In order to restore law and order and to maintain Akintola in power, the northern leaders called upon the army. But the middle-grade officers, many of them Ibos, who were expected to execute this unpopular and personally repugnant task, decided, instead, to overthrow the politicians whose actions were responsible for the civil disorders. In the coup of 15 and 16 January 1966 Prime Minister Balewa, Chief Akintola, Sir Ahmud Bello, the foremost northern leader, and some other northern politicians and officers were assassinated. The stated purpose of the rebellious army officers was to end corruption, nepotism, gangsterism, and violence.

The chain of events from the first army coup to the secession of

Biafra in May 1967 and the Nigerian civil war was both complex and tragic. In these months, Nigerians experienced another army coup, two waves of Ibo massacres in the north, and the repeated failures of negotiations on Nigeria's future constitutional structure. Even though the top northern leaders had been killed, northern society had remained unchanged. Their policy of maintaining NPC control in the north against the alien encroachments from the south had deep roots in popular fears, religious sentiment, and aspirations. If the monolithic Northern Region was to be broken up into smaller units in order to provide the non-Hausa Northern minorities with greater autonomy, to prevent the perpetuation of NPC-NNA domination in the federal government, and to assure Ibos in the north security through federally-backed civil liberties, some concrete benefits had to be extended to the Hausa citizenry in compensation. Failing that, heightened fears and dissatisfaction among ordinary Hausa folk would make them manipulable by the political class in the north, who would be the major losers from these reforms and, therefore, eager to stage a comeback. These concrete benefits would have to be economic: more jobs for northerners, a higher standard of living, higher crop prices, better educational opportunities, and more honest administration. If this had been done, and there is always the question whether it could have been implemented in a short time, the military government could have appealed directly for the support of the northern masses, bypassing the northern political class, and it might have gained time for the needed constitutional and political restructuring of the country. In addition, visible reassurances would have to have been provided that northern interests and aspirations were represented in the military government by giving some northerners top positions within it. Save these measures, only a tough, united, military administration could have governed effectively, but the Nigerian army contained the same tensions and divisions found in the wider society.

As it happened, the first military government under Major-General Aguyi-Ironsi did not take any bold steps to dissociate itself from the previous regime, nor did it undertake economic reform to create a base of support among the Hausa citizenry. The Ibo officers responsible for the assassinations went unpunished, and the Lagos government seemed remote, unresponsive, and Ibo dominated. At the end of May, public opinion was unprepared for a unification decree abolishing the federal regions and unifying the regional civil services. Northern civil servants, fearful that Ibos would now have access to civil service positions from which they had been hitherto excluded, demonstrated against the decree. Two days later the first attacks against Ibos occurred against the background of a poor harvest, end-of-the-dry-season price increases, and an economic recession. According to O'Connell (1968), the anti-Ibo riots were encouraged by those who had lost power since the January coup:

> In the months after the military took power, ousted Hausa-Fulani po-
> litical leaders, some bureaucrats, and a few embittered traditionalists
> fostered the targeting of Ibos in their midst as somehow responsible for all
> the frustrations facing northern society—from rising food prices to the
> decline of Northern power in the central government. The violent out-
> burst against Ibos, in which hundreds were killed and thousands fled
> the region, was incited and organized by these elements.

Aguyi-Ironsi had not dared use the army to protect the Ibos; nevertheless, many Ibos who had fled during the massacres returned to the
north. Ibo confidence in their future security and prospects in Nigeria
was again shaken by the mutiny of northern noncommissioned officers
against their Ibo officers on 29 July when Aguyi-Ironsi and many Ibo
officers were killed. Many Ibo federal civil servants and professionals
returned home from Lagos and Ibadan to the Eastern Region where they
became a powerful party in favor of secession. To block this eventuality,
the new military government under Gowon called a constitutional conference of all parties and groups in Lagos at the end of September. As
the price of keeping Nigeria one country, the northern delegation reversed its original stand and agreed to a breakup of the Northern Region
into several smaller units. As news of this reached the north, a second and
more organized, widespread, and bloody massacre was unleashed against
the Ibos in the north. As many as twenty thousand Ibos may have been
killed, many brutally; many more were wounded, and all had to flee,
leaving their property and jobs behind. In this exodus, 1.2 million destitute
Ibo refugees left the north and crowded into the already overpopulated
Ibo heartland. Ibos were now in virtual secession. Oil revenues collected in the east on behalf of the federal government were retained in
the Eastern treasury for the relief of refugees. The non-Ibo tribes in the
Eastern Region feared and opposed these developments since an independent Biafra would leave them at the mercy of an Ibo majority. At the
same time, the Ibo heartland by itself could not form a viable independent state since it lacked an outlet to the ocean and since all of the
oil was located outside of it. If the Eastern Region were allowed
to secede, it was expected that the west would follow suit because in a
truncated Nigeria it could not hope to maintain alone a balance against
the vastly larger north. To block the dismemberment of Nigeria, the federal military government declared a state of emergency and divided the
country into twelve states: in addition to the West, Mid-West, and Lagos,
the Northern Region was split into six states, two in the hands of non-
Hausa northerners, and the Eastern Region was split into three states,
with two states for non-Ibo easterners. To the Ibos this partition of the

Eastern Region was nothing less than an attempt to cut off their economic base in oil and a call to non-Ibo easterners to resist the Ibos with federal support. When the Ibos proclaimed Biafran independence, the military government of Nigeria started military operations to stop secession. The outcome of the war is now history.

SUMMARY

The Nigerian crisis can be traced to the efforts of the northern ruling class to maintain its privileged position by any means, force and fraud, if need be, through the policies of its political arm, the NPC leadership. To remain a viable ruling class, it had to control the pace of social change and retain its vast patronage powers. Thus, the new men created by increased commercial and government activity either would be drawn from its own or its followers' ranks, or would be dependent on and co-opted into the ruling class itself. The key to this strategy of gradual and controlled change was political control through the NPC at both the federal and regional levels. Yet, the northern ruling class rested on an insecure foundation. Nigeria was a vast and plural society. The social strata in the south that were challenging its control at the federal level were increasing in numbers and importance as a result of economic and social changes that could not be arrested. Within the northern region opposition groups based either on non-Hausa ethnic aspirations or class divisions within the highly stratified Hausa society were being rapidly mobilized as a result of the formation of modern political parties based on universal adult male franchise. Each election provided anew an occasion for challenging the entrenched position of NPC leaders. No doubt the northern leaders acted not only from narrow selfish interests, but from a deep religious conviction about the inherent worth of northern society and its way of life. Many of the ordinary Hausa folk shared their fears about a growing southern presence within their midst. Competition against skillful, educated aliens has never been welcome and has usually been the occasion for hostility and negative stereotyping. These beliefs and sentiments were exploited by the ruling groups to draw attention away from their own shortcomings and the class tensions inherent in northern society.

Crises of national unity resulting from similar circumstances are not a peculiarity of Nigeria or the new states of Africa. The secession of the Southern states in the America of 1860–1861 can be analyzed along the same lines. Like Nigeria, the United States was a plural society. Southern society, based on slavery and a monocrop agricultural economy, was not keeping up with the more dynamic, commercial, and industrial capitalism of the North. In the competition for western land and territory, the South was rapidly losing out as many more Northerners were settling there. As a result the delicate political balance in the Senate between free and slave states was being threatened. Yet, the defense of the institution of slavery and of Southern economic interests rested on predominant Southern influence within the federal government—on Southern control of the Democratic party and a Democratic administration in Washington. Abolitionist sentiment was growing in the North; the attacks on slavery were increasing. Under this strain, the Democratic party was breaking up along sectional lines which would spell the end of the Southern grip on the federal government. Just as important, and parallel to the dilemma of the northern Nigerian ruling class, the Southern plantocracy was not secure within its own section. Less than 20 percent of the population in the South had a direct property interest in slaves. In 1860, the pro-union Constitutional Union party won Kentucky, Tennessee, and Virginia and barely lost Maryland and Missouri. After Lincoln's election, the state referenda and conventions called to decide on the question of secession or union were closely contested in many states. Nevertheless, the upper class in the South managed to create a majority sentiment for slavery and for secession by playing on the poor whites' fear of competing against liberated black labor. To make sense of the events of the 1850s in the United States and of the 1950s and 1960s in Nigeria, one must realize that the central actors in both cases were the political representatives of regional ruling classes bent on maintaining their political and economic power even as they were in decline at the national level and fearful of losing control within their own region.

Chapter *IV*

MOBILIZATION:
THE FORMATION
OF CONFLICT GROUPS

INTRODUCTION

One of the central problems in the theory of social conflict and of collective behavior is to account for the mobilization of people with grievances into a social movement or some other conflict group. Mobilization refers to the process of forming crowds, groups, associations, and organizations for the pursuit of collective goals. Frequently, enduring social units are thus formed with new leadership, loyalties, identifications, and goals. Another way of looking at mobilization is to focus on the increase in power that mobilization produces for a collectivity, as in Etzioni's (1968a: 243) definition of mobilization as a "process in which a social unit gains relatively rapidly in control over resources it previously did not control." Mobilization theory is concerned with how people with little individual power collectively resist or challenge established and organized groups that have a vested interest in maintaining the status quo.

At the present time, mass society theory provides an explicitly stated theory of mobilization that is frequently used by sociologists. The purpose of the following pages is to take a critical look at its explanation of the growth of social movements and to present an alternative and hopefully more valid theory of mobilization based on an extension of Mancur Olson's theory of groups (1968). After describing mobilization processes as hypothesized in mass society theory and formulating a number of testable empirical statements implied in it, it will be shown that this theory is contradicted by the available evidence on the formation and growth of extremist movements and bitter community conflict in the U.S. and in Weimar Germany, namely, McCarthyism, the Radical Right, fluoridation controversies, and the rise of the Nazis. The alternative theory presented will account for the rise of all manner of social movements, including extremist and antidemocratic ones.

Mass society theory is well known and does not require another comprehensive exposition. Mass society is characterized by Kornhauser as "a social system in which elites are readily accessible to influence by non-elites, and non-elites are readily available for mobilization by elites" (1959:39). The availability of non-elites depends on "the extent to which members of the society lack attachments to independent groups, the local community, voluntary associations, and occupational groups." Mass society is further characterized by the isolation of personal relations (1959:90) and the centralization of national relations, that is, the growth of centralized bureaucratic organizations at the expense of locally controlled intermediate groups (1959:93). In the mass society context, a high rate of mass behavior can occur, and the ground is prepared for extremist, antidemocratic mass movements that are readily penetrated and changed into totalitarian movements.

There are two testable empirical propositions that follow from this conception of mass society and mass behavior. First, extremist movements will flourish in societies with a low number and thin network of intermediate groups, where few people participate in voluntary, occupational, religious, civic, and other associations; and second, it is the alienated, uprooted, nonparticipants in intermediate groups, those with the weakest attachments to class-based organizations who will be the most susceptible to extremist appeals, who will be the first to join extremist movements, who will join in large numbers and become the activists (Kornhauser, 1959:48–49, 182). A third testable proposition actually follows from both mass society theory and pluralist theory. Multiple membership in intermediate groups will inhibit participation and total involvement in extremist movements because it fosters crosscutting solidarities and the integration of group members into the society. Multiple group affiliation will act as a checks and balances mechanism for preventing the rise of any one movement that seeks to capture the total allegiance and involvement of its adherents. In particular, the leaders of intermediate groups, who are known to have more tolerant views than the rank-and-file citizens (Stouffer, 1966) will openly and actively oppose the nondemocratic extremists, will stand up for due process, free speech, and other democratic norms, and oppose witch-hunt type tactics and violence. How do these predictions stand up against the empirical evidence in the U.S. and elsewhere?

MASS SOCIETY THEORY AND
EXTREMISM IN THE UNITED STATES

Although it was not a fully developed mass movement since Senator Joseph McCarthy did not mobilize a cohesive, organized, popular following that pursued his political aims, McCarthyism (both McCarthy's own activities and the local witch-hunting activities that he stimulated) was an example of antidemocratic extremism frequently analyzed by mass society theorists and used by them to demonstrate the validity of their approach. Nevertheless, Rogin's (1967) most detailed and comprehensive study of McCarthyism fails to support mass society theory. He found that McCarthyism grew out of conservative rural politics, the politics of rural, conservative, local Republican elites, not out of mass politics in any meaningful sense, and that "most of those who mobilized behind McCarthy at the national level were conservative politicians and publicists, businessmen and retired military leaders discontented with the New Deal, the bureaucracy and with military policy. . . . These men had been part of the Republican right wing before McCarthy" (Rogin, 1967:250). These right-wingers as well as other Republican leaders hoped to use McCarthyism for unseating the Democratic administration that had kept them from power for the last twenty years. Though they thought McCarthy's tactics objectionable, these leaders found it expedient to remain silent and not to risk their personal position by openly opposing and condemning the Wisconsin senator.

McCarthy's appeal among rank-and-file citizens was specifically to the single issue of anticommunism at the time of the Korean War and was not the diffuse appeal that is characteristic of mass behavior (Rogin, 1967:242). Opinion polls consistently showed that the variable that produced the greatest percent difference between a favorable and unfavorable opinion of McCarthy was not socioeconomic status, occupation, demographic attributes, or some other variables that might be related to alienation and massification, but party affiliation: Democrats opposed McCarthy while Republicans supported him (Rogin, 1967:232–39). In sum, support for McCarthy cannot be explained with reference to mass society theory, and the much admired checks and balances of pluralist politics in the U.S., including the greater tolerance and support for civil liberties of political and community leaders, did not operate effectively, or only operated too late, to check McCarthyism.

If we turn to the Radical Right of the 1960s, the best empirical evidence again fails to support mass society theory. Wolfinger and his colleagues collected data in Oakland, California, in early 1962 on participants in the "Anti-Communism school" run by Dr. Fred Schwartz's Christian Anti-Communist Crusade, the second most prominent Radical Right organization in the U.S. after the John Birch Society. Crusaders were predominantly an upper-status group, with businessmen and professionals making up over 50 percent of the participants, with above average incomes, and a higher proportion with college education than the population of the San Francisco Bay area. They tended to be Protestant, white, and Republican. They were obsessed with the threat of internal subversion from Communism and were isolationist more than aggressive in their foreign policy preferences. (Wolfinger et al., 1964: 267–75). A comparison of Crusaders' memberships in all kinds of organizations—church, civic, veterans', and so on—with a comparable national sample shows that they had higher membership rates. Therefore, they could not be called social isolates (p. 276). Attitude data, socioeconomic and demographic background data, and other information on which Crusaders' and comparable national samples were contrasted led the researchers to discard explanations based on alienation, status anxiety, ethnic hostility, cultural resentment, excessive down mobility, political apathy, and other processes that have been linked with mass society theory (pp. 276–86). The researchers suggest that the Radical Right is a phenomenon associated with extreme conservative Republicanism, religious fundamentalism, and an obsession with internal subversion in regions where political party organizations are weak and lack continuity, such as is the case in California and the Southwest.

Turning now to community controversies in the U.S., Crain and associates (1969:220–28) in their study of fluoridation controversies in over a thousand cities find mass society theory and alienation explanations wanting. It is communities with a high level of education, a dense network of voluntary organizations, and high rates of citizen participation in civic and political affairs that have most difficulty in resolving the fluoridation issue (p. 215). The restraining effects of enlightened community leadership and of cross pressures due to multiple group affiliation do not operate to check the mobilization of the citizenry into bitter and protracted conflict, because elected political leaders and local civic and professional notables are unwilling to take sides in a controversial issue from which they stand little to gain and much to lose, while extremist leadership is not similarly restrained. The rank-and-file citizens, on the other hand, are readily mobilized into the controversy through the associations to which they belonged (Crain et al., 1969:13, 57, 148, 208, 222–23, 226). It is not apathy and alienation, but overparticipation in local community affairs that spells trouble for the acceptance of fluoridation and fuels the development of controversy. In communities with weak executive centralization of local government combined with a participatory tradition of citizen involvement in local affairs fluoridation has the lowest adoption rate (p. 204).

Coleman's study of community conflict of a decade earlier supports the fluoridation study findings. Conflict tends to take place in affluent suburbs with a participatory tradition; the upper and middle classes are readily mobilized into controversies through their associational ties; local leaders and organizations fail to check the growth of conflict as pressures build up against their involvement in controversial issues (Coleman, 1957:7, 11–13, 18, 21–22). Gamson finds in his study of fifty-four community controversies over schools, zoning, fluoridation, and the like in eighteen New England communities that the pivotal variable for explaining why controversies become rancorous in some towns but remain routine and normal in others is the existence of a prior cleavage in the community over a threatened shift in political control between two groups. The absence of solidary groups, economic strain, absence of shared background, lack of organization membership, and a participatory political structure have less or little explanatory power (Gamson:1966). Variables expected to produce an effect according to mass society theory had but minimal impact, although Gamson did not address himself to testing explicitly the mobilization mechanisms implied in mass society theory.

In reflecting on the failure of mass society theory to provide explanations for extremist behavior and unusually bitter community controversies, three shortcomings should be pointed out. Pinard (1968) has recently dealt with the first one to be discussed. The mobilizing potential and mobilizing effects of intermediate groups are not adequately recognized in mass society theory. Pinard notes that (1968:687) "under severe strain, and given that no other institutionalized channels for the redress of grievances are available, conformist components of the intermediate structure can become elements which encourage rather than limit the growth of a new movement. Moreover, members of intermediate groups may be the early, not late joiners in the movement, much earlier than the atomized mass, contrary to mass society theory."

The second point is most aptly stated in Gusfield's critique of both mass society and pluralist theory. It is based on the failure to distinguish between two types of social structure, both compatible with a dense network of intermediate groups and high rates of citizen participation in them, between linked pluralism and superimposed segmentation (Gusfield, 1962:29). In linked pluralism, each individual is affiliated with multiple groups but memberships in any one intermediate group cut across memberships in others, and all groups draw their members from a variety of social groups, status groups, or classes. It is only in this type of social structure that cross pressures act to moderate conflict and prevent the division of society along lines of superimposed cleavage.

Superimposed segmentation, on the other hand, means that although there may be high rates of participation in intermediate groups and many such groups and associations, memberships in these groups draw predominantly or exclusively from particular social classes, strata, or status groups. Thus, each class or stratum is highly participatory and bound together in dense but mutually exclusive networks of intermediate groupings. Superimposed segmentation allows for rapid mobilization of classes and strata against each other. Weimar Germany, as we shall see below, was characterized by superimposed segmentation, not the absence of intermediate groups, and it is precisely this fact that enabled the rapid mobilization of the Nazi movement, not the social isolation and apathy of the German people. As Gusfield summarized it (1962:26), there exist certain social settings in which "extremist politics is developed and conducted by well structured groups, representing discrete and organized parts of the social structure, acting to secure group goals related to group needs . . . while such groups are alienated from the existing political institutions, they are not socially disintegrated or unrelated to the society and its political system. They function within a pluralist framework in which their values receive short shrift." Coleman (1957:21–22) had already noted that a high density of organization ties in a community may not result in crosscutting cleavages integrating ethnic groups or old and new residents, if each group is highly organized within itself with few membership overlaps among them. In this situation, high levels of intermediate group membership provide for rapid mobilization of each stratum or class against the other(s) without countervailing mechanisms for conflict moderation and containment.

A third point of criticism is the tendency of mass society theorists to ignore the importance of political structures and institutions in the development of extremist movements and community controversies: the struggle for political control pointed out by Gamson; the weak centralization of executive authority in local government noted by Crain and associates; the key support provided to McCarthyism through the backing of conservative local and national political leaders and the encouragement of other Republicans who sought to exploit it to regain power described by Rogin; and the continuity between conservative Republicanism and the Radical Right in a context of weak party organizations and traditions noted in Wolfinger. This is not to say that socioeconomic, social-psychological, and demographic processes are unimportant for providing an explanation of why people are dissatisfied and have grievances. But so far as a theory of mobilization is concerned, political institutions have more importance than mass society theorists have been willing to grant.

MASS SOCIETY THEORY AND
THE RISE OF THE NAZIS

We now turn to the case of the Weimar Republic and the spread of Nazism, the very movement which gave rise to mass society theory itself and popularized its use among social scientists. The basic empirical questions that will be discussed are whether Weimar Germany was a mass society in the first place, whether it lacked or had but a thin layer of intermediate groups, whether those individuals who were social isolates, uprooted, or but weakly involved in this layer gave early and strong support to the Nazis, all of which one would expect to be true according to mass society theory. We are not concerned with a comprehensive analysis of the rise and victory of the Nazis but merely with establishing whether mobilization of Nazi electoral support took place in the manner specified in mass society theory.

Was Weimar Germany a mass society? If, following Kornhauser, mass society can be characterized by an absence or thin network of intermediate groups and associations that leave a large section of the people uprooted and atomized, the answer must be no. Germany was rather a good example of a society with a high degree of superimposed segmentation in which each class was caught up in its own dense network of intermediate relations, but with few links across them. Allen's case study of a town of about ten thousand inhabitants in Hannover where the Nazis gained an absolute majority in the 1932 elections (it was therefore an early Nazi stronghold) shows that it had an unusually large number and active network of voluntary associations consisting of twenty-one sports clubs, twenty-three religious and charitable organizations, twenty-five veterans' and patriotic societies, forty-seven economic and occupational associations, and forty-five special interest groups, such as singing societies and drinking circles. (Allen, 1965:17). However, membership was strictly along class lines. Each social stratum had its own shooting, gymnastics, veterans, singing, drinking, occupational, and political associations. The working class was a closed subculture dominated by the SDP (Socialist party) and its allied associations from youth groups to *Reichsbanner* (the paramilitary corps for the defense of the republic), cooperatives, trade unions, shooting societies, and so on.

Such a high level of participation in intermediate groups and superimposed segmentation was typical of Germany as a whole. At the first meeting of the German Sociological Society in 1910, Max Weber proposed to his colleagues an empirical investigation of organizations and associations in Germany (*Soziologie des Vereinswesens*): "those social units . . . that one conventionally designates as 'associational', that is, everything between the polity—state, community, official church—on the one hand and . . . the family on the other, . . . from bowling clubs to . . . political parties, religious, artistic, and literary societies" (Weber, 1924:441–42). Weber considered this phenomenon as characteristic of Germany as of the United States and cited as an illustration to his audience that "for instance in single cities of 30,000 inhabitants there are 300 different associations, or one per hundred inhabitants and one per 20 heads of family" (Weber, 1924:442–43). Each class and major social grouping in Germany had its own political party and associated network of organizations that mobilized its supporters behind its leaders (Lepsius, 1966:379–87). The Conservative party relied for half a century on the Union of Agriculturists (later Agrarian League, still later German Agrarian League) with 5,500,000 members to mobilize the small and middle peasantry behind Junker leadership on the tariff issue and for broader social and political goals (Gerschenkron, 1966:52, 105; Lepsius, 1966:386). The Catholics, with the *Zentrum* party, used a comprehensive network of church associated organizations (Lepsius, 1966:383–84); the Liberals based their leadership and mobilizing potential on prestigious local notables and civic groups in which judges, civil servants, professors, lawyers, and editors predominated (Lepsius, 1966:386), while the Socialists drew on their numerous trade unions and associated organizations: "party, unions, cultural, welfare, sports, and recreational associations integrated the proletariat into a political subculture that formed the base of a collective consciousness" (Lepsius, 1966:380). In addition, in areas that Prussia had recently annexed, such as Hannover and Schleswig-Holstein, anti-Prussian local patriotic parties and associations flourished and later played a key role in the rise of Nazis in rural areas. The stability of the German political party system from Bismarck to the depression of the 1930s demonstrated by Lepsius was based on its link with these enduring, highly organized, but closed subcultures (Lepsius, 1966:378–82). Even the white-collar class was highly organized and unionized in Germany. According to Schoenbaum (1966:8), fully 81.7 percent of the white-collar labor force was unionized through the Socialist *Gewerkschaft der Angestellten,* the National-Liberal Hirsch-Duncker unions, and the Christian-National associations such as the *Deutschnationaler Handlungsgehilfenverband.* These unions were tough negotiators preoccupied with securing salaries for previous wage workers, long-term labor contracts, and generous pension schemes. Weimar Germany, therefore, cannot be described as a mass society; rather, it was a highly organized class society in which, however, communities based on preindustrial divisions such as that between Protestants and Catholics persisted and in which the leadership of conservative Junkers in Prussia managed to integrate lower-middle strata of small farmers with the large landowners over the issue of agricultural protectionism in the absence of an attractive agrarian program offered by the Socialists (Gerschenkron, 1966). The Nazi neutralization, dissolution, and take-over of these extensive networks of intermediate groups in 1933 even go by the special name of *Gleichschaltung,* another indication that these networks must have been prevalent to begin with.

To answer the second question of whether it was the socially isolated and uprooted, those but weakly involved in intermediate relations and previously apathetic people, who voted in disproportionately large numbers for the Nazi party, we have to examine the studies of the German elections between 1928 and 1933. Although based on ecological analysis of very large electoral areas of between one-half to one million voters, the most plausible interpretation of the election returns is that the Nazis were especially strong at an early date in the rural Protestant districts between the 1928 and 1930 elections, that they picked up a considerable proportion of the nationalist conservative voters, some young new voters and previous nonvoters, and the supporters of regional splinter parties, and that after 1930 they made inroads among middle-class voters, in particular self-employed businessmen, small farmers, residents of small towns and cities, lesser civil servants and teachers, other lower rank professionals, and shopkeepers. The working-class and Catholic population tended to remain loyal to the Socialist party and the Catholic *Zentrum* respectively (Lipset, 1963:138–52; O'Lessker, 1969:63–69; Schnaiberg, 1969:732–34). Kornhauser states that (1959:157) "although it is true that there are other sources of mass tendencies, the very rapid expansion of cities and industries has constituted perhaps the most general source of social atomization in the modern world, in so far as they have inhibited the growth of new forms of group life to replace the village community, extended family and guild which they have destroyed." Lipset, on the other hand, cites studies that indicate the below average Nazi vote in the large cities, and reaches the conclusion that (1963:144) "these facts sharply challenge the various interpretations of Nazism as the product of the growth of anomie and the general rootlessness of urban industrial society."

The key to Nazi electoral successes was their ability to mobilize rural voters and their support in rural areas and small towns. Detailed studies of this process have been provided by Heberle (1945) for Schleswig-Holstein, and Loomis and Beagle (1946) in Hannover, who reach similar conclusions. The Nazis there were particularly strong in

1932 in the agricultural zone where small independent farmers pre-dominated. The farmers lived in small communities, relied on family labor, engaged in hog raising and dairy farming, and were particularly hard hit by the agricultural depression, the widely fluctuating prices for their products, and indebtedness. They resisted foreclosures and forced sales of their farms frequently by violent means. Before 1928, they had tended to support liberal parties and local anti-Prussian parties. They were highly organized in interest groups such as the *Bauernbund,* which opposed the conservative dominance of agrarian interests by the large landowner controlled *Landbund,* and in a multitude of other farmers' organizations, regional, cultural, folk, and ethnic associations such as the *Jungbauern Bewegung* and the *Jungdeutsche Orden* whose ideology stressed communal and local patriotic sentiments in opposition to big business, capital, Jews, and cities (Heberle, 1945:40–58). In no mean-ingful sense can this social stratum be considered massified: it was highly organized, active before the Nazis, and had a strong sense of identity and local patriotism supported by intermediary organizations and a tra-dition of defense of its interests. However, it was dissatisfied with the existing parties and their agrarian programs, felt that its interests were given short shrift in national politics, and was attracted to the Nazi party's agrarian program that promised "to stop exploitation of farmers by taxation, wholesale trade and oppressive interest rates" (Gerschenk-ron, 1966:145–46). They went over as a bloc to the Nazi party precisely because they were already highly mobilized and activists. Here again, as in Pinard's and Gusfield's criticisms of mass society theory, one finds that high participation in secondary organizations under conditions of superimposed segmentation provides for rapid mobilization into a pro-test movement when the people with deep-seated grievances are no longer hopeful of gaining relief through the existing political channels.

Allen's case study confirms this mobilization pattern for an urban setting in Hannover, where in 1931–1932 middle- and upper-class associ-ations backed by prominent citizens made common cause with the Nazis to wrest control of municipal administration from the Socialists in a context of constant political tensions, electioneering, and street fights. These groups seized an opportunity for getting rid of the Marxist "men-ace" once and for all with the help of Nazi thugs and electoral alliances, until in 1933 they themselves were purged from leadership in the city and their associations annexed and subordinated by the Nazis (Allen, 1965). The Socialists and trade unions put up a steady resistance to the Nazis' and their allies' efforts to destroy them. But unemployment rose steadily, construction work came to a halt, unemployment benefits were not paid because of a lack of funds, and the largest employer of orga-nized Socialist workers in the town, the railroad, came to be controlled by Nazi sympathizers who engaged in a wave of dismissals of Socialist railroad workers and in other means of economic coercion. Thus the Socialists' economic base was decisively weakened. It was impossible for them to resort to a strike when an army of unemployed was ready to be hired as replacements and the union treasury empty. It is true, as Kornhauser points out (1959:163), that the depression and unemployment weakened and demoralized intermediary groups of the working class, but it should be stressed that workers did not willingly submit as Kornhauser implies when he writes that "unemployment creates psychological tendencies which prepare people to participate in Fascist and Communist movements"; rather, it was a case of economic and physical coercion. Before the depth of depression had weakened Socialist organizations in the city Allen studied, they physically resisted Nazi strong-arm tactics during "three years of violence, . . . broken heads, split lips, and black eyes" (Allen, 1965:137–38), as his count of thirty-seven political fights, including four general brawls between 1930 and 1933 shows. Between 1 July and 20 July 1932, violence on a large scale erupted all over Germany, with 461 political riots in Prussia alone, during which 82 were killed and over 400 were seriously injured (Allen, 1965:113). This can hardly be called willing submission.

Therefore, it is hard to escape the conclusion that mass society theory does not explain in a satisfactory manner the growth of the Nazi movement in Germany. It is also evident that an alternative theory of mobilization will have to incorporate the mobilizing function of secondary associations in a social structure of superimposed segmentation. Another shortcoming of mass society theory is that it treats mass movements and its cousins, extremist, totalitarian, and antidemocratic movements, as a distinct phenomenon, with mobilizing processes different from movements that have nonextremist or prodemocratic goals. But no one has yet established that there are different processes of mobilization going on in movements whose goals and ideologies differ. In fact, Loomis and Beagle (1946:734) noted that "the manner in which the Nazis swept the farmer-peasant organizations of pre-Hitler Germany into the Nazi movement has parallels in the American Greenback, Farmer's Alliance, Populist and similar movements." One cannot help being struck by the parallel between the processes by means of which the Socialist CCF (Cooperative Commonwealth Federation) rose in Saskatchewan according to Lipset, and the Nazis rose in rural Schleswig-Holstein according to Heberle. Saskatchewan was marked by small farmers' communities specializing in wheat growing and therefore vulnerable to extreme price fluctuations. They had little internal stratification, strong bonds of solidarity, and a well-organized and highly participatory population before the CFF was formed (Lipset, 1966:245–47, 252). Heberle concludes that in rural Schleswig-Holstein, "where social stratification was not pronounced, where the village community was well integrated, the Marxists tended to be weak, the conservatives only temporarily strong, the liberal parties strong and relatively constant during the earlier years, the N.S.D.A.P. (Nazis) and its forerunners very strong during the end of the period (1928 to 1933) . . . ," and "other things being equal, the chances for the extreme parties were better the more specialized and therefore more sensitive to business cycles the farms were" (Heberle, 1951: 232–33). Therefore, it seems profitable to develop a comprehensive theory of mobilization applicable to all manner of conflict groups and social movements, whether leftist, rightist, or centrist, that seek to challenge vested interests, established leaders, and political parties.

OLSON'S THEORY OF COLLECTIVE ACTION

Olson's (1968) theory of collective action and of group formation deals with associations that exist to further the interests of their members by providing a collective good, namely, labor unions, cartels, farm organizations, pressure groups, lobbies, and the like. A collective good is any good whose benefits cannot be withheld from those in the collectivity who did not contribute to its cost, such as a wage contract covering all workers in an industry or firm, a tariff law resulting in higher prices for a certain type of commodity, roads, postal service, public education, and national defense, and, also, by extension, independence in the case of colonies, civil liberties, and political rights extended to negatively privileged groups. Although all the members of the collectivity have a common interest in obtaining the collective good, they have no common interest in paying the cost of providing it. For large collectivities, Olson finds that (1968:16) the "individual member . . . is in a position analogous to that of the firm in a perfectly competitive market, or the taxpayer in the state: his own efforts will not have a noticeable effect on the situation of his organization, and he can enjoy any improvements brought about by others whether or not he has worked in support of his organization." As a consequence, members of a large collectivity do not voluntarily, without the use of sanctions, or without some incentives and benefits distinct from the collective good itself, organize to attain a collective good that would benefit them all. Olson's analysis reveals, however, that (p. 34) "in a very small group, where each member gets a substantial proportion of the total gain simply because there are few others in the group, a collective good can often be provided by the voluntary self-interested action of the members of the group. In smaller groups marked by considerable degrees of inequality—that is, in groups of members of unequal "size" or extent of interest in the collective good —there is the greatest likelihood that a collective good will be provided."

Olson extends his analysis further by taking into account individual or noncollective goods and social incentives in addition to material incentives (pp. 62–63). Prestige, respect, leadership position, friendship, and the like, including psychological gratifications resulting from participation, group support, and doing the "right thing" out of commitment to a moral code—and, more generally, social sanctions and rewards—are individual goods that are used as selective incentives for mobilizing support in a collectivity in addition to the incentive provided by the attainment of the collective good itself. They can be analyzed in much the same way as individual monetary incentives are analyzed. Nevertheless, Olson thinks that (p. 63) "there is no presumption that social incentives will lead individuals in the latent group (the large unorganized collectivity) to obtain a collective good" because social rewards and sanctions cannot be effectively implemented in large collectivities.

Olson's theory accounts for the formation (or lack of it) of the main economic pressure-group organizations, but his theory is not (p. 159) "logically limited to any special case. It can be applied whenever there are rational individuals interested in a common goal . . . the theory of large groups . . . is not even limited to situations where there is self-interested behavior, or where only monetary or material interests are at stake." Although Olson does not think (p. 162) that his theory is especially helpful in explaining the formation of social, protest, and radical movements, I shall demonstrate below that a simple extension of Olson's basic framework can indeed be used as the foundation for a theory of mobilization of these movements.

As it stands, Olson's theory highlights the obstacles in the way of conflict group formation in large collectivities. Olson's theory would predict that large collectivities deprived of civil liberties and political rights will not develop from within an opposition organization for obtaining these goals if the members of the collectivity pursue their own selfish interests in a calculated, rational way and if they have complete freedom to join or not to join an opposition movement. In effect, each member of a large negatively privileged collectivity might as well wait until others take the risks and pay the price of mobilization and of opposition. But if each member follows this rule, then no opposition movement is ever likely to be formed. Nevertheless, we know from history and our own experience that opposition movements and conflict groups are formed quite frequently. Since Olson's theory is basically sound, one is led to question some of his assumptions with a view to modifying and extending his theory for the case of political opposition and conflict groups.

First of all, Olson assumes a society in which freedom of speech, assembly, and association are guaranteed, so that each individual is free to decide whether or not he will participate in an association or movement for obtaining the collective good. Yet we know that so far as protest and opposition movements are concerned, their members are frequently harassed, persecuted, outlawed, and repressed. As a result, in an authoritarian social setting, the obstacles to mobilization are even greater than in Olson's model, and these obstacles are especially powerful in the case of small groups who attempt to initiate mobilization in the early stages of opposition. This further difficulty turns out neither to contradict Olson's theory nor to complicate its application. Theorists, historians, and social scientists have often noted that protest movements emerge in a society not when a government is applying its repressive apparatus to the fullest extent, but, on the contrary, when a previously authoritarian regime is trying to reform and social control is loosened, allowing for greater freedom of association and speech and making opposition less risky. Thus, we can say that when conditions approximating Olson's assumption do in fact hold, an opposition movement is more likely to emerge than otherwise. Moreover, it is not when the economy is at its lowest depression or recession level and hardship is greatest that people tend to revolt, as has often been noted, but, on the contrary, when times are improving. In difficult times, people are too busy just making a living and are consuming all of their resources, but, in more prosperous times, they have a small surplus of time, energy, and material resources that they are able to "invest" in protest organization and behavior. Thus, negative economic sanctions available to incumbents are not likely to be as effective in more prosperous times than in depression, and the condition of free choice for participation in associations and social movements, which Olson's theory assumes, are approximated precisely when one observes empirically the formation of opposition movements and conflict groups.

Olson's theory also assumes that the members of the collectivity do not receive outside support for initiating and sustaining mobilization for attaining the collective good. But in many instances of protest behavior and opposition formation, outside help, both in the form of leadership and material resources, is pumped into the collectivity, at least in the initial stages of a movement. Wallerstein (1964:325) provides several illustrations of this in the case of African trade unions and political parties. Marx's theory of the bourgeois ideologists and intellectuals who join the anticapitalist movement of the working classes is also based on this notion. One does not have to subscribe to a conspiracy theory of history to note that this process is by no means infrequent. Thus, if one relaxes Olson's assumption to allow for outside support, the obstacles to mobilization are more likely to be overcome.

It is also true that in many instances opposition leadership and re-sources are drawn from within the collectivity and that the initiation of mobilization cannot be accounted for with reference to outside support. Must one relax the assumption of rational, self-interested behavior postu-lated by Olson in order to explain the emergence of inside opposition leadership in the face of incarceration, physical injury, and the ultimate fate? Olson's theory in no way implies that individual goods and selective incentives are not also present in group formation, and it is precisely individual goods and selective incentives that can account for the emer-gence of leaders and activists in a high risk situation. Olson writes that (p. 51) "selective incentives will stimulate a rational individual in a latent group to act in a group oriented way" and that "potential [or latent] capacity for action can be realized or mobilized [in large size groups] only with the aid of selective incentives." Although ordinary members in a negatively privileged collectivity only get the same bene-fits as all other members when civil liberties or political rights, the over-throw of a dictator or independence, are obtained, the leaders and activists in a successful movement obtain in addition high individual rewards such as political office, prestige, and leadership positions. The successful leader of a national or revolutionary movement certainly ob-tains a high individual reward when he assumes the presidency or some other top position in the new state. Thus, in order to explain inside opposition mobilization in high risk situations, one needs only to as-sume that individual rewards and selective incentives motivate the lead-ers and activists of conflict groups and that, given the same objective circumstances, some members of a collectivity will respond to these individual incentives in addition to being driven by the prospects of obtaining the collective good itself.

There are also other individual incentives for becoming an opposi-tion leader and activist that do not depend on the prospects of high future rewards, but on the desire to avoid the prospect of penalties and low future rewards. Once identified as a radical, troublemaker, outlaw, sympathizer, and sometimes only as a relative of opponents of the re-gime, one's usual career chances automatically become closed should one wish to change course, and continued opposition activity becomes an increasingly attractive alternative. One also wonders whether opposition activity is always such a high risk choice. It is true that for every Fidel Castro there are a Che Guevera and several other unsuccessful Latin American revolutionaries, but in the case of the African nationalists of the post–World War II period the success rate was strikingly high. A statistical study might shed light on this point. In any event, it will be shown in a later section that in the typical "colonial situation," or more generally in a society characterized by superimposed segmentation, the mobility chances of the most talented, qualified, and ambitious individuals in the subordinate groups are blocked or limited, as has so often been noted, and consequently the choice of opposition behavior is perfectly rational if individual incentives and variance of response to the same objective conditions are allowed. The point of view put forward here is again not in contradiction to Olson's theory but a simple elaboration of it. In fact, he explicitly writes that (p. 34) "in smaller groups marked by considerable degrees of inequality—that is, in groups of members of unequal size or extent of interest in the collective good—there is the greatest likelihood that a collective good will be provided." This precisely corresponds to the leader-follower relationship of small opposition groups in the initial period of formation.

A point at which Olson's theory must be modified and not simply elaborated to make it more applicable to opposition movements is in his assumption that the members of a large collectivity are unorganized individual decision makers similar to the numerous, small, independent producers in the market of the classical economist. This is but one possibility, and perhaps not even the most frequent one. Discontented groups can be members of a still viable or partially viable community, religious, tribal, ethnic, cultural and historical, into which they were born and which they accept as a matter of course because it represents the basis of their everyday life, their livelihood, their family life and kinship relations, and their most cherished beliefs. But it is precisely in this type of social structure that social rewards and sanctions are powerful incentives for participating in an opposition movement once the community leadership has decided on opposition, since one's livelihood and social life depend on maintaining good relations with other members of the community and since it is not possible for community members to disappear into an anonymous, undifferentiated multitude said to be characteristic of large cities. Furthermore, even if a collectivity is no longer a community in this sociological sense, its members might already be partially organized along associational lines for purposes other than opposition. Indeed, Olson himself analyzes this situation (p. 63) when he deals with the case of a federated organization resulting from the merger of preexisting small organizations that then provides the collective good for a large collectivity. It will be shown below that this is by no means exceptional but rather a very frequent way in which social movements are formed. Finally, one should not omit the possibility that members of the collectivity have already been partially mobilized against the goals of the protest movement, that counterorganizations or movements are created as the opposition movement gains in strength, and that attempts are made by the targets of the protesters to draw protesters or potential protesters away from the movement. Here again, this is least likely to happen in a society characterized by superimposed segmentation. The theory of mobilization put forward here is an elaboration of Olson's theory, with a few of his assumptions changed to reflect more realistically the social structure and social environment in which opposition movements are likely to occur.

In basing a sociological theory of mobilization on Olson's economic analysis, I am actually following a useful insight provided many years ago by Max Weber when he wrote (1947:122–23),

> many . . . especially notable uniformities . . . of social action are not determined by orientation to any sort of norm which is held to be valid, nor do they rest on custom, but entirely on the fact that . . . social action is . . . best adapted to the normal interests of the actors as they are aware of them. This is above all true of economic action, for example, the uniformities of price determination in a "free market," *but is by no means confined to such cases.* . . . This phenomenon . . . can bring about results which are very similar to those which an authoritarian agency, very often in vain, has attempted to obtain by coercion. . . . Observation of this has, in fact, been one of the important sources of economics as a science. *But it is true in all spheres of action as well.* (Emphasis added)

The very real theoretical gain achieved is that a theory of mobilization of opposition and conflict groups, social and mass movements, of protest behavior and collective political action, is essentially the same as the theory of mobilization for economic interest groups, and that the simple assumption of rationality in economic theory is sufficient in this theoretical effort. Thus, one need not make assumptions about individual motivation based on alienation or psychopathology, and a single theory spans the entire range of political and social movements, regardless of whether they are designated as extremist, leftist, rightist, centrist, or mass movements by their supporters and detractors.

A SOCIOLOGICAL THEORY OF MOBILIZATION

We now turn to the statement of a sociological theory of mobilization that draws on both Olson's theory and the theory of social change and, in particular, to an examination of social structural conditions favoring mobilization into opposition movements. The special conditions that account for the initiation of mobilization, the subsequent speed of mobilization, the conditions favoring sustained protest, or, to state the matter from the opposite side, factionalism and other processes making for demobilization, will be covered in later sections. It is taken for granted that a collectivity or quasi-group, to use Dahrendorf's (1959:179) term, with common latent interests, already exists and that the members of the collectivity are dissatisfied and have grievances (Merton, 1957:288–89; Gamson, 1968: chapter 2). We also assume a collectivity that is at least fairly large and geographically concentrated so that communication between members exists or can be established. The theory is concerned with substantial opposition movements and other forms of collective behavior such as riots and rebellion, and not with a sociology of sects, small deviant subcultures, and similar phenomena.

The guiding ideas of the theory are few and simple. The minimum conditions of collective protest are shared targets and objects of hostility held responsible for grievances, hardship, and suffering, augmented in some cases by more deeply rooted sentiments of collective oppression, common interests, and community of fate. These minimum conditions give rise, however, to only short-term, localized, ephemeral outbursts and movements of protest such as riots. For sustained resistance or protest an organizational base and continuity of leadership are also necessary. The organizational base can be rooted in two different types of social structure. The collectivity might be integrated and organized along viable traditional lines based on kinship, village, ethnic or tribal organization, or other forms of community, with recognized leaders and networks of social relations extending to its boundaries. On the other hand, the collectivity might have a dense network of secondary groups based on occupational, religious, civic, economic, and other special interest associations with leaders based on prominent roles in these associations and networks of social relations following associational ties. Both of these principles of social organization, and they are by no means mutually exclusive, produce horizontal links and sentiments of solidarity within the collectivity that can be activated for the pursuit of collective goals and the formation of conflict groups.

On a vertical dimension, the links between the collectivity and other collectivities in the society, especially those higher up in the stratification system, are also of central importance to a theory of mobilization. A structural feature facilitating mobilization into protest movements is obtained when the society is not only highly stratified but segmented. Under segmentation the collectivity whose potential for mobilization we are examining has few links and bonds, other than perhaps through exploitative relationships, with the higher classes or other collectivities of the society. Such a situation obtains when the traditional upper class or landed nobility no longer exercise protective, political, judicial, administrative, and diffuse social leadership functions among the lower orders, yet still derive their economic livelihood from the subordinate collectivity as landlords or employers, often in an absentee capacity, and the lower orders are cut off from the upper-status groups. Another instance of a segmented social structure occurs when colonial rule is imposed upon an indigenous society with few links between colonizer and colonized. It has also occurred in farming belts that have been self-contained and cut off from the power centers of the larger society except for market relations. On the other hand, if in a stratified society there exist strong vertical social and political bonds between upper and lower classes, mobilization into protest movements among the lower classes is not likely to take place. The landed nobility might still be fulfilling important roles in political leadership, protection, social welfare, religious ceremonies, administration, conflict mediation, and the like for the lower orders. They might still be the heads of local systems of patronage and exercise decisive influence in local associations. Ambitious and talented men from the lower orders are able to rise in the class structure and become co-opted and integrated into the upper strata. The lower orders in these circumstances look for leadership in problem solving to the upper class, and individuals are oriented for advancement to particular patrons and heads of local cliques, not to members of their own social stratum for collective action. Tocqueville (1955:81–84) makes a similar kind of distinction in his analysis of the contrasting relationships of aristocracy to bourgeoisie in France and England in the eighteenth century. In a modern context, a vertically integrated yet highly stratified system exists when the lower strata have access to power through their own associations and special interest groups and wrest a greater share of material resources through these associations. The legitimacy of stratification is then based on effective performance, the division of labor, and the opportunities for social mobility.

These ideas are elaborated in Figure 1, and the relationship between social structure and collective opposition further clarified. This figure is not meant to describe a typology of societies, but is only a means for classifying collectivities within a society. In any given society, there might exist side by side collectivities with different forms of vertical and horizontal integration.

FIGURE 1   Collectivities Classified Along Vertical and Horizontal
Dimensions of Integration

Horizontal Dimension: Links within the
collectivity

	Communal Organization	*Un-or weakly-organized*	*Associational Organization*
Vertical Dimension: links between collectivities			
Integrated	A	B	C
Segmented	D	E	F

The dimensions on which the classification is based are derived from theories of social change and social structure well known in the sociological literature. The horizontal dimension is based on the *Gemeinschaft-Gesellschaft* distinction, and the vertical dimension on the concept of "pluralism" in anthropological theory (Kuper and Smith, 1971). Tilly (1969:35–41) makes use of essentially the same dimensions when he discusses the topic of collective violence. He refers to the two dimensions as (1) the organizational basis of routine political life and (2) the relationship of groups to structures of power. The purpose of the figure is to facilitate the discussion of whether or not conditions for conflict group formation are present, the kind of leadership that conflict groups will tend to have, and the organizational forms that collective behavior will be expressed through.

The following hypotheses are applicable to each of the regions (*A* through *F*) in the figure. On the vertical dimension as we move from a vertically integrated to a segmented social structure, social control over the collectivity from outside weakens and shared sentiments of collective oppression and common objects of hostility are likely to increase among members of the collectivity with grievances. Thus, the minimum conditions for collective protest are more likely to be present as the group or collectivity becomes increasingly cut off from other strata in the society, i.e., as the collectivity is segmented. For predicting the organizational form that collective action and opposition will take, it is however the horizontal dimension of integration within the collectivity that matters. As we move from the center of the figure to the left or the right, from a state of un- or weak-organization to communal or associational organization, the structural conditions for sustained and articulate opposition movements are present to an increased degree.

So far as leadership is concerned, it is more readily available from within if the collectivity is in a segmented rather than an integrated social structure, since talented and ambitious individuals will tend to remain trapped within the collectivity with few prospects of upward mobility. Looking at the horizontal dimension, communal groups have their own leaders who can initiate mobilization whereas in collectivities with a strong associational network, the leaders of these associations represent the existing preopposition leadership resource. It is the un- or weakly organized collectivity that finds it difficult to supply its own opposition leadership, and it is in this situation that leaders and resources must be injected from the outside for substantial and sustained social movements, at least during the initial steps of mobilization.

If a collectivity is a solidary community under conditions of vertical integration (region *A*), collective protest is not likely to take place against upper-status groups because the community has access to the problem-solving centers of the wider society through its own leadership for the redress of grievances. However, communal riots can occur between two or more such solidary collectivities led by or with the support of their respective leaders if the society is split along racial, ethnic, religious, or other lines. Under conditions of vertical integration but weak horizontal bonds within the collectivity (region *B*), a context approximating the "amoral familism" noted by Banfield (1958) for the rural south in Italy, members of the lower classes are internally divided, suspicious of each other, in competition with each other for prestige and material resources, and not likely to form associations to protect their common class interest against landlords, since they are individually oriented for protection and advancement to local bosses and notables who monopolize local leadership positions. While the lower classes are certainly aware of being poor, ignorant, and despised, their private feelings do not translate into an active collective consciousness that might serve as the foundation for collective action. The lack of ties between families and villages together with the monopolization of leadership positions by members of upper-status groups blocks the emergence of opposition organization by means of strong social control mechanisms from above, often including physical coercion. Huizer (1969) has recently analyzed the way in which patron-client relations block protest mobilization among the peasantry in Latin America. Nevertheless, it is possible for social banditry to emerge in this context. Hobsbawm (1959: chapters 2 and 3) has shown, however, how these bands can be co-opted by the local squirearchy to be transformed into landlords' bandits, as was the case with the original Mafia in Sicily.

If a collectivity is both vertically integrated and has within it a dense network of associations (region *C*), collective opposition outside of institutional channels is not likely to take place because its common interests already receive attention through political parties, trade unions, and other class-based organizations with an access to power.

In the case of a solidary communal group that is segmented or cut off from upper-status groups (region *D*), we can expect an especially rapid and intense defense of common interests by means of collective action. This situation corresponds to rebellion against the imposition of colonial or foreign rule by still viable tribes, ethnic groups, or nationalities. As ties based on community weaken under the impact of social change, and inasmuch as vertical integration breaks down as well, (region *E*), collective protest of an unorganized, short-lived, but violent type such as the peasant *jacquerie* or the preindustrial urban riots described in Rudé (1964) emerges as the typical response to social dislocation and grievances. The lower-class urban riots of the 1960s by black slum dwellers in the U.S. are an example of these collective outbursts devoid of leadership, organization, and explicitly articulated goals that arise in a collectivity that is both segmented from the rest of society and weakly organized within itself.

If incipient associational ties are emerging in a previously disorganized collectivity (boundary region between E and F), the protest response will be more continuous, with more explicit leadership and the formulation of collective goals. Such is the case of millenarian and other religious movements of protest among colonial peoples centered on prophets and separatist native churches. Yet, because communal ties can no longer be extensively activated and associational ties are not yet strong enough, these movements are localized and are but precursors to a full-fledged nationalist movement. It is under conditions of strong associational ties and segmentation (region F) that the possibility of the rapid spread of opposition movements on a continuous base exists once more with particular force. Whether such movements will be peaceful or violent does not depend so much on their manner of mobilization as on whether they obtain recognition by the authorities or upper strata and on a number of other variables described in a later section.

The thrust of the theory of mobilization outlined here is precisely opposite to that of mass society theory and some theories of modernization, both of which emphasize the link among the dissolution of the traditional social structure and communal ties, the lack of integration into new forms of association, and the potential for collective disturbances. According to these theories, such conditions are found in mass societies and in transitional societies, both of which are characterized by instability and violence. These theories are based on imprecisions and oversimplification. In a transitional society, not all groups and collectivities are equally caught up in the process of disintegration, and, according to the present theory, it is precisely the groups least disintegrated that mobilize most rapidly and most effectively to promote their corporate interests. Although the experience of Western Europe would suggest that societies pass through a phase of disintegration and relative disorganization and segmentation so far as their lower classes are concerned before associational networks develop and once more provide horizontal bonds of solidarity, eventually leading also to vertical incorporation into the social structure, a more rapid and smoother transition from communal to associational ties is certainly not impossible and may even be more characteristic of some non-Western societies modernizing in the twentieth century, as was true for Japan.

A still viable network of communal relations can be the foundation and breeding ground for the rapid growth of modern associational networks. Associations need not emerge on the wreck of traditional society as some theories of modernization imply; on the contrary, they may grow out of its vitality and strength. It is possible that in a context of a partially viable traditional society, traditional leaders who still maintain the allegiance of many ordinary citizens may seek to block the emergence of a new elite of educated men who are in competition with them for leadership and whose positions rest on new forms of association. Yet, it is often individuals or sons of individuals who are prominent in the traditional social structure who also become prominent in the modern forms of association that spread during modernization, thus providing continuity in leadership and in legitimacy. Mass society theory emphasizes the mutual access of elites and non-elites to each other as conditions favoring the growth of mass movements. The present theory, which is not concerned with mass movements specifically, stresses segmentation as a favorable condition of mobilization. It implies rather that the members of the collectivity are no longer available for mobilization by elites outside of their collectivity, while the members of the collectivity no longer seek out elites for the defense of their interests and for solving their problems. It is to "inside" leadership based on still viable communal bonds within the collectivity, or based on newly cemented associational ties, that members of the collectivity look for leadership. Our theory agrees with Marxist analysis on the difficulty and effort required to establish a sustained opposition movement led by outsiders, intellectuals and other middle- or upper-class defectors, in a disorganized or only weakly organized lower class or peasantry.

The limitations of the theory of mobilization should also be pointed out. The theory deals here only with mobilization within collectivities. To explain the outcome of a period of social or revolutionary upheaval in an entire society, it is not enough to analyze serially the mobilization processes in each collectivity, class, or social stratum. It is also necessary to analyze the synchronization and mutual interdependence of the various mobilization processes, the shifting alliances and coalitions entered into by the leaders and most organized sectors of the various groups, the role of the armed forces and other groups having primary access to the means of violence, and, last but not least, the international context in which the movements occur and which can decisively influence the timing, sources, and amount of foreign intervention, both for and against the unfolding social movements (Brinton, 1952; Huntington, 1968; B. Moore, 1966; Wolf, 1969).

HYPOTHESES ABOUT MOBILIZATION

It is useful to formulate a few hypotheses based on the theory in more formal terms since the sort of empirical evidence that can sustain it or cast doubt on its validity will then be spelled out more concretely. The first hypothesis deals with the case of vertical segmentation and associational ties, that is region *F* of Figure 1.

Hypothesis 1. In a segmented context, the greater the number and variety of organizations in a collectivity, and the higher the participation of members in this network, the more rapidly and enduringly does mobilization into conflict groups occur, and the more likely it is that bloc recruitment, rather than individual recruitment, will take place.

Under conditions of segmentation, as Gusfield and Pinard have noted, secondary groupings can have a mobilizing effect rather than the restraining effects due to multiple group affiliation hypothesized in pluralist theory. Stinchcombe has hypothesized (1965:185) that "the greater the number and variety of organizations in a communal group, the more solidary it is likely to be." Hypothesis 1 is in full agreement with Stinchcombe's view, for the defense and pursuit of common interests based on shared sentiments implied in a process of rapid mobilization should certainly be more feasible if a group has a great deal of solidarity. The presence of numerous organizations ensures a preestablished communications network, resources already partially mobilized, the presence of individuals with leadership skills, and a tradition of participation among members of the collectivity. The hypothesis implies that in opposition movements it is not just the subsequent leadership group that has undergone a prehistory of participation in sects or associations, a fact frequently stressed for revolutionary leaders, but that such a prehistory of participation exists already for some of the subsequent rank-and-file members of the movement. Rapid mobilization does not occur through recruitment of large numbers of isolated and solitary individuals. It occurs as a result of recruiting blocs of people who are already highly organized and participants. In fact, many movements result from a sudden merger of a number of preexisting associations, what Olson (1968: 63) referred to as the "federated" group pattern.

The Populist party and movement had been preceded by an outpouring of farmers' organizations. According to Hicks (1961:16–17),

during the late seventies and eighties, a whole new crop of farm orders appeared in the old Granger states of the Northwest, the National Farmers' Alliance began to grow; in the South, the National Farmers' Alliance and Industrial Union, shadowed presently by the Colored Farmers' Alliance, made notable headway; in Illinois and neighboring states, the Farmers' Mutual Benefit Association; in Michigan and elsewhere in the old Northwest, the Patrons of Industry, and even in the Northeast, a Farmers' League, all—not to speak of numerous minor orders —gave promise of ever increasing vitality.

The Populist party was then quickly formed out of a merger of these preexisting organizations. At the St. Louis organizing conference of the

People's party in 1892, each farmers' organization invited was entitled to twenty-five delegates at large from the U.S. and one additional delegate for each ten thousand members. In the end, 800 delegates, representing twenty-one different orders, were awarded seats. (Hicks, 1961:224–26). Lipset (1966:252) notes a similar process for the CFF in Saskatchewan:

> Though it was a new radical party, the CFF did not have to build up an organization from scratch. It was organized from the start by the local "class" and community leaders of rural Saskatchewan. The fact that the province was so well organized on an occupational basis enabled the new party leaders to obtain the support of the politically conscious community leaders. By the early 1940's, the CFF committees, composed in the main of the same people who were the officials of the other rural organizations, were operating in almost every district in the province. It was this "machine" that brought the CFF to power.

For another century and continent, Crane Brinton's (1930) account of the rise of the Jacobins in 1789 and 1790 stresses the preexisting organizational network of literary societies and, to a lesser degree, Masonic lodges. These literary societies (*Chambres Littéraires*) had been established in French provincial towns in the latter part of the eighteenth century and "included representatives of all branches of the middle class, merchants, lawyers, doctors, rentiers, and not merely men of scholarly leanings" (Brinton, 1930:11). Many of them were already linked through committees of correspondence before the Revolution and had a tradition of active participation in civic and political affairs. "There is no doubt about continuity between these clubs and the various 'Societies of the Friends of the Constitution' [the Jacobin clubs] which spring up everywhere in the provinces in the late fall of 1789" (Brinton, 1930: 13). They merely changed their name and secured affiliation with the Paris Jacobin club.

A similar process can be shown for the Montgomery bus boycott of 1955–1956 that brought Martin Luther King, Jr., into prominence as a civil rights leader. The boycott was conducted by the newly formed Montgomery Improvement Association (MIA), built around several committees for transportation, finance, program, strategy, and negotiating. Over half of the committee members were ministers (King, 1964: 42–43, 53–57, 203–204). The predominance of ministers is not surprising. They were the only black community leaders not subject to white economic pressures since their jobs and salaries were not dependent upon the white community, as were those of black teachers, social workers, and other professionals. The rapid formation of the MIA and the successful implementation of a bus boycott by 17,500 daily black bus riders was only possible because of the preexisting organizational network centered on autonomous black churches in which most Montgomery blacks were caught up in one way or another. When King arrived in Montgomery a year before the boycott and became pastor of the Dexter Avenue Baptist Church, he immediately set about expanding the civic and political functions of his church by activating a set of committees in which many of his parishioners became involved: a social service committee for helping the sick and needy; a social and political action committee to encourage voter registration; a committee for raising scholarship funds, and so on. As a result, his church membership grew, the income of the church tripled, King got to know the members of his congregation, they became a more cohesive group, and a set of intermediate-level black leaders, active in these committees, was formed. These active members of King's congregation later played a key role in the MIA boycott committees (King, 1964:11–12, 15). These organizing activities stimulated by King increased the density of associations and participation among the previously divided and unorganized Montgomery blacks. After the Rosa Parks precipitating incident this network allowed for rapid mobilization in support of the boycott. Black churches provided technical resources for mobilization: meeting places and rallying shelters; focal points for communication centers; printing facilities for handbills and leaflets; lists of addresses and telephone numbers; the formation of a car pool to provide alternative transportation, and so on. The later Southern Christian Leadership Conference was formed in a similar manner of merging and drawing upon preexisting black associations and leadership, especially autonomous religious bodies free of white control.

In a similar way the overnight rise of the Free Speech Movement (FSM) at Berkeley in the fall of 1964 was possible only because of the existence of a prior network of political, civil rights, and special interest groups in an already highly politically mobilized and ideologically sophisticated student population. All groups, right and left, felt their interests threatened by the sudden ban on political campaigning at the Telegraph-Bancroft entry to the campus during the 1964 national election campaign. The FSM grew out of an overnight merger of these various campus groups. On a campus where most students are social isolates and organizational networks weak, the rapid rise of a student protest movement would have been impossible (Lipset and Wolin, 1965).

One important corollary of hypothesis 1 deals with the special case of a totalitarian society where the intermediate groups are controlled by and subordinate to the Party and therefore not available for the activation of protest movements by opposition groups. Nevertheless, such movements can take place even in a totalitarian setting, as occurred in Poland and Hungary in 1956 and in Czechoslovakia in 1967–1968. In all of them, intermediate groups played an important and indispensable function. Hypothesis 1a is:

Hypothesis 1a. In a totalitarian society, opposition movements can occur only when mobilization is initiated by dissidents from within the Party who gain temporary control of some organizations and associations normally under Party control and use this base for further mobilization.

The dissidents have frequently been intellectuals, artists, writers, and students. The growth of dissidents and of an intraparty opposition is itself only possible if the top Party leadership is divided, and in the case of the Eastern European countries, if the Soviet leadership itself is divided and unable to stick to a consistent policy toward the satellites. This phenomenon of a divided ruling group and the "desertion of the intellectuals," as Crane Brinton called it, are general structural conditions facilitating the mobilization of opposition movements anywhere. Hypothesis 1a only stresses the fact that where freedom of association is absent the control of already existing organizations is crucial for mobilization. Without it intellectuals cannot draw the wider citizenry into the movement.

An appropriate illustration for the hypothesis is the preparatory phase of the Hungarian revolution of 1956 that started with the New Course in 1953 following upon Stalin's death and the temporary eclipse of Stalin's faithful henchman and top leader in Hungary, Matyas Rakosi. The Communist intellectuals, especially writers and poets, managed slowly to break from Party discipline and establish control of several literary magazines, later also one of the main Party newspapers, and even more important, the Hungarian Writers' Association, despite temporary setbacks during Rakosi's and Stalinists' comeback in the winter of 1955 and early spring of 1956. In the summer of 1956, in alliance with student groups, they successfully captured the Petöfi Circle, a public debating forum, from the Communist Youth Organization. This occasioned open public meetings during which the Party leadership was criticized in a free debate with thousands of ordinary citizens in attendance (Tamas Aczel and Tibor Meray, 1959; see also Paul Kecskemeti, 1961: chapters 4 and 5). These developments were only possible because the Kremlin leaders themselves prevented the Hungarian Stalinists from reinstating a policy of repression. In the subsequent revolution, these left-wing intellectuals quickly lost control over the direction of the popular movement they had been instrumental in creating. The revolution was molded through the rapid formation of revolutionary organizations and in some instances the reestablishment of banned organizations, the most important of which were the old political parties, the armed resistance forces and national guard, the workers' councils in industrial establishments, and numerous revolutionary committees that ousted Communists in municipalities, collective farms, government offices, and economic establishments. It is interesting to note that despite seven years of Communist rule, the old political parties were reestablished in a matter of days after their leaders surfaced from prisons and assembled in the capital (United Nations, 1957:chapter XI, pp. 97–99, 91–94). The workers' councils, although patterning themselves after the Yugoslav Workers' Councils that were well known in Hungary, showed a leadership and organizational continuity with the pre-1947 independent Socialist trade union organizations. As a general point, one might conclude that under favorable circumstances (such as divided leadership and loosening of repressive social control), just because there exists a dense network of secondary organizations in a totalitarian society, mobilization against the regime can be rapid since control over some of the organizations brings with it considerable resources and an existing communications network. On the other hand, chances of lasting success of a popular movement are slim since these revolts will be suppressed ruthlessly by foreign military intervention as soon as they threaten the international power position of the Soviet Union.

Moving now to region *D* in Figure 1, hypothesis 2 is

Hypothesis 2. The more segmented a collectivity is from the rest of the society, and the more viable and extensive the communal ties within it, the more rapid and easier it is to mobilize members of the collectivity into an opposition movement.

The conditions specified in the hypothesis ensure that traditional social relationships founded on community can be activated for mobilizing purposes by "inside" leadership, that potential "outside" leadership will be either absent or not perceived as favorably disposed to solving the collectivity's problems, and that solidarity and shared sentiments of oppression and a community of fate based on ascriptive ties are already present in the collectivity even before mobilization begins.

As has been noted earlier, strong communal bonds also facilitate the emergence of secondary associations linking members of the community, so that if these are present as well, one would expect especially rapid mobilization by virtue of the joint applicability of hypotheses 1 and 2. That such is the case can be seen from recent studies of nationalist movements in Africa and political mobilization in India.

The Rudolphs (1966:447–50) found that in India the traditional communal organization of castes has provided a very effective mobilization soil for the growth of caste associations to further caste interests in the modern polity:

caste remains a central element of Indian society even while adapting itself to the values and methods of democratic politics . . . the shared sense of culture, character, and status, tends to create a solidarity of a much higher order than is usually found among voluntary associations where the multiplicity of social roles and plurality of interests of its members tend to dilute the intensity of commitment and of identification.

Similarly, Kenneth Little (1965) has shown how the large number and multiplicity of voluntary associations in West Africa (tribal, ethnic, occupational, religious, burial, mutual aid, and political) that have sprung up among recent migrants into towns provide for them a principle of integration into urban life and keep providing strong links between city dwellers and the rural villages. Since migrants participate in the associational network of people who come from the same tribes and rural districts, the new urban environment has tended in some respects to make ethnic and tribal consciousness stronger in cities than in rural areas. The continuities between rural community and urban associations is especially well described by Middleton (1969) in the case of the Lugbara in Uganda and Ibo in Nigeria. He concludes that (pp. 48–49)

> it is misleading to talk of "urban" associations as though they were distinct from the countryside. . . . I suggest that [the associations'] principal historical function is to link town and countryside into a single social and political system wider than either.

The nationalist movement initially centered on the towns and was led by educated Africans. But it grew rapidly by incorporating these associations and their members into the movement (Hodgkin, 1957:86–87, 146–47). As Zolberg (1966:35) observed, "[nationalist movements] grew by successfully incorporating a variety of ethnic and other groups." African nationalism grew so rapidly after World War II precisely because traditional communal, ethnic, and tribal organization had not been successfully disrupted by the Europeans in most instances and was a fertile mobilizing ground for the formation of modern associations, interest groups, and political parties that built on these associations and merged them into an overall movement to get rid of colonial rule. Coleman (1954:408) writes that

> in some instances, kinship associations and separatist religious groups have been the antecedents of nationalist organizations; in others they have provided the principal organizational bases of the latter (e.g. The National Council of Nigeria and the Cameroons was first inaugurated as a federation mainly of kinship associations and the African National Congress of the Rhodesias and Nyasaland was the product of the fusion of several African welfare societies).

Wallerstein (1964:331–34) provides many more illustrations as well as a general review of the role of voluntary associations in nationalist mobilization. These developments are by no means confined to the African postwar experience, as the case of ethnic associations and urban politics in U.S. cities during the period of heavy immigration would indicate (Handlin, 1951: chapters 7 and 8). One might also cite the case of Catholic political parties, trade unions, and other associations that readily grew out of a preindustrial and preurban religious community everywhere in Europe during the nineteenth century.

An interesting recent case of the reactivation of traditional social relationships for mobilization purposes is the overthrow of the Tutsi overlords by the Hutu in Rwanda. According to Lemarchand (1968:41), the modernized Hutu elites were able to activate and politicize traditional ties of clientage between themselves and the peasants in their drive against the Tutsi:

> [the fusion of urban and rural interests] expressed itself in the resurgence within the same ethnic stratum of traditional client-patron relationships, or, better, in the reconversion of this relationship into an instrument of political mobilization. By shifting the forms of clientage ties away from the context of caste relations to that of intracaste solidarity, the revolutionary elites were able to claim from their followers the same type of personal, reciprocal allegiances as the Tutsi patrons were once able to command from their Hutu clientele.

The revolutionary movement was more deeply rooted, strong and swift in northern Rwanda where the Hutu leaders had claims to authority based on traditional Hutu lineages in addition to their elite status based on Western standards of achievement.

That viable traditional communities can be the base for protest movements has also been noted for the Balkans by Stavrianos (1957). Nationalism was possible there because ethnic communities and identities survived relatively intact during the centuries of Ottoman rule. The Ottoman empire was a conglomerate of numerous self-sufficient peoples with considerable autonomy in matters of law, administration, culture, and religion. These surviving ethnic communities and solidary groups later served as the foundation blocs for nationalist mobilization. Barrington Moore, Jr., (1966: chapter 9) has noted as much in his analysis of conditions favoring peasant movements. According to him, where the landed upper class had successfully turned to agricultural production for the market and in that process had destroyed peasant social organization, peasant revolts have tended to be weak. But in areas where the landed aristocracy had severed its traditional links with the peasantry and left peasant society damaged yet still viable, peasant revolts were more frequent and achieved greater success. These revolts were often led by the upper crust of the peasantry who would activate social links and solidary sentiments within the peasant community against landlords or foreigners. This situation corresponds precisely to region *D* of Figure 1 in that the peasantry had become segmented from the upper strata yet maintained its traditional form of social organization based on community.

Another appropriate constrast between the mobilizing potential of intact versus partially disintegrated traditional social structures is that between the Mau Mau movement in Kenya and the resistance against the arbitrary exercise of British colonial rule in nearby Buganda during the 1950s. Buganda had a strong centralized traditional social structure based on the kingship, which British rule modernized yet left relatively intact from the point of view of authority and legitimacy. No white settlers disrupted the economy and agriculture of Buganda as they had in the White Highlands of Kenya. When Buganda demanded a separate state upon the advent of independence in opposition to the British plan for a unitary state in independent Uganda, the British summarily deported the *Kabaka* (king) in 1953 in order to force him and his people into compliance. Overnight a movement of noncooperation with the colonial government arose among the Ganda that forced the British to return the *Kabaka* in 1955 and to grant Buganda far-reaching concessions incorporated into the first constitution of Uganda when it achieved independence. By contrast, the Kikuyu in Kenya had never been as centrally and as strongly organized as the Ganda even before the advent of the British. Because of the white settlers' land grab in the Kenya Highlands and an intensive colonial penetration into the life of the Kikuyu in connection with supplying cheap labor to white farms and controlling native agriculture, Kikuyu social structure became much more weakened and disorganized under colonial rule than was true for Buganda. Kikuyu protest associations can be traced back to 1919 with the founding of Harry Thuku's East African Association, but it was not until the Kenya African Union (KAU) was founded in 1944 that mobilization of the masses against colonial rule started. In the face of British opposition to reforms and disregard of petitions and other peaceful means of protest at a time of increased hardship, the KAU leaders gradually lost control over the Kikuyu opposition movement, which in 1952 erupted into violence against Europeans and was later designated as Mau Mau by its opponents (Rosberg and Nottingham, 1966). The point of this contrast is that in a context of partial disorganization and rapid worsening of economic conditions and demographic pressures, without a corresponding rapid reorganization of the Kikuyu along new associational principles, a mass movement of opposition to the colonial power was much slower in coming into being than in Buganda and, when it did arise, was soon out of the hands of Kikuyu leaders.

While hypotheses 1 and 2 link preexisting communal and associational ties with rapid mobilization of conflict groups and ability to defend collective interests effectively, it is nevertheless true that collective protest actions of an ephemeral and violent form are possible even in a state of disorganization or lack of organization within the collectivity. The minimum requirement for collective disturbances are shared sentiments of collective oppression, and common targets of opposition and of hostility. Hypothesis 3 is based on these notions.

Hypothesis 3. If a collectivity is disorganized or unorganized along traditional communal lines and not yet organized along associational lines, collective protest is possible when members share common sentiments of oppression and targets for hostility. These sentiments are more likely to develop if the collectivity is segmented rather than vertically integrated with other collectivities of the society. Such protest will, however, tend to be more short-lived and more violent than movements based on communal or associational organization.

The pattern specified in hypothesis 3 corresponds to the riots in black urban slums in U.S. cities of the 1960s that from the point of view of common leadership, organizational involvement, and personal life of the inhabitants as manifested in stable family relations, steady employment patterns, and associational participation were but weakly organized. The pattern has also characterized peasant outbursts in different parts of the world. As Wolf (1966:106–108) wrote:

Simplified movements of protest among the peasantry frequently center upon a myth of a social order more just and equalitarian than the hierarchic present . . . [such a myth] often can and does move peasants to action, but it provides only a common vision, not an organizational framework of action. Such myths unite peasants, they do not organize them. If sometimes the peasant band sweeps across the countryside like an avalanche, like an avalanche, too, it spends itself against resistance and dissolves if adequate leadership is not provided from without.

Jayawardena (1968:425–26) has similarly noted that the common consciousness of being an underdog in a highly stratified society favors the emergence of strong egalitarian sentiments and values among the underdog collectivity and can serve as the foundation for leaderless, spontaneous collective protest, despite the absence of strong community organization or associations for pursuing common interests.

As is apparent in this discussion, the central problem in creating an enduring movement is not the development of novel beliefs and of opposition ideas, but the cementing together of an organizational network, which is always an easier task when some group networks already exist. Ideas and beliefs that have a revolutionary potential are usually present and are available for use by a protest leadership. Sentiments of oppression, of being wronged, are also frequently present in the lower orders and can be easily linked with more elaborate ideologies and world views. Such potential opposition ideas are very often part of the central, dominant, and legitimate belief system of the society. The Bible is subject at once to the most reactionary interpretations for legitimizing the status quo as well as to the most revolutionary and utopian interpretations that seek to change the existing order of society in a fundamental way. Secular ideologies such as Marxism can be used to justify revolution as well as to legitimize the privileges and newly secured positions of a new class. Tocqueville (1955:13) expressed this idea when he wrote that

> it must not be thought, however, that the methods employed by the [French] Revolution had no precedents or that the ideas it propagated were wholly new. In all periods, even in the Middle Ages, there had been leaders of revolt who, with a view to effecting certain changes in the established order, appealed to universal laws governing all communities and championed the natural rights of man against the state. But none of these ventures was successful; the firebrand which set all Europe ablaze in the eighteenth century had been easily extinguished in the fifteenth.

Millenarian and other religious protest movements built on common sentiments of oppression and utopian and egalitarian ideas propounded by prophets have been reported from all corners of the world as a response to colonial rule and show that opposition ideas are never in short supply (Lanternari, 1963). The reason many of these movements tend to be short-lived has to do with their lack of organization and the fact of their repression by the authorities, although on the scale of organization they rate higher than most riots and peasant uprisings. Hobsbawm (1959:91) notes in the case of millenarianism among the poor peasants of Andalucia that "just because modern social agitation reached the Andalusian peasants in a form which utterly failed to teach them the necessity of organization, tactics, and patience, it wasted their revolutionary energies almost completely." The availability of protest ideas and opposition sentiments in a region as poor and remote as Andalusia constituted no problem for the unfolding of a protest movement. Literate villagers who assumed the role of village preachers and prophets readily drew upon and reformulated the political ideas of Bakunin and other anarchists while widespread knowledge of Christian beliefs was drawn upon to elaborate and legitimize millenarian expectations. On the other hand, the equally poor Sicilian peasants who were mobilized into peasant leagues by means of an urban-based socialist leadership showed greater endurance and continuity with modern forms of political protest despite equally ruthless repression because an organizational base was created there with outside help (Hobsbawm, 1959:98–102). In the lower Congo enduring forms of millenarianism such as Kimbangouism and Amicalism based on African separatist sects were associated with the creation of an elaborate form of hierarchic organization modeled after the military structure of the Salvation Army. Here again, ideas and beliefs for creating a protest ideology against white rule were no obstacle since religious leaders could draw upon both traditional religious ideas and the biblical texts introduced by Christian missionaries, in particular the ideas of the Old Testament (Balandier, 1955:427 ff.). After Congolese independence the Mulelist rebellion in 1964 in Kwilu province spread in areas where Kimbangouism had been entrenched at an earlier date (Fox et al., 1965–1966). Talmon's (1962:141) view that millenarianism is a prepolitical phenomenon, a precursor to political awakening, and a forerunner of political organization is a valid one. Continuity between millenarian sects and secular political protest movements is probably stronger when an elaborate organization base allowing for recruitment along nonascriptive lines has been associated with them.

A HYPOTHESIS ABOUT PARTICIPANTS

Although mass society theorists and some writers on modernization stress the social isolation and atomization of participants in mass movements and in violent protests (Kornhauser, 1959:182), this point of view is too simple and is contrary to much available evidence. Hypothesis 4, in opposition to such views, is

> Hypothesis 4. Participants in popular disturbances and activists in opposition organizations will be recruited primarily from previously active and relatively well-integrated individuals within the collectivity, whereas socially isolated, atomized, and uprooted individuals will be underrepresented, at least until the movement has become substantial.

For weakly organized collectivities such as the black urban slums of the 1960s in the U.S., the most comprehensive studies have shown that active participants in riots represent a cross-section of the male population living in them and do not draw disproportionately from among the disorganized, unemployed, and criminal element (Fogelson and Hill, 1968; Oberschall, 1968). Similarly, the work of Soboul, Rudé, Tonensson, and other historians of the French Revolution concerned with popular participation in revolutionary demonstrations, popular disturbances, and patriotic associations confirms hypothesis 4, as recently summarized by Tilly (1964b:114–15): "The findings imply very little participation in either ordinary political activity or revolutionary outbursts by misfits, outcasts, nomads, the truly marginal, the desperately poor." Although questions of subsistence, in particular the provision of an ample and cheap supply of bread and price controls, were a central concern of the Paris working people throughout the revolutionary period, "the shortage of bread mobilized a population already politically conscious, active, and organized." Rudé's research extends these patterns of participation for a wide class of riots, demonstrations, and popular disturbances in the late eighteenth century and first half of the nineteenth century in Western Europe (Rudé, 1964: chapter 13). Just as important for mobilization theory is Tilly's emphasis on the mobilizing potential in Paris of the still viable social organization and solidarity within small shops and the traditional crafts binding masters and apprentices, small employers and their employees, in a neighborhood setting in which competition for local leadership by "outside" bourgeois elements was absent (Tilly, 1964b:115–16). This neighborhood setting in revolutionary Paris is another example of a segmented structure that favors the emergence of both solidary sentiments and inside protest leadership. Such a pattern was also found in Saskatchewan by Lipset, in Schleswig-Holstein by Heberle, and during the Montgomery bus boycott. In Montgomery, since the black community was segregated and the black churches controlled from within, black leadership centered on these churches did not have to overcome competition by outside white leaders in their endeavor to mobilize the black population. In Saskatchewan, because the farmers were geographically isolated in communities with little internal stratification and because the small-town professional and business groups were still linked to and identified with the farmers through kinship ties and economic bonds, no other competing outside groups were available to head the school boards, marketing agencies, and local government that constituted the organizational base of the later CFF.

Hypothesis 4 is not confined to working- or lower-class movements. Crane Brinton (1930:50–64) has shown that throughout France the Jacobins came from a predominantly bourgeois rather than working-class background, drawing heavily from the notables and substantial citizens and property owners in provincial towns and cities—lawyers, teachers, physicians, ex-priests, shopkeepers, merchants, and officers. These certainly cannot be called the less successful members of the bourgeoisie, let alone be designated as an outcast, marginal, uprooted element. In his later comparative study of revolutions, Brinton (1952:100–105) confirmed a similar pattern for other revolutions so far as the social origin of middle-level revolutionaries staffing revolutionary bodies and associations is concerned. Nor are these findings surprising from the point of view of the theory of mobilization, since hypothesis 1 implies that those who are already participants in premovement networks of association become activated in the movement as these associations and leaders merge into the movement.

CONDITIONS FAVORABLE TO THE INITIATION OF MOBILIZATION: THE LOOSENING OF SOCIAL CONTROL

The initiation of mobilization of conflict groups often takes place from the outside through the activities of upper-status groups in opposition to the government or ruling groups. Brinton (1952: chapter 2) has long ago emphasized the importance of divisions among the old ruling class, one faction of which initiates opposition and resistance to the government and, in the course of these events, starts mobilizing popular support for its struggle against the authorities. The "aristocratic revolution" before the outbreak of the French Revolution of 1789 and the campaign of banquets led by the Republican parliamentary opposition in France just prior to 1848 illustrates this process. These groups, of course, very rapidly lose control over the popular movement they helped to create and that soon turns against them after the *ancien régime* has been toppled. By stressing division among the upper class, Crane Brinton put his finger on the very general and widespread pattern of the loosening of social control preceding mobilization. In Hungary before 1956, as we have already mentioned, it was division within the Communist party hierarchy, in particular the desertion of the writers and intellectuals, that eventually led to mobilization of wider circles as the social control apparatus of the party and especially the secret police were seriously weakened and immobilized due to indecision within both the Hungarian and Soviet Communist leadership on how much and what kind of reforms and liberalization to allow under the new policy of destalinization.

The Mexican revolution was precipitated by President Diaz's announced intention in 1908 not to seek reelection in 1910, which was later reversed, Madero's imprisonment on the eve of the election when he refused to withdraw his candidacy in opposition to Diaz, and the subsequent Madero movement to stop Diaz. In Morelos, the district where the Zapata rebellion broke out, intense political activity took place with the help of Mexico City political clubs in the campaign for governor in 1909 after Diaz's announced retirement. All political factions sought to elect their candidate in anticipation of the end of the Diaz era. When Diaz reversed himself and imposed his own and the large plantation owners' candidate upon Morelos, the unpopular Escandon who had few local ties, Diaz managed to antagonize all the remaining groups who continued to mobilize their supporters in opposition to Diaz and Escandon despite repression. Mobilization was further helped by Escandon's ineptitude and partiality to the planters (Womack, 1969:10–35).

In Rwanda, the Belgian administration reversed its previous policy on Tutsi-Hutu relations in 1959 by initiating a purge of Tutsi elements from the police and the administration in preparation for Rwanda independence. It also gave tacit approval to the January 1961 coup against Tutsi rule. It is these events, initiated or encouraged by the colonial power, that resulted in loosening social controls and set the stage for the subsequent revolution (Lemarchand, 1968:35–36).

The importance of freedom of association, speech, and, in general, of oppositional activity based on civil liberties, cannot be overemphasized in a theory of mobilization. Writing in 1954, Coleman observed that (1954:44)

> the comparative freedom of activity (speech, association, press, and travel abroad) which British Africans have enjoyed—within clearly defined limits and varying according to the presence of white settlers— has been of decisive importance [to African nationalists]. It is doubtful whether such militant nationalists as Wallace-Johnson of Sierra-Leone, Prime Minister Kwame Nkrumah of the Gold Coast, Dr. Nramdi Azikiwe of Nigeria, Jomo Kenyatta of Kenya, and Danti Yamba of the Central African Federation, would have found the same continuous freedom of movement and activity in Belgian, Portuguese, and French Africa as has been their lot in British Africa.

In the U.S., the 1954 Supreme Court school desegregation decision marks a far-reaching reversal on race relations: it is considered the most convenient starting date of the civil rights movement. In all these instances, the actions of the authorities or some groups within the ruling class legitimize the demands of the protesters while at the same time they loosen social control and allow mobilization of the protest group to proceed. Prolonged or unsuccessful wars also result in a loosening of social control by the mere fact of exhausting the resources an authoritarian regime can raise to suppress opposition.

CONDITIONS FAVORABLE TO THE INITIATION OF MOBILIZATION: FOCAL POINTS

There is a class of precipitating conditions of protest movements that signal hope of success and the weakness of existing social control mechanisms with the success of a protest movement occurring at some focal point in the national or international system. In 1848, revolutions broke out in Vienna, Berlin, Budapest, and other cities shortly after the news of the successful toppling of the Orleanist regime in Paris. In 1960, military coups d'etat took place within a week in Turkey, Korea, Peru, and somewhat later in other Latin American countries. In 1956, the Hungarian revolution followed shortly upon the successes of Gomulka and the anti-Stalinists in Poland. In the U.S. urban riots of the 1960s, major riots not only occurred each summer in rapid succession, but set off smaller disturbances in adjoining cities and suburbs where no precipitating incident involving a policeman and residents occurred. Again in the 1960s, student unrest on campuses seemed to spread swiftly within a country and also across national boundaries. These instances are to be distinguished from the case of coordinated, simultaneously planned, and centrally led outbreaks led by highly organized groups such as the 1948 Communist risings in Southeast Asia following shortly upon a conference at which these risings had been planned. Social contagion, with its unfortunate connotation of an emotional and irrational process, is a poor term to describe this phenomenon.

Rather, what happened in all these instances is that prior to the outbreaks there had grown up a complex and often international system of orientation, communication, and social control with focal points. Both the potential participants in conflict groups and the social control agencies had learned to focus their expectations on and take cues from these focal points. Thus in 1848, and ever since the French Revolution, the eyes of revolutionary and reactionary groups alike were focused on Paris. Paris had the most highly developed, liberal and radical clubs and circles. European liberals and radicals everywhere in Europe were taking their ideas and fixing their hopes and expectations on Paris. Events there were bound to be repeated elsewhere. Similarly, within Germany itself, Prussia and Berlin were secondary focal points. When the king of Prussia made certain concessions and promised reforms as a result of popular disturbances, the other kings and princes in the German states followed his lead, even where large-scale riots were not taking place. When the king was successful in repressing the popular movement, other states followed his lead. In quite the same way, in 1956, the Kremlin's reaction to destalinization efforts in Poland was the crucial factor in the timing of opposition efforts elsewhere in Eastern Europe. The Hungarians were encouraged by Gomulka's success in Poland and the Soviet reception of the Polish changes. In the nationalist movements in Africa, the constitutional developments in Ghana and Ghana's independence stimulated hope of success elsewhere in the British colonies, since it was correctly assumed that Britain would have no more cause to repress nationalism elsewhere than it had in Ghana. The military coups d'etat that follow each other in quick succession actually all have a focal point in the U.S. State Department, whose reactions to the first coup d'etat are carefully weighed: does the State Department merely voice the usual platitudes about a return to civilian government at some future unspecified date, or is it applying stronger pressures against the regime by cutting off military and other aid and withholding recognition of the new military regime for an unusual length of time? In these illustrations, Paris and Berlin in 1848, the Kremlin, the British Foreign Office, the U.S. State Department, are focal points for an international system of social control that conditions the responses of both regime opponents and the agents of social control located at peripheral points. Successes of insurgents at the focal point signal the loosening and weakening of social control at its center of greatest strength, and therefore provide the hope of success for protesters and a clear-cut precipitating occasion on which all attention is centered. The outbreak of protest movements and their initial success at focal points is therefore another condition favoring the initiation of mobilization elsewhere.

CONDITIONS FAVORING MOBILIZATION:
THE RELATIONS BETWEEN CITY AND COUNTRYSIDE

Many protest movements among peasants, agricultural workers, and rural peoples receive urban-based support for mobilization. The activities of urban professionals and intellectuals in mobilizing rural people into nationalist movements in Africa have already been commented upon, as well as the socialist-backed creation of peasant leagues in Sicily. Even some famous rural risings during the Middle Ages received some support from townsmen. Pirenne (1958:196) reports that the rising of western Flanders from 1323 to 1328 "was excited and supported by the craftsmen of Ypres and Bruges," and that the English insurrection of 1381 was the common work of townspeople and those of the countryside. George Totten (1960) has described the help that the Japanese tenant farmers received from the Socialist trade unions after World War I during their attempt to form the Japan Farmers' Union and to engage in protest activities such as strikes. In Morelos just before the outbreak of the Zapatista movement, the Mexico City based Organizing Club of the Democratic Party and the Leyvista Liberal Political Club and other urban political groups helped mobilize the anti-Diaz forces in the cities, small towns, and villages against the Diaz-sponsored candidate for governor in Morelos (Womack, 1969:20–25). Later on, the Zapatistas received the services of urban radicals to help create a revolutionary administration in Morelos, to draw up new laws, to institute land reforms, and to negotiate with the central government (Womack, 1969:166, 193). The ill-fated "La Violencia" period in rural Colombia, precipitated by the

1948 assassination of Gaitan, the popular leader of the radical reform wing of the Liberals, followed upon disturbances that were egged on initially by national leaders in the capital as Conservatives initiated a nationwide purge of Liberals upon their return to power (Anderson et al., 1967:113–15). These leaders soon lost control over the rural bosses, their followers, and the rural people as a vicious cycle of reprisals and a bloodbath killing at least two hundred thousand was started for the next decade. Elsewhere in Latin America, Petras and Zeitlin (1967, 1968) have shown from election returns the radicalizing impact of miners and other organized left-wing groups upon the surrounding traditionally conservative rural population in a context of strong class divisions and a weakening feudal order headed by landowners. As in the case of Japan, no doubt kinship ties and the occupational mobility between agricultural proletariat and miners facilitated the establishment of direct lines of influence. In Morocco, short-lived and frequent rebellions among the desert tribes have resulted from the extension of political links and patronage ties from an urban-based, rival political leadership into the rural hinterland, each faction aligned with competing rural factions and each calling for a demonstration of local support in connection with tests of strength in the capital (Gellner:1962).

The rural-urban interchange in mobilization is not, however, completely one-sided. In France and Italy there exist rural areas with a tradition of anticlericalism and political radicalism from which population migration takes place into cities for industrial employment. These dechristianized rural population centers provide a reservoir and recruiting base for the Communist party in the cities as the newly arrived "preradicalized" migrants get fully drawn into the network of Communist party associations and subculture (Hamilton, 1967; Dogan, 1967). Because migrants frequently return to their villages of origin at election time, at least in the south of Italy, and because they influence their kinsmen and fellow villagers, the transfer of manpower from rural areas to the cities has increased the Communist vote more rapidly in the countryside than in the cities.

One should not underestimate the crucial role of a peasantry in making for success of an urban-based movement, especially of a revolutionary movement. Barrington Moore, Jr., (1966:480) has written that "the peasants have provided the dynamite to bring down the old building" with reference to the major revolutions of modern times. Huntington (1968:293) agrees when he writes that in the Chinese, French, and Russian revolutions "the peasants more or less spontaneously acted to overthrow the old agrarian political and social structure, to seize the land, to establish a new political and social system in the countryside. Without this peasant action, not one of these revolutions would have constituted a revolution." It is the peasantry, unchecked by the authorities who are tied down with urban revolt or unable to mobilize and deploy their forces fast enough, that destroys or weakens the old regimes. It is the countryside that plays the crucial "swing role" in revolutions, to use Huntington's term. If the government is able to make far-reaching concessions to the peasantry in revolt and deactivate them before it is totally incapacitated, as happened with the abolition of feudalism in 1848–1849 during the revolutions in Germany and the Austrian empire, or if it is able to crush the urban uprisings first and then turn its undivided attention and resources to reestablishing order in the countryside, as happened in Russia in 1905–1906, the probability of success of revolutionary movements is much diminished.

Not much is actually known about the specific circumstances that make for a successful timing and joining up of peasant and urban movements of protest. In Huntington's view, a revolutionary peasantry cannot be created by urban leaders, but an already restless and dissatisfied peasantry can be successfully organized, disciplined, and mobilized by urban leaders to support the wider aims of an urban led movement. The ideological bridge between urban intellectuals and the peasant masses rests on nationalist sentiments and appeals, not on class interests (Huntington, 1968:303–304). And it is certainly true that in the modern world, whether in African nationalist movements or in Vietnam, China, and elsewhere, peasants or farmers have readily responded to urban and intellectual nationalists.

A theory of rural-urban links and interchange is very much at the heart of any theory of social change. The most promising approach to rural-urban interrelations has been developed by Tilly (1964a), Wolf (1955, 1969), Moore (1966), and Foster (1967). Peasant communities have a considerable degree of economic and occupational differentiation. They possess a distinct culture, a peasant way of life. Yet they are not self-sufficient, autonomous communities cut off from the rest of the society. They are strategically linked to administrative centers and urban markets. The extension of capitalist market opportunities and market relations has a differential impact on various rural groups—subsistence cultivators, agricultural wage laborers, independent small farmers, tenants, artisans and craftsmen, rural cottagers, and so on. In particular, they affect peasant corporate structure and peasant response in different ways depending upon differences in land tenure patterns, family structure and property inheritance rules, land shortage and population pressures, and the opportunities for labor migration. The networks of credit and social control cutting across class lines and the rural-urban continuum as they are mediated by landlords, patrons, bosses, and small-town brokers are also important. Because of these differences, peasant response and mobilization patterns may be quite different in Middle America, Southern Europe, and the Near East from what they are in most of rural Africa.

CONDITIONS FAVORING
DISINTEGRATION

Paradoxically, the very same factors that account for rapid mobilization also account for the centrifugal forces that lead to the dissolution of opposition movements. A central idea of the theory of mobilization is that of group recruitment and group joining as opposed to the recruitment of isolated individuals. In group recruitment, members of the group provide each other with social support and negatively sanction those who would hesitate to join. The premovement group leaders take the initiative in mobilization, and the movement builds up rapidly through a merger of such groups. Thus, a heterogeneous leadership and membership, loosely held together in their pursuit of some common goals, comes into being, joined by others who are attracted by the initial successes of the movement. Yet, the movement will have little central organization, and the primary loyalties of the members may be to the component groups, leaders, and associations, and not to the overarching movement itself. Each group seeks to have its leaders recognized as the top leaders of the entire movement. There are no preestablished norms for choosing or establishing the top leaders, and their authority does not rest on institutional positions. There are no agreed upon, legitimized procedures for reaching collective decisions. The movement presents the picture of heterogeneity and confusion, a fact recognized by Killian when he describes a social movement as an "emergent collectivity" (Killian, 1965a: 439–46). Each group seeks to orient the entire movement to the pursuit of its goals and may not be strongly committed to achieving the goals of other component parts of the movement that it does not share. Thus, as the movement succeeds in some of its goals, the interest and commitment of some groups may be waning and entire groups drop out of active participation in the movement. Support for the movement and active participation in it fluctuate widely. Peasant armies are notorious for melting away once the initial goal of repelling or expelling outsiders has been successfully accomplished. This often coincides with the start of the planting or harvesting season when labor is required in the village fields. Radical movements linked ideologically and organizationally to outside movements centered in a foreign country such as the Soviet

Union or China split and fractionalize when ideological or tactical controversies emerge in that country, or when the requirements of an international strategy conflict with nationalist and local objectives. Lack of success or partial success in a movement also tends to produce divisions that may result in the breakup of a movement into smaller groups and factions, which then often spend as much time and resources attacking each other as in pursuing their original goals.

There are three processes that counteract these centrifugal forces: the presence of charismatic leadership, the formation of a subculture common to all the component parts of the movement, and the creation of an overarching organizational framework. Whereas initially all the members of the movement share only common enemies and sentiments of being wronged, a charismatic leader can build a cohesive movement by directly orienting the loyalties and commitments of members to himself personally rather than through the groups and group leaders that were in existence at the time of the creation of the movement. In time, also, especially in the face of continued resistance and the frustration of shared goals, a distinct subculture may emerge, with distinct dress, speech, life-styles, heroes, history, and traditions (Killian, 1965a:438–39), shared by all the component groups and thus creating the unity of purpose and of culture upon which cohesion rests. Finally, if the movement can successfully build up a centralized organizational structure accepted by all, the choice of leaders and collective decision-making can become regularized and the resources of the members fully exploited for the pursuit of the movement's goals. However, little is known about the specific conditions that favor or impede these processes counteracting dissolution. These problems are severe in the case of movements based on associational ties alone or on associations themselves based on still viable communities where subcultures and local leadership are especially strong and have to be weakened or neutralized before their members can be fully enlisted behind the overarching leadership and organization of the wider movement.

In conclusion, it should be pointed out that the theory of mobilization presented here stops short of providing an analysis for the institutionalization and internal organization of the movement. Certainly, a lot depends on the reaction of the authorities and their success in containing or repressing the movement. A movement that is illegal and that has to operate in secrecy to protect its members will develop a different organizational structure than a similar movement operating in a liberal environment. Movements that seek to expand their membership base as opposed to those wishing to maintain their hold over an already mobilized membership must by necessity be organized along different lines. The degree of heterogeneity of members reflected in ethnic, class, religious, and regional composition, as well as the availability of historical models and outside resources, all have an impact on internal organization processes. For its further extension along these lines, the theory of mobilization can draw upon considerable knowledge and insights developed in sociology, political science, administrative sciences, and political sociology.

Chapter V

MOBILIZATION: PARTICIPATION IN OPPOSITION MOVEMENTS, LEADERS AND ACTIVISTS, OPPOSITION IDEAS

OPPOSITION AND PROTEST LEADERS

Participation in a social movement can be of varying intensity and involvement. It is useful to distinguish several levels of participation: the top leadership, a more numerous secondary level of leadership, the rank-and-file members, and, finally, the rest of the public not taking an active part in the movement and ranging from sympathetic supporters through passive observers and indifferents all the way to active opponents of the movement who may even be part of an organized countermovement. The leaders are intensely concerned with the promotion and achievement of the goals of the movement. They are in positions of decisionmaking for working out the strategy and tactics of confrontation. They formulate "an analysis of the situation . . . specify an ideology containing their particular brand of explanation for problems and solutions, . . . give short cut expression to grievances" (Killian, 1965a:440). The leaders must convince their potential following that the movement can succeed. They have to prove through personal sacrifice and example their commitment to the cause; they must create pride and faith among the rank and file. Leaders may for a long time attempt to get a movement started by formulating a social philosophy, a program, and by recruiting a following prior to its actual start in the perception of the general public. Leaders, in sum, are the architects of organization, ideology, and mobilization for the movement.

Many questions have been asked about the leaders of opposition movements and revolutions concerning their motivations, personality characteristics, socioeconomic background, ability to actively shape and influence the course of the movement, and the existence and effectiveness of different styles or types of leadership. On a different level, it can even be asked whether relatively leaderless movements are possible at all. Dogmatic and unsupported answers have frequently been given to these questions, colored by the personal likes and dislikes of the commentators for the goals of opposition movements they are describing and their conceptions of the social psychology of the masses, such as, for instance, an alleged need for hero worship among the masses. Much information on leaders is simply lacking, especially on their motivational and personality attributes.

Leaderless episodes of collective behavior are common, and precipitating incidents in wider social movements may well occur without leaders or against the wishes of the leaders. For the urban riot wave of the 1960s in the U.S., the Kerner Commission reports that (U.S. Riot Commission, 1968:202)

> on the basis of all the information collected the Commission concludes that the urban disorders of the summer of 1967 were not caused by, nor were they the consequence of, any organized plan or "conspiracy." Specifically, the Commission has found no evidence that all or any of the disorders or the incidents that led to them were planned or directed by any organization or group, international, national or local.

Similar conclusions have been drawn about the Watts riot of 1965 (Oberschall, 1968:324–26), and this pattern may in fact be typical of riots. It is true that in localized incidents that occur at a street corner or in a neighborhood, a few individuals take the initiative in assaulting police or throwing rocks, and they may even address and harangue a crowd of people. But these individuals were neither leaders prior to these incidents nor do they subsequently play a leader role in other incidents. The February insurrection in St. Petersburg in 1917 that eventually brought down the Tsarist regime was neither planned nor led by revolutionary groups. In fact, all revolutionary groups, including the Bolsheviks and the Mensheviks, were caught by surprise, and many of their top leaders were in prison, exiled, or hiding at the time. Those who were free and about counseled caution, since they looked upon the popular movement as premature and doomed to failure (Trotsky, 1959:113–14, 138–40). Leaders and organized opposition groups were subsequently present, however, to capitalize upon the collapse of the Tsarist government and to expand the initial protest movement in a revolutionary direction.

Although riots and precipitating incidents can be leaderless, a con-

tinuous movement of protest that seeks to obtain wide reforms or revolution presupposes both leaders and considerable organization. Killian
(1965a:447) has written aptly that "in the absence of leadership, the
most that can be expected to arise from . . . mass dissatisfaction is
sporadic crowd behavior . . . through which people give vent to their
feelings, but do not really attempt to change the social order. A leader,
or a number of leaders, is required to give the concerns of the many potential followers a unifying theme." In some cases it may well occur that
leaders emerge during the disturbances themselves when police arrest
individuals who then become martyrs and heroes and to whom people
then look for further direction, but this case is probably not frequent and
may in fact be taking place only when the arrested individuals were
already leaders of some group or seeking to become leaders prior to the
incidents that made them visible.

Much-has been written about the motivations and personality characteristics of leaders, their alleged compulsion to dominate followers and
to purge rivals, their craving for recognition and publicity, their bitterness and resentments traced to childhood experiences, social discrimination, blocked mobility, or social marginality. These speculations are often
coupled with a conception of leadership that views leaders as fully in
control of popular movements; they manipulate the masses effortlessly
to satisfy their psychological or pathological needs; they possess outstanding attributes such as public speaking or personal magnetism
through which they establish their grip and hold the loyalties of the rank
and file.

Contrary to these views, another approach seems more fruitful in
providing an explanation for the sometimes seemingly erratic, irrational,
or authoritarian behavior of leaders. The behavior of leaders is very
much a result of the context of their situation as leaders of movements.
Leaders in social movement do not have a firmly established, institutionally sanctioned position as do leaders in other walks of life. They
cannot invoke institutionalized sanctions to have their decisions implemented. They do not draw a regular salary as elected politicians or administrative elites do; hence, they are often in a precarious economic
position. Their positions are continuously open to challenge by lesser
leaders who seek to replace them. They are often persecuted, arrested,
jailed, or have to spend a good part of their life in exile or in hiding,
making it difficult for them to conduct an orderly personal and family
life. If they are successful, they may be the subject of adulation and a
cult of personality, surrounded by sycophants and hangers-on, who wish
to derive personal gain from the movement's success. Often their best
friends and early associates later turn against them over questions of
strategy and ideology. Put any ordinary, stable individual into a similar

position, and he, too, would probably exhibit what some observers consider confused or arbitrary behavior as a result of the pressures and dilemmas that one is continuously faced with as a leader in an uninstitutionalized and emergent organizational setting. This approach is more fruitful than one which seeks to trace leaders' behavior to pathological traits or early childhood experiences. In any event, if protest leaders are allowed by the authorities and incumbents to engage in lawful processes of mobilization and protest activity, one would expect a much lower incidence of erratic and authoritarian behavior than in situations where leaders are suppressed.

The marginality theory of leaders was popularized by Daniel Lerner in connection with the Nazi elite (Lasswell and Lerner, 1966: chapter 5). Lerner found that anywhere from 50 percent to 80 percent of Nazi leaders, depending on whether they were propagandists, administrators, police officials, or military leaders, were "marginal men" in the sense that they were atypical or of a minority status with respect to a number of social positions and social categories used to describe the German people. But Lerner's methodology has been criticized by Donald Matthews (1954:59), who points out that several of the criteria used by Lerner as indicators of marginality are completely arbitrary. Why should a man whose primary lifework is peasant or artisan, whose religion is Catholic, whose age at marriage was 18–21 or 35 and over, whose military status was that of an enlisted man, or who received his higher education abroad, be classified as "marginal"? Lerner is confusing the concept of atypical in the statistical sense of nonmodal with the concept of marginality. By his thirteen criteria, any one of which put a Nazi leader into the "marginal" category, it is probable that a majority of the German population would have to be classified as "marginal." What Lerner's data demonstrated and what other studies have also shown is that an unusually high proportion of Nazi leaders were born abroad in German communities such as Austria or in sensitive border regions such as Alsace-Lorraine and the Saar, and that Nazi leaders as well as the rank-and-file party members and Nazi voters tended to be considerably younger than leaders and supporters of the other political parties. In Matthews's view, with which I concur, "that the leaders of the Nazi movement tended to be marginal men or alienated men are both interesting hypotheses. Despite the data and interpretation of *The Nazi Elite* they still remain unproven hypotheses." (Matthews, 1954:53).

The careful historical scholarship of Crane Brinton on the leaders of the French, American, English, and Russian revolutions leads to conclusions at variance with the social marginality theory of opposition movement leaders. In referring to both the leaders and the rank-and-file Brinton (1952:127) writes that they were composed of quite ordinary men and women probably a bit superior to their less active fellows in energy and willingness to experiment, and in the English, American, and French revolutions, even in their crisis periods, people of substantial property. These revolutionists were not in general afflicted with anything the psychiatrist could be called about. They were certainly not riffraff, scoundrels, scum of the earth. . . . Nor were their leaders by any means an inferior lot suddenly elevated to positions of power which they could not worthily occupy.

Brinton (1952:107) notes for instance that of the fifty-six signers of the Declaration of Independence thirty-three held college degrees and only about four had little or no formal education. Nearly all were affluent. The social origins of the leaders of the moderates in the English revolution were definitely upper status, and even the radicals had among their ranks a good number of gentlemen and others from "good" families. The 648 representatives of the Third Estate in the French Constituent Assembly of 1789 were composed of 278 officials and civil servants from all levels of government; 166 lawyers and notaries; 85 merchants, bankers, and former businessmen; 31 other professionals, mostly physicians; 67 individuals described as property owners, bourgeois, cultivators, or farm laborers; and 21 from other miscellaneous occupations. Such data scarcely suggest a marginal or deprived socioeconomic background (Palmer, 1959:154–56). Even the "Left" in the 1791 Constituent Assembly was made up mainly of these social groups and an additional contingent of sixty-eight nobles and ninety priests and bishops (Palmer, 1959: 154–56). Brinton notes that "after 1792, extremely few new leaders came to the top. The men who ran France in 1793–4 were . . . not of very different social origins from the men who really ran the old France—the literate bourgeoisie from which were ultimately recruited the bureaucracy" (Brinton, 1952:107). The Russian revolutionaries, especially the leaders of the proletarian parties, were drawn from a wider spectrum of social origins, but were not predominantly of working-class or peasant origins. Of the 137 outstanding Russian Communist leaders in the 1920s whose official biographical sketches Jerome Davis examined and where one might expect a bias in favor of over-reporting a "proletarian" background, father's occupational status was as follows: fifty-six or 41 percent were laborers and peasants; thirteen were teachers; four intellectuals; two were priests; twenty-three doctors, lawyers, or engineers; thirteen were minor government officials; three were important officials; and the thirty-nine remaining fathers of Communist leaders were of upper-class status such as wealthy proprietors of estates or factories, nobles, officers, and businessmen. In contrast, in the late nineteenth century, 93 percent of the Russian labor force was classified as peasants or laborers (Davis, 1929). Of the Communist leaders themselves, two-thirds had either attended a university or were university graduates.

Lipset (1950:360) found in his investigation of the social background and career of over 600 delegates to the Saskatchewan CCF provincial conventions of 1945 and 1946 that "the statistical data . . . demonstrate that in Saskatchewan a radical movement for economic reform was led at the grass roots by the people with status within the farming and working classes. The local leaders of the party were not marginal or deviant members of the society, but rather were the old class leaders . . . the class and community leaders were largely the same people. . . . The C.C.F. was able to grow rapidly in Saskatchewan because the 'normal' class leaders were the first to become C.C.F.-ers."

Research on other revolutionary or protest movements has tended to confirm the pattern of findings emphasized by Crane Brinton. Ming T. Lee has examined the characteristics of the fifty-two founders of the Chinese Communist Party and found that 69 percent of their fathers had been of the landlord-gentry stratum, 10 percent had been officials, 10 percent teachers, with only 6 percent (or three leaders) of peasant background. Forty-two percent of the leaders themselves were college graduates, another 40 percent had attended college, and another 10 percent had attended secondary schools (M. Lee, 1968:115, 118). North and Pool found in their study of the social origins of top Chinese Communist leaders and the top Kuomintang leaders in the 1920s and 1930s that a majority of both groups came from an upper- or middle-class background, namely, from a background of landlords, scholars, officials, or some combination of these. Only about a quarter of the top Communist leaders had fathers who were peasants or workers. In both groups, a substantial proportion had attended universities, often abroad in Japan, France, and the United States. The differences in the educational attainment and father's social stratum between the Communist and Kuomintang leaders are certainly not as great as the ideological differences and history of conflict between the two parties might lead one to expect (Lasswell and Lerner, 1966:376–82). In Guatemala, according to Schneider (1959:89) "with few exceptions, the leadership of the [Communist] Guatemala Labor Party [in the 1940s and early 1950s] came from among the young intellectuals from the lower middle classes who were finishing or had recently finished school at the time of the [1944] Revolution." They had far more education than most members of their class. In the 1960s in Guatemala, Petras notes that the leadership of the revolutionary MR-13 (Revolutionary Movement of November 13) and the FAR (Rebel Armed Forces) groups are by origin former military men from the traditional middle class (Petras, 1968:333). Elsewhere, the Brazilian rural revolutionary leaders Francisco Juliao and Father Francisco Lange both were from large landowning families. Camilo Torres, the Colombian revolutionary, was the son of one of the oldest aristocratic families in Colombia. The key leadership groups of the MIR of Venezuela and

Peru, the FALN of Venezuela, and the Caamaño forces in the Dominican Republic were composed of "defectors from traditional institutions and elites" (Petras 1968:334–35). An examination of the social origins of other revolutionary leaders of the working class or the peasantry would probably reveal much the same pattern of "outside" leadership by the educated sons of the traditional ruling classes or new middle class. Michels' (1937:120–21) reformulation of Marx's original insight, namely, that "class movements are led by members of the classes against which they are aimed," is substantiated in these figures. Protest leaders, whether of the left or right, whether members of elected assemblies that take revolutionary action or members of small conspiratorial or guerrilla groups, are mostly drawn from the educated strata and from among the sons of the well-to-do, if not the top ruling groups. They are certainly not representative of the rank-and-file of the movement, nor can one infer from the social origins of leaders of a movement or protest party the ideological position it takes and the goals it pursues without detailed information about the class structure and the historical context.

If one examines the occupational and social background of protest and opposition leaders in greater detail, it appears that farmers or people with an agricultural background are almost totally absent, that merchants and businessmen vary considerably from movement to movement in the production of leaders, but that the free professions, especially lawyers, students, teachers, and civil servants are almost always in the majority. In nationalist movements occurring in predominantly rural countries, farmers or cultivators seldom play a leadership role and constitute but a tiny minority of the new indigenous elites after independence is secured. Reflecting on the situation in Africa, Foltz writes that (1970:7)

> the Nationalist Middle Class is the group that everywhere in tropical Africa has dominated the politics of the first years of independence; it is greatly similar to the nationalist groups that have come to power in most of the rest of the underdeveloped world. In stricter terms of class analysis, this is a non-proprietary, petty bourgeoisie dependent on its white collar skills and training for its status. The group includes the lower-level civil servants, primary school teachers, journalists, veterinarians, male nurses, clerks in private business, and labor union leaders who constituted the new elite that emerged in Africa after the second World War. They are usually men with good, but not particularly prestigious education . . . most of them combined both rural and urban experience . . . although their standard of living was higher than that of any simple peasant, their life patterns were not so far removed that they were unapproachable.

The Ghana House of Assembly after the 1954 elections included only 4 farmers out of 104 members, in contrast to 30 school teachers, 18 members of the liberal professions, 18 merchants or petty traders, and 18 salaried white-collar employees from the civil service or the private sector (Hodgkin; 1961:29). The Legislative Assembly of former French West Africa, after the 1957 elections when nationalists established control, had but 3 percent farmers, but 22 percent were teachers, 27 percent were civil servants, and another 20 percent were of the liberal professions (Hodgkin, 1961:29). In Tanzania, only 8 out of 106 members of parliament were farmers after the 1965 elections. Most of the representatives were either professional politicians or civil servants and teachers (Bienen, 1967:401).

In predominantly peasant movements, it is educated "outsiders" and the more prosperous strata within the peasantry that take the lead. According to Barrington Moore (1966:474, 479), "by themselves, the peasants háve never been able to accomplish a revolution . . . the peasants have to have leaders from other classes . . . one of the greatest dangers of an *ancien régime* during the early phases of transition to the world of commerce and industry is to lose the support of the upper crust of the peasantry." And Wolf writes on the same topic that (1969:290–91)

> poor peasants and landless laborers . . . are unlikely to pursue the course of rebellion, *unless* they are able to rely on some external power to challenge the power which constrains them . . . the only component of the peasantry which does have some internal leverage is either landowning "middle peasantry" or a peasantry located in a peripheral area outside the domains of landlord control.

Even slave revolts are no exception. Looking over the social background and prerevolt careers of the leaders of the San Domingo uprising, C. L. R. James comments that 1963:19) "the leaders of a revolution are usually those who have been able to profit by the cultural advantages of the system they are attacking, and the San Domingo revolution was no exception to this rule." In the United States, according to Hofstadter (1955:101–102), the leaders of the Populist movement tended to be professional men, rural editors, professional reformers, and rural party veterans, not farmers. At a secondary level of leadership, it was the rural middle class of small merchants whose livelihood depended on the prosperity of the farmer community that undertook organizational tasks. There are exceptions. The leadership of the CCF (Lipset, 1950:343–48) was almost three-fourths farmers by occupation, most of them the wealthier and more successful farmers, but even in Saskatchewan more than two-thirds of the rural CCF leaders held some public posts in local government or in the cooperatives in addition to farming. And among Nazi leaders (but not the top leadership circle) and party members in the years 1930 to 1933, the proportion of farmers—excluding agricultural laborers but including landowners—varied between 9 percent and 18 percent, compared to 21 percent for the total gainfully employed population in Germany in 1933, and one would guess an even higher percent of farmers in the Nazi electorate since the Nazis fared very well in rural areas but poorly in the large cities (Gerth, 1940:106; Schoenbaum, 1966:29–44, 71; Doblin and Pohly, 1945–1946:46–47).

Merchants and businessmen, surprisingly enough, do participate in some opposition movements, but it is their educated sons who do not follow in their fathers' footsteps who are more likely to provide leadership in opposition movements. Hofstadter reports that (1955:144) many leaders of the Progressive movement were businessmen and proprietors of fairly substantial enterprises, though college-educated, Protestant professional men were in the majority. About a fifth of the members of the Third Estate in the French Constituent Assembly of 1789 were merchants and businessmen or property owners, as we have seen. Crane Brinton found that in samples of Jacobin clubs, merchants, businessmen, and shopkeepers constituted from 20 percent to 25 percent of the members throughout the revolutionary period (Brinton, 1930:50). They were also well represented among the leaders and activists of the American revolution, but that is not so surprising since these revolutions included movements aiming to benefit the property-owning classes. Roughly 15 percent to 20 percent of the Nazi party leaders and Nazi Reichstag deputies in the years 1930 to 1933 were drawn from the ranks of independent businessmen, merchants, and craftsmen (Schoenbaum, 1966:29–44). In countries dominated by feudal and landowning aristocracies and a state bureaucracy, especially where the business element in the middle class is weak, the business community plays but a marginal role in revolutionary assemblies. The 1848 Frankfurt Assembly included only about 50 representatives out of 830 deputies from the world of industry, commerce, transportation, and crafts (Ringer, 1969:44). The 1905 Russian Duma had but a handful of merchants and industrialists sitting in it (Weber, 1906:367–70). On the other hand, the sons of businessmen do participate in protest movements. Sorokin (1927–1928) found that 14 percent of the American labor leaders' fathers and 18 percent of foreign (European) labor leaders' fathers were professionals, managers, or businessmen; these figures are less than labor leaders' fathers who were skilled workers but higher than fathers who were semi- and unskilled workers.

By contrast, members of the free professions, especially lawyers, and the civil service, including teachers in many countries, supply the bulk of revolutionary assemblies and of leaders in social movements. This is true to an overwhelming degree for the representatives of the Third Estate in 1789 and the Frankfurt Assembly of 1848. In the 1905

Duma, roughly half the delegates were professionals, teachers, and officials (Weber, 1906). Professionals made up about 20 percent of the membership in the Jacobin clubs. In the Progressive movement they were the most numerous occupational stratum represented. Among the top Russian Communist leaders, Davis found a greater number of sons of professionals and officials than of workers and peasants (1929:48). And, as has already been reported, the great bulk of elected members of assemblies in Africa nearing independence were drawn from these groups. Among Nazi party leaders and Reichstag deputies, 10 percent to 20 percent were former teachers and civil servants, depending upon the year and leadership group. Members of the liberal professions were few among these Nazi leaders, but the white-collar employees, an occupational classification not yet existing in eighteenth- and early nineteenth-century society, formed the most numerous single occupational category (Schoenbaum, 1966:29–44).

It is difficult to escape the conclusion that the upper and middle strata in society supply the substantial bulk of opposition leaders to all manner of social movements in proportions far above that of their percentage in the population at large. But this is equally true for political leaders in political parties and in other institutionalized groups that have access to political influence and decisionmaking. In the United States, from the 1930s to 1950s, professionals, especially lawyers, supplied the majority of senators, representatives, and state governors, and over one-third of state legislators, as compared to about 20 percent to 25 percent for proprietors and officials and a much lower proportion for farmers. Wage earners and farm laborers are conspicuous by their absence from the political elite in the United States (Matthews, 1954:30). In France, men of law dominated the assemblies of the Third Republic, and other professionals, academicians, men of letters, journalists, and higher civil servants exceeded by far businessmen and landowners, not to speak of small farmers, lower civil servants, workers, and white-collar employees (Dogan, 1961:69–72). Parliamentary leadership appears, however, to draw a high proportion of its representatives from among the more prestigious and high income professions typical of the upper middle class. Social movements of protest and opposition tend to draw more than parliamentary leadership from among the teachers and lower civil servants of the middle and even lower middle class. It is my impression, however, that once a lower-class movement has settled into stable parliamentary opposition, the proportion of its leaders from a lower-class background becomes higher than it was during its earlier social movement phase. In any case, the social origins of protest leaders are rather similar to, instead of strikingly different from, the social origins of leaders of established parties with whom they clash.

How do the sons of the well-to-do and of officials get recruited into opposition movements? It appears that many of them are recruited during their student years at the university, frequently a university abroad. Davis's study of the official biographies of top Russian Communist leaders shows that two-thirds attended or graduated from the university, that they first engaged in radical protest action at the relatively early age of fifteen to twenty-one, that the character of these early activities was frequently participation in a student circle, student demonstrations, or student strikes, and that among the radicalizing stimuli reported, influence by fellow students and teachers is second only to that of books and periodicals (the two are by no means mutually exclusive) and far exceeds all reported family stimuli to radical activity (Davis, 1929:49–55). Once drawn into radical activities as students, most of the leaders were arrested several times and the process of continuous revolutionary activity begun. It is quite plausible that once arrested and known to the police as a radical, the student's career chances, in the Tsarist civil service especially, were seriously impaired. This pushed him further into revolutionary activity whose success would open up for him a bright future. Prisons often keep political offenders together in separate sections where they further educate and reenforce each other's political views, make new contacts, and are frequently afforded a great deal of time for reading and study. According to Shils (1961:40), "many of the Indian intellectuals now over 40 got their best education in prison during periods of civil disturbances . . . Indian Marxism had its training establishments in Arthur Road Prison and similar institutions all over India." Should the radical escape and go into exile abroad, he again tends to become part of a close-knit group of radical expatriates who reenforce each other's political views. Underground activity and multiplicity of social relations with equally radical individuals who sustain each other similarly tend to strengthen an esprit de corps. The founders of the Chinese Communist party almost all went to a university, often in a foreign country. Fully 46 percent of the fifty-two founders of the Party had been resident abroad, and 50 percent of them, though never living abroad, were educated in the new Western curriculum rather than the traditional Confucian higher education. Fifty-two percent were students at the time they entered the Party, another 18 percent were in teaching, and 21 percent were in journalism (M. Lee, 1968:115–18). The top leaders of the Guatemala Communist party of the early 1950s were all just finishing or had just finished studies at the University of San Carlos at the time of the revolution of 1944 and were active in radical student groups in the law faculty (Schneider, 1959:89–92). Top African, Asian, and West Indian nationalists were also recruited from among the tiny minority of foreign-educated university graduates and were influenced by Marxist circles in Paris and London, or by the Pan-Africanist movement in the United States. Emerson states about the top nationalist leaders that (1962:196–97)

> [they] were all men who had become familiar with the West in one or another fashion, but not all those who had even full-scale exposure to the West were nationalists. . . . Any sample of the leading figures in the nationalist movement would demonstrate the immense preponderance of men who went through the process of Western education and who may decently be assigned to the middle class.

After listing over thirty names that read like a list of postindependence presidents and prime ministers of the former colonial countries, Emerson concludes that (1962:198)

> the revolution against imperialism has been carried on primarily under the leadership of Asians and Africans in whose intellectual formation the West itself had a very large share.

Students from colonial or underdeveloped countries studying in European capitals were struck by the easier and more open race relations among student groups in the metropole in contrast to the behavior of whites in the colonies. They were keenly aware of the limited possibilities for advancement that a return to the colonies would mean despite their qualifications. They realized, for the first time perhaps, that a range of alternatives other than the traditional or colonial society was open for their country, that not all Europeans were superior to them in education and ability and that many metropolitans were in sympathy with nationalist aspirations. This, added to the influences of radical circles and of the great philosophic traditions of the Enlightenment and of Marxism, opened the way for a desire to change the colonial and traditional social order upon their return home. Oxaal (1968: chapter 4) has written the most subtle and penetrating portrait to date of "the education of young colonials at home and abroad" with special reference to three outstanding intellectuals and anticolonialists, all born and raised in Trinidad—C. L. R. James, George Padmore, and Eric Williams.

RISKS, REWARDS, AND RESOURCES

In accounting for these observations and generalizations about leaders and active participants in social movements, the sociological theory of mobilization can once more be drawn upon as a starting point. Although the social marginality theory of leadership and activism does not account for the bulk of the data, it nevertheless provides useful insights when it is further respecified and restricted to certain specific social contexts. It is useful to think of opposition and protest leadership as a scarce resource that has to be developed, often with considerable help from outside the collectivity or social strata that are the principal carriers of the social movement. Failure of leadership to emerge depends as much on the lack of outside support and the operation of social control as on psychological and cultural characteristics and their distribution in the potential opposition groups. Potential opposition and protest leaders as well as opposition ideas are almost always available prior to the movement's start. It is not so much their origin, but rather their development and coalescence with a following into a social movement that have to be accounted for. Leadership rests on skills that have to be learned through education and the trial and error experience of activists as the movement unfolds. Whether able and talented individuals will seek leadership positions in social movements rather than institutionalized leadership positions is largely determined by the mobility opportunities and openness of the society. However, leaders cannot create a substantial following and a social movement if there are not already widespread shared grievances experienced by a collectivity or groups in the population.

The actions and decisions of leaders consist of goal-directed behavior under complex conditions and considerable uncertainty. Outside pressures and internal constraints, incomplete information, the necessity to keep the movement from splitting up, the desire to maintain one's leadership position in the face of challenges, a precarious financial base, and other similar factors weigh heavily on the overall strategy and the day-to-day tactics and moves. The model of a fanatic leader driven by some inner compulsion in the pursuit of a long-standing irrational goal and thirsting for power and domination over men is a caricature not useful in sociological analysis, true as it might be in single isolated cases. Nor is a sociological theory concerned with the explanation and clarification of a particular sequence of specific historical events. The theory put forward here is not concerned with why X rather than Y became the top leader and what difference that would have made to subsequent events. Rather, the theory is concerned with specifying the conditions necessary for opposition and protest leaders to emerge, the likelihood that both X and Y and other potential leaders are drawn from a specific social class or social stratum and undergo certain experiences that tend to push them into opposition, the probability that individuals like X and Y should choose opposition activity rather than some other activities, and the range of choice open to any leader faced with certain situations, whether he be X, Y, or someone else, given the pressures and constraints they all face.

In Olson's theory (1968) the benefits accruing to all members of a collectivity from a collective good are not a strong enough inducement for them to organize to obtain that good if they behave like rational actors, especially in a large collectivity. So far as the attainment of collective goods is concerned in a situation where negative sanctions and coercion can be applied against those individuals who start organizing, the prospects of mobilization are even dimmer than Olson would have it. Furthermore, if the members of the collectivity are negatively privileged, lack economic autonomy, and possess few organizational skills due to lack of education, they will be extremely vulnerable to the social control mechanism and agencies of the society and even less likely to organize for the attainment of a collective good.

In these circumstances, outside help to initiate mobilization is one important way in which the obstacles to it are overcome. The other way is for a smaller group of individuals, the leaders and activists, to initiate mobilization. Leaders are the agents of group mobilization and the architects of organization. They are exposed to considerably higher risks and penalties and have to expend more time, energy, personal resources, and make more economic sacrifices than the followers who subsequently join a social movement when its nucleus is already formed. While the followers spend the bulk of their time and energy in the usual pursuits of making a living, raising a family, and so on, the leaders are frequently full-time activists who must make a living from the opposition activities themselves. Because they are involved full-time and because their activities entail higher risks and potentially higher rewards than for followers, leaders must be understood from the point of view of the individual incentives, gains, risks, and opportunities for advancement that participation in a social movement represents for them. Social movement leaders are political entrepreneurs just as politicians are. If successful, leaders obtain individual benefits and rewards in addition to the benefits that accrue to all the members of a social movement when the goals they seek have been achieved. Some may object that this view of leaders' and activists' motivation is too simplified or does violence to social reality since these individuals may be moved by ideology, altruism, a sense of outrage at social injustice, and so on. Granted that such an objection has some validity, one suspects, nevertheless, that few people are moved by ideals and noble sentiments alone, and many are moved by them to a far lesser extent than they themselves proclaim or wish others to believe. No one is in a position to disregard where his next meal is coming from and whether he is going to have a roof over his head. Leaders and active participants in social movements are no different from other people: they fear punishment; they are vulnerable to social and economic pressures; they seek social support and economic security;

some can be co-opted, others corrupted. At any rate, the theory here is not concerned with the few remarkable individuals who subsequently become the heroes, saints, and martyrs of history, but with analyzing the forces that explain the participation rates and patterns of the large majority of activists in a social movement.

The question of whether leaders of opposition movements will be new leaders or already established leaders and whether they will be drawn from within or without the collectivity that becomes the carrier of the movement can be analyzed from the vantage point of the previously introduced distinction between the vertical and horizontal dimensions of integration. The horizontal aspect of integration can be described along a community—unorganized collectivity—association dimension, bearing in mind once more that one is dealing with a continuum rather than sharp discontinuities and that any large collectivity or social class such as the working class or the peasantry is usually composed of groups and social strata falling along different points of the continuum because of regional variation, ethnic and economic differences, and so on, rooted in past history. A collectivity at either end of the continuum has already preestablished communal or associational leaders developed in the normal everyday course of social processes. These leaders are the most likely source of protest and opposition leadership should the interests of the collectivity be threatened or receive short shrift. An exception might be the case of organized groups whose members are so dispossessed, economically vulnerable, and dependent that they are unable to muster sufficient resources to produce their own leaders without outside support. But it is the un- or weakly organized collectivities, especially if they are economically dependent upon the groups they seek to revolt against, that find it difficult to produce their own "inside" leaders for sustained social movements. Here the availability of outside leaders and resources for mobilization is a necessity.

Looking at the vertical dimension of integration of a collectivity into the wider society—again to be thought of as a continuum without sharp gradations—inside social movement leadership is more likely to emerge in a segmented context, since talented and ambitious individuals will be blocked from social ascent by the ceilings built into the social structure for the negatively privileged groups. Thus, they will tend to accumulate in the collectivity with nowhere to move. They might as well actively pursue the goal of overthrowing or loosening the system of subordination they are subject to. In the integrated structure, able and talented individuals will have channels of mobility for rising in the class structure other than the more long-range and risky prospects of social movement leadership, even in an unorganized or weakly organized collectivity. In organized communities, whether they be communal or associational, leaders in a vertically integrated structure will have access to the societal elite and will be able to influence the top decisionmakers in order to solve the problems of their groups through institutionalized channels rather than through opposition activity.

As for the type of outside resource that is made available and that is sometimes necessary for the development of protest leaders, it is often education, both secondary education and university education abroad, as has already been described in the case of nationalist leaders. But help comes in other ways too. For instance, during the black movement for civil rights and equality in the United States, the bulk of the money and much of the manpower flowing into protest activity, civil rights, and political drives to advance the black cause came from white liberal groups, college students, and the federal government itself. Moreover, an elaborate network of government agencies and semiofficial associations, bodies, and boards, was created in connection with the War on Poverty, enabling protest entrepreneurs to earn a living as protest leaders, to build up a following, and to acquire a quasi-official organizational base for their activities. In former colonies, the introduction of civil liberties and freedom of political and trade union activity even within limits made available a large number of elected municipal, regional, and national legislative positions to be filled by potential opposition leaders who would then use the newly created legitimate base for their nationalist activities. In colonies with a relatively underdeveloped indigenous business sector, the financial rewards of such political office might be as much as ten times the salaries for lower level civil servants, clerks, teachers, and small traders, not to speak of cultivators and unskilled laborers. As one might expect under such highly skewed rewards, competition for political office by a large number of potential leaders outbidding each other in militancy was keen. In the United States, quite apart from the financial resources pumped into civil rights organizations by Northern liberals, the mass media and liberal universities played a further independent role in adding to the opportunities available to protest leaders. It was, and still is, possible to make a viable career as a spokesman for radical or militant groups, from appearances on television shows, conferences, workshops, seminars, lectures, magazine stories, and university appointments, once mass media publicity had catapulted a vocal dissenter into the national limelight. This is also true for the radical student movement.

The likelihood that leaders and activists in a social movement are drawn from certain groups and social strata can be established with reference to the risks and rewards that participation entails for them. Rewards might consist of social status, prestige, personal satisfaction, and so on, in addition to financial and economic rewards. Nor does it refer to rewards in an absolute sense, but to the rewards of participation in a social movement relative to the rewards and satisfactions enjoyed in the normal, everyday course of life. Risks of participation include not only economic risks such as loss of one's job but prosecution, imprisonment, and loss of life and limb of the participant, and sometimes even danger to his family and kin. The basic idea is that the lower the risks and the higher the rewards for an individual and members of a group or social stratum, i.e., the lower risk/reward ratio, the more likely are they to become participants in a social movement of opposition, of protest, or of rebellion. We assume, of course, that the individual or the groups under discussion have grievances to begin with. Because of individual differences in personality, motivation, social support, and so on, one would expect a certain amount of variation in the responses of group members even under the same conditions of risk, reward, and intensity of grievances. The ideas so far discussed and the dynamics of participation can best be presented with reference to Figures 2a and 2b.

FIGURE 2a:
The likelihood of participation associated with various regions of the risk/reward field.

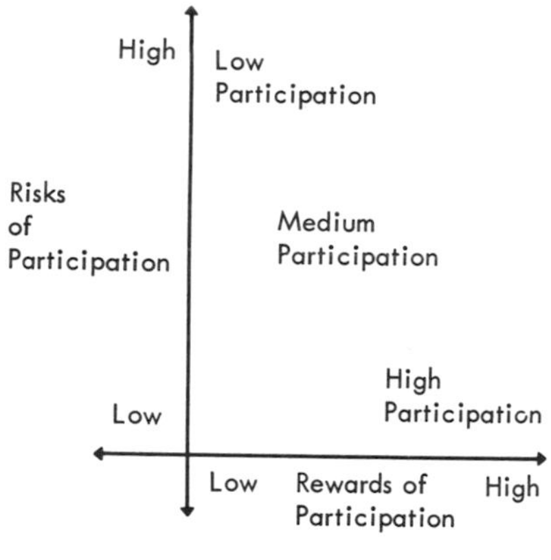

FIGURE 2b:
Time path of participation associated with changing risk/reward ratios: An illustration

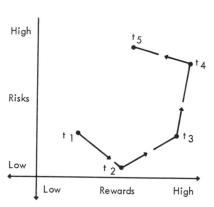

In Figure 2a in the upper left corner, individuals and groups subject to high risks and relatively low rewards from participation or joining a social movement will have low rates of participation. When rewards are high and risks low, as they are in the lower right region we predict high rates of participation. When there is an even balance between risks and rewards, we predict a rate that is in-between the two previous situations.

A diagram such as Figure 2a can also shed some light on the timing of participation of various groups and individuals. Those falling into the lower right hand corner can be expected to be the early participants, and those in the upper left region the last to join. What often happens, of course, is that as the movement gains momentum, the risk/reward ratios for other groups change because of a change in the balance of forces. Thus a high risk, low reward group might be initially unresponsive to mobilization attempts, but as the risks of participation become lower, and/or the rewards higher, it moves into a region with a higher probability of participation. This is illustrated in Figure 2b where the time path of the likelihood of participation is traced out for a hypothetical individual or group. At t_1, the premovement state, the risks of active opposition are considerable, and the rewards low since no viable institutional alternative for making a living or achieving political influence yet exists. Suppose the authorities institute reforms from above when they relax social control and create appointive and elective political offices for social strata previously deprived of the franchise. A group then finds over time (t_2 and t_3) its risk/reward ratio favorably changed in the direction of increased participation. If the incumbent government now takes fright at the growing power of the opposition and of social protest that it has allowed to surface, it may well increase social control once more (t_4) and may even abolish the positions and alternatives it had earlier made available (t_5), thus increasing risks and lowering rewards and forcing the group back into the region of low participation probability.

The figures also clarify the concept of the loosening of social control introduced earlier, which plays so important a role in the theory of social conflict. The fastest way to produce high rates of social movement participation is to lower risks and increase rewards *simultaneously*. A previously authoritarian or repressive regime may create a dangerous situation for itself when introducing far-reaching democratic reforms all at once by allowing both civil liberties and opposition rights and by establishing political offices that opposition leaders can compete for. On the other hand, the gradual relaxation of either dimension followed by a gradual relaxation of the other, but not both at the same time, will probably result in a slower emergence of opposition movements and a greater capacity of the incumbents to control it and to relinquish their monopoly of power in graduated steps while still remaining firmly in the saddle. An especially alert government will want to make certain that it opens up opportunities and channels of social and occupational ascent to able and ambitious individuals in potential opposition groups, and only then introduce greater freedom of expression, civil liberties, and tolerance for opposition, since it will then be able to keep the rewards of opposition participation relatively low compared to the opportunities it is able to provide, and thus can proceed safely to lower the risk dimension. The principle of co-optation of unruly and vocal elements in situations where a government or incumbents are unable to raise the risks of opposition essentially involves their manipulation of the reward dimension, the only other alternative. By lowering the rewards of opposition relative to the rewards and opportunities they are willing to provide through institutionalized means, they manipulate a dangerous situation by moving it from the high probability of participation region to one with medium or fairly low participation probability. Nevertheless, it often happens that an authoritarian regime will bar students and other youth from civil service jobs and other opportunities for making a living if they have at any time engaged in opposition activity. It thereby creates a situation in which the rewards of protest and of opposition involvement remain high for these groups since the rewards from other types of legal activity remain very low. Even if the regime keeps cracking down—that is, moving risks from the lower end to the higher end of the dimension— it can at best move these groups from a high to a medium probability of participation. Thus, it can look forward to years of fluctuating unrest on the part of activists who at some point might establish leadership of a larger social movement of opposition when social strata and classes in the population experience increased hardship.

The approach described here can now be applied to the explanation of previously described high rates of participation of free professionals, students, and intellectuals in opposition leadership, and the low rates of participation and relative absence of businessmen and members of the most deprived social categories.

Members of the free professions, especially lawyers, journalists, artists, writers, professors, physicians, and students who are training to become professionals, have frequently taken the initiative and most active role in opposition and protest movements. Aside from possessing intellectual and organizational skills by virtue of their education and an initial economic resource base that can be drawn upon, these groups can build up a following from their clientele upon whose welfare their own social status and economic standing depends. In a segmented society, their rise to the top of their profession and to the top of the society might be blocked because of ascriptive factors and discrimination. If a certain amount of open opposition is allowed, these groups can gain a lot by achieving high political office at relatively low risk—low risk because they have the skills and means of legal defense and the regime cannot muzzle them without a trial and without publicity, as it might ordinary people. If these groups are repressed and have to go underground, their means of livelihood, their access to their clientele is cut off, and they have little choice but to continue in opposition. The rewards of opposition are now even higher when compared to any other alternative. One thing that repression cannot do is to take away their intellectual and organizational skills on which their leadership potential rests. In difficult times, because their relatives and friends usually do come from among the well-to-do, they can frequently fall back upon assistance from their kin and associates who for a time can afford to support them. If they are prosecuted, punishment will not be as harsh as for ordinary people because professionals are usually members of associations and of organized bodies that will rise up in defense of their members. Thus the risk/reward ratio for professionals in many situations is such as to favor their active involvement in opposition when compared to the situation that other social strata are normally faced with.

Business groups are in a far more vulnerable position since they have fixed, nonmovable assets, and the gains or rewards of active protest involvement are relatively small compared to their usual expected economic gains. Care must be taken to distinguish larger from smaller businessmen. Owners and managers of large industrial enterprises, substantial merchants, and so on, are seldom in the position of being severely deprived or lacking access to the centers of power of their society. Therefore, one would expect them to show up with low frequency in the ranks of opposition groups and movements. Rather than engage directly in politics, large businessmen make the more rational decision when they influence the elites and the authorities through economic lobbies and other similar means. Faced with an opposition social movement that grows in strength, businessmen may well wish to reach an accommodation with it no matter how distasteful the goals and the ideology of the movement are to them, and this often entails making financial contributions to the social movement as well as to other political groups as an insurance policy. Substantial merchants and business groups do, however, find themselves in situations where the rewards stemming from opposition may outweigh risks if the rewards of business activity were low to begin with because of a long-term economic depression or restrictive and discriminating policies often instituted by a foreign or colonial power or by a government under the influence of such a power. If metropolitan or foreign businesses are favored at their expense, if their profits are taxed at a high rate, if the government is unwilling to provide local businesses with tariffs and protectionist policies, large businessmen and merchants do rally to a nationalist or opposition movement, as they did in the American revolution. Last but not least, once a conflict has already started, businesses tend to profit from outfitting and supplying the antagonists. Picking the winner at an early date might mean enjoying a later monopoly position with respect to government contracts and favorable government intervention in their behalf. They therefore tend to gain from joining an already successful opposition movement.

Small businessmen, merchants, traders, and the like are in an entirely different position from large businessmen, substantial merchants, and industrialists. Through licensing arrangements, permits, inspections, bank loans, suppliers, creditors, and so on, they are extremely dependent on the authorities, and the financial institutions and the large businesses in whose good graces they must remain to make a living, so that their risk of opposition is high. Their small margin of profit and limited material resources do not give them much of a resource base to draw upon for opposition. Nor do they possess organizational and leadership skills by virtue of education or experience. At the same time when their income has been low, because of the competition from larger businesses, foreign enterprises, "Jews," or similarly entrenched economic minorities, or during a depression period, the rewards of opposition, if successful, appear very high compared to their usual economic prospects, because competition can be eliminated through political means and because achieving political office leads to a more comfortable life-style than does marginal small business activity. The marginality theory is most applicable in these situations. However, the crucial variable is reduction of risk, for even marginal groups do not become activated if the risk/reward ratio stays high. The typical situation therefore is the mobilization drive of a right-wing and "nationalist" movement among these groups when the government relies upon right-wing support as a means of strengthening itself against threatening developments on the left. Small businessmen are most likely to be drawn, as in the Nazi case, into a right-wing rather than a left-wing opposition movement under conditions of government encouragement of the right. However, it is not inconceivable that an antiestablishment, left-wing opposition movement might mobilize support from these groups, unless such a movement is directed against all property owners rather than only large businesses and unless the working class is already so strongly organized and numerically preponderant that small business groups have but a small chance of being collectively heard and represented in an opposition movement of the left. Indeed, such was the case for the late eighteenth-century and early nineteenth-century artisans, craftsmen, and small business groups who were still linked through numerous social, familial, and economic bonds to journeymen, apprentices, and ordinary working people and whose livelihood was being threatened by the increased competition from factories and other modes of production based on large capital investment and wage labor.

Lower civil servants and white-collar employees, including teachers in those countries where they are civil service employees, are in much the same high risk position when joining opposition and protest movements as small businessmen are, since their positions are controlled by large, bureaucratized employers in a monopolistic market. They are economically vulnerable. On the other hand, they carry their resources with them as learned skills, as do the professionals, and they have excellent prospects for social mobility and achieving high organizational and political position should the opposition movement be at all successful. Although they may normally find themselves in a high risk, high to medium reward context that is not particularly conducive to opposition leadership and protest activity, the situation can change when social control is loosened, as it is with the introduction of even limited civil liberties and opposition rights. The risk of protest is suddenly much lowered, and the rewards of achieving office could be financially several times higher than the usually low clerical and civil service pay scales. Thus, for these groups a sudden shift in the risk/reward ratio can very much increase the probability of active opposition. In the colonial situation, as has already been pointed out, students trained as professionals had to start and remain for a considerable time in clerical, white-collar positions often working under less competent and less educated foreigners. Even if they were able to progress there were upper limits to their social ascent and economic opportunities. The relative deprivation and degree of marginality of these groups were therefore higher than for ordinary clerks, and the risk/reward ratio was for them a favorable inducement for opposition. The natural direction of protest was into nationalist movements that would eliminate the foreign superordinate group and open up mobility channels to the very top.

In other situations, however, civil servants, teachers, and students can ally themselves with movements of the fascist type, as is likely to be the case for small businessmen. This is going to happen in a society where the government bureaucratic sector dominates the private business sector and where there are sharp discontinuities between the property-owning and highly educated upper middle class and professional groups, and the lower middle class. A right-wing movement can democratize recruitment and increase mobility opportunities in the state apparatus and in political leadership so as to favor the lower middle class at the expense of the upper bourgeoisie while at the same time it curbs working-class organizations and parties. Whether lower civil servants, white-collar employees, and teachers will be left- or right-wing mobilizable depends, therefore, primarily on whether they are in a "colonial situation" or in a more economically advanced society dominated by the state bureaucracy. However, the risk dimension must be lowered before mobilization takes place, and this is usually accomplished with the introduction of opposition rights and elected offices in colonies or with the connivance of a nationalist–right-wing government that seeks to buttress its position against a real or imagined working-class challenge. In those countries where there is an overabundance of educated clerks and administrators dependent on government employment for making a living and where the ruling groups are not threatened by an organized working-class movement and therefore not in need of white-collar support, white-collar groups are in a particularly vulnerable position for forming an opposition, since the government can always replace them by dipping into reservoir of un- or underemployed clerks. The oversupply of educated "marginal" clerks in itself need not represent a threat to a regime. In fact, such a situation represents an opportunity for effective social control by an authoritarian regime.

Among the peasantry, agricultural wage workers or tenants are in a vulnerable, high risk position for protest since their livelihood depends on subservience to landlords, rural notables, plantation overseers, and local officials, and since they have no resource base to fall back on. Alternative employment, usually in the city, removes them from the rural scene altogether. "Outside" leadership and resources or an otherwise crumbling social order must precede organized and sustained opposition activity, although local riots, revolts, and social banditry are frequently endemic among them. Peasants tend to engage in frequent short-lived, localized, violent riots and rebellions as landlord or government exactions and exploitation are increased. Middle peasants, i.e., owners of small plots of land engaged in part in producing a cash crop for the nonlocal market, are much more likely to initiate and to lead sustained protest movements as a response to landlords' attempts to grab their land, to increased taxation, to decreases in the price for cash crops, to increases in interest rates, and to increased exploitation by middlemen and creditors that threaten to result in loss of their property and in down mobility into the class of tenants and wage workers. They also frequently have some education and organizational skills and some knowledge of the wider world needed for effective opposition activity. The rewards of protest for them are high since they might successfully consolidate land and secure land rights at the expense of landlords and foreigners. Other means of advancement for them are frequently blocked since securing credit at less than usurious interest rates and increasing production by technological improvements are not realistic options in their situation. If the risk of protest is lowered as a result of increased social unrest among other social strata that weaken the government's social control apparatus, the risk/reward ratio of the middle peasantry is much diminished and reaches the point of high probability of participation in opposition.

The probability of student participation in opposition movements can also be analyzed from a risk/reward perspective, although in the student case the ideological commitment, the gratification derived from peer group approval, and generational hostility must also be taken into account. A distinction should also be made between student protest acted out mainly on university campuses and directed at the university authorities—even if the rhetoric of protest has wider ideological and societal goals—and student participation in primarily off-campus and nonstudent movements. In the United States, campus protest activity has been of the low risk type up to and including the commitment of misdemeanors and milder forms of felony, especially at the high quality universities with a national reputation. University authorities and faculty disciplinary bodies have been lenient in their sanctions, most offenders receiving warnings, probations, and possibly suspensions, if they are at all apprehended. The worst one might expect during a campus police bust is a light injury; certainly not a permanently disabling injury or death. Because of the decentralized and multitiered higher education system, a student expelled or dropping out of a top university has a fair chance of completing his studies without jeopardizing his career chances at some other less prestigious but nevertheless good institution. Student militants receive considerable sympathy and often open encouragement and support from the faculty, especially the younger nontenured faculty. Scholarships or financial aid, even government fellowships, are not withdrawn for disciplinary infractions. Punishment for illegal and coercive student protest activity is meted out under the assumption that talented, sincere, and committed upper middle- and middle-class students should not have a permanent blot on their records because of a youthful escapade. Black students are not disciplined for fear of angering adjoining lower-class black populations.

Furthermore, in the early and middle 1960s the rapid expansion of higher education of the previous decade created a seller's market in most disciplines favoring the recent Ph.D. student and frequently even the students still a year or two from completing their dissertation when it came to getting a position as lecturer, instructor, or assistant professor. Militancy on the part of graduate students was therefore not of the high risk type. Students could easily shuffle their dissertation advisors to end up with sympathetic faculty and even get a fairly good position on their own. With the recent tightening of the job market for Ph.D.'s, the increased hesitancy of faculties to condone disruptive activities, and the resort to tougher disciplinary measures, the risks of student campus militancy have increased sharply.

On the reward side, the picture is less clear. Universities could do little to change national draft laws, stop the Vietnam war, bring U.S. capitalism crashing down, wage a private War on Poverty by extending health, educational, and other social services in the lower-class neighborhoods in which they are frequently located, and end their heavy dependence on government funds. On the other hand, the termination of ROTC, curricular reform, greater attention to undergraduate instruction, greater influence of students in university governance, special programs such as black studies, and other university reforms were by and large achieved, instituted and are being implemented to the satisfaction of a majority of college students. The rewards of student protest in the sense of creating a better university from the point of view of meeting student needs have been in the medium range. As of 1970, however, the rewards of further university-oriented protest activity have decreased while the risks of protest have increased for reasons already mentioned. Thus the risk/reward ratio has increased and represents a more unfavorable ratio for student protest than at any time in the last five years, and this change is indeed reflected in the diminished student campus protest activity.

So far as the risks and rewards of student protest in the wider society are concerned, the risks of prosecution were higher than on the campus, yet because the campus was a safe base to operate from—seldom if ever would a student's pursuit of a college degree be jeopardized by arrest or participation in militant political activity—the risk factor was not high. Rewards of protest, apart from psychological ones, were real insofar as the reversal of Vietnam policy meant a much lower probability of serving in the armed forces for an unpopular and immoral cause. Thus, while risks have remained constant, rewards from continued militancy have decreased after President Johnson was forced to give up running for a second term, Vietnam policy had been reversed, and troops began to be withdrawn. For the minority of revolutionaries who aimed all along to use student protest as a means of forcing present-day American institutions to the point of collapse, the dampening of the student movement was a real disaster since they had not been able to build up a following among blacks or working-class whites. The tactical choice made by this small revolutionary minority for bombing in the manner of the Russian anarchists is really a last act of desperation, as it has always been, and represents the abandonment of the original unrealistic goal of a large anticapitalist mass movement. Almost certainly the consequence of bombings will be to increase the risk of protest activity even further, as severe national laws will be passed and universities will no longer undertake to shelter revolutionaries. Only another reversal of the Vietnam policy can reverse the gradual demobilization of the student antiwar movement.

In other countries, the student movement has to be analyzed within the context of different historical and institutional settings, usually a far greater centralization of higher education with greater central government control over student discipline and career chances, but with a higher probability that students can form alliances with already established and powerful parties and other opposition groups.

These ideas can also be applied to the case of mobilization and leadership in social movements of negatively privileged minorities, to changes over time as a minority movement led by more militant leaders challenges the original "accommodationist" leaders who were content and forced to accept the group's subordinate position in the society. In terms of Wirth's (1957) typology of minority movements, the new assimilationist leaders who want integration into the majority on the basis of equality may be challenged in turn by secessionist groups and even militant groups who wish minority domination over the superordinate majority. In Kurt Lewin's "periphery" theory of ethnic leadership (cf. Bell et al., 1961:88–91) referring to the premobilization situation, the successful individuals in an ethnic group—successful in terms of the limited opportunities available to the ethnic group—will be oriented to the values of the majority and will strive to be accepted by the majority. Hence, the successful ethnic group member tends to isolate himself from the masses of the ethnic group to which he belongs. He is called upon and does perform leadership functions within his own group, as a result of majority pressures for using him as a safety valve mechanism and ethnic group pressures for using his limited influence in their behalf with the majority to obtain small favors and concessions. But he is unlikely to depart so far from a moderate-accommodationist style as to endanger his privileged relations with the majority and the substantial economic benefits he derives from these relations. All these processes result in the "lukewarm" ethnic leadership of the preprotest stage. At the same time populist leaders and nativistic prophets in close touch with the masses form sects and movements for the pursuit of otherworldly goals. Nevertheless, because the risks of protest are high and the reward from defying the system of subordination low and because many in the ethnic minority live at the margins of subsistence and many others are vulnerable to economic sanctions and legal and physical coercion, the masses of the premovement period appear apathetic and unresponsive. This is usually interpreted in cultural, racial, or ethnic terms and linked to explanations based on personality and socialization theory that allegedly explain the failure of leadership and the apathy and timidity of its potential following. Actually, as new social strata less dependent upon the majority come into being, as "outside" resources are pumped into the ethnic minority to beef up protest leadership and support nascent opposition organizations, and as social control is loosened by means of legislation and favorable government action, the risk/reward ratio for the ethnic minority can rapidly be changed in a matter of a few years, so that the previously leaderless and resigned subordinate group can now sustain a highly mobilized and threatening social movement that no longer is dependent upon outside support for its continuation. These processes will be illustrated in some detail with reference to the incidence and changes in leadership and the rhythm of mobilization that took place in the United States in the decades of the 1950s and 1960s in connection with the civil rights and black power movements. The mobilization theory put forward here can provide insights that Wirth's, Lewin's, the culture of poverty, and psychologically oriented theories of minority and ethnic leadership and protest have not provided.

LEADERS AND FOLLOWERS: THE
PSYCHOLOGICAL DIMENSION

In social movement and collective behavior theory, it has been quite common to stress the charismatic qualities of some leaders in order to account for their success in mobilizing a following and in maintaining a high degree of commitment and loyalty among them. Smelser's introduction of the psychological dimension into his value-added approach also leads to an unfortunate emphasis on the role of leaders as mobilizing agents and to a psychologistic, Freudian analysis of leader-follower interactions (Smelser, 1968:118–20). My approach throughout tends to emphasize the instrumental aspects of the leader-follower relationship, based on the mutual benefit that each derives from it. The actions of leaders are constrained both by the agents of social control and the characteristics of their potential following. Some collective behavior events, such as many riots, are leaderless to begin with; others prosper despite weak or multiple leadership; in still others leaders find themselves in positions of command against their own inclination or are desperately trying to keep a step ahead of their followers. In one of many turbulent events during the revolution of 1848 in France, Lamartine was seen by one of his friends hastily leaving the Chamber of Deputies in pursuit of a noisy crowd of Paris citizens bent on proclaiming still another revolutionary government from the balcony of the Hotel de Ville. When asked why he was leaving, Lamartine replied "Je suis leur chef. Il faut que je les suive!" *

Lamartine's dilemma may be much more frequent than is generally thought. One should not mistake mass media publicity accorded to lead-

---

* "I am their leader. I must therefore follow them!" The story may be apocryphal but it illustrates the point I am trying to make.

ers, or their own successful efforts at manufacturing praise and enforcing conformity, for genuine popular dedication, loyalty, and charisma. So long as they pursue group goals energetically, leaders do build up a fund of good will and loyalty that they can later draw on even after they cease to be effective or no longer vigorously represent their followers' interests. Yet, it is more likely that new leadership will challenge established leadership under these circumstances. The rank and file usually do know what they want, and they have a good idea of which leaders and activists represent their interests.

It is a misconception to think that leaders mobilize activist or hostile crowds on the spot, so to speak, by haranguing and urging them on to action. Contemporary and historical evidence does not support such a view. According to Rudé (1962:196–97), in eighteenth-century London, it was the established elites and their contending factions who made use of the time-honored device of "raising a mob" and not protest movement leaders such as John Wilkes.

> Wilkes only once put himself at the head of a London crowd—on 26 April 1773, when he marched with them to Westminster to make his annual claim to his seat in Parliament; on other occasions, he was conspicuously careful to avoid such contacts and to call on his followers to vote or demonstrate without disorders or violence.

Yet, Wilkes was enormously successful in mobilizing a popular movement of "the inferior sort of people" whose political aspirations simply did not figure in the politics of the time. During the French Revolution, the political education and mobilization of the Parisian "little people" took place by means of the pamphleteering activities of leaders such as Marat and Camille Desmoulins, in the clubs and popular societies, and through their membership in the National Guard and local assemblies (Rudé, 1967:212–13). Seldom did leaders directly address crowds of citizens in mass meetings. Writing about the leader-follower relationship in the period 1730–1848, Rudé remarks that (1964:249)

> communication between the topmost leaders and their followers was seldom direct. Displays of mass oratory were the exception rather than the rule . . . press, Parliament, and political club were more often chosen as a forum than the public square. Robespierre's oratory was confined to the National Assembly and the Jacobin Clubs; Wilkes wrote his addresses and manifestoes from the King's Bench prison; Marat used the columns of his paper, *L'Ami du Peuple;* and Ned Ludd issued his directives from his headquarters in Sherwood Forest.

The stage-managed mass meeting of party faithful during which the leader directly addresses thousands in a stadium—one thinks of the giant Nazi rallies staged in Nürnberg in the 1930s—is a ritualized and institutionalized event typical of social movements that have been triumphant and have eliminated their opposition and achieved a monopoly of communication. It is then that a "cult of personality" develops, managed from the top down, not from the bottom up. In revolutionary situations there is a tremendous outpouring of words, pamphlets, posters, and meetings, but communication and influence take place in small groups of neighbors, co-workers, associates, and so on. Trotsky marveled how anything was done at all during the Russian revolution because people spent so much time talking and debating with each other. According to John Reed (1967:39),

> hundreds of thousands of pamphlets were distributed by thousands of organizations, poured into the armies, the villages, the factories, the streets . . . Russia absorbed reading matter like hot sand drinks water, unsatiable . . . lectures, debates, speeches,—in theatres, circuses, school-houses, clubs, Soviet meetingrooms, Union headquarters, barracks . . . for months in Petrograd, and all over Russia, every street corner was a public tribune. In railway trains, street-cars, always the spurting up of impromptu debate, everywhere.

And in May 1968 in Paris (Seale and McConville, 1968:94–95),

> the most striking feature of those days was the sight of people talking to one another—not only casual exchanges, but long intense conversation between total strangers, clustered at street corners, in cafés, in the Sorbonne of course. There was an explosion of talk, as if people had been saving up what they had to say for years. And what was impressive was the tolerance with which they listened to one another.

It is this orgy of participation and of talk, conducted in casual meetings and small groups for the most part and in which a diversity of points of view are expressed, that is so characteristic of the early phases of social movements, and not the monopolistic leader-captive mass audience relationship on which the Le Bon and other stereotypes of the leaders' mesmerizing influence upon masses are based. Contemporary research has discovered the great importance of small groups and local influentials in routine mass communication processes (Katz and Lazarsfeld, 1955; Wright, 1959). Their importance is perhaps even greater in the period of mobilization for collective behavior episodes. Nevertheless, leaders and activists succeed in these times to direct popular enthusiasm and energies into more structured and focused collective action. As Trotsky remarked (1959:xi),

> without a guiding organization the energy of the masses would dissipate like steam not enclosed in a piston-box. But nevertheless what moves things is not the piston or the box, but the steam.

It is true that some groups do not demobilize after the partial attainment of movement goals, and some become a "pure conflict" sect. Smelser correctly notes the tendency that leads many movements to endure beyond their "natural" life, including some that "attempt to provoke authorities into hostile actions which presumably will breathe new life into the movement" (Smelser, 1968:118). Clearing up this common terminal feature of many movements can again be done without appealing to psychodynamics. Leaders and activists, as well as the rank and file, pursue selfish ends, not only group goals. Some activists have risen in status and have obtained other tangible rewards from being thrust into leadership position during the mobilization and confrontation phase. These personal rewards are now diminishing as the rank and file become demobilized. If the activists pursue selfish goals, they have a stake in continued agitation and provocations that might result in incidents around which the rank and file can be remobilized. Olson's and my own approach can deal effectively with these terminal situations without invoking Freudian explanations.

There still remains the basic issue of what the importance of psychological processes is in the overall explanation of collective behavior and group conflict. The matter can be clarified in the following terms. Collective behavior, as all other behavior, is embedded in a group context. Although people do pursue goals rationally with a deliberate choice of means, and although they are by and large selfish, the goals they pursue are neither randomly distributed over all possible goals nor necessarily *private* or *personal*, but those that prevail in the groups and other collectivities and social units to which they belong or aspire to belong. Those individuals who pursue goals detrimental to group welfare or group cohesion will be subject to group sanctions. Since most people do derive tangible benefits from group membership, they will weigh very carefully the advantages of pursuing private ends in conflict with group goals with the disadvantages of losing group membership and being exposed to group sanctions. Within broad limits, variation in behavior, even in relatively homogeneous social units such as peasant villages, is ensured by the fact that a range of permissible goals is in practice always found and that goals vary for different age, sex, and other statuses within the social unit. As to the choice of means, they too are limited by group norms and, ultimately, the self-interest of the individual who cannot afford to violate these norms consistently if he wishes to enjoy the benefits of group membership. Indeed, lack of skills, limited resources, misinformation, misperception, and so on, also limit the choice of means.

In group conflict situations, many idiosyncratic factors that have to do with choice of means and ends do cancel out; and we are often interested in an aggregate group response primarily, e.g., one is concerned whether or not a certain peasant group rebels or a certain population group riots. For many purposes, if 20 percent, say, of the able-bodied males engage in rebellion at any given time, it *is* a rebellion. One need not know which 20 percent engage in it and how rapid the turnover rate is. We also want to know whether the other 80 percent are more likely to be mobilized to support the rebels or, on the contrary, support agents of social control in their efforts to quell the civil disorders. If we wish to predict precisely which 20 percent of the discontented group become the activists and who among the other 80 percent are their most ardent supporters and opponents, additional variables, including psychological ones, can be introduced as intervening variables to reduce the unexplained variance. Even in these situations, however, the basic postulates of rationality and of self-interest or, what amounts to the same thing, the careful weighing on the part of potential participants of the rewards and costs of collective action, can go a long way in explaining differential participation.

The following rules of thumb can be formulated. The more dense the group structure that forms the individual's social environment, the stronger the social controls operating on him. Also, the more homogeneous the group, the stronger the social control exercised upon him. Given a fairly uniform set of stimuli and opportunity structures, the choice of goal and of means is rather narrowly defined for all group members and the risk/reward ratios uniform. Thus, there is less likelihood that additional variables, e.g., psychological, need be introduced to explain differential participation. On the other hand, as social control in a group or collectivity becomes weaker, usually because of greater heterogeneity of group elements and a looser group structure, the scope of individual choice for both means and ends is greater. Thus, the risk/reward ratios resulting from external social control and opportunities for material gain and social ascent will elicit a greater variability of responses by group or collectivity members. Hence, intervening variables will be of help in reducing unexplained variance of behavior responses, including often psychological variables.

From these ideas it also follows that usually at the very top of the authority structure (the top leadership level of both the incumbents and their opponents) where individuals are more likely to be members of multiple groups, the range of choice is greatest of all. Hence, the necessity to introduce more and more information on specific individuals in leadership position may be necessary to the point even of a psychohistory, such as Erik Erikson has done for Luther and Gandhi. Even at the top leadership level, however, the range of options is considerably narrowed if one realizes that leaders are often subject to very strong group pressures and certain choices cannot be made if they wish to retain their following. The leader who is facing a divided public opinion has a greater range of choice than one who is facing a decision in a situation where group pressures on him coincide. In collective decisions reached by small groups such as a cabinet, the Supreme Court, a management team, or the executive committee of a professional association, knowledge of small groups research and of the theory of teams and of committees in economics also has to be drawn upon for an analysis of the decisionmaking process.

Even at the level of aggregate group response, such as rebellions and riots, the assumptions of rationality and self-interest go a long way in explaining behavior before the necessity for calling on additional intervening variables. Strictly speaking, only individuals can be assumed to be rational and self-interested, not groups, but the use of these terms allows one to express statistical regularities with economy of language. Collective behavior, whether the conduct of peaceful demonstrations or violent outbursts, is learned behavior, sometimes even to the point where it has become ritualized. Group support and group sanctions operate as in ordinary behavior; emergent norms, folk ideas and beliefs, past norms embedded in the historical tradition of a people, set bounds to what is permissible and uncalled for and specify the goals that are desirable and permitted. If anything has been learned from recent historical research on crowd behavior and from recent sociological analyses of crowd behavior, it is precisely this.

A demonstration or violent outburst as a whole might be characterized as non-rational if one could show that it is an inappropriate means to obtaining group goals and that other channels for seeking redress for grievances are available and are more effective. But recent history shows that collective behavior episodes have been effective and have been the only means of forcing policy reversals from entrenched elites. The antiwar movement managed to block President Johnson's reelection and reduced President Nixon's options to deescalation and U.S. troop withdrawal, though not at the rate activists had hoped for. Blacks in the U.S. discovered that channels of access to those in authority were opened and resources and reforms were enacted and enforced only after they took to the highways and the streets. Students did get campus reform, though not all some of them asked for. Historic crowds repeatedly have managed to topple oppressive, corrupt and illegitimate rulers, or at a more modest level, obtained relief from food shortages and high prices. Trade unions in the end got recognition in law after the violent strikes, sit-downs, and factory occupations of the 1930s. And all this *after* other means had failed.

Crisis management and response are not confined to collective behavior situations. Currency reform is not undertaken until the succession of monetary crises and balance of payment deficits threatens to upset the pattern of world trade; pollution control not until the air becomes too foul to breathe; welfare reform not until its cost is prohibitive even while the system perpetuates dependency; and so it goes, ironically, also in societies that believe in central planning and social engineering. Here, as elsewhere, collective behavior and ordinary behavior do not differ.

IDEOLOGY

Whatever term one uses, ideologies constitute an important element in the analysis of social conflict and of social movements. In McClosky's definition (1964:363), ideology refers to a "system of belief that is elaborate, integrated, more or less coherent, which justifies the exercise of power, explains and judges historical events, identifies political right and wrong, and furnishes guides for action." Converse (1964:207) prefers the term "belief systems," or a "configuration of ideas and attitudes in which elements are bound together by some form of constraint or functional interdependence." Heberle (1951) uses the concept of "constitutive ideas," i.e., those ideas considered most essential to a social movement that form the basis of its solidarity and of concerted action for the pursuit of common goals.

The role of ideas in social action has long been controversial and has been debated without in the least making converts in opposed camps. Crane Brinton has written (1952:51–52) that "ideas are always part of the pre-revolutionary situation . . . no ideas, no revolution. This does not mean that ideas cause revolution, or that the best way to prevent revolutions is to censor ideas. It merely means that ideas form part of the variables in a study of determinants and causes of collective action." This is so because, as Smelser has stressed (1963:16), social strain, grievances, and dissatisfaction have to be made meaningful to the potential participants in collective action. The sources of an undesirable state of affairs and appropriate responses to it have to be specified before collective behavior can occur. The notion that movements of protest are caused by subversive ideas spread by agitators in a peaceful, contented population who become aroused by extravagant promises made to them by those who would exploit them for their own private gain is perhaps quite common, but must be rejected in a scientific analysis, except as one of several working hypotheses. Such a view fails to take into account the very real force of objective grievances in social conflict. It expresses a view of the masses as subject to manipulation and ready to riot on the slightest pretext that is simply not borne out by history. On the other hand, ideologies do not simply narrowly reflect underlying social tensions and material interests of those who formulate and champion them.

Such a simple correspondence between the content of ideas and of interests is difficult to establish, though broad empirical uniformities linking ideas and interest do exist and will be described below. It is best to think of protest ideas and opposition ideologies as producing a collective response in conjunction with the presence of real or felt grievances, discontents, and suffering. The ideas serve to explain private wrongs and sufferings experienced by individuals in terms not of private shortcomings, of accidental events, or of eternal, unalterable states, but in terms of shortcomings of the society that can be remedied and of particular groups responsible for the collective welfare.

It is easy to be either naive or cynical about the analysis of protest ideas and political ideologies; naive, if one accepts the statements propounded in them as eternal truths like the law of gravity; cynical, if one thinks that all ideals are but thinly disguised masks and part of a plan for systematic deception on the part of a particular group or class to legitimize its aspirations or defend its share of rewards and privileges. The Declaration of the Rights of Man on 4 August 1789 proclaimed in part that (Palmer, 1955:352)

> men are born and remain free and equal in rights. Man's natural rights were held to be "liberty, property, security and resistance to oppression." Freedom of thought and religion were guaranteed . . . all persons were declared eligible for any public office for which they met the requirements. . . . Law must fall equally on all persons. Law was the expression of the general will, to be made by all citizens or their representatives. . . . Taxes might be raised only by common consent, all public servants were accountable for their conduct in office.

If we ask which groups or classes had most to benefit directly and immediately from the abolition of feudalism and the creation of new political and legal institutions along the lines suggested by the Declaration, it is clear that it was the bourgeoisie, especially the wealthier section of it. Yet it is a fact that some members of the aristocracy and the clergy joined the Third Estate in support of the Declaration. They must have believed in the natural rights of man as valid and true principles, and they must have been morally committed to these principles regardless of the immediate benefits or losses to them as occupants of the privileged strata. Once such ideals are embodied into institutional forms as constitutions or laws, their long-run significance is far wider than the immediate group benefits they extend to those who first enunciated them.

The same is true for nationalism. The principle of self-determination and the right to be governed by leaders chosen from among one's own people rather than by foreigners imposed from without is put forward at a particular time and place by groups who would gain from independence most: the new stratum of Western-educated, urban-based, professional and white-collar groups who are ready to assume political offices and take over civil service positions from the colonial administrators. In doing so they everywhere experienced a very rapid increase in their social status and material style of life. Nevertheless, the appeal and successes of nationalism can never be explained with reference to these groups alone, and the consequences of independence are far-reaching. Nationalism has always incorporated democratic and egalitarian ideals, since authoritarianism and inequality were associated with the condemned colonial regime and the need of nationalists to enlist the support of the masses necessitated an emphasis on more responsive and participatory government and a more egalitarian future society. Once these ideals are proclaimed in party platforms and later enshrined in constitutions and laws, they acquire legitimacy and become the norm against which the shortcomings of leaders and of the social structure are contrasted. Although these ideals can be subverted by the new strata who benefit most from independence, this is done only at the risk of losing legitimacy. Opposition groups can then appeal to democratic and egalitarian values to challenge the newly formed vested interests.

Principles such as those in the Declaration of the Rights of Man and democratic constitutions create new ideals against which societal realities can be measured. The gap between ideal and reality becomes more visible than earlier. At a future time, these ideals can be taken up by disaffected groups who wish to narrow the gap in order to improve their situation as well. Moreover, ideals proclaimed as universal principles are always subject to wide interpretations. If the eligibility to public office is to be based on qualifications, what specifically are these qualifications? Education, ability, the possession of property, the preference of the majority, seniority, are all candidates for qualifications even after criteria based on ascription are done away with. Thus, a struggle over the concrete interpretation and consequences of broad principles can now develop with each party favoring and pushing forward its particular interpretation. Finally, when new political institutions are established in one country they serve as models for people in other countries and represent a new base line of the political dialogue against which the possibilities of social change are evaluated. Even in countries where the intellectual strata or dissenting groups are few in numbers or too weak and disorganized, the rapid spread of ideas proclaimed somewhere else in the world is responsible for creating alternative conceptions and ideals of how society ought to be organized, often with explosive potential and consequences. It is often not new ideals and novel ideologies that have the most far-reaching consequences, but the demand that values and rights already enjoyed and taken for granted by some groups or classes, or enjoyed in some parts of the world, be extended to other groups or classes, or to peoples in other parts of the world.

A full-blown ideology consists of four parts that can be conveniently distinguished (Killian, 1965a:434–37). These are usually elaborated in the literature produced by intellectuals and interpreted in the pronouncements of the leaders of the movement. There is first the interpretation of the process that has led to the present undesirable state of affairs, and the blame for it is fixed on certain individuals, groups, or institutions. Heroes and villains are identified. Second, the ideology provides the blueprint of a desirable state of affairs that can be obtained if only the resistance of certain groups is overcome. The blueprint describes the goals of the movement and the means by which to achieve them. The blueprint provides a hope to end frustration and dissatisfaction as well as a vision of still greater frustrations should the movement fail. Third, the ideology will have a set of moral ideas associated with it, sometimes called its social philosophy (Heberle, 1951:24). These ideas express the justifications for the movement and its program. They spell out connections between the goals of the movement and the values of the larger society in an attempt to establish the legitimacy of the goals. Lastly, the ideology may provide a novel interpretation of the historical process and may be concerned with the moral revaluation of the protest group. If the protest group has been a negatively privileged, low status collectivity, as so often happens, a new sense of identity and pride necessary for collective self-assertion and militancy is fostered by the reassessment and rewriting of its history, by showing that it has had a glorious history, with great achievements and past heroic actions that have so far gone unrecognized and can be repeated once more. It is important to note that ideologies have an intellectual and cognitive component—that is, they contain statements purporting to describe the state of society and the motives and behaviors of certain groups that can in principle be verified empirically—as well as a moral component, that is, statements about right and wrong, what is desirable and undesirable, and who is to blame. The moral component is present in short-lived collective disturbances even when the intellectual component is either absent or has not been systematically developed beyond folk ideas.

While the history of ideas and of political philosophies tends to examine the intellectual component of political ideas as stated by its most articulate formulators, we are more concerned with ideologies as they are perceived and understood by the rank-and-file of social movements and conflict groups, and these are frequently composed of traditional conceptions of justice and of right and wrong, folk ideas about heroes and villains in which the moral component outweighs the cognitive elements of the protest ideology. Moral revaluation and cultural revival may precede the articulation of political goals and programs. Oxaal (1968:151–52) has shown for the case of Trinidad how the black middle class developed pride in its own ethnicity through the Creole culture movement of the 1940s and 1950s prior to their commitment to nationalism. Before the war local folk culture was seen as degrading and shameful. The ideal was represented by European life-styles and culture. But "in the postwar period, the educated Trinidad middle class discovered the artistic validity and prestige of local folk culture . . . [they] formed a congeries of patrons and publicists of local culture, and it helped pave the way psychologically for a middle class rapprochement with the masses." The middle strata championed and took pride in the carnival, the steel bands, the *Little Carib* modern folk dance theatre, and other elements of the folk culture of Trinidad. This cultural revival and moral revaluation of non-European traditions was a necessary preparatory step in the rise to self-assertion preceding the demands for political independence. This phenomenon is particularly well documented for European nationalist movements where romanticists, poets, artists, and intellectuals created a cultural renewal centered on a positive revaluation of folk culture, fairy tales, songs, sagas, and other aspects of national life looked down upon earlier by the men of letters of the Enlightenment (Kohn, 1955).

For illustrative purposes the ideologies of four well-known social movements can briefly be summarized according to the above scheme. In the case of the Nazi movement, the element of blame for the economic depression and Germany's other troubles was fixed upon the Jews, Communists and other Marxists, the foreign countries whose reparations policy had weakened the German economy, and the previous national leaders who had accepted the humiliating terms of the Versailles treaty and given in to foreign pressures. The blueprint of a better society was left much less precise, but it stressed that unity and order as opposed to the chaotic strife-torn present would follow from strong Nazi leadership only if the Jews, socialists, and Communists were suppressed. The Nazis also had a concrete program for industrial and agricultural recovery. The Nazis established their legitimacy and provided continuity with past values through nationalism. They stressed and later carried out the reconquest of territories lost after World War I and appeared in the guise of strong defenders of the national interest against the foreign enemy. Finally, the Nazis furnished a moral revaluation of the defeated German people in stressing the key role the Germans were to play in Europe, the link between the Third Reich and previous German empires, and the racial superiority of the German people over their neighbors and the Jews, and their energy and mission in history compared to the decadent Anglo-Saxons whose world historical leadership role was at an end.

The Wallace movement in the presidential election of 1968 tried to base its appeal on a wide range of fears and grievances among white lower middle-class and working-class voters over the integration or threatened integration of public schools, student antiwar and campus disturbances, and the level of taxation experienced by the small property owners who derive relatively few economic benefits from government spending while increased amounts of money are spent on welfare and the military-industrial complex. The hero of the Wallace movement was the "forgotten man," the "ordinary folks," the man who works hard and is trying to make ends meet in the face of oppressive taxation by a remote federal government, who is never in trouble with the police, who never lives off "handouts" and welfare, and who has been forgotten by the leadership of both political parties whose programs have no relief and no benefits to offer him. The villains of George Wallace were an assortment of Washington bureaucrats, pseudointellectuals—meaning the professional and academic people who staff government, the universities, and the news media—Communists, student and civil rights demonstrators and other "agitators" who are seen as causing, not reacting to, the social problems of the nation. Wallace tried to establish the legitimacy of his goals and continuity with past values by appealing to the tradition of states rights and the principle of local sovereignty against the encroachments of the federal government, to patriotism, and to the populist principle that ordinary people know what's best for them and can run their affairs without the interference of bureaucratic and technical experts who create rather than solve the problems the ordinary man is faced with. In short, the Wallace movement from a moral point of view was nothing short of an attempt to revaluate the white lower middle class and working class at the expense of blacks and other white social strata.

The Populists of the 1890s had a specific blueprint for solving their economic woes through free silver, legislation aimed at curbing the power of the railroads, and reform of the political parties and legislatures by means of the primary, the referendum, the recall, and the direct election of senators. Blame was fixed on corrupt legislators, the railroads, eastern bankers, and sometimes a wider international conspiracy of plutocrats organized to defraud the farmers. Their vision of the future was but a version of the Jeffersonian and American dream of independent, hard-working, self-governed, and prosperous farmer communities. The legitimacy of their ideal and program consisted in the Jeffersonian democratic ideal of direct participatory democracy and government immediately responsive to the people's will. Populism was a relatively short-lived movement that did not develop a full-fledged interpretation of the historical process.

The (early) civil rights movement concentrated heavily on specific goals such as school desegregation and its enforcement and the repeal of segregation laws. Its spokesmen linked these goals with the central American values of equality and freedom as manifest in the Constitution, the Bill of Rights, and Supreme Court decisions. Nonviolent direct action, acts of civil disobedience, was justified in the context of a higher religious morality and Christian brotherhood that enjoyed widespread public support and sympathy. The blueprint of the future desirable state of affairs was integration, an extension of the idea of America as the melting pot society that was in conformity with basic principles and values that all Americans pay at least lip service to. Blacks did not want anything that the white majority did not already have as a matter of right. The heroes and villains of the movement emerged as a result of the confrontations in the South between sheriffs, local officials, and state governors and the rank-and-file demonstrators and civil rights workers who were subject to abuse, beatings, arrest, imprisonment and sometimes death. The last element of ideology, moral revaluation of blacks (black is beautiful) and a reassessment of their history and cultural heritage, did not emerge markedly until the civil rights movement was challenged by the black power movement, but it was present nevertheless from the beginning. In all these movements it can be seen how important a component of ideologies the moral revaluation of a previously negatively privileged stratum is and how every effort is made to legitimize the specific goals and broader orientations of the movement with respect to already widely accepted and shared ideals and values embedded in the culture.

SOCIAL CLASSES AND
CONCEPTIONS OF THE SOCIAL ORDER

That social class is a most useful organizing concept for a wealth of empirical data and uniformities that bear upon politically relevant opinions and attitudes as well as party membership and voter's choice is one of the most firmly established principles of political sociology. Granted that social classes in the contemporary context are no longer marked off by sharp boundaries and can be thought of as a vertical continuum consisting of some modal categories alternating with smaller transitional strata, there is nevertheless a substantially high correlation between social class, however measured, and ideological and behavioral variables that express and reflect political processes. Lipset (1963: chapter 7) argues in fact that the normal state of politics in Western democracies consists of the social class linked competition for political power by political parties. One can place party programs and ideologies on a left-right continuum. The parties of the left represent themselves as instruments of social change in the direction of greater equality—that is, they will support programs and legislation for reducing income differences, for leveling the style of life differences between the well-to-do and ordinary citizens, and for abolishing privileges and inequalities in political and civil rights—and they draw the bulk of their voters from the working and lower middle classes. The parties of the right draw the support of the well-to-do and support programs and legislation for maintaining the material advantages enjoyed by them. Parties of the left will tend to proclaim republican, secular, liberal, progressive, and socialist ideas, whereas parties of the right have been associated with the principles of monarchy, clericalism, conservatism, capitalism, and tradition. Left parties, especially in the contemporary setting, have been more concerned with establishing social justice and equality of fact; right parties with protecting freedom and equality of opportunity. The simplest explanation for these broad ideological differences that are expressed concretely in a number of national and regional variations is that they broadly reflect the economic interests and political aspirations of the bulk of the supporters of the respective political parties (Lipset, 1963: chapter 7).

Social class is both an objective reality, in the sense that social class of origin is correlated with one's subsequent life chances for education, income, occupation, quality of health care, life expectancy, even mental illness, and a subjective reality in the sense that awareness of social class exists. However, class awareness should not be confused with class consciousness. Class awareness refers to one's awareness that one is, for example, from the working class, that there are other people or groups who are better off materially and whose children get a better education, and so on. This awareness of differences need not be translated into hostility toward other classes or into a sense of victimization, and even when it is, need not lead to political action. Class consciousness, according to Mills (1951:325) means rational awareness and identification with one's own class interest, awareness and rejection of other class interests as illegitimate, belief in some basic Marxist doctrines, and readiness to use political means to realize common goals. Much of the support that political parties of the left receive from rank-and-file citizens is not based on class consciousness in Mills's specific sense, but on class awareness and folk conceptions of equality and inequality, moral ideas about what is right and what is wrong, what is deserved and undeserved, fair and unfair, in relation to material differences and life chances. Hadley Cantril has found that even hard-core Communist voters in France and Italy in the middle 1950s did not subscribe to most of the basic tenets of their party and of Marxism (Cantril, 1958). A higher proportion expected societal change to come about by evolution rather than by revolution. The vast majority were not concerned with workers' movements in other countries and did not identify with the struggles of the proletariat elsewhere. A majority even agreed that the employers they worked for were making normal rather than excessive profits. Nevertheless a majority were class aware, resentful of their low social status, and expressed a sense of injustice and of victimization. These emotional and moral sentiments precede and are more basic than the intellectual component of class consciousness, yet are nevertheless sufficient to lead to political behavior in support of the most antisystem and anticapitalist political party.

Research in the United States especially has established that although political party leaders and the college-educated population do have a fairly well spelled out and internally consistent ideology which corresponds to the world view of conservatism, liberalism, socialism as elaborated by political philosophers, the majority of the electorate when faced with a choice of party or candidate or with supporting or opposing concrete programs and legislation does not think and respond along ideological lines. Converse (1964:218) finds that only 11 percent of a random sample of American adults in the mid-1950s had an ideological or near-ideological level of conceptualization of the political process in the sense that they used a left-right, liberal-conservative yardstick consistently in their preference for parties, candidates, and legislation and in explaining the reason for their choices. By contrast 42 percent of the sample had a level of conceptualization described by Converse as expressing "group interests." It consists of an evaluation of parties and candidates in terms of their expected favorable or unfavorable impact upon different groups and social strata. People with this evaluative framework are aware of a conflict of interest between different groups such as business and labor, or rich people and working people, in the competition for scarce societal resources, and they locate parties and candidates according to whether they favor one or another of these groups. On issues that directly affect them and that have been subject of publicized controversy by the political leaders and opinion leaders, these rank-and-file citizens know where their own group interests lie and favor by and large a resolution of the issue in accordance with their own interests. But on other issues that do not affect their interests directly and visibly they do not consistently take a position consonant with their class position and with the ideology that "fits" their class position. The rest of the citizenry, almost one-half of the total adult population, do not respond to political issues within the framework of ideologies, class interests and group benefits.

Lest one think of the U.S. electorate as exceptional in this regard, similar studies in France lead Converse and Dupeux to write that (1967:3)

> the familiar characterization of French political culture as involving a number of highly ideological and principled political sub-cultures may be more a characterization of political elites than of the political mass. The French electorate appears to be quite a bit less ideologically oriented than one would expect from a consideration of the nature of political debates in the National Assembly of the Fourth Republic.

Indications are that this phenomenon is not a recent development due to a dampening of class conflict, the moderation of radical political leaders and the increased standard of life of the working class. One of the earliest studies of the aspirations and political views of workers conducted in 1908 in Germany found a similar state of affairs (Levenstein, 1912). At the time, Germany was a class society with the largest, best organized, and Marxist-oriented Socialist party supported by roughly 80 percent of the urban-industrial working class in the country. Yet, according to Levenstein, the hopes and wishes of over five thousand workers in the iron and steel industry, textiles and mining, was centered not on revolution but higher wages, socialist victories at the polls, better life for one's children, and the like. Max Weber commented on the 1908 Levenstein findings (1909:956) that "this material confirms at least for me the old experience that the manner of perception of the proletarian . . . is far more similar to that of the 'bourgeois' than the *a priori* class theorists think." Nevertheless, class awareness, perception of social injustice and of victimization, and the pursuit of group benefits was then and is still now a sufficient force to organize the electorate behind political leaders and parties who take a more calculated, rational, and consistent ideological position in the quest for political office and leadership.

It must be stressed at the cost of repetition that in understanding the appeal of social movements to the ordinary man, more than even the appeal of established political parties and orientations, it is the images of society, of right and wrong, justice and injustice, success, and other moral components of their view of the world and where they themselves are situated in it that actually matter and upon which the perceived legitimacy of their protest and demands rests. It is also the moral component of political ideologies that can shed light on the fact that those privileged strata who are a numerical minority in the population nevertheless are able to remain in political leadership positions even under conditions of universal suffrage. "Legitimacy," in Lipset's view (1963:64), "involves the capacity of the system to engender and maintain the belief that the existing political institutions are the most appropriate ones for the society." Legitimacy is provided through beliefs, values, and norms established between rulers and ruled about their mutual rights and obligations. The rulers, according to traditionalist views, are supposed to protect the people from foreign enemies, administer laws justly, maintain domestic peace and unity, make life bearable for ordinary people by creating favorable conditions for earning a decent living and by being accessible to ordinary folks with justified grievances. The people, on the other hand, are supposed to obey the laws, pay their taxes, show deference and remain loyal to the rulers, and engage in an orderly way of life. So long as the rulers followed the prescribed ways in which they were supposed to behave according to traditional views, their authority rested on a secure legitimate base. The rulers' or ruling groups' authority can of course be increased by the personal popularity of the incumbents, but popularity of leaders is not the same as legitimacy, since one can be opposed to a particular ruler or incumbent in office without questioning the legitimacy of institutional authority arrangements as such. As Weber has pointed out, authority can rest on other foundations than legitimacy alone, e.g., on fear, habit, and the material benefits it confers on those in subordinate positions. Yet any lasting and stable authority relationship will have a component of legitimacy. The drive to secure firmly and stabilize authority relations by the incumbents of privileged statuses accounts for the elaboration of systems of belief and moral ideas upon which legitimacy rests. In Weber's words (1958:271),

> the fortunate is seldom satisfied with the fact of being fortunate. Beyond this, he needs to know that he has a *right* to his good fortune. He wants to be convinced that he "deserves" it, and above all, that he deserves it in comparison with others. . . . Good fortune thus wants to be "legitimate" fortune. If the general term "fortune" covers all the "good" of honor, power, possession, and pleasure, it is the most general formula for the service of legitimation, which religion has had to accomplish for the external and the inner interests of all ruling men, the propertied, the victorious, and the healthy.

The most fundamental distinction in understanding the conception of society as a moral order is the concept of positively and negatively privileged social strata that Weber used throughout his sociology of religion, but which plays an equally key role in the analysis of secular ideologies.

> Strata in solid possession of social honor and power usually tend to fashion their status-legend in such a way as to claim a special and intrinsic

quality of their own, usually a quality of blood; their sense of dignity feeds on their actual or alleged being. The sense of dignity of socially repressed strata or of strata whose status is negatively valued is nourished most easily on the belief that a special "mission" is entrusted to them; their worth is guaranteed or constituted by an *ethical imperative*, or by their own functional *achievement*. (Weber, 1958:276)

Aristocracies have emphasized that their privileges and monopolies of political office and superordinate social positions are based on superior ascribed qualifications possessed by virtue of birth and heredity, i.e., that they were born to rule. Such a conception emphasizes the eternal, inevitable, God-ordained fact of inequality among men in society. Society works satisfactorily if all groups, no matter how exalted or humble, perform their God-ordained tasks in a satisfactory manner. The nobility should rule justly, and the garbage collector should collect the garbage regularly. The end result will be social harmony, and benefits will flow to all people, though benefits will necessarily be unequal in a hierarchic social order. So long as people do not aspire beyond the station into which they were born, the society will perform in a satisfactory manner for the common good. As long as subordinate groups accept this view of the social order and their own innate social and biological inferiority, the ruling groups' authority and privileged positions are secure. These conceptions of rights and duties and of the social order were typical of caste societies and of Western medieval political life based on estates rather than social classes. In medieval society, rights and liberties were not accorded to individuals but to groups, such as corporations and estates. Representation was through estates. The lowest-status people, journeymen, laborers, tenants, servants, had rights and enjoyed protection only by virtue of being members of a group headed by an upper-status master or lord who stood up for the welfare of his subjects (Bendix, 1964:55). The crisis in the medieval order occurred when the privileged groups increasingly evaded their traditional responsibility to their subjects, yet insisted on retaining their customary privileges at the same time. This development occurred both as a result of the economic changes associated with the growth of towns, commerce, and industry that led to the formation of new social strata that did not readily fit into the estate system and as a result of the growth of a national monarchy whose power rested on a centralized bureaucratic administration that took over the functions of justice, administration, public order, formerly exercised by the nobility (Schumpeter, 1955:144–45). Where the traditional patriarchal relations between lords and peasants on estates were replaced by a capitalist exploitation of estates based on wage labor without a corresponding shift in the conception of society and social relations, the medieval world view increasingly became a "false consciousness" in the sense of conceptions that no longer accurately mirrored the realities of relations between superior and subordinate and was bound to be challenged by alternative conceptions sooner or later, as happened in eighteenth-century Europe (Mannheim, 1936:96).

The medieval-aristocratic view of the social order was challenged by the bourgeois view of society as organized on the principle of the division of labor, social classes, and of unequal rewards based on individual achievement rather than on ascribed criteria (Heberle, 1951). In this view first put forward systematically by the Scottish moral philosophers, the division of labor necessary to operate the economy if it is to produce wealth and economic progress produces social strata and classes that enjoy unequal material rewards. However, location in the division of labor and the unequal system of rewards should be based on individual ability and achievement, not on inherited status. To develop the productive capacities of the society, the most able and hard working individuals should be able to rise to the top and thereby the entire economy and population would benefit. If there are differences in wealth and power between merchants and artisans, manufacturers and workers, landlords and tenants, it is because there simply is not enough wealth to reward everyone equally. Besides, if working people were to enjoy higher rewards for their work, they would stop working and production and progress would be brought to a halt to the detriment of all. Differences in material incentives and rewards must exist so that talented individuals are motivated to work hard and aspire to be upwardly mobile, thereby benefiting the entire society. By the same token the social system should be "open" in order to allow for the upward mobility of talent. The task of government should be to abolish all feudal and artificial privileges and monopolies that interfere with this ideal pursuit of happiness and personal advantage. People of low status should find this system acceptable, since through hard work and perseverance they can improve their social position and material level of living. The limits to inequality are given by the laws of supply and demand in a free market. Inefficient producers will not long be able to compete since they will be ruined. If an activity is particularly profitable for a time, many will enter this line of production and thus diminish the rewards obtained in it.

The ideology of economic liberalism, as it has frequently been called, was individualist rather than collective. It was future and progress oriented, stressed equality of opportunity but was tolerant of inequality in fact (Marshall, 1965). To be sure it did not hold that some people are naturally inferior and born to serve, but it blamed the losers for their misfortune. They were lazy or stupid, incapable or unwilling to take advantage of opportunities and self-improvement. Therefore, their lowly rewards were deserved. The image of society expressed in economic liberalism is that of a ladder or that of an elevator in a tall building by means of which hard working individuals can rise to higher rungs or floors where they obtain increased social status and material rewards. Although conservatives and humanitarians of the eighteenth and nineteenth centuries never accepted the legitimacy of this conception of the social order, it did become the prevailing view during the Industrial Revolution in Western Europe. Nevertheless, since the equality of opportunity proclaimed in it was a distortion of reality, the self-correcting economic mechanisms for checking the growth of steep inequalities did not operate as anticipated, and unhindered economic progress was set back by frequent depressions and a growing class of proletarians living at subsistence level, the middle-class conception of the social order was in its turn challenged by socialism.

According to the socialists, the source of all inequality is private property. Society is split into two camps, the property owners and the propertyless between whom a wide gulf exists. Property creates a permanent advantage to those possessing it and it provides them with the means of controlling the state and its officials. Capitalism is not a progressive economic system: it cannot stop periodic economic crises from lowering the overall material level of society nor can it raise the standard of life of the working masses. It is not that the individual capitalists are evil men who are personally to blame for the sad condition of the workers. They themselves are trapped by the system. If they paid higher wages than was prevalent in their industry because of humanitarian inclinations, they would be ruined by their competitors. If private property were abolished by socializing the means of production, the sources of inequality would be abolished. In a socialist and progressive economic system, economic crises would no longer occur, and there is no reason, moral or economic, why a factory worker, accountant, and manager could not live in the same type of home and enjoy equal hours of leisure. The class struggle was inevitable since private property would not be abolished by persuading the bourgeoisie to surrender their material and social advantages without the use of force. The socialist view is that failure to improve one's social position and material condition is not due to personal shortcomings but to the flaws inherent in a class society based on the capitalist mode of production. The working class has a historic "mission" to accomplish, namely, to usher in the classless society with its equal distribution of rewards. While the division of labor is necessary, its efficient operation need not rest on unequal incentives and rewards.

These three conceptions of society as a moral order were not formulated by any one writer or philosopher; rather, they are a synthesis of the thoughts of many individuals associated with the conservative, liberal, and socialist philosophies formulated and reformulated during the nineteenth century. Each of these conceptions in its many different variations is still held by some groups, and each is grounded in basic values that enjoy widespread legitimacy. That the principles of equality and of achievement or of freedom and social justice can all be considered legitimate and desirable, yet lead to contradictions, different goals and institutional arrangements, and social conflict in concrete implementation and application, derives from the fact that values are only very generally defined and are subject to differing interpretation and that the value system of a society is made up of potentially inconsistent elements if pursued to their ultimate logical consequences (Parsons, 1951:293–97). Therefore, it is not surprising that ordinary individuals in the same social class or groups do not all hold the same conception of the social order and may, indeed, hold views that historically and objectively are associated with the rise and position of a social class other than the one they belong to. Thus, an aristocracy might maintain itself in political power even under conditions of universal suffrage because large sections of the peasantry and some sectors of the working and middle classes accept as legitimate its conception of the social order and its claim to leadership by virtue of superior qualification based on heredity and tradition. Other groups accept the world view of the class they aspire to belong to rather than the class they in fact objectively belong to. Still other people do not have any definite conceptions at all, are basically apolitical or religiously oriented. Most countries have regional differences in economic and social structure, with some areas considerably more traditional and backward than the most economically developed areas. Movements of population from backward to developed areas ensures that conceptions of the social order associated with an earlier historical period might still be found in the advanced regions, continuously brought there by the migrants' families.

Much useful empirical information on conceptions of the social order has been summarized by Dahrendorf (1959:280–89). In particular, he refers to a study of unionized steel workers by Popitz in the 1950s in West Germany, a group among whom one might expect a high degree of class awareness and political sophistication. Popitz and his collaborators found that roughly 10 percent of the steel workers had a conception close to what has been described as the medieval-aristocratic. Society is seen as a fixed order into which individuals are born. Their self-esteem and material rewards result from a proper execution of the tasks, no matter how lowly, to which they are assigned and which they always will perform. Twenty-five percent had a conception close to "bourgeois" economic liberalism, the conception of a hierarchic yet open social order in which an individual can improve his life chances by hard work and perseverance and thus rise to a higher status. Another 25 percent had a socialist conception that stressed the gulf that separates workers from the middle and upper classes, although the element of class conflict was not prominent in it. In this view, the workers are in a perpetual underdog position that can only be improved through collective class action. The remaining 40 percent of the steel workers had either no clear conceptions of the social order or other mixed and partial perceptions. In particular some 10 percent tended to blame their subordinate status not on the social system but on their own intellectual or moral shortcomings. These findings illustrate the survival and perpetuation of world views developed in earlier centuries in conjunction with the rise of other social classes among contemporary working people.

In the United States, except for Lane's (1962) study in depth of fifteen New Haven working-class males, little in the way of probing the conceptions of the social order has been done. In line with earlier findings, Lane found that his respondents supported specific measures embraced in the formula of the "welfare state" that have egalitarian consequences in terms of income distribution, yet they also believed that what a man gets should be a result of his own efforts and that, by and large, what they are getting and what others are getting are deserved. He found little sympathy extended to those who are in the lower and under-class, who were thought to have only themselves to blame for their misfortune. Lane also uncovered the belief that complete equality of income would deprive men of an incentive to achieve and to develop their skills (Lane, 1962:60–69).

An unpublished study by Elinson (1967) in a prosperous working-class area in Los Angeles county supports Lane's earlier findings for New Haven. Elinson in particular noted that most of his respondents could point to a life of hardship, perseverance, and hard work during which they rose to their present status as skilled and well-paid workers and as home owners. There was little sympathy or understanding expressed for the plight of the black urban poor who were thought to be living off welfare and other handouts paid out of the pockets of law-abiding, respectable, hard working, and financially squeezed working people. The under-class, in this view, is an under-class because it simply does not make the effort needed to improve its condition. On top of that, rather than being grateful for welfare and urban programs, the ghetto dweller riots. These conceptions of American working people reflect the nineteenth-century view of economic liberalism rather faithfully.

In sum, most people do not possess an articulated and intellectualized political ideology. Class-based politics and the competition for political power and office proceed without, and do not need to be sustained by, a consistent political ideology on the part of all rank-and-file citizens. Simplified versions of competing and conflicting world views survive in the collective consciousness of social classes and strata together with religious ideas and folk conceptions. A large number of working people will subscribe to views formulated by upper- and middle-class publicists and ideologists and not to views formulated during the rise of the labor movement by socialist and labor leaders. It is a reasonable assumption that a majority of negatively privileged groups and classes do not ordinarily have a "revolutionary" ideology or conception of the social order and that they are in fact frequently inclined in a conservative direction. The notion that equality and freedom will automatically appeal to those in subordinate positions is mistaken. They only become acceptable after some preexisting and competing conceptions have been shaken and displaced. To many traditional peasants, the idea that they are equal to or ought to have equal rights with noblemen or townspeople is at first a totally foreign conception contradicted by their daily experience. When in the 1860s and 1870s in Russia, the young populist idealists "attempted to go to the people [as revolutionary agitators, or for social service as doctors or nurses, or simply as manual workers], the peasants in many instances received these missionaries from the other orders of society with a marked suspicion, and in certain cases even betrayed them to the police" (Robinson, 1967:139). Following these unsuccessful attempts to mobilize the peasantry, the professional revolutionists turned to assassination and terror as the means of overthrowing the Tsarist government. Nevertheless, after four decades that saw the 1905 revolution, the First World War and the 1917 revolution, and during which considerable mobilization took place, these same peasants, in November of 1917 in a relatively free election based on universal suffrage, voted in overwhelming numbers for the two most revolutionary parties, the Bolsheviks and the Social Revolutionaries, the direct successors of the populists of the 1860s and 1870s, because these parties stood for ending the war and turning over the land to the peasant (Radkey, 1950).

The traditionalist views of negatively privileged groups are, therefore, not unalterable, nor do many protest and opposition movements take place under the stimulus of novel, revolutionary ideas. Indeed, as Rudé has shown (1964: chapter 14), the ideas of protesters are frequently backward looking and traditionalist; nevertheless, their actions undermine the present order and help usher in a new one. Other opposition movements are simply a reaction to oppressive conditions, increased hardship, and violations of traditional norms and custom on the part of the authorities or ruling groups. To state the matter differently, ideas that can justify opposition and protest are never in short supply, for traditionalist, religious, and conservative conceptions and norms can be and often have been invoked to sustain protest in the absence of revolutionary ideas. Whether a movement can do more than merely disrupt the social order or correct immediate abuses depends on the presence of leadership and organization that can channel and sustain popular energies in a constructive direction. Ideas, values, and goals are never inherently revolutionary. It is the means used to implement these values and goals that may or may not have revolutionary consequences, and the means used grow out of the confrontation itself. The means used depend not on the goals, but what reception the goals and demands of the protesters get in the society. If legitimate, peaceful means are used, but the protesters are repressed or fail to get satisfaction, the chances of illegitimate and violent means increase, whatever the goals of the protesters. The partial repression of a peaceful movement or its inability to achieve goals will tend to bring to the fore a new orientation in the movement, an orientation to acquire "power" as a prerequisite for securing the original goals (Turner and Killian, 1957). The shift from Martin Luther King's "I have a dream" orientation to the black power ideology within the black movement in the U.S. is an example of this process.

PEASANT SOCIAL ORGANIZATION, IDEOLOGY AND REVOLT

To illustrate the point that revolutionary ideas and radical ideologies are not required to create revolts and rebellion, it is useful to examine the relationships between peasant social organization and peasant conceptions of the social order and to describe how peasant folk ideas can come to legitimize movements of revolt among rural folk. Peasants have generally been characterized as conservative and tradition bound, xenophobic and suspicious of outsiders, opposed to novel ideas and to innovation. Yet, recent history abounds in peasant uprisings and peasant movements that have contributed to the major social changes of our time. There need be no paradox if it is understood that peasants revolt in order to resist changes forced upon them from the outside and to defend and reestablish their time-honored way of life. Peasants, like other groups, strive for security, which their communal way of life has provided for them. Changes forced on the peasant do not usually enhance their material welfare and their sense of security. Therefore, they will collectively resist most such attempts. While the clock cannot be turned back in the way the peasant intends, the force of peasant resistance and revolt can undermine the social control apparatus and weaken the economy of a regime to such an extent that other opposition groups are given the opportunity of overthrowing the ruling classes and of instituting a new social system. This crucial "swing role" of the peasantry in a period of wider social upheaval has been recognized especially by Huntington (1968:291–93). Unfortunately the peasants' lot does not necessarily improve even when they have been the major instrument of political and social change.

At the outset one must distinguish between several classes of agricultural producers. Farmers are the owner-operators of a family business enterprise dealing in agricultural commodities. They are fully committed and dependent upon the market economy. They obtain their capital, their means of production, and labor over and above the family through the market. They reinvest part of their earnings in their business; they buy consumer goods, much of their food and services, from merchants and professionals located in small towns. Farmers are well known for their capacity to form associations and political parties for defending their interests against urban-based banks, land speculators, the railroads, the urban consumer, and other nonfarm interests upon whom their livelihood depends. Farmers seek easy credit, cheap storage and transportation costs, high prices for agricultural commodities, tariff protection against low cost foreign agricultural producers. They are opposed to the expenditure of public funds to finance costly social welfare projects benefiting the urban masses. When their main opponents are urban-based financial monopolies and their local agents who seek to control the marketing of agricultural commodities, agricultural credit, transportation, and the distribution of consumer and capital goods needed by the farmers, they will band into cooperative marketing associations, sponsor credit unions and farmers' banks, open cooperative stores, and form political alliances with left-leaning political parties that are opposed to the same financial and industrial organizations within the context of nationwide class-linked party politics. If, on the other hand, the farmers' main opponent is a socialist government that favors the urban working class by keeping food prices down and instituting costly, subsidized social welfare programs, farmers will seek out allies on the political right. Farmers get considerable help in leadership and organization from small-town merchants and professionals whose own prosperity and careers depend largely on the standard of life of the farming communities that surround them.

Unlike the peasants who are conscious of being in a negatively privileged, low-status social category and are looked down upon as ignorant country bumpkins by city people and officials, the small independent farmer becomes frequently the bearer of a positive social ethos that glorifies the virtues of hard work, self-reliance, advancement through individual effort, and the moral integrity, simplicity, and neighborliness of the rural community. These positive traits are contrasted to the decadent, morally corrupting ways of the city where vice, greed, and moneymaking prevail, where the profit motive is king and financial gain takes precedence over all human relationships. During times of social dislocation and national crisis, urban intellectuals in the grip of social malaise romanticize and glorify these rural virtues that in their eyes have accounted for the glorious achievements in the nation's past. To them, the uncorrupted farmers still form the moral backbone of the nation, a last bastion that must be saved at all cost and must become the rallying point for a moral crusade against Communism, Marxism, Jewry, foreigners, capitalists, and all the other underminers of national strength, corrupters of ethnic purity, and agents of material and moral decadence. Under conditions of extreme economic hardship and insecurity, when small independent farmers are collectively threatened with loss of land and livelihood, it can happen that they become susceptible to these intellectuals' and propagandists' appeals and thus come to play a reactionary role in national political life, as indeed happened in much of rural Germany at the end of the Weimar Republic. When farmers are not under such economic strain and not so readily accessible to outside political propaganda, their moral energies are spent in local political disputes and controversies. The conflict between the fundamentalist church and the saloon so characteristic of rural communities in the American Bible Belt is a typical example of this process.

In contrast to farmers, peasants are poor and illiterate and make use of a low level of agricultural technology. Nevertheless, it is their labor and their agricultural output that sustain the ruling classes, the court, and the officialdom of preindustrial societies. Unlike agricultural laborers who constitute a landless rural proletariat, peasants do retain considerable control of land through ownership, undisputed squatter rights, and customary rights governing the rental and use of land (Wolf, 1955:454). Peasants live in a partially monetized economy and do produce partly for the external world to which their standard of living and economic well-being are thus linked. They have frequently revolted against excessive taxation and exactions, forced military conscription, and encroachments upon their communal lands and traditional rights. Peasants have had little reason to expect anything but trouble and hardship from the agents of the outside world. They have therefore been hostile to outsiders and intensely local in their concerns and orientation. It is outside groups, the state and its officials, the local nobility and landlord class, foreign settlers following upon the heels of missionaries, traders, and colonial military conquest, who have set in motion the assaults on the peasants' way of life, which eventually result in collective movements of resistance and revolt.

According to mobilization theory, organizational and ideological conditions favorable for resistance against the imposition of foreign rule exist when peasant communal solidarity is strong and the relationships between peasant commoners and their chiefs or traditional rulers are still viable and mutually beneficial. On the other hand, peasant revolt against an indigenous ruling class will be likely to occur when the vertical links between lord and commoner have been severed but for one-sided exploitative economic relationships even as peasant social organization is still vigorous.

The relationship between peasant commoner and indigenous chief or local nobility rests on traditional authority and is regarded as legitimate and mutually advantageous for both groups. While the commoner's labor sustains the superior life-style of the ruling group and deference is paid to their superior status, the exploitative potential of the superior-subordinate relationship is circumscribed and limited by the collective rights of the peasants. The ruling groups are responsible for the administration of justice, for mobilizing and leading the community against outside invaders, for organizing raiding parties against neighbors, and for distributing the war booty. They carry out ritual functions necessary for ensuring the prosperity of the community according to the prevalent religious beliefs. Commoners can count on material assistance in case of need. They derive a sense of ethnic identity and local pride from the power of their chiefs and rulers. These beliefs and sentiments set them apart from neighboring peoples. There are, of course, good and bad overlords. While the social control exercised by commoners upon the ruling group varies a great deal from place to place, bad rulers can usually be resisted and deposed and others vested with authority by resorting to means sanctified in tradition. Such peoples and communities are frequently at war with other neighboring peoples similarly organized. The rules for succession to chieftainship and for assuming privileged status are flexible enough to give rise to frequent rivalries and open clashes within the ruling group. It is these weaknesses that are exploited by a foreign power during the imposition of colonial rule when it makes alliances with subject peoples or the losing faction in a succession struggle. Thus, a numerically small band of well-armed foreigners can conquer a vast indigenous population with the help of local allies, as has happened on the occasion of the Spanish conquest of Mexico, and so often since then.

In addition to the relation of superior to subordinate, the horizontal links binding the peasants to each other must be described in order to understand peasant social organization. The peasant community is composed of all adult males or heads of households who collectively exercise control over communal lands either directly or through a symbolic intermediary such as a chief. There exist clearcut boundaries separating insiders from outsiders. Membership is ascribed and includes rights that guarantee the means of livelihood through access to land, to pasture, to water and firewood, though the concrete details of these rights vary a great deal. Members, however, do not have the right to sell communal land assigned to them as their share. Thus there exists but an imperfect market in land for the community well senses that unchecked private property in land would spell its doom. In Latin America, a variant of this form of social organization, the "corporate peasant community," has been well described and analyzed by Wolf (1955). In Africa, it has continued to exist after the imposition of colonial rule and has come down to the present, except where foreign settlers have forcefully expropriated African land. In prerevolutionary France and Russia, even in the face of commercial exploitation of rural properties by landlords and the growth of a class of medium peasants with individual property rights in land, elements of this form of social organization were preserved. Historically the peasant community was given legal status and political and administrative functions by a central government interested in limiting the local power of landlords, a hereditary nobility, or immigrant settlers. At the same time such an arrangement could be utilized to make collective labor and financial demands upon the peasant community as a whole while keeping the costs of administration low.

The peasant community is at once egalitarian and conservative. It is egalitarian since it ensures that every member shall have a guaranteed minimum means of livelihood and that no member shall become enriched at the expense of others. It is conservative since it negatively sanctions individual ambition, innovation, and enterprise in order to prevent any of its members from consolidating a permanent advantage over others. The institutions through which the leveling of wealth and social differences is accomplished have been observed in many peasant communities throughout the world (Nash, 1966:78–79; Wolf, 1955:458): systems of inheritance that result in the distribution of accumulated goods among a number of heirs; the custom of forcing prosperous peasants to expend their wealth on communal ritual rather than on private ends; the norms pressuring individuals to support needy kinsmen; periodic redistribution of communal lands. The detailed operation of these institutions differs from place to place. These practices are supported by institutionalized envy, malicious gossip, witchcraft beliefs and accusations, the threat of boycott and ostracism, and even the use of violence. Strongly internalized community norms backed up by social control perpetuate the conservative and egalitarian aspects of peasant society. At the same time these institutions assure its continuity in time and its tenacity against inside and outstide forces seeking to undermine it.

The peasants' conservative institutions are reenforced by a pessimistic world view that has been called the "image of the limited good" by George Foster (1965:296–97). It is a conception of the world in which all of the desired things in life such as land, wealth, health, friendship and love, manliness and honor, respect and status, power and influence, security and safety, exist in finite quantities and are in short supply, as far as the peasant is concerned . . . in addition, there is no way directly within the peasant power to increase the available quantities . . . it follows that an individual or family can improve a position only at the expense of others. Hence, relative improvement in someone's position with respect to any "good" is viewed as a threat to the entire community.

Such an outlook reflects the realities of poverty and low productivity resulting from the low level of agricultural technology, exploitation by outsiders, scarcity of land, high mortality rates, vulnerability to natural disasters, and the uncertainties of the weather.

Thus, the peasant community is by no means the harmonious utopia described by romantic writers. There is a great deal of envy, mistrust, character assassination, competition between families, disputes over land, and other forms of interpersonal conflict. Individual success is thought to have been gained at the expense of others; failure is explained with reference to the malevolence and machinations of particular individuals. Leaders are mistrusted and are expected to exploit their position at the expense of ordinary folk. Followers are attracted to leaders because they might gain an immediate advantage and readily shift their allegiance to others if it is not forthcoming. In such a community, it is very difficult to create associations for the pursuit of community welfare and improvement. The concept of disinterested service for community-wide goals is lacking (Bailey, 1966; Banfield, 1958). Nevertheless, the peasants are attached to their way of life and stubbornly defend their communal institutions and rights against the forces of change.

The degree of resistance put up by peasant peoples against foreign rule will vary. If foreign rule means foreign settlement of land that is the basis of livelihood, if the people are forced to supply labor for settler agriculture, mining ventures, and public works, if they are forced to become economically productive by having to grow crops that will benefit the colonial interests of the conquering power, and if their chiefs or rulers who resist this process of subjugation are humiliated and deposed, revolt led by the chiefs and existing military formations will erupt in the name of defending the independence and integrity of the traditional community. If, on the other hand, foreign rule does not threaten land and livelihood, if the indigenous ruling groups are continued in office under a policy of indirect rule and their authority is recognized by means of alliances more or less freely entered upon, or else if foreign domination means protection against the raiding parties of more powerful neighbors, foreign rule can be gradually extended without military conquest and may even be welcome. In short, to the extent that the basic peasant social organization is not threatened by foreign rule and the peasants' security and means of livelihood are maintained, primary resistance movements are less likely to occur.

Peasant revolts against their traditional overlords occur when the earlier relationships based on reciprocity and mutual advantage have yielded to purely economic relationships between a landlord class and a peasantry still maintaining strong horizontal communal bonds. In terms of mobilization theory, the peasantry's vertical links with other social classes have been broken with the result that redress for peasant grievances can no longer be obtained through access to upper-status groups who used to defend the peasant interest. The peasantry is then forced back on its own internal resources to stand up for its collective rights.

Such a development is frequently the end product of a long chain of events. During the long period of struggle for power between a central government and the provincial nobility that typifies the emergence of an absolutist state from a feudal society, royal officials of the central government take over the administrative, judicial, and welfare functions formerly exercised by the hereditary nobility. The nobility and gentry nevertheless remain on the land in the capacity of landlords. They maintain their claim on the peasants' output and manage to take their economic surplus but provide them nothing in return. Consequently the legitimacy of the overlords' hereditary status and traditional rights is increasingly questioned not as a result of novel ideologies spread by the urban intelligentsia but because the norms of reciprocity and equity on which lasting social relationships are founded are unilaterally ignored and abrogated (B. Moore, 1966: chapter 9).

There are additional factors that at the same time increase the hardship of the peasantry. The process of state formation is an expensive undertaking. The central government raises additional revenue to pay for an expanding staff of officials, a modernized army, and for ambitious programs of public works and improvements. A large portion of the needed revenues are usually squeezed out of the peasantry. As the nobility and gentry are stripped of their leadership roles, they take up residence at the court and in towns where their expenditures increase to the point of perpetual indebtedness to merchants, bankers, and the urban middle class. Consequently, they seek to reverse their declining economic fortunes by increasing peasant dues and reviving long-forgotten feudal rights. Some may seek to exploit their estates in a more profitable commercial way; others sell or rent their land to urban creditors who then proceed with large-scale commercial exploitation of the newly acquired properties. The best local land may thus pass into the hands of outsiders. During this process, many peasants are evicted from the land in violation of their rights of tenure; the commons are enclosed or encroached upon; a market in land develops. Peasants are collectively forced to become agricultural laborers or to accept the insecurity of new tenure arrangements. Some become rural cottagers, others migrate to the towns. Much land in the meanwhile may be held uncultivated for speculative purposes while demographic pressures aggravate the land hunger of the small peasants.

The more fortunate richer peasants manage to buy some of the land. They become the capitalist exploiters of medium-sized holdings and hire the labor of their less fortunate neighbors. Their economic security and material well-being no longer depend on the security provided by communal rights and the reciprocity relationships of peasant social organization but on their own abilities, their own individual effort, and on their property rights. Thus, the decline of the nobility and the penetration of commercial agriculture and capitalist exploitation of the land create social classes within the once relatively undifferentiated peasantry—the peasant community is threatened from both within and without. As Eric Wolf (1969: Conclusion) has emphasized, peasant revolt is a defensive reaction against the loss of social and economic security resulting from the weakening of the traditional peasant community under the impact of market forces at a time when the traditional ruling groups no longer protect the peasant against these disruptive changes and have in fact turned against him. Depending on how far the process of class formation has proceeded, peasants take up arms either to reestablish the traditional peasant social organization or to establish themselves as a class of small holders.

There is no lack of ideas and precedents for revolt in peasant folk culture. The figure of an outlaw-hero who takes from the rich to distribute among the poor is well established in peasant folklore. So is that of the good king, benevolent Tsar and protector who would punish wicked officials and come to the peasants' rescue if he only knew the hardships they suffer. Peasants frequently address petitions to their supreme protector for the redress of grievances, and only after their voice goes unheard do they rise in revolt. But while such figures provide the peasant movement with models of personal heroism, feats of courageous opposition against exploiting outsiders, and with anarchist goals for destroying all outside authority that has been imposed upon them, they do not serve as models for organizing the peasant movement itself or the wider society that is temporarily at their mercy.

Peasant social organization and communal solidarity, with its strong egalitarian bias and sanctions against individual differences of status, wealth, and power within the community, is incapable of becoming the foundation for lasting and hierarchic organization needed for the implementation of major social changes against determined opposition. According to Womack (1969), the Zapatista movement during the Mexican revolution was concerned first and foremost with the restitution of communal lands grabbed by the *hacendados* to the villages and with the abolition of the hacienda system of landlord exploitation. It lacked a broader conception of a Mexico-wide social revolution. The Zapatistas were at a loss on what strategy to pursue once they were in control outside of their home state of Morelos. In this the Zapatistas were typical of many peasant movements. Peasants will burn manors to the ground, they will make bonfires of the documents in which their debts and feudal obligations are recorded—then they will return to their villages and fields believing that they have rid themselves of oppression. Peasant bands melt away during the months when their labor is required for tilling, planting, and harvesting in their villages, or else they disperse after each defensive action to reassemble on the occasion of another threat. The fury of peasant revolt and the specter of anarchism frighten potential allies into backing the authorities, and more often than not a peasant rebellion is repressed in a bloodbath that exceeds in savagery the worst of the peasants' own previous actions.

Chapter VI

MOBILIZATION, LEADERS, AND FOLLOWERS IN THE CIVIL RIGHTS MOVEMENT IN THE UNITED STATES, 1950 TO 1970

AN OUTLINE OF EVENTS

It is not my intention to provide a complete descriptive account of every aspect of the civil rights movement and black revolt. This has frequently and competently been written and has been updated continuously by many authors and commentators. Instead, I wish to bring to bear on this movement some of the tools developed earlier in order to clarify certain questions that have so far not been answered in a satisfactory manner: what accounts for the twists and turns, the timing of various phases and changes in the movement's course? How is it that the lack of militant protest leaders in the 1950s suddenly gave way to an abundance, if not oversupply, of such leaders and to a proliferation of new protest organizations? What are the characteristics of the new leaders, and what sorts of people did they displace? Why did the black masses first become activated for the civil rights movement in the South rather than the North, and why did mass protest in the North erupt in riots in the middle 1960s? What factors account for the patterns of support for and opposition to the movement? Just what relationships were there between the economic standing, gains, and losses of various black social strata and their participation and active support of different aspects and phases of the civil rights and black movement during this period?

The period under investigation can be divided for the sake of convenience into several periods. During the depression class and labor issues predominated over race issues as the number one problem and focus of attention in the United States. Roosevelt's New Deal reforms benefited the blacks indirectly as one of several low-income, working-class groups. Indeed, these gains resulted in the blacks' massive support of the Democratic party in the North at that time. At the same time, because blacks were then still more rural than urban and heavily concentrated in the nonindustrial South, as a group they did not lose as much during the depression as other more urban and industrial groups. Many Americans at this time lived close to or on the margins of subsistence, and "outside" resources to be used in mobilization were being pumped into labor unions, not into black protest organizations as such. The combination of low economic level, lack of outside leadership and financial resources coming in from outside the black group, the absence of programs and goals that would benefit blacks specifically aside from goals and programs benefiting all working-class Americans, and the lack of national attention devoted to specifically black problems, all made for a relatively quiescent period during the depression up to 1940, so far as black protest and civil rights activities are concerned.

The following period, from World War II to about 1949, finds the black caught up in a high wage and low unemployment economy, which put him into a favorable bargaining position and which resulted in the large-scale migration from the rural South into the Southern and Northern cities. While class and race problems faded into the background in the face of the great national effort to win the war, black militancy was on the rise and the federal government, because of its increased power and involvement in running the wartime economy, was in an especially favorable position to initiate changes in race relations. As a result of black pressures, a willingness to act to preserve national unity in war, and the increased importance of black votes for the Democratic party, the federal government reversed its prewar policy of tacitly condoning established local racial practices. This period saw the March on Washington movement for jobs in national defense industries and for integration in the armed forces under Philip Randolph's militant leadership, the 1943 urban race riots that bore a striking resemblance to the World War I and 1919 riots and that resulted both from the frictions brought about by the sudden influx of Southern blacks into Northern cities and the increased competition for jobs and living space, the creation of CORE in 1943, and the push to establish a Fair Employment Practices Commission (FEPC), to integrate the armed forces, and to end discrimination in federal employment, which were all accomplished by executive orders of President Truman.

The third period of 1949–1954 is again a quiescent period insofar as a civil rights movement conducted by protest leaders and activities was lacking, though behind the scenes the NAACP was vigorously pursuing black civil rights and equality of opportunity goals in the courts. In fact not much was left of the mass protest movement of the previous period, and the NAACP membership declined to 200,000 from the wartime high of about 500,000 (Bennett, 1966:181) when dues were raised from $1 to $2. Why did the activism of the war and immediate postwar years not carry over into the early 1950s? First of all, the Korean war economic boom benefited the black working people in the North, and as a result of World War II and the subsequent economic and occupational changes the black middle class was beginning to expand and to consolidate its first gains. The Eisenhower administration appointed some blacks to high posts, black judges were put on the bench at all levels of government, public facilities in Washington, D.C., and a number of Northern and Midwestern cities were desegregated as a result of litigation and sit-ins conducted by the NAACP and CORE respectively. But these activities received scant publicity and national attention compared to the cold war hysteria and McCarthyism that was then sweeping the country and that put all "leftist" and protest organizations on the defensive: "The NAACP, the Urban League, and the liberal establishment began cleaning house, barring communists and silencing radicals. Picketing and mass demonstration became a dangerous form of dissent. The word masses assumed an ugly meaning; and polite protest was enshrined as the only means of struggle." (Bennett, 1966:168). The subsequent white allies of the black movement, the liberals, the upper middle class, the affluent liberal Protestant churches, and the students, were either on the defensive or apathetic. Meanwhile, the black migration into Northern cities continued unabated.

The next phase starts with the 1954 Supreme Court school desegregation decision and the one-year period of grace for its implementation, and extends until 1960 when the student sit-in movement began. The 1954 decision was a visible sign to blacks that the white establishment and federal government were supporting the legal road to changing their subordinate position. Nineteen fifty-four represents the reform-from-above plan that so often in history has preceded the more militant and active mass phase in the social movement of a negatively privileged group for greater equality and more rights that followed its checkmate. The checkmate in this case resulted from the Southern resistance and countermovement, ranging all the way from the Southern governors and legislatures to the White Citizens' Councils and widespread illegal repression and terror. The high hopes and wait-and-see attitudes of blacks after 1954 gave way to increased disillusionment and dissatisfaction with the substance and pace of desegregation sponsored by the federal government, the white liberal establishment, and the NAACP and moderate Northern leadership. The Montgomery bus boycott movement, which in its tactics and mass base belongs to the subsequent period, also revealed the modest gains that could be achieved at a high price in the face of Southern resistance. At the same time, on the economic front, the Eisenhower recession took effect, with the 5 percent nonwhite national unemployment rate in 1951–1953 edging up to a 7–9 percent rate in the years 1954 to 1957 that was to jump to a 10–12 percent nonwhite unemployment rate in the last years of the Eisenhower administration and the Kennedy years 1960–1963.

The next period, 1960 to 1964 and 1965, starting with the black college student sit-in movement and continuing until the defeat of the SNCC voter registration drive in the South and the Los Angeles-Watts riot of 1965, sees the active mass protest phase led by the new militant but nonviolent civil rights leadership with the Reverend Martin Luther King, Jr., in prominence and the proliferation of new civil rights associations and leaders helped by liberal white churchmen and students. Their activities captured the support and enthusiasm of liberal and progressive world opinion. Their finest day was the 1963 March on Washington, and their greatest legislative victories were the 1964 Civil Rights Act and the 1965 Voting Rights Act. At the same time, while the desegregation of public accommodations in the South both prior to and following the 1964 Civil Rights Act resulted in very concrete benefits to Southern middle-class blacks, and the black middle class made impressive occupational and economic gains, the economic condition of the majority of lower-class urban blacks either remained stationary or worsened at a time of increased national prosperity, despite the War on Poverty. The legislative victories provided no tangible benefits and relief for the central problems facing Northern working- and lower-class blacks, beyond symbolic satisfaction. Attempts by the new civil rights leadership and organizations to mobilize the black urban masses remained by and large unsuccessful because these organizations had a Southern base and because their efforts at improving housing and job opportunities for blacks in the North were met by increased resistance from Northern whites whose enthusiasm for the black cause was considerably weaker when the satisfaction of black aspirations would require a change in their way of life rather than of Southerners, and because the solution to the problems produced by de facto segregation and the goal of integration are considerably more intractable and costly than was true for desegregation in the South.

The next and final period here considered, which was coming to an end about 1970, covers the urban riots extending from 1964 to the riot wave following Martin Luther King's assassination in 1968 and saw the rise of militant-radical leaders and organizations outbidding each other in their extreme demands and militant rhetoric and turning against the moderate leadership; the falling apart of the early 1960s civil rights coalition with white students and radicals, who were becoming far more concerned with opposing the Johnson administration over the Vietnam war; the rise of black nationalism among the black students; the increased use of threats by black militants to keep in the limelight; and the acceptance of the philosophy of violent self-defense and violent overthrow or at least attack upon the structure of American society by a small yet substantial proportion of young black and white activists. At the same time, in the latter 1960s, the Northern migration of blacks slowed and later halted for the first time since World War II, and the economic standing of the black working class, but not of the "underclass," improved markedly. The oft-predicted white backlash never materialized on the scale predicted by most observers, blacks made impressive gains in voter registration in the South, won positions at all levels in government everywhere including the Deep South either on their own or in coalition with liberal white voters as in Cleveland and some other cities, while the Nixon administration and police all over the country began a policy of suppressing militant white and black groups such as the Chicago eight and the Black Panthers. What the future has in store for the black movement and what the economic and integration prospects of blacks are will be outlined after a more detailed analysis of the mobilization processes and leader-follower relationships during the two eventful decades of the 1950s and 1960s.

Any such analysis must begin with a recognition of the fact that blacks did not constitute in 1950 nor did they twenty years later constitute a homogeneous and undifferentiated mass of people with similar economic and political interests, but that considerable regional and class variations have existed and, indeed, have become accentuated among them. Following from this observation one must recognize that many of the problems of the blacks that have been perceived and discussed both in popular and in scholarly discourse under the label of "race" problems and white racism were and are in fact class issues and class problems not peculiar to blacks as such in the United States but similar to problems faced by lower-class, low income people everywhere regardless of race or ethnicity. Perceptive black and white intellectuals like Bayard Rustin and Arthur Lewis, Nathan Glazer and Daniel Patrick Moynihan, have always recognized this fact, but theirs has been a minority point of view. Furthermore, so far as blacks in the United States are concerned, and no matter which social stratum they are from, it has never been in dispute that throughout the period 1950–1970, or indeed throughout their history in slavery or in freedom, they have been a negatively privileged, exploited minority with many legitimate grievances, who, despite a facade of acceptance of their subordinate status, had nevertheless to be kept down by superior force, physical and economic coercion, and legal sanctions where segregation existed. Although the social and economic position of various black strata did change up and down over time, the common and constant level of legitimate grievances was certainly high enough throughout the period to provide potential mass support for protest movements. What then explains changes in the intensity and scope of protest activity among blacks and its geographic distribution at any given time are changes of leadership, of outside support, government policies, public opinion support, the loosening of social control and its impact on the risk/reward ratios, which are all linked to changes in the socioeconomic position of various black groups.

THE BLACK SOCIAL STRUCTURE

What were the social structure, the leadership groups, the associations and the community characteristics, the resources of the black population in the 1940s, and how did these change during the period under review? In the 1940s, most black men were still heavily in agricultural occupations; others were in semiskilled and unskilled jobs; and only a tiny minority of less than 5 percent were professionals and otherwise enjoyed a middle-class life-style by American standards. Blacks were thus a lower-class population group with no independent economic and geographic base. Studies of black leaders (Winston, 1931–1932; Monahan and Monahan, 1956) indicate that they were found in medicine, the ministry, education, and only a small fraction in business. In time, the absolute size of the black leadership group as well as of the middle class increased somewhat. More of them were in government, in the civil service, in social agencies, in race relations organizations, and in teaching, especially in the South. Yet the precarious economic base and vulnerability of the black population at all levels stand out sharply. Teachers, educators, and civil servants were in positions dependent upon white-controlled agencies and boards. The black working class was in the lowest paid income category and dependent upon white employers, in the cities as well as on the farms.

By 1960, changes in the black labor force composition (down to 15 percent in agriculture and a roughly twofold increase in the percentage of middle class and professional occupations) reflect the large migration from rural South into Southern and Northern cities and increases in education. Commenting on these changes, C. Eric Lincoln has written (1964):

The Negro middle class is made up primarily of Negro professionals, with school teachers constituting the largest single block. Teachers, along with doctors, lawyers, college professors, small businessmen, ministers and postal workers have traditionally made up the bulk of the Negro middle class. . . . However the recent availability of new kinds of jobs . . . technicians, politicians, clerical and sales personnel, social workers, labor union officials, minor government bureaucrats, and an increasing managerial class in such agencies as Federal housing and local units of national corporations have helped broaden the occupational range of the Negro middle class.

The peculiar thing about the blacks' total socioeconomic standing in the United States, and especially of black middle-class males, is the greater occupation and income differences between them and whites than the differences in educational attainment (Blau and Duncan, 1967: 208–13). As late as 1966, the ratio of nonwhite to white median income for adult men was .80 for those with only elementary education, but it was .60 for those with one or more years of college education (Bureau of Labor Statistics, 1967:21). The same is true of occupational differences. In Blau and Duncan's words (1967:210–11),

the highly educated Negro suffers more from occupational discrimination than the less educated Negro. . . . The difference between the mobility chances of whites and non-whites becomes larger with increasing education until after high school. Education, a path to upward mobility for all, is not as effective a route up for non-whites as it is for whites. . . . Although educated Negroes achieve occupations superior to those of the less educated, the more education a non-white man acquires, the further does his occupational status fall behind that of whites with comparable education.

In the North, especially, this growing stratum of educated but under-rewarded blacks played an important part in challenging the accommodationist black leadership as it existed in the early 1950s. Since they were qualified on grounds of education and skill, they stood everything to gain from a loosening of occupational discrimination. And they had some skills, resources, and time to invest in protest activity.

Regional variations are also important. In the rural and small-town South, in the Black Belt or Deep South especially, we find that as late as the early 1960s the political and economic position of blacks had not changed substantially since Myrdal's description of twenty years earlier. Blacks were engaged in farm tenancy, as resident sharecroppers, as agricultural wage workers, laborers, and domestic servants, living in poverty or at its very margins. All family members had to work to contribute to family income during the cotton season. Voter registration rates varied between 0 percent and 15 percent, black political power was nil, and rural blacks especially had an extremely precarious and dependent economic base. In Myrdal's view (1944:727), black leaders tended to be made and unmade by whites, had to conform to the proper deferential attitudes on the race question, and had to be accommodationist in orientation within the segregation framework. Blacks singled out for leadership would derive certain individual benefits from their patrons but were not in any position to improve the condition of the black community. In fact, the adoption of tractors and mechanical cotton pickers in the 1950s in the cotton growing areas, gradual as it was, and the reduction in cotton acreage imposed by federal government programs were the major push factors for the migration of the black, yet still there remained a surplus of black workers, un- or under-employed for much of the year, not a situation conducive to a strong bargaining position for raising wages or for pressuring whites into easing the segregation pattern (Dillingham and Sly, 1966). Advancement for a black family could be accomplished only through migration into a Southern city or to the North, especially in the case of blacks trapped in rural counties with a high proportion of blacks, where social control was stifling (Matthews and Prothro, 1966:115–17). All in all, one can conclude that the economic dependence of blacks upon whites for jobs, income, credit, and supplies in such communities is so strong, both for tenants, laborers, schoolteachers, small businessmen, professionals, and even black ministers in small-town congregations whose church property was often mortgaged to banks, that unless massive outside resources are poured into them and protection from physical violence is extended to the first blacks who break the pattern of subordination, protest against the segregation structure is not likely to come about simply from within.

In Southern cities, research (Ladd, 1966; Hunter, 1963: chapter 5) indicates that especially in the peripheral South and Atlanta, a Bourbon-Negro alliance in politics frequently was formed at the expense of the "crackers" or working-class whites and resulted in substantial welfare gains and some political posts for blacks. Yet, even in Atlanta, black leaders tended to be older men, accommodationists in their operations, and unable or unwilling to challenge the segregationist institutions of the city. These leaders derived considerable benefits from segregation despite indignities and the frustration of being unable to rise to the top. The conserving strategy of these leaders impeded the mobilization of the black community for wider collective goals. They were to be challenged shortly in the 1950s by more militant groups.

Whereas in the South desegregation was desired by almost all black groups, urban and rural, middle and working class, since all would derive some immediate tangible gains from its termination, the situation of the blacks in the North was different. Class divisions and conflicts of interest were pronounced. Public housing would benefit middle-class blacks who could afford to live in it while it meant "Negro removal" and further crowding for the lower-class families who were required to vacate their dwellings. Increased and aggressive police patroling and an emphasis on law and order in black neighborhoods would protect the better-to-do families from lower-class crime at the expense of increased police harassment and arrests that lower-class blacks, especially male youths, had to put up with (Banfield and Wilson, 1966:297–98, 309). In the North the black middle class consisted of a higher proportion of the total black population than in the South though it was still heavily outnumbered by the working and lower classes.

In 1960 black women were just beginning to break into professional, semiprofessional, and clerical occupations in sizable numbers. Typically both the head of the household and his wife would be in the labor force. But the business and industry base of the black middle class was weak: it depended for employment and advancement on white corporations and industries and the federal, state, and municipal governments and agencies. Because most of the black population was compressed in contiguous high density sections of the city almost exclusively, black votes did translate into elective offices and appointments in municipal government, public agencies, and some safe congressional seats, though nowhere near the proportion of black inhabitants in the city, many of whom did not bother to register or were barred from registration because of residency requirements or other barriers. However, election or appointment of blacks to public office could not easily be translated into tangible benefits for the average black voter in the North except in cities dominated by a political machine because the problems resulting from de facto segregation and large urban ghettoes are resistant to rapid solutions at the city level, depending as they do on national programs, federal funds, the cooperation of private industry and labor unions, and the overall performance of the American economy.

The employment and advancement opportunities of working- and lower-class blacks in Northern cities in the 1950s and early 1960s were governed by several negative factors: inmigration of low-skilled, poorly educated persons at a time of lackluster performance of the national economy and of increased automation for unskilled jobs; the demographic pyramid of black population which contained a high proportion of youths and young adults, many of them with an inferior ghetto education; the resistance of the skilled craft unions and building industries unions to black entry; and the increased professionalization of lower municipal employees such as police and firemen, requiring higher admissions qualifications and seniority, all tended to keep black unemployment rates high and more than double that of the white unemployment rate. Prospects for advancement were slim, especially for young black males. Their situation was considerably less favorable than that experienced by other immigrant groups earlier in the century.

The main support within the black community, in terms of staff, membership, and resources, for the NAACP and the Urban League, came from the black middle class. These organizations were part of the white liberal, labor, and black alliance at the national level operating within the framework primarily of the Democratic party. At the local level, this alliance was subject to considerable internal factionalism and disputes with local labor unions and both white and black politicians, especially in machine cities such as Chicago. Although the overall contributions of the slowly expanding black middle class to these organizations and other race-advancement activities were modest compared to its overall resource base in the North (Wilson, 1960; Banfield and Wilson, 1966: 294–312), it is nevertheless true that the black middle class was to be the primary support base and source of organizational activity in favor of civil rights in the late 1950s and early 1960s within the black community. As Eric Lincoln wrote (1964),

> despite criticism, . . . the Negro middle class has borne the brunt of the civil rights protest. . . . The civil rights fight, at least in so far as it visualizes an integrated society, is a middle class fight. The NAACP, CORE, the Urban League, and the followers of Martin Luther King are all middle class. Indeed the lower class Negro has yet to be stirred by the promise of integration. He is more concerned with such immediate needs as jobs and housing.

The single most important failure of the middle-class black and the civil rights organizations was their failure to mobilize and to organize the lower-class black community. But this failure has to be seen against the background of conflicts of interests between middle and lower class, and the difficulty, short of national programs and massive federal resources, of making a dent in the socioeconomic problems of the ghetto. In the 1950s only the Black Muslims had a certain amount of success in organizing the black lower class and providing tangible and lasting benefits to them, both material and psychological (Lincoln, 1961). In Silberman's words (1964:163),

> the Muslims' success in transforming the lives of its members dramatizes the failure to date of traditional institutions—the Negro church, the civil rights groups, the white settlement houses—to make any real headway with the psychological, social and economic problem of the Negro poor.

However, it must be remembered that even the Muslims reached out only to a small fraction of the lower-class black population.

APPLICATION OF MOBILIZATION THEORY

Given this resource base and given the divisions and regional variations in the black population in the 1950s, what can a sociological theory of mobilization say about the manner in which the civil rights movement came into being and the various twists and turns and changes in leadership, membership, ideology, goals, and effectiveness it has experienced since? First, one must realize that a negatively privileged minority is in a poor position to initiate a social protest movement through its own efforts alone. Especially in the early phases of a movement, outside support and the impact of outside societal events play an important role in bringing about a loosening of social control, which permits mobilization of the collectivity's resources. We shall document the extent to which the federal government, Northern liberals, college students, churches, and a host of other public and private associations, plus the effects of national news media coverage in generating broad public opinion support for increased federal government involvement and congressional legislation, had a decisive impact upon the civil rights and black movement. Second, the theory of mobilization predicts that substantial social movements must have a prior base grounded either in associations or in communal groups that are already formed and active prior to the start of the movement. We shall document the extent to which the Northern-based NAACP, CORE, and other civil rights organizations provided a key support base for more grassroots and mass-oriented protest organizations and the extent to which the black church and clergy in the South, the closest thing to an independent communal and associational base not controlled by whites in the South, played a decisive role in mobilization. The next important issue is to explain the geographic diffusion, the time sequence, the rhythms of involvement of various social strata and classes within the black population, and the emergence of new leadership and competition for leadership position. Here the key idea is to consider the protest potential of various social strata and groups along the risk and reward axes, and the changing risk/reward ratios for different groups. Finally, some light will have to be shed upon the Northern riots of the 1960s and the fragmentation, both ideological and organizational, of the mid- and late 1960s civil rights movement. Here the theory predicts that when unorganized groups without leaders become activated, the probability of violent confrontation sharply increases. Fragmentation occurs when outside resources are progressively withdrawn, social control is once more tightened, and when the successes and gains achieved by the movement that are unevenly distributed within the collectivity lead to the deactivation of previously mobilized groups and a keener competition for the remaining scarcer resources among the remaining activists.

THE IMPACT OF OUTSIDE EVENTS

As for the impact of outside events and the outside support that played an important role in loosening social control and providing the resources for black mobilization, we have already seen how the pattern of increased federal executive and judiciary activity in the 1940s—FEPC, the integration of the armed forces, the desegregation of Washington, D.C., fair employment in the federal government and, increasingly, in local and state governments outside the South, the requirement of nondiscriminatory employment and hiring in private industry holding government contracts—resulted from the increased power of black voters, pressure groups, and civil rights organizations within the framework of successive Democratic administrations, as well as from a deep concern and support of the liberal and governmental establishment for changing the most visible sore in American society, which was at the same time a blatant injustice by accepted American values and a source of international embarrassment at a time when the United States was assuming the leadership role of the Western democracies and courting the new states emerging from colonial status. The McCarthy period halted this trend momentarily, for the liberal forces and the government were on the defensive and interested primarily in protecting themselves. But in 1954 the Supreme Court desegregation decision marked the great divide of this period because the federal judiciary unequivocally put its stamp of law and legitimacy upon a fundamental reversal of U.S. racial policy that over the years had already been quietly undermined in many parts of the country without, however, making a dent in the South where a majority of the black population still lived. That the 1954 Supreme Court school desegregation decision had a tremendous psychological impact on blacks and that it raised their hopes and expectations have been stressed by every observer and commentator. At the same time the decision created bitterness among Southern whites. In a sense, the decision marks the high point of a program of reform-from-above by means of legal and institutionalized channels for bringing about social change sponsored primarily by the progressive elements within the ruling groups and elites that so often is followed by the mass action and confrontation phase of a social movement subsequent to the reform's failure.

The failure of nonviolent, legally sponsored school desegregation

was due to the growth and strength of the Southern resistance movement that outside of the Border states led to but token compliance and
in many areas to outright repression or violence against blacks. In the
words of a Southern Regional Council report (1966:17),

> since 1954 and before, reaction to federal court decrees and law affecting
> segregation has been of three kinds—a grudging, but good faith ac-
> ceptance, an effort to evade through administrative delay and cheating,
> and all-out resistance with violence and terroristic intimidation and re-
> prisal. All three reactions could and did occur in all eleven states. Some
> states, like Tennessee, were characterized by a predominance of the first;
> some, like Virginia and South Carolina, by a predominance of the
> second; and some, like Alabama and Mississippi, by a predominance of
> the third. These were old and familiar configurations in the South.

Whereas school districts in Washington, D.C., Baltimore, Wilmington,
St. Louis, and Kansas City, and, generally speaking, also school districts
in Delaware, Maryland, West Virginia, Kentucky, Missouri, and Okla-
homa implemented desegregation peacefully, the reaction farther South
was something else again. The statistical record of the magnitude of evasion, violence, and repression is summarized in publications of the Southern Regional Council (1960) and fully documented in various volumes
and reports issued by the U.S. Commission On Civil Rights. The spread
and operation of the Deep South resistance movement is perhaps best
described in John Bartlow Martin's account (1957) appropriately entitled *The Deep South Says Never*. Martin documented how the White
Citizens' Councils spread from area to area by means of the service clubs
(Rotary, Kiwanis, Lions, and so on), many of whose local members joined
as a block upon the formation of a local Citizens' Council and by means
of friendships and political networks, how the Councils were representative of the respectable white middle class and how despite their lip
service to nonviolent resistance and their attempts to avoid Ku Klux Klan
entanglements their widespread resort to economic reprisals and pressures against black families was not only effective but gave encouragement to the violent repressers. As the Councils multiplied and became a
political force, open opposition to them by moderate whites decreased,
the local press fell silent, senators, congressmen, and state legislators
publicly supported them and Southern legislators, governors and school
boards laid out a complicated legal and administrative plan to block implementation of the school desegregation decision, from closing the
public schools to enacting state laws forbidding the expenditure of state
funds in desegregated schools and granting tuition from state funds to
pupils in private schools should the public schools close down. As a result the initial Southern white belief about the inevitability of desegrega-

tion turned to an optimistic assessment of the chances for maintaining a segregated way of life.

The consequences of successful Southern resistance were several. Faced with repeated outrages such as all white Southern juries returning verdicts of not guilty against known murderers, frightened black children having to be protected from angry white crowds by troops, churches being bombed, and so on, often occurring at a time when the U.N. General Assembly was convening in New York for its annual session and in full view of the international press corps, faced with openly defiant Southern governors and endless Senate filibusters against civil rights bills, the Eisenhower administration got progressively sucked into active federal enforcement of court decisions, into supporting civil rights legislation to protect the lives and property of individuals, into using administrative pressure for checking the growing Southern resistance movement and actively promoting the cause of civil rights. Thus, the pressures of domestic and world opinion and the force of events outweighed Eisenhower's reluctance to involve the presidency in the murky constitutional issues of federal versus states' rights, a reluctance further strengthened by his belief that laws would not really bring about a basic change in the attitudes and sentiments of men ("the hearts of men") necessary for improving race relations in the South.

The reaction of the white Northern liberal supporters of civil rights to the Southern resistance movement was to increase financial contributions and recruitment in favor of the desegregation cause, to involve various groups such as churches, bar associations, and individual spokesmen for various organizations to the point of taking a public stand against violence and illegality and in favor of civil rights, all of which in turn increased the pressure of public opinion upon the Congress and the federal government for becoming actively involved in the civil rights cause. The extent of this outside support for the civil rights and black cause throughout the 1950s and 1960s is impressive. Although the NAACP itself raised most of its budget from membership dues, the NAACP Legal Defense Fund got most of its funds from white liberal individuals and organizations. It was the Legal Defense Fund that bore the brunt of civil rights litigation, of bailing out and defending the numerous activists in the sit-ins, freedom rides, SNCC campaigns of the 1960s, and so on. While the freedom rides cost about $20,000, the legal expenses growing out of it came to about $300,000, all of it borne by the NAACP Legal Defense Fund (Lomax, 1963:166). So far as CORE is concerned, in 1961 at the height of its growth and activities, it had forty thousand members, half of them white, second only to the NAACP in size of membership and budget, the bulk of which came from Northern white contributors, many of them students. The Urban League was and is primarily supported by foundation grants, the contributions of industrial enterprises, and liberal individuals and so is the Southern Regional Council. The bulk of the financing of the Southern Christian Leadership Conference (SCLC) was white liberal, though the speech-making and fund-raising activities of Martin Luther King at freedom rallies brought considerable sums into its coffers. SNCC was originally financed by the NAACP, CORE, and SCLC, and subsequently the friends of SNCC groups on Northern campuses helped finance its activities. SNCC, as we shall see, also had a sizable white membership and kept being beefed up by white student volunteers on its summer freedom projects in the rural South in the years 1961 to 1964 (Lomax, 1963:162, 194, 196; Silberman, 1964:212). The black college student sit-in and protest movement of 1960 and 1961 throughout the South was initially supported by CORE and later by over 100 associations and groups—national religious organizations, local church-related groups, national labor unions and local affiliates, student and faculty groups at white colleges and universities, and others—many of whom issued public statements endorsing the sit-in movement, made financial contributions, and sent participants to join the protests (Southern Regional Council, 1961). Other civil rights and urban ghetto organizations seeking to mobilize poor people were also financed by white liberal money and federal government War on Poverty funds. Some of the organizers of these campaigns were whites, especially students, often drawing a salary from War on Poverty or VISTA budgets. "Mobilization for Youth" on the New York Lower East Side was financed by the federal government, state and local government agencies, and the Ford Foundation. The Woodlawn Organization in Chicago was organized by Saul Alinsky's Industrial Areas Foundation with the help of many Woodlawn community, church, and business associations and was financed with grants obtained from the Catholic Archdiocese of Chicago, the Presbyterian Council of Churches, and the Schwartzhaupt Foundation (Silberman, 1964:328, 350). In fact, even the early radical student movement was at times supported and financed by the institutions it was to turn against: for instance, a grant of $5,000 in 1963 from the United Auto Workers to the Students for a Democratic Society enabled Tom Hayden and other SDS leaders to organize ERAP (Economic Research and Action Project), an effort to mobilize poor white and black people in Newark and a dozen other sites (Newfield, 1966:101). Of the many civil rights and black associations and groups, the Black Muslims and the black churches stand out as producing all of the resources expended for organization, leadership, and their activities from within the black community. There can be little doubt that massive outside support and the loosening of repressive social control brought about by increasing federal government involvement and support for civil rights created the conditions making possible the mobilization of the black movement. In Pettigrew's words (1964:193),

> even if federal authorities have sometimes been too late with too little help, as in Albany, Georgia and other Black Belt sites, the fact remains that the current Negro protest takes place within a generally permissive national atmosphere. . . . Moreover, this special type of revolution is supported to a considerable degree by white American public opinion.

Indeed, the effect of increased and continued Southern resistance was to increase and deepen outside support for the black drive and the civil rights cause.

THE END OF PATERNALISM AND THE START OF MOBILIZATION IN THE SOUTH

Equally important was the impact of the Southern white resistance movement on the Southern black population. The theory of mobilization outlined earlier emphasizes the importance of a social structure of segmentation along the vertical integration axis that favors mobilization from within the collectivity for common opposition goals. As long as members of an oppressed and subordinated minority are oriented for their own limited advancement to individual patrons and benefactors in the superordinate group and to the accommodationist brokers within their own collectivity, the likelihood of a collective effort from within against the established structure of subordination is slim. Aside from lack of resources and economic vulnerability, the clientage and brokerage relations act as mechanisms of social control against those who step out of line and as a mechanism for distributing modest but tangible rewards to those who conform. These institutions and mechanisms, often referred to as paternalism in the literature, soften the impact of the basically coercive and exploitative relationships on which the system is based, provide certain psychological satisfactions and feelings of security to many members of the subordinate collectivity, and confer a degree of acceptance and an aura of legitimacy upon the system of subordination itself. The Southern resistance movement against the Supreme Court desegregation decision weakened and, for some, shattered the trust, security, and legitimacy upon which paternalism rested. In Lomax's words (1963:85),

> We—particularly those of us who were Southern born—had faith in a class of white people known to Negroes as "good white people." These

were respectable white people who were pillars of the Southern community and who appeared to be the power structure of the community. It never occurred to us that professional white people would let poor white trash storm the town and take over. . . . We expected them to be law-abiding and to insist that their communities remain that way.

The crisis of confidence resulting from Southern noncompliance and open defiance of the Supreme Court decision also undermined the lukewarm accommodationist leaders who were up to that time the brokers and intermediaries between the black and white communities and provided an opportunity for new, more activist, protest leaders to emerge, gather and organize a following, and lead the way to a direct challenge of the segregation structure. The title of Lomax's book, *The Negro Revolt,* refers as much to the revolt against the established black leadership and race organizations as it does to a revolt against segregation.

But a changing mood of disenchantment and impatience is not in itself a sufficient cause for mounting a widespread social movement. Resources have to be made available and mobilized around an organized structure and a leadership group. The theory of mobilization predicts that such leadership and organization are most likely to emerge out of a preexisting community or associations, or both, controlled entirely by blacks and around leaders who are least vulnerable to physical and economic coercion, i.e., for whom the risk/reward ratio is lower than for other groups in the black population. The one institution and group in the South that stands out on all these criteria is the black church and the black clergy. According to E. Franklin Frazier (1966:85),

> the important role of religion and the Negro church in the social organization of the American Negroes has been due to the restricted participation of Negroes in American Society. And as a consequence, the Negro church has left its imprint upon practically every aspect of Negro life.

Furthermore, Frazier states in greater detail (1966:43–44),

> as the result of the elimination of Negroes from the political life of the American community, the Negro church became the arena of their political activities. The church was the main area of social life in which Negroes could aspire to become the leaders of men . . . it was the area of social life where ambitious individuals could achieve distinction and the symbols of status. . . . Monetary rewards which went with power and position in the Church were not small . . . within their Churches, especially the Methodist, [Negroes] could vote and engage in electing their officers. . . . Outside the family, the church represented the only other organized social existence. The rural Negro communities in the South were named after their churches. In fact, the Negro population in the rural South has been organized in "church communities" which

represented their widest social orientations and the largest social group in which they found an identification.

The picture that emerges from Frazier and other writers is that the churches were the black institution least controlled and penetrated by whites. They were numerous enough to reach out and involve in a network of social relations most members of this subordinate and segmented minority. The church communities were also organized as associations with a division of labor, a hierarchy, fund-raising activities, elections, and so on, which enabled talented individuals to acquire and practice leadership skills and provided the church members models and opportunities for organized activity. The fact that the black churches were decentralized and relatively small congregations weakly linked with each other is also important, for, according to Olson's theory, small collectivities are more likely to mobilize for obtaining a collective good than large collectivities. Black ministers were the least exposed group among blacks to white sanctions since their salaries and church property depended entirely on contributions raised within the black community, at least in the larger churches not mortgaged to banks or helped by small donations from white patrons. On top of that, the church members and their families shared a community of beliefs, symbols, moral precepts, and language based on the Bible, especially its Old Testament sections dealing with the oppressed, the dispossessed, and the disinherited. The writings and teachings of the Bible on matters dealing with social action and submission to or rejection of worldly authority are numerous, rich enough, and sufficiently ambiguous so that over the centuries, Christian leaders might draw several contrary inferences and moral guidelines from them. They might, for instance, draw entirely spiritual, otherworldly, and salvation-oriented guidelines for social action or, on the contrary, find inspiration and legitimacy for direct intervention in the social processes of the world, as did at various times the Puritans, the Anabaptists, the Jesuits, the Catholic worker-priests, the Social Gospel ministers, and other groups too numerous to mention. Any Christian community has available to it a reservoir of legitimate, sacred beliefs and guides to action that can legitimize direct collective action in the manner of a moral crusade for changing the evils of the world and for liberating oppressed social groups in the name of God and a higher divine law, if only a new leadership group in the clergy is able to wrest control of the congregation and the church from the usually tradition-minded and individual-salvation oriented conservative clergy.

However, not all black churches were in a favorable position to institute protest activity against segregation in the face of white pressures; the small-town and rural congregations with a majority of members dependent upon white employers for making a living were not. Ministers' homes and black churches could be bombed with relative immunity from arrest by white law enforcement agencies, and white juries could be counted upon to pass light sentences or free white segregationists in the infrequent instances when they were actually brought to trial. In the middle-sized and large cities, however, the position of the large and relatively affluent black churches was much stronger. Its ministers and finances were truly independent of white control. Its middle-class, professional congregation enjoyed social leadership and prestige within the entire black community and possessed considerable financial resources independent of white control. This was especially true in cities that had several industries and in which a Bourbon-Negro political alliance was effective. For lack of research it is not known why and how younger, better educated, and more social action oriented ministers such as the Reverend Martin Luther King, Jr., assumed leadership positions in large, urban, and middle-class black churches in the South in the 1950s. One would guess that it was the culmination of several trends including changes in the quality of education offered in black colleges and seminaries and the demand by a more educated, articulate, and increasingly numerous middle class for a different style of religious leadership that would satisfy its spiritual and social needs. In any case, the historical fact is that in the national context of loosening of social control urban middle-class congregations led by ministers such as the Reverend Martin Luther King, Jr., did spearhead the nonviolent direct-action phase of mass protest against specific segregationist institutions in Southern cities that was to come into its own in the 1960s with the student sit-in movement, managed to unite large sections of the black population behind it, challenged and in some localities successfully displaced the existing accommodationist black leadership, and, more importantly, pioneered a tactics of protest that was to advance the cause of equal rights more rapidly and effectively than all the other techniques tried out previously while at the same time increasing Northern liberal support and federal government intervention on behalf of the civil rights movement. Lerone Bennett wrote with great insight that (1966:194)

> King must be seen as a man who solved a technical problem that had stumped Negro leaders for generations. As a powerless group living in the middle of a powerful majority that hated and feared them, Negroes could not stage an open revolt. To go unto the streets under those conditions with open demands for change was suicidal . . . King and the sit-in students solved the technical problems by clothing a national resistance movement in the comforting garb of love, forgiveness, and nonviolence, a transformation that enabled Negroes to stage an open revolt without calling it an open revolt.

I have already described earlier the manner in which the Montgomery bus boycott was organized by the Montgomery Improvement Association (MIA) which in turn drew its resources, leaders, and organizational model from the churches and congregations that reached deep into the Montgomery black community. The Montgomery movement inspired similar movements led by young black ministers, who took King as their role model, against specific segregationist institutions in some other Southern cities. Some of these movements, such as the one in Tallahassee (Killian and Smith, 1960) and "Camellia" (Matthews and Prothro, 1966:180–200, 209) resulted in the overthrow of the accommodationist black leaders when they refrained from participation in boycott activities. The new leaders, many of them ministers, moved from issue leadership to occupy more permanent organizational leadership positions in the local branches of the NAACP, SCLC, and other race associations. In Little Rock (Cothran and Phillips, 1961), the leaders who rose to prominence were also ministers and not educators or businessmen, who were vulnerable because of the prospect of losing their positions, credit, and business permits.

The weaknesses and limited successes of the pre-1960 direct-action phase of the Southern desegregation movement are evident. As described by J. J. Clark (1961), antisegregationist organizations formed in the South after the Montgomery bus boycott like the Alabama Christian Movement for Human Rights, the Montgomery Improvement Association, or the revitalized Tuskegee Civic Association, were heavily middle class in membership, moderate rather than militant in their goals and the tactics for fighting segregation. Their members preferred lawsuits, low-key voter registration drives, and negotiations to picketing, boycotting, and direct confrontations with the white power structure. They favored nonviolent techniques and legislation as a means of achieving full citizenship. The effectiveness of their protest style depended upon enlisting outside support. In Montgomery, the bus boycott movement succeeded because the Supreme Court eventually sustained a decision of the U.S. District Court in declaring Alabama's state and local laws on segregation in buses unconstitutional. The suit had originally been filed by the NAACP. After that decision, white segregationist violence in the form of shootings and bombings erupted for a time, white juries refused to convict the culprits and white leaders only reluctantly condemned the violence, and the City Commission of Montgomery passed several anti-black ordinances strengthening segregation in public parks and playgrounds. The MIA was not in a position to mount an offensive against these new segregationist measures. The overall historic significance of Montgomery and the church-based desegregation movement was to raise the Reverend Martin Luther King, Jr., into national prominence whence he could serve as a model for other ministers and college students, to demonstrate that a challenge to the accommodationist leaders and luke-warm race leadership in Southern cities was possible and had broad support within all social strata of the black population, to have developed a nonviolent tactic of protest and civil disobedience that had wide-spread public sympathy, and to demonstrate once more the depth and magnitude of the Southern resistance movement to all forms of change in race relations, which would be overcome only if massive outside support were mobilized in favor of civil rights.

DIRECT ACTION

The direct-action, mass movement phase of the civil rights and black movement for freedom and equality can be said to have truly come into its own with the sit-in movement of 1960. When four North Carolina A & T College freshmen in Greensboro, N.C., asked to be served at the lunch counter for whites at a downtown Woolworth store, they were refused but remained sitting until closing time and came back on the following days. This event started the sit-in movement that spread within a week to other black colleges in North Carolina and shortly thereafter to other Southern and Border states and broadened to sit-ins, protests, boycotts, pickets, marches, and later to the Freedom Rides at supermarkets, cinemas, libraries, swimming pools, beaches, parks, churches, bus terminals, and state capitols. According to a report of the Southern Regional Council (Cothran, 1965) a year and a half after its start, the sit-in movement had succeeded in integrating at least one establishment in each of seventy-six cities in the South, had involved about 75,000 demonstrators altogether, and had produced 3600 arrests. However, the movement was not successful in the Deep South. In the twelve months of 1963, 930 direct-action protest demonstrations and sit-ins had taken place in eleven states and 115 cities, and had resulted in twenty thousand arrests, ten deaths related to protest activity, and thirty-five bombings by segregationists (Heacock, 1965:3). The extent of the successes achieved by direct action is revealed in a Justice Department report released in March 1964 which indicated that token integration was giving way to more rapid progress especially in communities where the white leadership had prepared for change and quietly come out in favor of desegregation of certain public facilities. The same Justice Department report cited a survey of 560 communities in Southern and Border states that showed that in 391 of them at least one privately owned public facility had been desegregated. By type of public facility, the changes over time were as follows:

Number of Southern cities (out of 560) in which at least
one facility has been desegregated by:

Type of Facility	27 May 1963	13 November 1963	11 February 1964
Theaters	109	253	284
Restaurants	141	270	298
Hotels-Motels	163	222	259
Lunch counters	204	304	344

In addition, civic or human relations committees dealing with race relations were meeting in 180 of these cities. All of these events occurred
well before enactment of the Civil Rights Act of 1964.

We do not possess as much information as we would like about what
long-term changes and precipitating events account for the high rate of
support of the sit-in movement among black college youth in 1960 and
1961. Black colleges in the South were by and large ill-financed and ill-
staffed. The quality of the education received in them was much inferior
to that offered in the leading universities and colleges in the U.S. The
atmosphere was authoritarian so far as instruction and students' rights
were concerned and there was an emphasis on athletics and sororities
and fraternities (Jencks and Riesman, 1968:406–11). There were some
exceptions—Fisk, Howard, the Atlanta group of colleges—but it was not
in them that the sit-in movement originated. The private and public
black colleges were white financed and controlled. College presidents
and faculty were in a vulnerable position. For them to openly sympa-
thize and support, let alone initiate or join, an active student-led challenge of the segregation structure was to put their positions and the
budgets of their institution on the line. In fact a Southern Regional
Council count in September 1961 reports that at least 141 students and
58 faculty members were dismissed by Southern colleges and universities
as a result of sit-in activity (Cothran, 1965). Because students are not
yet in established careers and do not have to provide a living for a family,
they have everywhere been less afraid to take risks than older people.
Students are moved far more by ideals and a just cause than other
groups, especially when they receive peer group support for their activities. Whatever the explanation for the new mood among the black college
students in the South, and many speculations have been advanced, research indicates that the sit-in movement was not born of frustration,
alienation, and despair, that an overwhelming majority of the students
openly supported the movement while a substantial proportion participated actively by walking a picket line or engaging in a sit-in, and that
students from a professional and middle-class background were more
active in it than those from a working-class or farmer background
(Searles and Williams, 1962; Matthews and Prothro, 1966:407–33). The

sit-in activists, compared to other college students, tended to be better informed politically and somewhat more optimistic about improving the status of blacks in the South; they tended to be humanities and natural science majors rather than oriented to a vocational education or business administration career; and so far as participation rates in different types of black colleges are concerned, students in higher quality, small, private institutions, located in a large community with a smaller proportion of black population, had a higher rate of participation than students in other colleges and other communities (Matthews and Prothro, 1966: 424–28). Here again one might point out that the lower-class student with a vocational orientation to education or business, and who was probably under considerable family pressure to get a job after college to help support his family, was in a higher risk-taking position should he be arrested and blacklisted than students from a more affluent background.

The success of the sit-in movement was due in part to the early financial, organizational, and manpower support it received from existing organizations, especially CORE, which had pioneered the sit-in technique after World War II in the North, the support it got from white Northern and Southern university students, the new black protest leaders in the urban South, the liberal Protestant clergy, and the favorable and highly visible coverage given by news media. The new national mood of hope, idealism, and activity generated among college youth by President Kennedy's inaugural address and the supporting activities of his administration for civil rights, in particular the civil rights division of the Justice Department under Robert Kennedy and Burke Marshall, helped sustain the drive of the Southern civil rights movement. Continued Southern resistance as manifested in the savage beatings and burnings of the Freedom Riders in the Deep South, the resistance of Governors Barnett and Wallace to the admission of blacks at Old Miss and the University of Alabama, and other acts of defiance sustained the public opinion pressure on Congress and the administration for continued and increased intervention in favor of civil rights in the South. Thus, the Interstate Commerce Commission outlawed segregation on all trains, buses, and terminals. Even so, direct-action mass confrontations led by Dr. King himself were not sufficient to desegregate public facilities in Albany, Georgia, in the summer of 1962. Still, in many towns and cities outside the Deep South, the combination of direct mass action and increased political power based on rising black voter registration made possible by the 1957 and 1960 Civil Rights Acts and more militant black leadership did lead to significant changes in the segregation structure.

Equally important were the accelerated emergence in Southern cities of new black leaders favoring militant protest activity and the eclipse of the accommodationist leaders. Research by Ladd (1966) shows that these new leaders tended to be much less vulnerable to white social control than the leaders they displaced (Ladd, 1966:223–25, 229):

> [In Winston-Salem, N.C., in 1963,] the large majority of Negroes recognized as top leaders by the members of their subcommunity are dependent upon Negroes rather than whites for their income. No Negro prominently associated with protest organization activity in Winston-Salem is an economic vulnerable. . . . No vulnerable ranks among the top leaders in Greenville, S.C. . . . to be effective in a deep south city like Greenville, a Negro leader must at times antagonize local whites. Greenville Negroes are seeking extensive modification of the existing race relations structure, and whites are intransigent in their opposition to many of those changes. Racial conflict in a quite intense form cannot be avoided. The vulnerable in Greenville cannot stand much conflict.

In many Southern cities in the early 1960s a permanent, self-sustained, organized black political and civic base that could no longer be used as a tool by the white segregationist leadership for their own purposes was created. Its support had to be enlisted for the election of citywide officials and the appointment of municipal committees, and its decisionmaking power on matters affecting race relations in the city was considerable. All of these developments were further beefed up and institutionalized with the passage of the 1964 and 1965 Civil Rights Acts. Nor can the clock be turned back to an earlier accommodationist leadership by co-optation or economic coercion. Not only did the absolute size of the black leadership group increase together with the size and economic independence of the black middle class, but a certain degree of differentiation and competition within the black leadership group and organizations assured continued dynamism and activism on race relations and civil rights issues. With each new issue and confrontation, as earlier protest leaders tended to become more moderate or conservative by virtue of their newly gained standing and position on committees, boards, and associations, new protest leaders would arise to outflank and threaten the recently established leaders and force them into a more militant stance. Indeed, the effectiveness of conservative black leaders in dealing with the white community was increased, since they could always point to more militant and intransigent leaders ready to step into an issue should it remain unresolved and black demands frustrated (Ladd, 1966:134–35, 228).

SOCIAL CONTROL IN THE DEEP SOUTH

While progress on civil rights was already being made before the Civil Rights Act of 1964 in the Border states and in the cities, the story in the rural Black Belt from Louisiana to Georgia was something else again. It was the defeats and checkmates there of the community organization and voter registration efforts of SNCC and other organizations that led to increased tensions and factionalism within the civil rights movement and, within the national context of urban ghetto riots in the North, to the eventual split between the black power advocates symbolized by Stokely Carmichael and the moderates symbolized by Dr. King and his philosophy. Increasing black voter registration and translating the votes into political offices and power was the Kennedys' preferred technique for producing fundamental changes in race relations in the South. It had worked for the Irish in Boston in an earlier era; in fact, it had brought the Kennedy family into prominence in Boston, then in Massachusetts, and finally in national politics. Yet the Civil Rights Acts of 1957 and 1960 did not provide a sufficiently strong legal and administrative foundation to implement such a policy successfully in the rural South where the resources of the whites and their power over the black population were formidable. Research by Matthews and Prothro (1966:116–48) has documented the fact that the strongest single correlate of low black registration in Southern counties among a large number of social, demographic, economic, and political characteristics is the proportion of black population in the county: the higher the black population, the lower the black registration and the more difficult it is to increase it in the face of segregationist opposition. Southern communities containing a large proportion of blacks tend to be located in the Black Belt, tend to be rural, tradition-bound communities where tenant farming predominates, where local blacks are poorly educated and have very low incomes. The legal requirements for voter registration were purposely kept complex. Registration was administered by white segregationists. It was almost impossible for a black to work his way through this obstacle course in the rare instances that he had sufficient courage to attempt it. Economic sanctions were used against nonconforming blacks. In a depressed agricultural area where there is surplus labor and many of the people live at subsistence and poverty levels, economic sanctions tend to be extremely effective. But violence and harassment by law enforcement officers were also commonplace (Matthews and Prothro, 1966:303–4). In a closed social system where the judge, law enforcement officers, employers, political leaders, and other local community leaders and their agents belong to one and the same privileged, threatened, and determined group, it is impossible for a subordinate and exploited group without resources, even when a numerical majority, to defy the power structure. The risks involved for the few willing to initiate protest and mobilization are too high; the rewards of even successful protest are comparatively low. It was this tight structure of domination that SNCC and other organizations intended to crack in the years 1961 to 1966. The theory of mobilization predicts that only a massive infusion of outside resources can effectively bring this about, and only if it is at least able to provide physical safety and security from economic reprisals to its potential following. SNCC proved unable to do either.

SNCC was formed originally in 1960 to facilitate concerted action among the 1960 sit-in college youth and to inject some resources into the sit-in movement from organizations such as the NAACP, CORE, and SCLC. In 1961 SNCC made the decision to take the movement into the rural Black Belt, to mount extensive voter registration drives, to build local leadership and organization on a permanent basis, and to do this by having its organizers live and work in the local community itself. The ultimate goal of SNCC was to overthrow the caste system in the Deep South altogether. In 1965 SNCC had over 200 paid field secretaries and 250 full-time volunteers, mostly black, in rural communities. Its $800,000 budget was provided by foundations, churches, colleges, the Northern student movement, and various friends of SNCC groups (Laue, 1965: 125).

Whereas the 1960 sit-in college youth tended to come from middle-class homes, half of the SNCC field workers whose backgrounds Howard Zinn (1964:9) checked in 1963 were college graduates or college dropouts from working-class family backgrounds. SNCC started as an interracial civil rights group with integrationist aims. In the summer of 1961 in Amity County, Mississippi, under the leadership of Robert Parris Moses, and later during its 1962–1963 voter registration drives, it ran into the realities of Southern resistance and violence when its staffers and supporters were shot, beaten, jailed, and whipped. The turning point came however in 1964 with its community and political organizing efforts in Mississippi, the murders of Goodman, Chaney, and Schwerner, and the Mississippi Freedom Democratic Party (MFDP) delegates' failure to be seated in full at the 1964 Democratic party convention. Having tried to work within the system only to be offered an unacceptable compromise, SNCC turned inward and leftward in its ideology. It adopted the clenched fist salute of the nineteenth-century Russian social revolutionaries who tried to organize the Russian peasants for the revolution and was thinking in terms of a national alliance of the black and white oppressed classes. The defeat at the polls in 1965 of the Lowndes County Freedom Organization after a year and half of dangerous grass roots organization in a county that was 81 percent black finally brought to leadership within SNCC a nationalist and radical group that no longer believed in integration, that no longer sought the help of white liberal or radical organizers, and that liberal whites could no longer support. With Carmichael the black power movement was born (Newfield, 1966: 48–75).

Before this turn of events, considerable disagreement and increased factionalism within the civil rights movement had already taken place. The younger SNCC staffers were impatient with the slower, more cautious methods and long-term perspective on change manifested by the NAACP, and they resented the news media publicity and credit that Dr. King received when he would arrive in a community to head freedom marches after SNCC had been sweating in the field for months with little notice (Lomax, 1963:107–10; Jacobs and Landau, 1966:20). Nevertheless, the multiplicity of civil rights organizations using different styles of protest, appealing to different constituencies, mobilizing different social strata, and in vigorous competition with each other, did result in a kind of dynamism and steady civil rights activity that a well-organized, hierarchically led, better financed mass organization might not have provided in these years. August Meier wrote perceptively that (1965:56, 58)

> King's failure to achieve a position of power on a level with his prestige is fortunate because rivalries between personalities and organizations remain an essential ingredient of the dynamics of the movement and a precondition for its success as each current tries to outdo the others in effectiveness and in maintaining a good public image. Without this competitive stimulus, the civil rights revolution would slow down.

The NAACP was an effective fund raiser for the more activist organizations and provided them with much needed legal aid when their activists were arrested and jailed; SCLC was effective in enlisting the support of the liberal clergy; CORE and SNCC were engaged in programs that would attract the active, committed college youth, black and white, from all over the nation; and the Reverend Martin Luther King, Jr., had the international prestige and standing that would draw the news media instantly to wherever he went to publicize the plight and local efforts of other unnoticed civil rights groups and drives. The presence of more militant activists on King's left who absorbed the labels of "radical," "dangerous," and "irresponsible" made King's program and demands look like the moderate and respectable solution that had to be supported, so far as the Congress and the mainstream of American public opinion were concerned. Yet, despite several large-scale civil rights projects in the Deep South in the years 1964–1966—the most important were COFO (Council of Federated Organizations), SCOPE (Summer Community Organization and Political Education), and the Lowndes County Freedom Organization—in which many white college youth and some lawyers, ministers, and physicians participated, the results measured in terms of increased voter registration, in the face of arrests, shooting, bombings and burnings, and equally important, in the face of black fears of reprisals, were meager indeed (Watters, 1965). Perhaps the most important event was the murder of several white civil rights workers, which outraged public opinion and hastened the passage of the 1965 Voting Rights Act with strong enforcement features backed up by federal registrars. Equally significant was the radicalization of idealistic white college youth who returned to their campuses in a disillusioned and frustrated mood ready to initiate and participate in the unfolding campus and antiwar movements (Lipset and Altbach, 1966:322).

The temporary checkmate of the voter registration and community organization drive in the rural Deep South and the rejection of the MFDP challenge by liberal Northern Democrats, at that time more concerned with attempting to hold the South in the face of the Goldwater challenge, led to a great deal of internal bickering, antagonism, and soul-searching within SNCC. Tensions within SNCC between black and white staffers and volunteers increased, the break with the NAACP and those organizations within the civil rights movement willing to work with the liberal Democrats was completed, the black nationalist faction within SNCC led by Carmichael came out on top, and what is known in the sociological literature as goal displacement took place: integration was rejected, the search was on for a more responsive and mobilizable constituency and following than the low-income rural blacks, the new ideology of black power was elaborated and the tactics became revolutionary in aim and rhetoric, if not in action, as liberal white support was discounted as hypocritical and ineffective for achieving a fundamental transformation of the racist society, North and South. Instead of continuing the broad liberal coalition of the early 1960s, SNCC strategy became the development of a small but threatening vanguard aiming to mobilize only the potentially revolutionary groups in American society. The largely unorganized ghetto population seemed a likely prospect for this undertaking. These changes have to be assessed against the backdrop of the urban ghetto riot wave of 1964, 1965, 1966, and 1967, and the emergence of the Vietnam war and antiwar movement as another focus of national attention.

THE NORTHERN SITUATION

The anticipated 1964 Northern white backlash against the liberals, the civil rights movement, and the Johnson administration did not develop because President Johnson emerged as the "peace" candidate and because Goldwater's and the conservative Republicans' record on unionism, social security, and the popular New and Fair Deal programs and legislation was unacceptable to the majority of working- and middle-class Americans. But when President Johnson's Vietnam policy was reversed in the context of broken campaign promises and escalation followed escalation, the draft expanded, and war casualties mounted steeply, the white student movement channeled its manpower, resources, and attention into the antiwar movement at the expense of its participation in civil rights activity. Peterson's (1968:38) nationwide study of student protest reported that while "campuses experiencing organized student protest of the Vietnam War almost doubled in the interval between 1965 and 1968, . . . civil rights activism among college students has declined significantly. White student activists are leaving prosecution of the ongoing civil rights revolution to black activists." Thus, one major outside resource that had sustained the black movement diminished in these years.

President Johnson had initiated the War on Poverty, but as Vietnam became the number one problem confronting his administration, and since he pursued a policy providing both guns and butter, the War on Poverty became caught in a financial squeeze and the administration devoted less and less of its time to civil rights and urban ghetto problems. Implementation of the existing War on Poverty programs ran into organizational difficulties, black militancy, and local white sabotage and lack of support. Faced with increased radical rhetoric and ghetto violence and threats, liberal money for the black movement began to dry up. More important yet, the black lower and underclass in Northern big city ghettos and increasingly also in medium-sized cities vented their anger and grievances in riots, arson, and looting.

How did this state of affairs come about? The gains of the civil rights movement in the South in the years 1954 to 1965 did not translate into tangible, nonsymbolic gains for Northern blacks who were not disenfranchised and who were faced with discrimination and de facto segregation equally troublesome as that experienced by their Southern counterparts. Adam Clayton Powell commented subsequently that (Barbour, 1968:306–7)

> black leadership in the North and South must shift its emphasis to the two-pronged thrust of the Black Power Revolution: economic self-sufficiency and political power. The Civil Rights Act of 1964 (with the exception of Title VII or the FEPC title) has absolutely no meaning for black people in New York, Los Angeles, Chicago, Philadelphia, Detroit or any other of the Northern cities.

and Bayard Rustin commented (1965)

> What is the value of winning access to public accommodations for those who lack money to use them?

Even in the South, the major gains benefited the middle-class and urban blacks far more than the lower-class and rural blacks whose problems were first and foremost due to poverty, low wages, a poor education and few skills, and a declining agricultural sector creating a large labor surplus that was only partially diminished through out-migration. In the North, the impressive national economic progress of the years 1961 to 1966, measured in terms of rising family income and growing GNP, did not filter down to make a dent on the standard of life and conditions experienced by the black lower class, especially the youth living in the ghetto. Unemployment was at depression levels, and incomes decreased.

The special census survey taken in South Los Angeles shortly after the Watts riot makes for sorry reading (Current Population Reports, 1966). At a time of increased national prosperity, the median family income (adjusted for price changes) actually dropped by 8 percent between 1959 and 1969. Fully 42 percent of the Watts population lived below the poverty level. In 1967 in nine major metropolitan areas a government report indicated that while the total labor force unemployment rate varied between 2.1 percent and 4.4 percent, black ghetto unemployment rates varied between 8 percent and 15.5 percent. The nonwhite teenage unemployment rate was several times higher yet, in the 20 to 30 percent range (*New York Times*, 7 August 1967).

The lower-class segment of the black population remained by and large unorganized and unmobilized. For years many of the resources of the black civil rights movement and the white liberal groups had been pumped into the South to advance civil rights there. The total financial, manpower, leadership, and organization resources at the disposal of the liberal forces in the U.S. were not unlimited. The Northern ghetto, increasing in size and declining economically, remained by and large neglected. After the passage of the 1965 Voting Rights Act, Dr. King and the SCLC, the NAACP, and the Urban League were increasingly sensitive to the fact that lower-class ghetto grievances were reaching an explosive stage. Yet their belated attempts to build an effective direct-action, nonviolent protest movement in the North were unsuccessful. In the North, the class cleavage between the middle- and lower-class blacks was far greater than in the South, the preexisting network of black churches and communal organizations that might have been used to flesh out protest organizations was not present to anything like the degree it was in the South. Moreover, the mood, rhetoric, and ideological focus in 1965, 1966, and 1967 changed from the nonviolent moderate philosophy prevailing in the late 1950s and early 1960s. The militant nationalist and antiwhite posture of Malcolm X and the Muslims was more attuned to the psychological needs and frustrations of the Northern lower class than Dr. King's Gandhian philosophy and Roy Wilkins' politico-legal orientation. Yet even the Muslims, especially after the split between Elijah Muhammad and Malcolm X, were not able to organize and discipline the vast majority of ghetto residents into an effective movement. All the evidence we have points to the accuracy of Jacobs and Landau's statement when they wrote that (1966:26)

> the masses of poor Negroes remain an unorganized minority in swelling urban ghettoes, and neither SNCC nor any other group has found a form of political organization that can convert the energy of the slums into political power.

The combination of failure of a reform program, absence of an organized protest movement to enlist angry men, increased economic hardship, and heightened expectations due to the much publicized yet ineffective War on Poverty, all made for a high probability of violent confrontation between the authorities and the black urban lower-class population. No attempt will be made here to explain the causes and spread of these confrontations. The Kerner Commission's Report (U.S. Riot Commission, 1968) has provided a detailed, comprehensive, and competent account of its causes and its extent. It remains, however, to analyze the social, political, and economic context in which the riot wave occurred and the changes that have taken place in the years 1965 to 1969, especially the gains and losses to various social strata, in order to make sense of the events of these years and to chart the future of civil rights, of integration, and the black power movement itself.

Some recent analyses of the 1964 to 1968 riot waves have consisted of explanations based on rising expectations, the discrepancy between aspirations and achievements, and the growth of separatist and nationalist consciousness among black youth, often drawing analogies with African nationalist movements. Other researchers have attempted to do cross-sectional correlation studies contrasting conditions in cities where riots occurred with cities where there had been none by a certain date, only to see their nonriot control cities riot the following summer. These analyses have missed the primarily lower-class character of these hostile outbursts and their nationwide character reflecting a basic similarity in the condition of the lower-class black urban masses in these years. Bayard Rustin (1965) was correct in his assessment when he wrote that "last summer's riots were not race riots; they were outbursts of class oppression in a society where class and color definitions are converging disastrously." According to one count, a total of 215 cities had experienced at least one hostile outburst between 1964 and 31 May 1968 (Downes, 1968:509). Whether or not a hostile outburst would be a short-lived affair with no fatalities, only a few arrests, minor property damage, and lasting but one evening, or whether it would be a major riot lasting several days in the manner of Los Angeles, Detroit, and Newark, had a lot more to do with the size of the ghetto, ecological and situational circumstances, and most of all, the reaction of the police and authorities handling the disturbances, than it had with variations in the socioeconomic condition or degree of frustration of the ghetto population itself. No one can deny the fact that the riots had political significance in the sense that they became major political issues affecting public policy or that intellectuals and black leaders provided political and ideological interpretations for the actions and goals of the rioters. Yet, in no instance were the rioters' intentions or actions designed to overthrow the presently constituted municipal and state authorities, let alone the federal government itself, and at no time did the riots ever threaten to do so. The riots were directed at local law enforcement authorities and ghetto merchants primarily. The destruction of alien white property in the ghetto and physical assaults against the alien white agents of social control were its characteristic trademark, not the seizure of city halls, the proclamation of new governments or political manifestos, the destruction of life, or assaults at white populations residing in the fringes of the black ghetto. Nor did the more affluent, middle-class sector of the black population riot anywhere: Watts rioted, but not the "Ivory Ghetto" adjoining the Los Angeles slums. Civil rights and other black organizations, black politicians and black leaders, did not incite, join, or provide leadership to the angry crowds, not even the Black Muslims, although many subsequently acted as spokesmen in articulating black grievances and frustrations and attempted to recruit ghetto residents into their organizations to channel their energies into a more effective political direction. The major short-term losers of the rioting were the merchants and businesses located in the ghetto and the ghetto population itself. It is they who sustained the bulk of the casualties, lost jobs and homes, were arrested and jailed, apart from suffering temporary losses of income and other inconveniences. In the long run the benefits may outweigh the losses that were incurred. National attention was focused on the Northern low-income population; police departments are being restructured; the police are being educated to change their objectionable preriot practices in the ghetto; the courts and the administration of justice will probably be overhauled and humanized; the outdated welfare system has a good chance of being completely changed; and increased organizational penetration in the black inner city is being translated into greater collective political power as black mayors and municipal administrations more responsive to the needs of the black urban masses are elected and appointed.

The primary goal that remains to be accomplished despite important gains is the provision of more jobs, better paying jobs, and jobs with advancement opportunities for black people that would lead to an acceptable American standard of living for the black masses and would bring in its wake a more stable family life, self-respect, and social standing for the black breadwinner and family head and lower crime rates and other improvements reflected in other indices of social disorganization. White resistance to integration and white prejudice—nowadays referred to as "racism"—will be much diminished through the adoption by lower-class blacks of the American middle- and working-class life-styles and attitudes. It is more likely to be diminished through economic security and higher incomes than it is through continued activity based on threats and militant rhetoric. Much of the resistance to integration is based not on specifically racial attitudes and prejudices but on class hostility and fears that even middle-class blacks manifest toward lower-class blacks. This is not a novel prescription or insight. James Wilson (1961:300) wrote back in 1961 that

> an argument can be made that increasing the net disposable income of a minority group is, over the long run, the best way to make possible those larger gains which seem to elude protest action at the moment . . . increased income, held over time and in conjunction with other factors (such as education), will work in the long run to reduce the *class* differentials which amount for part (although certainly not all) anti-Negro feelings.

Much will depend on the overall performance of the national economy (Tobin, 1965), and the continuation of favorable trends in black income, occupational, and political status that started to emerge in 1965, 1966, and subsequent years (Glazer, 1968; Current Population Reports, 1969).

I do not wish to minimize the sizable gap that still exists between blacks and whites, that black youth male unemployment was still at depression levels in 1970, and that the inner cities contain large absolute numbers of the so-called underclass. But the emptying out of low-skill black families from the rural South into Northern cities has come to an end, and the absolute number of blacks living below the poverty line has in fact decreased from 9.6 million persons in 1966 to 8 million in 1968, the first such reversal in this trend for decades. These figures mean that the black middle class is gaining within the black population, the underclass is diminishing, and the lower middle and working class is better off and more economically secure than it has ever been.

Corresponding to these gains there have occurred a decrease of violent, spontaneous, urban ghetto riots and hostile outbursts since 1968 and a great deal more organized protest actions designed to increase black community control of school, social agencies, and other institutions located within and servicing black populations. Nevertheless, the militancy, the revolutionary rhetoric, the use of threats, the mood of defiance and hostility, of many protest groups had not diminished in 1968 and 1969 as one might well expect with the diminution of economic hardship. This paradox can actually be clarified from the point of view of the mobilization theory outlined earlier. It has a great deal more to do with the competition by numerous political entrepreneurs for increasingly scarce War on Poverty and other "outside" resources pumped into agencies and programs dealing with the ghetto than it has to do with the frustration, anger, and militant black consciousness of the ghetto masses. These developments were analyzed by Meier and Rudwick (1968) with great insight.

When SNCC turned northward and adopted the black power ideology, white liberal money funding the direct-action civil rights organizations began to diminish. Correspondingly the antipoverty program became an important source of employment for black activists, local community leaders, and white college youth, and it paid very well. The Office of Economic Opportunity (OEO), responsible for implementing the War on Poverty, encouraged the idea of creating local community organization at the grassroots for solving the problems of lower-class blacks. The combination of funds and institutional positions made available for political entrepreneurs and activists precipitated a struggle for the control of these resources between city hall and the War on Poverty staffers, and also among the political entrepreneurs themselves since there were not sufficient funds and positions to go around. On top of that the established black leaders and organizations in the ghetto were themselves threatened by the War on Poverty sponsorship of a set of new potential leaders. The resolution of these complicated power relations and competition was to increase the militant rhetoric, the volume of protest activity, and the disruptive direct-action movements in the inner city. Frustrated by the efforts of the white and black politicians and the city bureaucracy to contain and increasingly control the War on Poverty programs such as Head Start, neighborhood service centers, legal services, health centers, job placement and work training programs, and other similar activities, activists used "community action funds to promote marches and demonstrations against city hall. . . . Other community action funds were expended to attack school boards or welfare departments. . . . In other communities program workers were fighting the welfare bureaucracy on behalf of their clients" (David, 1969:101). Side by side with the dedicated civil rights activists and War on Poverty staffers there grew up a group of civil rights hustlers and political entrepreneurs making a living out of protest activity and disruption. The quickest way for them to get on the payroll was to outbid each other in radical rhetoric and the use of threats in an attempt, frequently successful, of being co-opted into the War on Poverty agencies, political organizations, or municipal administration. These entrepreneurs actually had little following and influence in the black community itself, but mass media publicity, the paper organizations they set up, and the continuous social disturbances made them credible and successful. At the same time, other organizations and political entrepreneurs were in a similar manner taking advantage of the university and foundation circuit. Liberals were ever willing to listen to "spokesmen" and "representatives" of the masses harangue and threaten them for fat fees. As OEO funds were being cut back with the increased tempo of the Vietnam buildup, the competition became more keen and the rhetoric more extreme. At the same time OEO programs were by and large ineffective in solving or ameliorating the fundamental problems faced by the black low-income population. Meier and Rudwick write that (1968:442)

> the OEO programs unintentionally serve to increase the frustration and discontent among the black poor. The aims and the rhetoric of the anti-poverty program further escalated the expectations of the Negro masses; yet OEO failed to deliver anything substantial . . . at worst the OEO projects were obviously make-work ones designed to "cool it" for a summer. Poor people involved in these projects came to view them as just another "hustle," and attention was often centered on fighting over which groups or cliques . . . would share in the limited available resources. Ironically, it is even likely that the failure of OEO to achieve anything near what it had seemed to promise, may have been a significant factor in augmenting the climate of angry discontent that produced the widespread rioting of 1967.

Thus it came to pass that even while most of the social and economic indicators measuring the welfare of the black population started improving in 1967 and 1968, protest, disruption, and disturbances did not start diminishing until sometime later.

THE FUTURE

It is very likely that the 1970s will see a great deal less social turmoil, civil rights activism, rioting, than was the case in the 1960s as the economic position of blacks keeps improving and their political power at the local and state level expands and becomes consolidated. In other words, the civil rights and black power movement is going to become partly institutionalized and shift its center of gravity from direct-action protest to conflict through the usual channels of political competition for office, for resources, and for programs to better the condition of lower-class blacks. These developments will not necessarily slow the pace of tangible benefits gained by the black population, nor will it undermine the gains already achieved in the 1950 to 1970 period. Short-term protest activity, both nonviolent and violent, will flare up in the inner city mainly as a result of short-term economic downturns that will increase the unemployment rate and hit certain specific groups especially hard, such as youth in the ghetto. The danger of urban guerrilla war carried out by armed militant groups, supported by a sympathetic black population, has been exaggerated, and so has the danger of a nationwide right-wing reaction that will suppress black, radical, and liberal dissent and undermine the gains achieved during the "Second Reconstruction." This is not to say that at the end of the 1970s America will be a peacefully integrated or harmonious multiracial society. Desegregation in public education and in housing will not have been achieved in a substantial way. But by that time blacks will have control over the inner-city public schools, social agencies servicing blacks and their problems, public housing, and even private housing, to such an extent that de facto segregation in the inner city and in the institutions and services located there will not be experienced as objectionable as they now are.

These predictions are based on an optimistic assessment of political and economic trends. The black middle class will continue to grow and to bridge the gap between itself and the white middle class in income and life-style terms. The major mobility escalator for blacks will be in the service sector, especially in public employment, in federal, state, and local government, in education and the semiprofessions, and in the medical service industry in particular. Inasmuch as one would expect that public employees will continue to unionize and will achieve the right to strike, conflict over the standard of living enjoyed by public employees, both black and white, will be pursued along the lines of institutionalized labor-management conflict and will not be perceived in race conflict terms alone. These jobs will be protected by the unions and will not be cut back in response to economic downturns as is the case for jobs in manufacturing where blacks so often were the last ones hired and the first ones fired. The position of the black under-class and lower class will not improve dramatically unless the present welfare system is scrapped and an effective family allowance or income maintenance system is substituted for it. This will probably happen. Beyond that, the long-term "solution" of much of the "black problem" in the United States will not come about until the black lower class is transformed into a working class with the same job opportunities, job security, and material standard of life that the white working class now enjoys. In Moynihan's words (1970),

> the Negro lower class must be dissolved. . . . By lower class I mean the low income, marginally employed, poorly educated, disorganized slum dwellers who have piled up in our central cities over the past quarter of a century. I would estimate they make up almost one half of the total Negro population. They are not going to become capitalists, nor even

middle class functionaries. But it is fully reasonable to conceive of them being transformed into a stable working class population: truck drivers, mail carriers, assembly line workers—people with dignity, purpose, and in the United States a very good standard of living indeed. Common justice, and common sense, demands that this be done.

As Moynihan himself explicitly states, this will take a long time to accomplish, longer than a decade. Yet the trend in 1967 and 1968 has been in this direction, and if the economy in the 1970s performs as well as in the 1960s the trend will continue. The danger is that inflation, recession, and measures to combat both probably will have adverse effects on the rate at which the black working class is increased and the lower class diminished.

The political power of the black population will continue to increase in the 1970s, and with it, that of the black politicians and officials at the expense of the civil rights leaders and the black militants. One thing the past decade of civil rights protest has provided the black population with is an abundant supply of leaders with experience and skills. There exists now a sizable number of black leaders and potential leaders, with a diversity of points of view, backgrounds, styles of operation, and constituencies. Competition among them is going to block the reemergence of "accommodationist" leaders who might be tempted to abandon the vigorous pursuit of black goals. Political mobilization within the black community based on institutionalized electoral and political party processes has now reached the stage where it is no longer dependent on outside leadership, manpower, and resources to sustain itself. Still, to maintain the momentum, the 1965 Civil Rights Act on voting will have to be extended for another five years to protect the gains in the South against the reaction of the Wallace forces. Despite repeated predictions of a white backlash ever since 1962 and 1964, the fact remains that a substantial minority of whites is willing to cast a vote in favor of black political candidates, and it is ultimately on white electoral support of black candidates for office and of black electoral support for moderate white politicians that the growing political power of blacks is and will continue to be founded.

Bayard Rustin's well-known programmatic article of five years ago on the future of the civil rights movement is on the way to realization, even though it did not come about as rapidly as he had hoped it would. At that time, Rustin wrote that (1965:65)

neither the civil rights movement nor the country's twenty million black people can win political power alone. We need allies. The future of the Negro struggle depends on whether the contradictions of this society can be resolved by a coalition of progressive forces which becomes the *effective* political majority in the United States.

Within the black community the militants will keep losing power. The Panthers are being suppressed and are internally split. They are spending most of their resources and energies on their own defense. The extent of their mass following in the ghettos has been exaggerated to begin with. So far there have been no outbreaks of violent disorders after police raids and shoot-ups of their headquarters. The arrests and exile of the top Panther leadership have considerably weakened their organization discipline and effectiveness. In some instances local Panthers have engaged in extortion rackets within the ghetto, a fact deeply resented by the more affluent segment of the ghetto population. Their adoption of revolutionary, radical, and Maoist ideologies and rhetoric attracts a few white radicals but is not understood by the black masses. The coalition of the oppressed black and white lower classes in the United States led by the Panthers and the white radicals is an unrealistic and absurd goal that can only lead to a waste of their resources and energies. When black politicians and pressure groups come to control more city administrations, social agencies, and institutions in the inner city, the militants' work will be seen as undermining the effort for community control and political power by the black community. As the risks of militancy increase and the threat of riots decreases, some militants will join the black administrations and pressure groups. The remaining others will be increasingly controlled and subdued from within the black community. Black community control and black self-assertion, cultural consciousness, pride, and identity will become an accepted reality that will not be perceived as a threat by other groups. The chief beneficiaries of all these developments will be the black middle class and those of the working class who are going to swell the middle-class ranks when they seize the opportunities now available to them by virtue of their education, skills, and effort. Community control will be black middle-class control. As a result, class conflict within the black population will increase since black control of public education and the social and community agencies is not going to solve overnight the problems that at present exist. This division may take some time to develop because of the initial honeymoon period extended to the new leaders and the lasting unifying effects of black cultural pride and black nationalism. The fate of the lower class will, however, depend largely on the state of the U.S. economy and national legislation on welfare, family allowances, and income maintenance. In the foreseeable future, the average working- and lower-class black family will still live in segregated residential areas and will have to send their children to schools that are at best integrated in token fashion. In this sense, though the political power and economic position of the black population will keep increasing, racial integration in the full meaning of that term will be no more achieved at the end of the 1970s than it has been at the present time.

Chapter *VII*

SOCIAL CONTROL

AND

CONFLICT REGULATION

THE CONFLICT PROCESS

A theory of social conflict that only deals with the causes of conflict and not its course would be an incomplete theory. Yet such is the present state of social conflict theory that Harry Eckstein observed for the case of internal wars (1965:136):

> the theoretical issues raised by internal wars can be classified according to phases through which they pass: they include problems about their pre-conditions, the way they can be effectively waged, the courses they tend to take, the outcomes they tend to have, and their long-term effects on society. . . . Curiously enough, the later the phase, the less there is to read about the issues involved . . . but in regard to etiology, to "causes," we are absolutely inundated with print.

It is the task of the theory of social conflict and of social movements to formulate statements that can be empirically verified or rejected about whether issues at conflict will be pursued through institutional or extra-institutional channels, whether the means resorted to will tend to be nonviolent or violent, what strategies and moves are available to contending parties and the consequences of these choices, the probabilities of successful outcome, the manner in which conflict can be regulated or resolved, and what the consequences of conflict are for the individuals and groups involved in it and the larger society in which it takes place.

In any process of confrontation between an opposition group that demands certain changes and the established groups, often represented by the government from whom concessions and changes are sought, one must distinguish several separate issues. When demands have been formulated and voiced or after some precipitating incidents have occurred, the authorities are faced with the decision whether to bargain and negotiate or whether to repress the protest group. If they decide to negotiate, they still have to decide with whom to negotiate, what issues to negotiate, and under what rules and circumstances the negotiations should take place. The decision whether to negotiate at all, as opposed to repressing the protesters and treating them as an outlaw group that ought to be prosecuted, is the most basic decision and involves the *recognition issue.*

Recognition is the minimum condition for institutionalizing conflict. It is possible that the authorities or established groups upon whom demands are made decide to negotiate in bad faith, with no intention of remaining committed to any agreement reached and only using negotiations as a means of gaining time for the mobilization of the forces of social control. But in this special case one might say that the authorities are making use of negotiations as an auxiliary tactic of repression, not of bargaining. The decision to negotiate means that the authorities publicly acknowledge the opposition and their representatives and, in that sense, acknowledge the legitimacy of the opposition, though they may not agree to their specific demands and manner of protest. It can also mean that the authorities have been forced by circumstances against their inclination to negotiate rather than to repress, for instance because they were weak and ill-prepared. Nevertheless, whatever their motives and reasons, the act of entering negotiations represents a decision not to resolve the issue by destroying the opposition, but to include them as a party in a public decision that will affect both groups and the society at large.

The recognition issue is the most difficult hurdle to jump in the process of confrontation, yet it has the most far-reaching consequences for the institutionalization and peaceful resolution of the conflict. If denied, recognition may become the fundamental issue that will be contested, with the discontented groups remaining unsatisfied even if their substantive demands are met by unilateral concessions. The protesters may want to have blocked channels of political participation and influence opened up and normalized once and for all; they may want not only to be listened to from time to time, but to have a continuous voice in the formulation of public policy and decisions affecting them. The employers who refused to allow their employees to be represented by a trade union in collective bargaining on the terms of the labor contract, the Southern city council that refused to negotiate with the NAACP or any other body of black citizens who came forward as spokesmen of the black community to demand desegregation of public accommodations, the refusal of the U.S. and South Vietnamese governments to consider the National Liberation Front as anything else but a front set up by the North Vietnamese, are all instances of the complexity and fundamental importance of the recognition issue in social conflict. Failure to solve the recognition issue in a satisfactory manner tends to coincide with the most violent stage of confrontation, during which open hostilities occur, the authorities seek to destroy the organization of the opposition, arrest their leaders, and even set up stooges that allegedly speak for the population from which the protesters are drawn, while the opposition may seek to overthrow the government or force it into meeting its demands by violent means, or engage in other coercive actions designed to protect their very existence.

Even after recognition has been decided in good faith, it is by no means obvious with whom the authorities ought to negotiate. Social movements are amorphous and heterogeneous and lack procedures for formalizing and legitimizing leaders. Self-appointed spokesmen, members of rival factions, marginal groups, and other elements may clamor to be included in the negotiations or deny the right of representation to other groups, while it may be in doubt that leaders have sufficient command over the rank-and-file members to enforce the terms of future agreements. If a negotiating group is formed, the opposing sides have to agree on procedural rules under which talks will take place before the substantive issues can be discussed, including the often troublesome question of what precisely ought to be negotiated, the negotiators' safety from arrest, the order of the agenda, the presence of mediators, or even preconditions that either party might make such as, for instance, the nonnegotiable character of some of the demands or tokens of good faith before the initiation of negotiations.

The sharp difference between fully institutionalized conflict and incompletely or uninstitutionalized conflict is best seen in the contrast of routine collective bargaining with other kinds of confrontations. In routine collective bargaining, the date of termination of the existing contract is the predictable and anticipated precipitating event that sets off the negotiations. Since union and management both recognize each other as the legitimate representatives of the employees and the employer, and the negotiators have been elected or appointed according to law and precedent, both the recognition issue and the composition of the negotiating parties are resolved. The format and procedures for collective bargaining are set down in law and by precedent; thus, the procedural issues are also resolved. The negotiations can concentrate right from the start on the substantive issues in the renewal of the labor contract. After agreement has been reached, union members are required by law to vote for its approval or rejection; thus, acceptance of the terms is based on the legitimate principle of majority approval. Should the union rank and file reject the terms, a strike vote must be taken prior to direct mass action. Precedent and law exist for bringing mediators into important negotiations to help bring about agreements. Because every step in the confrontation between union and management is initially known and accepted by both parties and backed up by law and precedent, the conflict is regulated and bounded with penalties to those who step out of the institutionalized channels. Finally, as Dahrendorf has written, rules for changing the rules of negotiation are also available. In the case of the polity, they are specified in the constitution of the country (Dahrendorf, 1959:227). Nevertheless, wildcat strikes do occur, strikes are undertaken by union members against the advice of their leaders, and a certain amount of violence may occur in routine strikes. Even fully institutionalized conflict processes do not run like clockwork, and the relations between leaders and rank and file in any organized body are not without conflicts of interest.

In contrast, in the early phases of a nationalist movement, the colonial authorities ban or impede political activity and brand the leaders of the indigenous majority as agitators and troublemakers. The government's reaction to popular disturbances consists of "law and order" and might be accompanied by formal co-optation of "safe" natives into local government bodies. Commissions of inquiry may be appointed to look into the causes of disturbances and recommend legislation and administrative reform in unilateral moves. In any case, recognition of the movement is denied in the early stages and can become the main issue at contention. Similarly, in the California grape pickers strike against Shenley, DiGiorgio, and other wineries and agricultural enterprises in the early 1960s, recognition of the Chavez-led National Farm Workers Association as the Mexican-American agricultural laborers' collective bargaining agent became the main issue. The companies imported strikebreakers, locked out Chavez's men, and used local police to harass and arrest peaceful pickets. Even after some growers agreed in principle to union representation, the representation issue became a new hurdle. Some of the growers set up rival company unions and insisted that a vote be taken among their imported strikebreakers. In guerrilla war, the government is reluctant to enter into visible negotiations with the insurgents and thereby confer on them the status of a rival government or a legitimate opposition, whereas the insurgents claim to speak for the entire population and refuse to negotiate with a government they consider illegitimate (Huntington, 1962:21). In all cases of confrontation involving uninstitutionalized conflict, the negotiations can break down at every stage and new issues over recognition and procedures emerge to add to the already heavy load of substantive matters under contention.

SOCIAL CONTROL

When an elite or the government is faced with demands and social disturbances, it must decide upon a course of action. Will it resort to repression, will it implement reforms, or will it use a mixture of both; will it extend recognition to the protest groups and enter into negotiations, or will it be concerned first and primarily with the reestablishment of order and the prosecution of the opposition, will it meet the challenge to its authority with a hard or soft response, and so on. These are the questions to which a theory of social control seeks to provide answer. Social control is here used in a more restricted sense than in sociological theory where it refers to the processes of socialization, the internalization of norms, social support for conformity and social sanctions for deviant behavior, the operation of custom and of public opinion. We are concerned more specifically with the handling of open, uninstitutionalized group conflict, especially the response of the authorities and of the political leaders. The processes referred to as the erosion of legitimacy, which are but imperfectly understood at the present time, the concept of the loosening of social control that has already been discussed in the mobilization chapter, and the development of a revolutionary situation, will also receive some attention in the discussion.

We begin with Etzioni's distinction between physical power, material power, and normative and symbolic power to which correspond, respectively, coercion based on fear and force, compliance based on the material benefits and losses due to conformity or nonconformity, and compliance based on ideological commitment, conviction about right and wrong, justice and injustice (1968b:396–97). Put simply, people comply with group norms, organizational commands, and the authorities because they derive material benefits from participating in social units and from submitting to authority, because they believe that those in command positions have a legitimate right to command and they themselves a duty to obey, and because they are afraid of the consequences of noncompliance, in particular the application of coercive power by the agents of social control. From an early age, through the influences exerted by their family and later on by the school and through social pressures, most people internalize their rights and obligations in such a way that by and large they do not experience positions of subordination as stifling. As they move through the various stages of the life cycle and of a career, they are constantly evaluated, screened, and directed, in a process of selection and self-selection, to positions for which they have at least a minimum of competence and legitimacy of incumbency that others recognize. Much of the time, for most people, and in most situations, the social system is self-policing and does not require the intervention of the state. For instance, a library has a self-policing system of social control. Users have been taught at an early age to respect the regulations of public facilities and they recognize by and large the necessity and legitimacy of the regulations imposed upon them. By a process of self-selection, probably only those people use the library who value books and learning to begin with. Although every user might derive selfish benefits from stealing books, cutting out pages, failing to return them on time, and hiding them in the library for their own exclusive use, a rather mild schedule of fines and penalties and the awareness that if many people started behaving in a selfish way the service the library would provide would deteriorate to the point that no one, including they themselves, would any longer benefit from it, is in fact sufficient to keep the library operating as a public service. This is not to say that people do not engage in deviant behavior, but that its incidence is far below what they might get away with considering the low degree of coercive social control at the disposal of the library staff. In the case of the library, individual acts of deviance do not receive the social support of a deviant subculture or group. However, self-policing social control systems break down when people no longer derive material benefits from conformity, when they come to look upon the norms as illegitimate and unfair, and when they receive group support for defying the norms and regulations that they are expected to put up with. Under these circumstances, the agents of social control are called in to enforce compliance by means of punitive measures based ultimately on the coercive power of the state.

This is precisely the case with group conflict. When talented youth from a colony receive a university education in the metropole during which they absorb the philosophic, moral, and economic arguments against colonialism, and after they are prevented from assuming the positions of responsibility and prestige for which their education and technical training have prepared them, the processes of socialization and of selection can be said to have broken down from the point of view of social control for maintaining the colonial regime. When peasants are pushed off lands in which they had traditional rights of ownership, cultivation, and grazing, and when they are forced to eke out a living at a bare subsistence level from fragmented and overcrowded small plots, the system no longer delivers the material benefits that they have been accustomed to, and the state enforces new laws and regulations that are looked upon as unjust and illegitimate. When an opposition movement is formed, group support for resisting these changes and for opposition action are further legitimated with reference to modern ideologies and values. Thus, the major mechanisms of social control are undermined one after another, and the system will have to be increasingly maintained by the threat or use of force. As simplified as this brief illustration is, it points up the diversity of social control processes.

Just as the opposition group has to mobilize in order to be able to initiate and sustain a confrontation, so the authorities and the state have to assemble resources if they seek to increase social control, and they have to decide the allocation of their resources among various means of social control. However, there are constraints that operate on the authorities when they seek to mobilize resources or to reallocate them, just as the mobilizing potential for opposition of various collectivities differs depending on whether or not they are communities, relatively unorganized groups and individuals, or able to draw on associations and organizations already present in them. One of the merits of Stinchcombe's (1968: chapter 4) discussion of power is to focus attention on the importance of the extent to which "the powerholder can call upon sufficient other centers of power, as reserves in case of need, to make his power effective." One of the weaknesses of the usual approach to power and to social control is to deal exclusively with the responses of the people over whom power is exercised. The question of stability and social control is then discussed within the framework of the "popularity" of the government or the legitimacy of authority. Stinchcombe points out, however, that the effectiveness of power depends as much on the other important power holders in the system as on the person over whom power is exercised. The police officer may well manage to arrest an alleged offender, but for sanctions to become applicable, the judge has to uphold the actions of the policeman (1968:160):

> the "authority" of the policeman thus consists of the probability that his action will be backed up by other concentrations of power, and it is limited because the conditions under which others will back him up are limited.

As a matter of fact, one of the reasons that the police will frequently harass, curb, and interfere with what they define as threatening and socially harmful actions that have a high probability of leading to hostile reactions in lower-class neighborhoods, both black and white, is that they know that the judiciary will not uphold their social control actions and that they might even come in for some criticism. The police engage in a considerable amount of preventive social control prior to the actual violation of law, and they consider this strategy as a more effective one for keeping peace and order than the apprehension of offenders after the law has been broken—indeed, the only effective strategy if their actions have a low probability of being backed by the other centers of power in the system. They might also do this in order not to overload the courts and the jails. At any rate, the authorities' capacity for social control depends a great deal on the extent to which various parts of the social system are self-policing to begin with and on the extent to which other centers of power back up and support the actions of the state's agents of social control.

Faced with a period of social disturbances and unrest resulting from group conflict, what processes of social control can be activated by the authorities? Socialization, in the short run at least, is not a viable strategy of control. Socialization is usually exercised through families and, at a later stage in the life cycle, through the educational institutions and frequently also the major religious organizations and orders. Even a totalitarian regime has relatively little influence on socialization within the family, though it would, of course, exercise effective control over education. But most governments in liberal societies or authoritarian systems where religious orders handle education have relatively little influence on the education system. In any case, at a time of unrest, greater influence over socialization processes cannot have an impact on social disturbances, since the adult protesters are already out of the reach of socializing agencies. The manipulation of socializing processes is at best a long-term strategy for social stability in the future. And since the intrusion of the state into the moral development of children that the family and religious orders have been responsible for and have had an exclusive right to is going to be resented and opposed, only a strong regime is going to attempt it, but hardly at a time of unrest when it seeks to create support for its policies, not enemies.

Selection processes, i.e., the directed movement of people into social positions and social units for which they have been trained and which they expect to reach by virtue of their achievements, skills, and the aspirations they develop during the socialization period, are largely tied to socioeconomic processes that operate in a highly decentralized fashion through thousands of organizations, groups, and social units that are for the most part self-policing with organizational elites and professional and occupational associations exercising effective control. Yet, in most political systems the political leaders have some room for the manipulation of selection and of mobility through systems of patronage, the expansion of the government bureaucracy, putting potential or actual opposition leaders on a government payroll, and co-optation in its many forms. In the extreme case, a totalitarian regime has the power of making political loyalty and conformity the primary criterion of advancement and incumbency down to the lowest rungs of the social pyramid. But even in other systems the dismissal of unpopular ministers or officials, the appointment of new officials who have earned the people's confidence, is perhaps the most visible short-term response that the government can undertake, at relatively low cost and with a good chance of at least buying time, when faced with group conflict and social disturbances. To the opposition these appointments and dismissals indicate good prospects of recognition and of negotiation, an implicit admission that their grievances have substance and are legitimate, and a symbolic commitment to reform by the authorities. In the long run, of course, the underlying causes of the grievances and dissatisfactions will have to be dealt with successfully. Selection processes can also be manipulated by the top political leaders to weaken other competing centers of power, as when military commanders and district officials are kept rotating from area to area and from position to position. In some instances, the political leaders can directly intervene to even out the supply and demand of certain services and skills. For instance, by exercising influence on budgets, examinations, student stipends, and university expansion, a government can within a couple of years reduce the total number of students in higher education for the purpose of quashing a troublesome student movement and floating population of unemployed graduates that it has brought into being and subsidized. As can be seen from these examples, a weak government, or one which operates in a pluralistic institutional context, can use selection processes for the purposes of social control in only limited fashion, since various groups and elites will control selection in their own institutional spheres. Many governments are not able to demote, promote, and rotate the military brass around at will without taking a heavy risk of being toppled.

A third option for the authorities is to manipulate the structure of material benefits and penalties in order to generate greater material commitment of the population for the system. Here again there are severe constraints upon most governments. Landlords, industrial elites, bankers, foreign investors, international markets, the groups who hold the state debt, have considerable power in setting economic policies or blocking the execution of policies that might have an immediate impact on the standard of living of a population that is caught up in social unrest. As Crane Brinton (1952) noted, the classic revolutions were precipitated by prolonged government fiscal crises during which the social and economic power centers refused to bail out the political leaders without the concession of major political reforms. The Weimar government was caught up in a worldwide economic depression over which it had little control. Smaller states with underdeveloped economics must frequently yield to the policy recommendations of foreign investors, foreign governments, or international agencies even if they expect the recommended belt-tightening policies to be unpopular and to add to popular unrest. Short-term measures to relieve material discontent such as increased wages in the public sector, higher minimum wage legislation, price controls, may have an adverse effect on the economy shortly thereafter.

Long-term economic reforms depend on the cooperation of other power centers, an efficient bureaucracy, and the ability of the government to raise the necessary funds through higher taxation, indebtedness, nationalization of property, and so on. Economic reforms are frequently ineffective for lack of funds, bureaucratic bungling, and the noncooperation and sabotage of powerful groups upon whom their success largely depends.

Normative power based on the political system's legitimacy and the ideological commitment of the people to the political leaders and institution represents a considerable resource in the hands of the authorities. Legitimacy gives the incumbents considerable time before cumulative dissatisfactions lead from demands for relief to attacks on the political system itself. However, the inability of a system over a period of time to deliver material benefits and ensure peace and order so that the safety of its citizens and the normal flow of goods and services are maintained leads to a gradual erosion of legitimacy (Lipset, 1963:68–71). Legitimacy can also be eroded independently of these processes by the desertion of the intellectuals and other shapers and guardians of societal values and ideals upon which legitimacy ultimately rests when previously accepted values, ideals, and principles are questioned and criticized publicly without anyone rising to their defense (Brinton, 1952:41–52). It can even come about that the incumbents themselves and other powerful groups no longer believe in the system's legitimacy, that they adopt the rhetoric of the opposition even while they defend their privileges and vested interests that are now shorn of their ideological justification. Legitimacy can also be eroded when a traditional upper class adopt foreign manners and become absentee landlords residing in the capital, divesting themselves of the traditional obligations owed to the lower classes while claiming and maintaining the right to the material benefits and services enjoyed by those in high social positions. Thus, a previously legitimate system of rule based on mutual rights and obligations and reciprocated benefits can yield to unilateral exploitation (Eckstein, 1965). This process of estrangement of ruling groups from the people is due to long-term social trends over which the political leaders have no control once they are faced with crises.

It is possible to beef up or restore legitimacy by extending recognition, citizenship rights, political rights, a constitution, and so on to hitherto excluded groups, but this is tantamount to yielding major political power to the opposition. As a tactic of splitting a united opposition it can be effective, however, as the English Reform Act of 1834 and the promise of constitutional government embodied in the October Manifesto of 1905 in Russia have shown. In both instances, the middle-class opposition were more concerned with liberal constitutional reforms and the extension of political rights to themselves than with revolutionary transformation and, consequently, shifted from opposition to support of the government in order to take advantage of the newly won rights. However, the extension of civil and political rights to disaffected groups entails a risk, since the newly won political power can be used to increase opposition mobilization as has so often happened in colonies. It is a strategy of social control that paradoxically rests on a loosening of coercive social control and the abandonment of some coercive power by the state. The hope is, of course, that the newly formed vested interests and beneficiaries of the political reforms will now become supporters of the regime and will in fact contribute to social control through their influence and control powers in different groups and institutions. If successful, increased legitimacy will add to the total social control capacity of the system even while the political authorities divest themselves of a portion of their share of it.

There remain to examine physical power and coercive social control. Since the state already has a coercive social control apparatus for purposes of dealing with crime, enforcing the law, and keeping social interaction peaceful and orderly, a coercive response to social disturbances is the cheapest and most immediately available means of control to the authorities. The state is expected by the citizens and is required by law to protect life and property and to arrest the perpetrators of illegal actions. It has little choice but to use its coercive power when protesters and opponents themselves use coercive or violent tactics. But what about the repression of peaceful and nonviolent dissent? Paradoxically, a weak government—that is, a government that cannot enlist the support of other power centers for social control purposes—is more likely to fall back upon coercive social control since it is the only option left for it. A government that cannot implement reforms because it lacks the means, that is unable to transfer some of its political power to the opposition for fear that it would be fatally weakened, can only resort to force when faced with a serious popular or opposition challenge. Stronger governments can afford a period of growing opposition and the transfer of resources to the opposition before the long-term effects of reform and increased legitimacy result in a lower incidence and intensity of opposition and of conflict. It seems possible also that an authoritarian regime can survive with a smaller coercive social control apparatus than a democratic government, since the opposition is not allowed to mobilize and initial outbreaks of protest are nipped in the bud. A democratic government must allow mobilization of the conflict groups and can count less on the support of other centers of power who are independent of the political authorities. Thus, democratic societies will experience more open conflict and by more highly mobilized and powerful opponents and, therefore, might have to invest in a larger coercive social control apparatus to keep conflict within manageable bounds.

Coercive control requires command over the agents of social control —the police, the army, the courts, the prison system, and the other law enforcement and military agencies and organizations. These groups not only have a legal obligation to carry out the orders of the top leaders but make a living out of it. They derive material rewards for implementing coercive social control, they have been trained, socialized, and selected for that purpose, and they frequently develop an ideology of social control in which they represent themselves as the ultimate bastions of law, order, stability, and justice against the forces of anarchy, violence, disruption, and chaos. As such, they can develop into an important power center of their own that the political authorities can no longer control by selection, budgetary manipulations and material rewards, and by appeals based on legality and legitimacy. A period of social disturbances that leads to an increased and prolonged period of coercive response necessitating an expansion of the social control apparatus will bring about a major drain of societal resources that might have been used for reform purposes and will also lead to the emergence of a social control elite and specialists as a center of power autonomous of the political leaders. Once such a development occurs, the return to other strategies of social control becomes exceedingly difficult. The new vested interests will resist a cutback of the material rewards, power, and size of operations that they have enjoyed and come to count on. The specialists of coercion are also apprehensive of the possibility that they will be called upon to account for their repressive actions and that they might be prosecuted for excesses. And since considerable resources were invested into coercive social control, chances are that the reform capabilities of the government apparatus have become weak for lack of personnel, facilities, and experience, so that a coercive response as a solution to all social problems by means of the well-greased, large coercive apparatus that has to be supported in any case may appear as a convenient and realistic policy. Thus, a government can become boxed into a policy of continued coercive control and end up being toppled by the army and coercion specialists when it seeks to change these policies. This type of "right wing" takeover is, however, less likely to occur in a totalitarian regime. Totalitarian regimes always develop a coercive social control apparatus directly under the regime's chain of command separate from the army and the police and other law enforcement and military agencies. Thus, they make certain that they never lose their grip over coercive social control and that they have a coercive means of controlling the coercive social control apparatus itself.

SOCIAL CONTROL IN REVOLUTIONS

Revolutionary terror is perhaps the most dramatic example of the application of coercive social control. Much as one might object to its exercise on humanitarian grounds, it may be the only means available for a revolutionary government to consolidate its position and to fend off the challenges of those who seek to overthrow it, usually by violent means. In the eyes of large segments of the population, a new revolutionary government will be illegitimate. Typically, some groups will refuse to submit to the new authorities; often they will engage in direct acts of sabotage and prepare for armed risings and invasions from a foreign base with foreign support. The economy is likely to be in serious difficulty if not chaos, so that immediate material rewards are unavailable for extending social control. As many have noted, amidst revolutionary chaos and postrevolutionary disorganization, the responsibility for continuing or for reestablishing the normal flow of goods and services is a serious drain on the resources and energy of the incumbents. Reliable and competent staff to implement reforms are also lacking. The purge of opponents from important positions, which is necessary for the extension of revolutionary control and for ensuring that new policies are executed, is likely to create a disgruntled and opposition-minded group of losers. In order to restore the economy and to organize national defense against foreign threats, the new government has to increase taxation and might have to institute forced levies for labor and for the armed forces. To many groups, these actions increase hardship and are violations of their traditional rights and obligations to the central government; hence, they will be resisted by force. Socialization as a means of revolutionary control is only a viable strategy for increasing compliance in future generations. Thus, by default, coercive social control is the only means of staying in power and of reestablishing normality. The greater the threat to the incumbents and the weaker their economic position, the more reliance will have to be placed on terror, that is, the physical elimination of their opponents.

Terror may not be the irrational policy it is often depicted to be. During the French Revolution, according to the careful statistical analysis by Donald Greer (1935) of the incidence, victims, ecology, and time path of the terror, revolutionary terror was applied in direct proportion to the threat that opposition represented to the life of the revolutionary government (1935:68, 70–71, 81, 85):

> the terror barely brushed those *départements* which manifested little or
> no opposition to the Republic or had no traffic with the foreign enemy.
> On endangered frontiers and in the *départements* of local disturbances,
> the repression was more severe, and it became harsh on the fringe

of civil war areas and in the departments where serious insurrections occurred. In the civil war regions themselves, the terror wrote its record in blood and reached a peak of severity where the eruption of counter-revolution was most violent . . . 81% of victims of the terror were condemned to death in the territory where the Revolution and the counterrevolution, republican France and monarchical Europe, were locked in a death struggle . . . it would be difficult to ignore the inference that the terror was an instrument of political repression used principally against the bitterest enemies of the Republic . . . [it] was directed against those who opposed the revolution in act or word.

It was only during the final phase of the Terror, just prior to the fall of Robespierre and Saint-Juste, and principally in Paris, that the Terror became an irrational and unnecessary policy of eliminating potential opponents and upper-class Frenchmen regardless of their actions and of the threat that they represented to the regime (Greer, 1935:119–21). The purges undertaken by revolutionary governments after they have consolidated their positions and are no longer threatened by foreign enemies and armed resistance—Stalin's purges in the 1930s and the Nazi's final solution for the Jewish "problem" by extermination—represent the most clearcut cases of coercive social control run amok. This can happen only when a government has already a monopoly of power in society so that its fate no longer depends on the cooperation and the accountability of its actions to the people and to autonomous elites and centers of power not under its control.

The approach to the theory of social control presented above also allows for a further discussion of what is meant by a "revolutionary situation." According to Crane Brinton (1952), Trotsky (1959), and many other students of revolution, a revolutionary situation develops when the government is caught up in serious and recurrent fiscal difficulties for the solution of which it has to enlist the support of the economic elites; when the elites, upper classes, and other centers of power are themselves divided, with one section mobilizing for opposition and working to undermine the authorities; when the legitimacy of the system of government has been eroded over time as a result of the intellectuals' deserting the regime and sowing doubts in the minds of the upper classes and the incumbents themselves; and when the government is losing its grip over the agents of social control who no longer can be counted upon to put down social disturbances and popular uprisings. From the point of view of the theory, the revolutionary situation develops when all the means of social control have become inoperative or ineffective and legitimacy has been eroded, and with it the reserve of patience, goodwill, and trust that a government might count upon to buy time until the corrective measures take effect. Reforms are difficult, if not impossible, to implement if the treasury is empty and important power centers fail to support them; in fact, some power centers may be working to undermine reforms -and may be supplying material and leadership resources to growing opposition. Thus, social control based on increased material benefits and inducements also becomes inoperable. Since the only other means left, coercive social control, is also being undermined, the weakness of the incumbent government is plain. The revolutionary situation must be distinguished from the revolutionary seizure of the government by some opposition group. A revolutionary situation can just as well be the occasion for an armed forces takeover as for the seizure of power by a revolutionary group or a broad-based social movement. The opposition groups must neutralize the coercive social control apparatus through troop defections, the distribution of arms to their supporters, the organization of citizens' militia or professional armed forces under their command, and they must seize control of an administrative apparatus through which they can issue authoritative commands, requisition resources, and build up their own executive and legislative powers that the population will submit to in lieu of that of the government. In guerrilla movements, the creation of dual sovereignty or dual power will proceed on a territorial basis. In the classic Western revolutions dual sovereignty will develop out of revolutionary bodies (soviets, councils, committees) that grow up parallel to the government structure and from the seizure of existing organizations and institutions after revolutionary groups take executive charge of communications networks, transportation services, production facilities, and so on.

VARIETIES OF SOCIAL CONTROL STRATEGIES

Revolutionary situations developing from the loss of all means of social control are relatively infrequent. The authorities and ruling groups usually do have the choice of combining various strategies of social control. The means used will depend not just on the constraints that other powerful groups impose upon the government but on the characteristics of the subordinate classes and protesters as well.

Viable communities and groups based on kinship, neighborhood, ethnic membership, religious bonds, and other primary group ties possess distinct beliefs and a way of life that set them apart from other groups, classes, and communities. For such groups ascriptive membership delineates visible boundaries within which a dense network of social relationships extends to every member. There exists little internal differentiation in economic status because specialization and the division of labor are but poorly developed. Leadership is not open to all group members but restricted to certain families or descent groups. Leaders are bound to uphold the traditions and interests of their community or else face ouster. When such a community is incorporated into a larger society, as is the case with colonial conquest or the extension of central government authority in outlying districts, compliance with the superimposed outside authority will not be based on legitimacy, but rather on the fact that the new authority is imposing only few demands that do not necessitate a change in the accepted way of life. The least expensive method of social control is to recognize and deal directly with the existing community leaders who already enjoy legitimate authority and leave them by and large to work out their own internal problems. Outside authorities have virtually no means of influencing socialization processes. Interference with selection processes, for instance, the forcible ouster of leaders who are uncooperative and the imposition of others who are more subservient and manipulable, creates the likelihood of open revolt and will also undermine the system of self-policing because the authority of stooges will be resisted. The manipulation of economic rewards is at first limited since such a community is by and large self-sufficient and has but limited needs for engaging in economic exchange with the outside. The effort by an outside power to make such a community economically productive—e.g., to exploit its land, labor, and natural resources with a view of realizing profits for outsiders—will usually have to be backed by coercive social control.

Opposition to the imposition of foreign rule and of exploitative economic relationships will take the form of risings under existing leaders with the ready participation of most members of the community. The likely outcome is repression based on collective reprisals and scorched earth policies in a context of low visibility, low accountability and an ill-informed public opinion. Paradoxically, too much success in repressing opposition—resulting as it does in the fatal weakening of the community social structure and hence also of the basis for self-policing social control —will have to be followed by large expenditures on administration and social control. If, however, the suppression of risings does not fatally undermine the structure of leadership, or else if the changes demanded from without were few to begin with and did not precipitate armed opposition, the policy of indirect rule by means of traditional leaders can be introduced as the foundation for social control. From the point of view of the outside authorities, this policy sets severe limits on the extent to which change can be introduced from without. A cheap and weak form of social control limits the opportunities for remolding and exploiting a subordinate group. When several such communities previously warring amongst themselves are brought under the control of a single foreign or central authority, the new overlord frequently institutes a policy of divide and rule so that a state of tension and a balance of forces is maintained between the various groups. Under these circumstances the likelihood of massive opposition to the outside authority is much diminished, and local resources can be mobilized to control emerging local opposition.

In contrast to the relatively limited choices of strategies for social control in segmented communities, the lower classes and subordinate groups in an integrated though stratified society are subject to more varied influences for ensuring conformity. These societies will have religious specialists exercising a great deal of influence on socialization processes and on the legitimation of beliefs stressing submission and obedience to those in authority. Acceptance of subordinate status based on beliefs in the inherent inferiority of common folk and the superior qualification for rule of the high-status groups is common. Talented and ambitious individuals who might become opposition leaders if their careers and plans are blocked can be incorporated into the lower echelons of the administration or rewarded through patronage. Nonconformists can be ruined and pressured to emigrate. Selection and the manipulation of economic rewards create social and economic differentiation in such a way that the more privileged members of the lower classes benefit from the existing structure of stratification and have a vested interest in its persistence. Coercion need therefore be applied only sparingly and infrequently, for social control will be exercised by local notables and their clients at early stages of discontent and protest. The absence of open protest is used by the higher strata to support their claim that the lower orders are happy, contented, and well looked after. In fact the risks of open opposition will be too high to bear, and the resource base for mounting an opposition movement will be lacking because of organizational skills not found among the lower strata. Therefore, the integrated and highly stratified social system will tend to be durable and stable, until as a result of broad social changes new groups have emerged that no longer fit into the stratification pyramid and that are no longer economically dependent upon the upper classes. More often than not even these new groups will need considerable outside help to sustain an open opposition movement in the face of a comprehensive system of social control.

The social control of relatively weakly organized subordinate collectivities will have to be based on a combination of coercive control and the manipulation of economic rewards. In highly mobile populations lacking structure and internal differentiation there is the temptation of using a giant propaganda apparatus for creating an ideological commitment to the regime. Mass indoctrination to spread conformist attitudes has, however, yet to be proven effective in the absence of a police state to back it up. It is more likely that appeals based on patriotic sentiments and nationalist aspirations can enlist the loyalty of the population when there exists a real or manufactured foreign threat. Subordinate social strata possess their own subculture and socializing institutions, which are impervious to penetration by outside agencies. Not having the means of expressing grievances through institutional channels and their own leaders and associations, there will take place periodic outbursts of unorganized protest and social disturbances. These will be repressed, misunderstood, and overreacted against by the authorities who lack a means of keeping informed about the frame of mind of the lower classes except through the misleading reports of paid informers and undercover agents. Social control will boil down to the Roman strategy of *panem et circenses*, backed up by coercive social control. The idea is to keep bellies full and minds distracted in nonpolitical pursuits; hence, the emphasis on sports and mass entertainment in the contemporary world. Such a system of social control prevents the emergence of permanent opposition organizations and leaders who champion the interests of the lower orders. It stands a good chance of boxing itself into a spiral of mounting coercion when faced with increased popular discontent. The strategy is doomed when rivalries and competition divide the once united ruling group and one faction mobilizes a popular following to prevail over its rivals.

The social control of collectivities organized along associational lines relies a great deal on the conservative tendencies inherent in large-scale organizations described long ago by Robert Michels (1959), i.e., on the internal self-policing that association leaders exercise over the membership. In a vertically integrated society, association leaders have regular access to the centers of power and have a recognized sphere of influence. Indeed, they will become a component part of the ruling groups, whose life-styles and way of thinking they will come by degrees to adopt. Much time and energy will be devoted by these leaders to maintain their top positions against challengers from within the organization. They will take care not to make extreme demands phrased in offensive ideological terminology so as not to jeopardize their ready access to and smooth relations with the ruling groups. The dominant tone of the influences that are transmitted from the top leaders through the middle ranks to the rank-and-file membership will therefore be moderate and conformist. The membership will in turn be submissive to their leaders so long as they keep obtaining tangible material benefits through these arrangements. Dissident elements within the organization who insist on a more militant style and ideology are crushed in the name of preserving unity and organization strength. These associations can become powerful vested interests in favor of their members to the detriment of those who are not allowed entry. Although the strategy of social control through internal self-policing ensures a nonrevolutionary political orientation, at the same time it seriously limits the capacity of ruling groups for instituting reforms when faced with the demands of other, less organized, smaller collectivities hitherto excluded from these preferential arrangements, as has been and still is the case of black workers excluded from the white dominated trade unions in the United States.

In a segmented society where the lower classes are strongly organized through an antiestablishment movement whose leaders have been excluded from direct political power, the conservative and oligarchic orientation developed in large-scale "militant" organizations such as the French and Italian Communist parties results in an even more powerful means of social control. The leaders of these giant organizations occupy comfortable and privileged positions whose continued enjoyment rests on their gradual and cautious actions despite their radical ideological pronouncements and openly defiant posturing. The larger such organizations and the greater their material resource base, the more able they are in supporting a numerous body of cadres, organizers, ideologists, and professional careerists who might stand to lose a great deal if their organization were suppressed by the authorities. In fact a successful opposition career can be worked out entirely within the confines of the network of associations linked to the party without ever running afoul of the authorities. Caution and delay can be justified with reference to learned historical analyses demonstrating the dire consequences of premature revolution that would set back the progressive forces and strengthen the reactionaries. The staying power of these organizational giants and their immunity to efforts by other groups to weaken their hold on their following rests on their own high degree of internal social control over members. The sheer size and potential power of these large opposition organizations will discourage the authorities from provoking and repressing them. Both sides will be quite content to establish a modus vivendi and have an interest in avoiding confrontation.

A negatively privileged collectivity that is not thus monolithically organized but that nonetheless contains a number of competing associations and leaders provides a more likely context from which a vigorous and growing opposition movement can emerge. Competing with each other to gain followers and obtain outside resources and allies, disagreeing with each other on goals, tactics, and ideology, too insignificant to be co-opted and too numerous to be repressed, the leaders and activists in an emerging, decentralized social movement maintain a high level of tension and dynamism that propels the movement forward. Conservative tendencies are not given a chance to build up around vested interests since with each turn of events novel leaders and organizations, ideas and strategies, are thrown up to occupy the center of the stage and to undermine the process of consolidation. New layers of the population hitherto unmobilized become restless and have to be drawn into the movement by formulating new goals and adopting novel tactics. Leaders who wish to rest content with partial gains find that their erstwhile followers are deserting them and are shifting their support to more radical activists.

Some of the main points in the discussion of social control can now be summarized. In a given society, the means of social control resorted to depend both on the capabilities of the authorities and the characteristics of the subordinate social strata. Just as an opposition movement has to assemble material and moral resources, from within and from without, so the authorities have to assemble resources for exercising control and have to operate within a framework of constraints set by the interests of other elites within the upper social strata, the strength of public opinion, and the degree of autonomy of the agents of social control themselves. Much of the time the strategy of social control of subordinate groups rests on the manipulation of material rewards and selection processes and on self-policing made possible by internalized norms and attitudes. When social disturbances break out, the authorities are bound to intervene to protect life and property, reestablish the normal state of affairs in which routine living can be pursued, and punish those responsible for breaking the law. Some use of coercive social control is inevitable in every society. The question is whether coercion alone will be used to suppress discontent or whether an effort will be undertaken to deal with the underlying causes of the disturbances by some other means and how effective these measures will prove. Thus, the question of social control shades into the topic of conflict regulation and conflict resolution, of social reform and of conciliation. The disaffected groups have to avoid a situation in which they appear to be dangerous, unyielding, irresponsible radicals against whom repression without restraint becomes a welcome and legitimate enterprise. They have to establish the credibility of their grievances and the legitimacy of their demands in such a way that a response based on coercion alone will be impossible to undertake. The authorities, on the other hand, have the aim of reestablishing domestic peace and creating self-policing social units within the lower orders, so that constant intervention and large expenditures on coercive control will not be required. To raise a hitherto powerless and excluded group into full-citizenship status cannot be accomplished without loosening the screws of coercive control and transferring resources and delegated authority into their hands. The risk involved is that newly won freedoms and resources might be used to strengthen the opposition movement to the point where it is powerful enough to undermine the government or overthrow the ruling groups. The hope is that new groups having a stake in social stability and gradual change are created and consolidated ahead of those groups who benefit from continued mobilization of disaffected elements and from social disturbances.

CONFLICT REGULATION

When social disturbances break out, the authorities or the target group of the demonstrators has to decide whether or not to adopt a conciliatory policy, a policy whose aim is "to avert or discontinue conflict without either asking or offering surrender" (Turner, 1969:823). The essence of conciliation is to recognize and to negotiate with the leaders, representatives, or spokesmen of the protest group in order to reach an enforceable agreement on the basis of which hostilities can cease. The protest group in turn has to decide whether to desist from further confrontations during negotiations by calling off demonstrations, provocative and coercive actions that have been used in order to voice grievances publicly and to press for negotiations. For both sides conciliation means abandoning the goal of injuring or crushing one's adversary and of extorting unilateral concessions and gains at his expense. Whether conciliation will be sought depends on the costs and benefits that both sides expect from a negotiated agreement weighed against the costs and benefits of continued confrontation. For instance, if one side estimates that by refusing to conciliate it may have to deal with more intransigent and dangerous opponents at some future time, it may well decide in favor of conciliation. On the other hand, should one of the conflict groups use confrontation as a means of gaining notoriety, recruiting followers, and strengthening the resolve of its members, then its chances of reciprocating a conciliatory opponent are slim (Coser, 1956:95–104).

What benefits does the protest group seek to obtain through conciliation that it might not gain in continued confrontation? Most immediately, protesters seek to obtain redress for their grievances through actions and measures to which their target group will publicly commit itself in a negotiated agreement. They seek the creation of institutional arrangements whereby a greater share of resources will be diverted to solve their problems. Oftentimes protesters seek to obtain some influence in shaping hitherto unilateral administrative decisions affecting their welfare. Conciliation is a means of opening blocked channels of communication to the higher levels of authority by negotiating directly with important officials rather than the lower echelons who were routinely concerned with their problems. Protesters also seek to obtain personal security for themselves by entering into negotiations instead of risking injury, arrest, prosecution, and penalties likely to result from continued confrontation. Leaders may also wish to protect their organization from

being banned and destroyed by the authorities. A third gain from conciliation is the opportunity for building an image of moderation and restraint
through which allies can be recruited and public opinion can be favorably influenced. Finally, the protesters may wish to maintain continuing
cooperative relationships with their opponents because they need to
enlist their support for the solution of their problems or of future problems (Turner, 1969:823–25).

The authorities or target group on its part stands to gain from a
termination of overt conflict in a number of ways. Coercive social control
may be a source of embarrassment and of weakness if the authorities
base their legitimacy on the consent of the governed and the support of
the people. This is why authorities who refuse to negotiate typically
minimize the number of protesters and emphasize "outside" agitators
who have stirred up and misled an otherwise loyal and contented popu-
lace. The authorities are also under pressure to reestablish the normal
round of daily activities so that people can go about their business without fear of personal injury and the destruction of their property. If coercive control triggers widening social unrest, conciliation may be a means
of reestablishing domestic peace. Third, the authorities may hold that
the cost of continued confrontation and coercive control is an expensive
undertaking that diverts resources into nonproductive channels. Finally,
they may want to maintain or reestablish good working relations with the
members of the protest group and others sympathetic to the protesters,
since they need such collaboration for joint undertakings. These might
be economic, for instance, increasing production, or political, for instance, obtaining votes for reelection.

It follows that the greater the expected benefits from conciliation
to both sides, the more likely it is that an arrangement for regulating and
resolving the conflict by negotiation will be reached. In particular, if
the potential of the protesters for disrupting everyday routine socioeconomic activities is great and if the costs of repression are considerable,
the prospects for conciliation look good. If the protesters do not, however,
enjoy public support and sympathy, if their moral credit in the eyes of
public opinion is low, then the necessity to be conciliatory is absent.
Such protesters can readily be defined as dangerous and irresponsible
hooligans, criminals, delinquents, and outlaws against whom an appropriate response is severe punishment. Again, if a government or authority
does not rest its authority on democratic principles, if public opinion is
weak and inarticulate, or if repression can be carried out in relative
secrecy, the pressures for conciliation are that much less. From the protesters' point of view, if continued confrontation is not likely to lead to
injury and negative sanctions, if the target group is fairly incapable of
providing redress for grievances and relief from hardship, the benefits

from terminating confrontations and entering negotiations are not impressive. These last two conditions are typical of weak and inefficient regimes on the verge of collapse, as in revolutionary situations; the agents of social control refuse to engage in coercive actions to contain the insurgents, and the administrative apparatus of the incumbents is so inefficient and corrupt that reforms with a chance of success cannot be implemented.

Even if both sides find it in their interest to undertake a conciliatory approach, it might still happen that negotiations will break down, that an enforceable, mutually acceptable agreement will not be found, and that overt conflict will be resumed. Any conciliatory enterprise is complicated: on top of the substantive issues causing the conflict in the first place there arises the question of allocating responsibility for the injuries that both sides have inflicted upon each other during the confrontation period, of punishment for those held responsible, and of compensation for damages and injuries incurred. Not only do negotiations take place against a background of past humiliations, broken promises, recriminations, injuries, and disappointments, but the atmosphere of hostility and mistrust is reenforced by new incidents that lead to doubts about the good faith of one's opponents, that call for retaliatory action and thus might be the occasion for resuming full-scale overt conflict. Such incidents strengthen the complementary negative images of the adversaries and the position of the hard liners in both camps who were opposed to conciliation to begin with (Deutsch, 1969).

Consequently the chances of fruitful negotiations are enhanced to the extent that both sides are highly organized, united, and strongly led, with leaders able to enforce discipline down to the rank-and-file who man the front lines, since then the likelihood of injurious incidents poisoning the conduct of negotiations is low. Dahrendorf (1959:226) reaches a similar conclusion from a different perspective when he maintains that regulation of conflict is impossible so long as the conflicting forces are diffuse aggregates. This requirement applies to the authorities as much as to their opponents. The higher authorities have to be able to control the actions of lower level field commanders and of the executors of their orders. Indiscipline, ambiguous instructions, confused lines of command and of communication can wreck the prospects of successful negotiations. By the same token, to negotiate with leaders who cannot restrain the demonstrators for whom they purport to speak is also less likely to lead to a successful conclusion. After each clash resulting in loss of life and property, the pressures on the authorities for coercive control increase, and the issue of responsibility, of blame, and of bad faith surfaces once more. It is also apparent that a movement rent by factionalism and leadership rivalries will be difficult to negotiate with. Some lesser leaders may not have a stake in restraining their followers. They hope to increase their influence in the movement by taking a more militant and intransigent stance; they may wish to deprive their rivals of the prestige and added stature that a successful agreement would confer upon them. In fact, when faced with an amorphous, spontaneous social disturbance typical of unorganized or weakly organized collectivities, there may be no one with authority and influence over protesters to negotiate with. The target group may find itself in a position of proclaiming well publicized, unilateral concessions. If disturbances continue, it is faced with the unpalatable prospect of making further concessions that appear to reward the demonstrators for illegal and injurious actions. The temptation to turn to coercive control is then great.

Much the same conclusion can be reached by focusing on the prospects for enforcement of an agreement. From the point of view of both sides, a major benefit of an agreement resulting from negotiations is the cessation of social turmoil and the diminished risk of injury and damages. If either side is incapable of enforcing the terms of an agreement, the authorities can claim a mandate for arresting the leaders of their opponents and for suppressing their organizational base, whereas protest leaders may find it necessary to call for renewed disturbances in order to pressure the other side into compliance and to maintain their grip over their rank-and-file supporters. To the extent that both sides are highly organized, united, and strongly led, the prospects of enforcing an agreement are good and the likelihood of renewed overt conflict diminished (Coser, 1957:132–33).

Negotiations are more likely to get under way and to be successful if they are preceded by goodwill gestures. Tensions must be eased, a measure of trust between adversaries must be reestablished, the mutually negative images that the two sides have formed of each other must be counteracted. Thus, the withdrawal of particularly hated troops and police identified with past repression, the reassignment of hard line officials to positions and responsibilities removed from the conflict, the appointment of others more responsive to the needs and voices of the protest group, restraint and fairness in prosecuting demonstrators and protesters, are common ways in which an atmosphere conducive to successful negotiations is created. On the other hand, unilateral threats, extravagant charges and claims, setting down preconditions to negotiations, unrealistic negotiating positions, nonnegotiable demands, an unwillingness to discipline and restrain one's disgruntled and trigger-happy followers, all have the opposite effect of maintaining a high pitch of tension not conducive to negotiations.

Mediators and mediating bodies can do a great deal for conflict regulation. In Boulding's (1966:246) view, conflict management and regulation have to be learned much as any other skill and technique, but "conflict management is . . . something which does not necessarily arise out of the conduct of the conflict itself. It has to be fed into it from the outside." This is precisely what third parties, mediators, outsiders can accomplish. Mediators are particularly effective if they have not been identified previously with either side, if they speak with a united voice, and most crucial, if they have a mandate for representing the public whose interest and point of view have been drowned in the charges, countercharges, and staking out of positions by the adversaries. Mediators may thus possess considerable moral authority before which both sides are able to moderate their stand without losing face and giving an appearance of weakness. Mediators might be able to persuade both sides to abide by the principle of reciprocity in negotiations: in the give-and-take of bargaining, gains and losses to both sides should balance out (Dubin, 1960:501–18). Once such an "ethic of symmetry" is established as a norm of conflict regulation, neither side can in good conscience push the other up against the wall with unrealistic demands and an uncompromising position. Mediators are helpful because they might be able to redefine the conflict such that past precedent suggests solutions; they can be an unbiased source of information that both sides have to reckon with; they can establish physical contact between adversaries, assume responsibility for an agenda and the procedures under which negotiations are conducted, including the safe conduct of the negotiators; they might even be called upon to ensure that the terms of the agreement are adhered to and that the cessation of open conflict is not exploited for the purpose of preparing another round of confrontations; they can suggest terms of agreement that the leaders of neither side dare openly voice for fear of appearing weak, of being too willing to yield. Last but not least, mediators might shoulder the burden of assigning responsibility and blame for past injurious actions resulting from the confrontation and of suggesting a reasonable schedule of penalties and reparations that become the starting point for reasonable bargaining positions. Mediators stand the best chance of success when both sides are sensitive to public opinion and wish to appear flexible and responsive to the public interest. If both parties appeal to different publics, within an already polarized society, then the mediators' task is made very difficult, since they will be lacking in moral authority. In such situations, a third party with superior force at its command might physically intervene in the conflict and impose a solution from above.

In the end, lasting conflict regulation requires more than ad hoc conciliation whenever disturbances occur; it requires institutionalization of the conflict. Institutionalization means that certain forms of protest are recognized as lawful and that consequently the agents of social control not only have no right to repress them but must protect the safety of the protesters against hostile interference. It also means that the leaders and organizations pressing for reforms are given the right to conduct their business, to recruit followers and raise resources, to publicly voice their position, in full freedom. It means that officials are bound by law and by public opinion to recognize these leaders as legitimate representatives of larger groups who must be received, listened to, bargained with in good faith. Institutionalization may further mean that a concrete sequence of steps and appeals is spelled out for resolving outstanding differences. Thus, the question of whom to negotiate with, when, under what rules, and which issues, is answered with reference to rights, to laws, to precedent, and not the bargaining power or goodwill of the adversaries.

CONFLICT REGULATION
IN THE CIVIL RIGHTS MOVEMENT

It is useful to illustrate the previous ideas about conciliation and coercion with reference to some well-known cases of social conflict. The Montgomery bus boycott of 1955–1956 was a typical instance of the conflict between a southern municipal administration and the black population over changing segregation institutions before the federal government became a major and active party to conflict regulation. The Montgomery Improvement Association wished to obtain a repeal of municipal ordinances in order to desegregate seating arrangements on municipal buses. Only negotiations with the city council could bring about the desired change. The tactic adopted for the purpose of pressuring the council into negotiations was the boycott of buses by black riders, not an illegal action. It was designed to minimize the probability of physical and material injury so as not to provoke retaliatory repression and give an occasion for arresting participants in the boycott movement. By maintaining a moderate stance, exercising self-discipline, yet demonstrating determination and a spirit of sacrifice, the relatively powerless black protest movement had the prospect of using its moral credit to build up support in public opinion and among groups who had some influence with the Montgomery authorities and white notables. For this purpose it was extremely important to demonstrate visibly that MIA leadership and the boycott movement had the support of the vast majority of the black community, that it was not masterminded by a minority out to gain an advantage for itself. Movements of subordinate groups lacking resources have to demonstrate in numbers and in unity what they lack in power. This goal was achieved through the total mobilization of the black population behind the boycott right from the start.

Since the protesters were not engaged in illegal actions, the authorities had no mandate and no occasion for employing coercive social control. At the same time, since the protesters were not disrupting the normal course of daily activity in the city, there was little inducement for the authorities to adopt a conciliatory position. The cost of the boycott fell heavily upon the boycott participants, many of whom walked to work over long distances. Only after months had passed did the loss of income from bus fares create a financial situation worrisome to the municipal administration. The response adopted to meet the boycott challenge was to use harassment tactics in order to increase the costs of protest to the point where the movement would collapse from within. It was expected that a lack of tangible gains by the MIA would in time discourage its supporters and create dissension within the black population. To yield even limited concessions to a peaceful challenge of the segregation system was considered by the white majority to be unacceptable because it brought into question the legitimacy of white supremacy as a whole. It was also thought that concessions would embolden blacks to seek further changes in segregation practices. Paradoxically, it is easier to yield on a matter of principle to superior power than it is to yield before a superior moral claim, since the principle itself is then not brought into question. In the end, the issue was litigated in the federal courts where the city lost its case. As is so often the case, an institution whose sphere of authority does include or comes to include the matter under dispute provides a means to terminate the confrontation, and without loss of face to the stronger party. To sum it up, the failure of conflict resolution through negotiations resulted from the fact that while it was in the interest of the MIA to negotiate, the white power structure did not derive any benefit from doing the same. The use of nonviolent, noncoercive tactics by the boycott movement resulted in insufficient disruption and did not force a decision to conciliate or to repress. It must be realized that the use of coercive tactics by blacks in the Deep South in the mid-1950s would have brought down on their heads a full-scale repression at a time when effective outside support, either from the Washington administration or from a mobilized public opinion, was weak or lacking altogether.

Why was conciliation so difficult in the civil rights movement to desegregate the South? There were, of course, hundreds of instances of nonviolent regulation of conflict in race relations, especially in the Border states, yet there can be no doubt that it was the numerous and repeated instances of violent confrontation that gave to this troubled period its characteristic stamp and had the decisive influence in shaping the course of events. First of all, the existing machinery of conflict regulation and conflict resolution was inadequate to serve as the framework within which major changes in race relations could be realistically expected. The resistance to the Supreme Court's school desegregation decision and the limited results achieved by the early 1960s were a visible demonstration of this fact. Subsequently, the breaking of unjust segregation laws, the arrest of those practicing civil disobedience, litigation in local courts, appeals to higher courts, the reliance on federal court orders lacking adequate enforcement machinery, were expensive, time consuming, and endangering the physical safety of the protesters who were exposed to the wrath of local law enforcement officials. Moreover, the costs of this means of challenging the segregation institutions fell entirely upon the black protesters; hence, the resort to nonviolent mass protest forcing a confrontation with local authorities and forcing some response, coercive or conciliatory, since it disrupted the normal cycle of community activities. The second element shaping the conflict had to do with the peculiar nature of the segregation institutions themselves: these were sustained by hundreds of local authorities and communities and were expressed in many different discrete forms. There was a lack of geographical focus and of a single outstanding issue on which segregation could be challenged decisively. The successful desegregation of public transportation in one town would not set a compelling precedent for a neighboring town, let alone a city located in another state. Within the same town the desegregation of a lunch counter would not be automatically followed by the desegregation of a theater, and perhaps not even the desegregation of other lunch counters. Thus, the movement against segregation had to be pursued by means of hundreds of discrete, localized, uncoordinated actions and campaigns, each of which had potential for violence. While in some communities the local authorities decided to conciliate the conflict in order to avoid a bad national image, the costs of repression and the interruption of business, an invasion by newsmen and outside organizers and activists, other communities for various reasons decided on an uncompromising stand.

A third factor was the absence of a strong, legitimate, superordinate authority that might either impose a solution from above or be able to compel the two sides to negotiate. Because the United States possesses a decentralized form of government, the federal government was neither responsible for local law enforcement, nor were segregation laws unconstitutional or contrary to federal law in the absence of national legislation before the Civil Rights Acts of 1964 and 1965. Moreover, whatever national laws existed conferred only limited powers upon the federal authorities. Only if federal court orders were defied by local and state authorities, or if the execution of these orders were interfered with by mobs whom the local officials refused to control and discipline, would there be an occasion for the direct intervention of the Washington administration. In the usual confrontation law enforcement was in the hands of officials and agents of social control who had a bias against the protesters and who in many instances encouraged the illegal use of force against peaceful and orderly demonstrations as a means of smashing the opposition. In this context of repression and lawlessness sanctioned by some local and state authorities, private citizens with an extremist disposition stood little risk of apprehension, prosecution, and conviction for engaging in physical assault, bombings, shootings, and murders. Negotiations and conflict regulation are, of course, difficult to pursue when they take place in an atmosphere of mistrust, recriminations, repeated injuries, and continued turmoil.

The fourth element in the situation resulted from both parties' stake in continued confrontation and a state of high tension. Many Southern politicians and officials could look forward to advancing their political careers by openly defying the federal authorities. By courting federal intervention they would emerge the champions of states' rights and local patriotic sentiment that had an appeal outside the South as well since it had deep roots in American history and traditions. Thus, the moral issue would be shifted away from centering exclusively on inequality and unequal justice on which their potential for mobilizing national support was weak. The civil rights leaders were caught up in a different set of dilemmas. They realized early enough that only national legislation would decisively demolish segregation throughout the South. In a series of local confrontations without federal help or intervention they would more often than not fail to emerge as victors and would in the process dissipate their meager resources. But congressional action could only be expected to materialize if Southern excesses of the Bull Connor variety would create a public outrage and nationwide clamor for civil rights legislation. Thus, for black leaders to call off their campaigns of mass action in the face of risks of violent confrontation would be to abandon the only weapon they possessed for achieving their goals. Moreover, the civil rights movement was by no means united: in the competition for leadership, for publicity, for outside resources and allies, for followers among an increasingly aroused black mass, it was difficult to back down from confrontation since it would mean a loss of influence in the civil rights movement, the rise of other leaders and groups bent on more forceful methods, and the possibility of spontaneous and uncontrolled crowd actions with a much higher potential for violence.

Finally, the civil rights confrontation occurred in a context where no highly respected group or national institution was regarded by both sides as an impartial mediator possessing compelling moral authority and a united voice that could be identified with the national interest. Congress was divided along sectional lines. The segregationists looked to Southern congressional leadership to block civil rights legislation and to maintain an uncompromising stand. The Supreme Court with its 1954 school desegregation decision had forfeited its claim to impartiality and moral authority in many Southern eyes. It was in fact perceived by many as the source of all the trouble to begin with. The president and the executive branch were increasingly drawn into the controversy in ways that favored the civil rights cause, though they did in numerous instances manage to persuade and pressure both sides into deescalating a dangerous confrontation, as President Kennedy did in Birmingham in 1963. Nor could the president in this case fail to assert executive leadership, since inaction in the face of mounting civil disorders and defiance of federal court orders were contrary to his constitutional duties and in any case would have appeared to be partial to the Southern resistance movement. In any event, only strong leadership in favor of reforms whose time had come could make possible the national legislation that eventually became the basis of institutionalized conflict regulation in Southern race relations.

CONFLICT REGULATION
AND AFRICAN NATIONALISM

As another example of the play of forces pulling in the direction of conciliation and of coercion, it is interesting to review how the nationalist aspirations of colonial peoples were handled by various European powers after World War II. In particular, why did Britain pursue a generally conciliatory policy in its African colonies while Portugal, a much weaker power by any standard, instituted and still follows a policy of repression? For Britain, coercive social control on the part of its colonial administration against a mass movement would be a source of embarrassment in international relations and at home. Its philosophy of colonial rule rested on the premise that self-government is a legitimate aspiration that would indeed be eventually granted when the Africans were ready for it. It was assumed that the British colonial government was at the time, and still for some time to come, more qualified than any potential indigenous counterpart to exercise the functions of government. A mass movement that had to be contained by force or a series of military actions against national liberation movements would clearly give the lie to such claims.

The benefit that Britain derived from its African colonies was based on economic and strategic factors. In World War II the colonies were a useful source of manpower, of raw materials, and of bases from which the British Isles could be defended against Nazi aggression. Immediately after the war, British economic recovery, though slow, was nevertheless made less painful through colonial economic policies that favored Britain at the expense of African economic development. By the middle 1950s the strategic and economic benefits from colonies were less obvious. Strategically, the United States was assuming most of the burden for containing Soviet expansion in Europe and elsewhere. With or without its colonies, Britain would have to rely on United States help to defend itself from threats and attacks directed at the British Isles. So far as the economic advantages of possessing colonies were concerned, it became evident that huge investments would have to be made in order to develop colonies at a pace that would satisfy the material aspirations of the African peoples. On top of that, the costs of coercive containment of nationalist movements would be high. Even if such repression were possible, one could expect the disruption of the pattern of normal economic activity from which many British corporations and citizens were deriving financial gain and a livelihood. The precedent of Indian and Pakistani independence proved that it was possible to maintain an economic presence and come to terms with postcolonial governments through goodwill earned by a conciliatory approach and the persistence of trade patterns. Thus, Britain had much to gain from conciliation and much to lose from repression.

The heart of British policy was to ensure that groups friendly and well-disposed toward her would assume the reins of power after independence. It was thought that the best way to achieve this goal was to demonstrate the benefits of a British-style parliamentary democracy during a period of transition under British tutelage and thus establish a tradition of Western government. Respect for civil liberties, property rights, and the rule of law represented also the best protection for British citizens and investments that would remain in the former colonies. Finally, by leaving behind a legacy of government that is justly admired and that has withstood the test of time, the loss of prestige resulting from diminished empire and worldwide influence would be compensated by pointing to the lasting contributions that Britain had made in the third world and in which Englishmen could take pride.

On the African side, confrontation based on mass pressures was crucial if the very leisurely and far from definite timetable for eventual self-rule was to be brought back from the distant into the near future. Another thing that became evident is that the British would be quite willing to transfer power to whichever groups were securely established and willing to adopt parliamentary democracy. This included traditional rulers, chiefs, and notables who in many countries had a sizeable following. The new groups, middle class, the urban professional and white-collar strata who wanted to obtain the top leadership positions after independence had to establish a political base by means of political parties with a mass following over which they exercised control. Only then would they be able to impress upon the British government that stable postindependence rule could not be ensured if they were kept from power. These nationalists had ambitious goals for their country, of accelerating socioeconomic changes, of a cultural revival, of an independent role in world politics as part of the nonaligned, third world nations. The more nationalist and socialist their economic program and the more independent their foreign policy, the more important it was for these nationalists to achieve a monopoly of support among the African population, for only then would the colonial administration find it futile to deal with other leaders and groups whose pronouncements and policies were more to their liking. The intense competition for support among the population by the nationalist parties did not proceed without its share of confrontations and coercive tactics against both the African opposition and the colonial government that set down tight rules within which the competition for political power was to proceed in orderly and gradual fashion. During these times of political awakening of the ordinary Africans it paid the nationalist leaders to be arrested and prosecuted for they might thus gain in stature as the champions of the common cause and as the victims of colonial oppression. Once the British had come around to deal directly with the nationalist leaders as the future leaders of their country, nothing was to be gained by not reciprocating a conciliatory policy: after years of living the unsettled and insecure life of a political agitator and organizer, the possibility of moving from prison and detention camps into positions of authority and responsibility that were financially rewarding was difficult to resist. It was also realized that for some years to come the British would be a useful and necessary source of skilled manpower and financial assistance. Hence, it was in the interest of the nationalist leaders to reestablish good relations with the British government. Thus, as soon as confrontation had forced the British to adopt a conciliatory attitude and to agree to a transfer of power to the nationalists, both parties became involved in the cooperative enterprise of effecting a smooth and orderly period of transition. By and large, therefore, and especially if seen against the backdrop of violence and turmoil so characteristic of major changes in world history, the achievement of independence of Britain's African colonies has involved little bloodshed and has not left behind it a legacy of bitterness and mistrust.

The transition did not proceed equally smoothly in all instances, notably in the case of "settler" colonies, Kenya in East Africa and Southern Rhodesia in Central Africa. Because in the 1950s Southern Rhodesia was part of the Central African Federation in which it played the dominant role, the white settlers' political aspirations interfered with the more orderly political evolution in the other two sections of the Federation as well, in Nyasaland and Northern Rhodesia, now Malawi and Zambia. In settler colonies the grievances of the Africans were greater to begin with: land had been alienated to European farmers; native reserves were kept in an undeveloped state in order to provide an abundant and cheap source of labor for a white-dominated economy; racial discrimination and segregation everywhere increased as the European community grew in size and could conduct its social life in self-imposed isolation from the African environment. The British government had contributed to the creation of these dual societies with its colonization policies and the concessions it had made to settler self-government. Because of settler opposition and a white-dominated economy the rise of an educated African social stratum was delayed. The Africans' aspirations for political rights and political participation kept being blocked. The colonial government felt responsible for the future of the settlers. It could not fail to grant some measure of political power to them, but in doing so it jeopardized its long-term commitment to majority rule when that majority would be ready to assume it, since the settlers used the power they had gained to make certain that such a time would never come about. Failing that, the settlers' goal would be to gain total independence from Britain, counting on the knowledge that it would be exceedingly difficult for any British government to use force against its own "kith and kin." In these efforts, the example of South Africa as a former British colony where white minority rule was achieved without British intervention served as an encouragement and as a model.

Unrest and open rebellion erupted among Africans, in Kenya during the early 1950s, in the Central African Federation at the end of the decade. Despite an endless series of reviews and reports, meetings and conferences, petitions and commissions of inquiries, it became apparent that the settler goal of minority rule and the African nationalist goal of majority rule could not be reconciled by any compromise formula. Because of the legacy of past injuries and conflict, neither side trusted the other sufficiently for even a temporary compromise to work. Faced with the mounting cost of social control, but unable to restore an orderly society and guarantee a stable future, faced with a situation where both parties were increasingly disenchanted and uncooperative with British overrule, the colonial government adopted the policy of yielding to the stronger, more determined, and more troublesome group. Given this tendency, the incentive for continued confrontation was high. Africans knew full well that with each increment in the power of the settlers at the expense of the colonial administration, the chances of achieving majority rule by peaceful and parliamentary processes of political competition were diminishing. Far preferable therefore to confront an authoritarian yet humane colonial regime than risk confronting an intolerant and unresponsive future settler regime that would respond to opposition with coercion. Africans also knew full well that the weak link in British colonial policy was British public opinion at home and British sensitivity to adverse worldwide reaction, especially on the occasion of social disturbances that had to be put down by military force. In Kenya, after Mau Mau, it was obvious that no viable settler government would stay in power without the support of a British military presence. This was also by and large true in Malawi and in Zambia. Here the Africans therefore prevailed. In Rhodesia the settlers were more numerous, their geopolitical position bordering upon South Africa more secure, the African opposition more disorganized and more openly repressed and less able to mobilize support for lack of political rights. In Rhodesia the settlers therefore prevailed.

Why did Portugal not adopt the British road to decolonization when faced with nationalist demands and risings instead of repression? Portugal is a small country not in the limelight of world attention; its colonial policies underwent much less scrutiny than British policies. Less information was available since the Portuguese authorities hid behind a cloak of secrecy (Duffy, 1963). In the absence of a free press, the right of association, and other essential civil and political rights, the Africans' point of view could not become public. All these facts conspired to keep criticism and moral pressure from without Portugal at a low level. Since Portugal is an authoritarian regime its government does not have to put up with open opposition at home. Hence, another potential source of pressure against its colonial policies was lacking. Moreover, the Portuguese regime does not believe in democratic institutions for its own people in Europe, consequently much less so for Africans in its colonies. Its position in Europe might become shaky if it were to extend political rights in the colonies that it does not consider desirable to introduce in Europe. Whereas the British did not deny the legitimate goal of eventual self-rule in their colonies, the Portuguese long-term goals were based on a nebulous cultural policy through which Africans would become civilized and assimilated to a European way of life and way of thinking. In this formula the alternative of self-government was not included. Thus, the Portuguese regime, unlike the British government, lacked the inclination, the precedent, and the institutional machinery for a devolution of political power to its colonial peoples.

On top of all this, a loss of colonies would represent a far greater economic blow and require a far greater ideological readjustment at home for Portugal than for Britain. In economic terms the colonies—or Overseas Territories as they were euphemistically designated—provided emigrants from a poor country with an opportunity to become settlers with far more affluence than would have ever been possible at home. Therefore, the colonies made less likely the accumulation of an impoverished and frustrated lower middle and working class at home. For individuals in the higher strata it provided a career in the colonial administration with more rapid advancement possibilities than at home. Colonial trade passing through Portuguese commercial houses enriched the metropolitan business community. Colonial markets protected against foreign competition helped nascent Portuguese industry. Portugal also feared that since it lacked the capital and resources to develop its colonies single-handedly, an independent African government would soon repudiate the pattern of exclusive economic ties to Portugal and seek resources for development elsewhere. This, too, would result in a major economic dislocation at home. On the matter of national morale and prestige, Portugal can take little national pride in any accomplishments apart from the past glories of empire and the Christian and civilizing influences it was able to spread as a consequence. The official justification for colonial wars rests precisely on the claim that these values have to be defended against Communism, barbarism, and chaos. Reduced to its metropolitan size and its status as the poorest and most backward country in Western Europe, Portugal would undergo a major crisis of national consciousness that the present regime might not survive. And lastly, even if the regime were inclined to change its policy of repression, the Portuguese settlers might well opt for a Rhodesian solution, i.e., declare their unilateral independence from Portugal and continue the policy of coercive control of Africans on their own.

On the African side, Portugal's immunity to worldwide criticism of its colonial policies and the absence of institutional channels for voicing grievances in an authoritarian system left no alternatives but confrontation. Armed rebellion was started in the 1960s and was met by armed retaliation. It should be noted that in situations where an opposition movement is kept from mobilizing potential supporters because of police control, where peaceful demonstrations and petitions might go completely unnoticed because of press control, where even mild forms of protest are going to be met by prosecution and harsh forms of punishment, only armed revolt stands a chance to penetrate the cloak of secrecy and to force the regime to reconsider its uncompromising stand. After ten years of rebellion, which seems to have become a stalemate at least in Angola and Mozambique, the prospects of a decisive victory are unlikely for either side, and since the costs of repression have been high to the Portuguese, a negotiated settlement should not appear unattractive to both sides. The major stumbling block would appear to be the present Portuguese regime's unwillingness to risk initiating major changes that it might be unable to survive in Portugal itself.

CONFLICT REGULATION ON THE CAMPUS

It is equally instructive to review the problems of conciliation in the typical campus confrontation between student radicals and the university administration into which the faculty and the majority of moderate students are inevitably drawn. A university is under ordinary circumstances an institution in which considerable reliance is placed on self-policing. Rules and regulations backed up by a mild schedule of penalties are administered in such a way as to provide the offender with ample opportunities to make good again. What keeps the university functioning smoothly is that the creation of new knowledge and the transmission of existing knowledge are goals considered desirable by faculty, students, and administrators alike. Each of these groups derives tangible benefits from pursuing these goals in cooperation with each other. The university is, however, not an egalitarian institution in which basic decisions are reached through a democratic process. It combines under one roof groups unequal in age, authority, accomplishments, expertise, permanence, and responsibility; no matter how cordial the relations between its various categories of members, the university remains a highly stratified social system.

By the 1950s and 1960s the major institutions of higher learning in the U.S. no longer concerned themselves systematically with character development and moral education. Apart from teaching respect for the idea of learning and the pursuit of science, the discipline of scholarship and the rigors of method, the faculty did not think it appropriate to transmit ethical and political values to the students. To be sure, since the scientific and scholarly approach is sceptical of established truths and the conventional wisdom, the process of instruction and of learning does foster a critical and speculative bent of mind. The shortcomings of existing institutions are exposed and alternative arrangements are proposed; rather less effort is spent on how reforms are translated into reality.

Under these circumstances the major influence shaping the political and moral outlook of the students came from outside the university: President Kennedy's call to idealism, the civil rights movement in which many participated, the visible needs of the lower classes, the poor, and minorities in the affluent society, continued cold war and the arms race that did not lead to any greater security for either side, the war in Vietnam. In the experience of the most active students every single cause that they had dedicated themselves to had ended in major setbacks: John Kennedy, Martin Luther King, Jr., Robert Kennedy were assassinated; the war in Vietnam was intensified by "peace" candidate Johnson; misery and rioting continued in the slums; integration did not seem to work in the megalopolis; black nationalists no longer wanted to put up with white liberals; the Johnson administration was utterly insensitive and unresponsive to peaceful and orderly mass protest; no issue was able to arouse a basically conservative, middle-class America concerned with its comforts. The students who took part in these campaigns and movements and who set the mood for the entire student body became angry young men and women. They became impatient with the slow pace of change through existing institutions, mistrustful of those in authority positions, intolerant of those who did not share their intense concerns and priorities, disillusioned with their elders. For some, earlier idealism had given way to a cynical, negative, and destructive orientation. Others thought the achievement of realistic goals less important than the sheer experience of participation in a movement, no matter what its goals. When these student activists turned upon the university, it was in part to correct abuses and shortcomings in the multiversity. But it was also in part a case of selecting a weak and exposed target against which the prospects of success were much higher than against the Pentagon, City Hall, Southern sheriffs, or the Washington administration.

In the campus confrontations the two sides had an unequal stake in conciliation. The administration was under pressure to reestablish the normal cycle of instruction and activities that were disrupted. It also wished to prevent a situation where the likelihood of physical injury to people and of damage to university property was high. Coercive social control was not within its means to execute without calling upon outside police or national guard troops and was in any case a highly distasteful alternative except as a last resort to most members of the university. It was a widely held conviction that even if coercion had become the major means for conflict settlement elsewhere in the society, the universities would remain the last refuge of reasonableness, common sense, and rational nonviolent dissent. Students pressed demands not under the banner obtaining narrow personal advantages, but in the name of correcting societal abuses, of justice for the underprivileged, of stopping the war machine, and other values and principles shared by the faculty and the administration. Under these circumstances, the image of student dissenters that prevailed, at least initially, was that of idealistic, dedicated, intelligent youth, temporarily misguided, but fighting for worthwhile causes, deserving support and guidance. Conciliation, not coercion, was thought to be the answer to such protesters even if their tactics were coercive. Lastly, important groups, especially in the faculty, held that a coercive atmosphere would permanently poison the free and cooperative atmosphere most conducive to learning and to intellectual exchange. Even if the concrete steps undertaken to conciliate the students were sometimes poorly chosen, the administrators of the university were under strong pressures to explore all means of noncoercive conflict settlement.

No corresponding pressures weighed upon the student activists. Their problem was that of a committed minority that seeks to force changes without a clearcut mandate from an ill-defined constituency. Confrontation was used by them as a tactic to build up a following among the silent majority of the students. Coercive tactics and an intransigent, defiant stand that would be met with halfhearted attempts at discipline and coercive containment could be counted upon to radicalize and unite many of the hitherto unmobilized students. Students engaging in illegal actions were fairly certain of not incurring severe physical injury or heavy penalties damaging to their subsequent educational careers, since they knew that many faculty members would favor mild disciplinary action. Nor were they concerned with maintaining good relations with administrators who, though regarded as liberals in the wider society, were held responsible for the university's uninvolvement in social reform and for its complicity and collaboration with the establishment. The replacement of these administrators by more intransigent, conservative people could always be used to increase the involvement of uncommitted students. Thus, the two sides in campus confrontations had an unequal interest in conciliation.

What of the substantive issues themselves? One set of demands dealt with academic matters and university reform. Students wished to participate more fully in intellectual discovery and enterprise, which the structure of large lecture courses, credits, requirements, grades, examinations, and a remote faculty was blocking. Some demands struck more closely at the principle of academic freedom and at the structure of authority: students wished to influence the subject matter that was taught and have a voice in the selection and promotion of faculty members. From the faculty and administration point of view, the danger in changing existing arrangements was twofold: certain courses might become little more than political indoctrination sessions or open forums for unstructured discussions void of intellectual content; the criterion of competence for faculty advancement that only colleagues were qualified to judge might be replaced by the criterion of conformity to the ideologies of whichever group was able to apply the greatest pressure at a given moment. Nevertheless, compromise on university reform was possible. Regular consultation with students over curricular changes and academic policies could be instituted. Greater weight could be assigned to teaching and community service in the recruitment and promotion of faculty. On ultimate control by the faculty over curricular content and appointments the faculty was generally united and agreed to hold firm. Because the student radicals needed faculty support for achieving other goals, they were quite willing to be conciliatory and stop short of revolutionizing authority relations altogether.

Another set of demands dealt with disengaging the university from its collaborative role with the military, certain government agencies and business institutions, and with redirecting its resources to support the causes sponsored by the student movement: support for blacks and the poor, support for the student movement itself. Some of the demands such as termination of ROTC were largely symbolic and did not require any financial sacrifices and the reallocation of resources, although here too the principle of interfering with some students' freedom of choice was involved. More black students might be admitted, special programs such as Afro-American studies could be instituted to meet some demands. More difficult to deal with were demands that struck at the economic foundations of the university. Much of the income of large universities derives from the federal government, in particular agencies such as the Atomic Energy Commission and the Defense Department who were held by student activists to be directly responsible for conducting the cold war and the Vietnam war. It would be impossible for institutions of higher learning as presently constituted to cease accepting funds from and cease doing research for these agencies. Neither would it be possible for universities to divest themselves of all securities and incomes from corporations that have defense contracts. Nor for that matter could the university commit major resources to urban renewal, health care, and public education in the ghetto without further undermining its precarious financial base. When student demands were more selective and specific, directed at particular suspect research projects and at specific abuses and problems limited to the university's immediate urban environment, negotiation and conciliation were possible.

The heart of the difficulty in redirecting university resources toward socially useful and desirable goals is that in the absence of a value consensus no criteria exist for identifying socially desirable and undesirable projects. Any project, no matter how innocent on the surface, might produce knowledge that one day could be used for purposes that some groups deem undesirable. Any advisory, consultative, or training function that faculty members perform for government agencies or business firms might conceivably lead not to a more enlightened elite but to one more capable of manipulating and deceiving the citizenry. If the principle of freedom of inquiry is abandoned and no agreement on alternative principles and criteria can be established, then the process of restricting university activities within any given limits would boil down to coercive control through vigilante activity, unsubstantiated accusations, guilt by association, the exercise of superior force, and other techniques more characteristic of a totalitarian state than of a free university. Hence, the preference of faculty for leaving the subject matter and funding of research to the discretion of the individual, under very loose supervision from his colleagues, the administration, and scientific and professional associations. Nevertheless, to student demands for discontinuing this or that suspect project, program, or source of support, the university administration has not usually responded with a last ditch stand of no compromise, though it has tried to protect the principle of free inquiry.

The most intractable aspect of campus conflict, the rock on which conciliation founders, is not the substantive demands themselves but the style of the confrontation, the injuries resulting from rule enforcement and disciplinary attempts, and the explicit student challenge to the legitimacy of authority relations. The typical campus disorder involves at some point unilateral coercive actions such as the seizure of buildings, the disruption of instruction, the invasion of offices, blocking a construction site, on the part of students who feel that they have already put their case before university officials long enough by peaceful means and have nevertheless been ignored. On their part administrators feel that they have been responsive but have not been in a position to render quick decisions because many other groups with an interest in the matter under dispute and with authority to take part in the decision had to be consulted.

Coercive student actions are taken in the name of the substantive demands, but they are complicated by further demands and proclamations: the demands are nonnegotiable, which on the face of it is a rejection of negotiations and an attempt to gain unilateral concessions by coercion; the coercive action will be continued until the demands are conceded; amnesty for the protesters has to be guaranteed; or else new disciplinary machinery has to be set up to deal specifically with the rule violations resulting from the coercive actions, on which students sympathetic to the protesters would be influential. These tactics strike at the legitimacy of authority relations, for they imply that the pursuit of certain ends justifies coercive means and that individuals in the pursuit of righteous causes should not be held accountable for their actions. Civil disobedience is a means of breaking unjust laws without disputing the right of authorities to hold law violators responsible for their actions. Making nonnegotiable demands, demanding amnesty, and refusing to stop coercive actions unless demands are fully met is a power play that frontally challenges the principle of authority and goes beyond civil disobedience. To cave in to such tactics means setting a dangerous precedent, since illegal behavior not only goes unpunished but is rewarded. Continued operation of the university, or any institution for that matter, is not possible if each minority by illegal means is able to exact unilateral concessions, or if conflict is settled to the satisfaction of whichever party poses the greatest momentary threat. If the radicals are not persuaded in frantic and usually confused discussions to modify their stand, the administration is likely to retort with its own ultimatum requiring the students to terminate their coercive actions and to submit to disciplinary procedure. The police bust that follows at this point stands a good chance of escalating the cycle of injuries, reprisals, recriminations, and coercive actions on the part of ever increasing numbers of demonstrators and law enforcement officials. When this point has been reached, the chances of conciliation have receded yet further. In all the campus confrontations where the students continue disrupting actions until their demands are unconditionally met and where they refuse to submit to disciplinary bodies, it is not possible to avoid the use of coercion to end coercion. Nevertheless, it makes a great deal of difference for subsequent conciliation under what circumstances and at what point the police were brought in, who assumes responsibility for the event, and the degree of restraint they exercise.

The faculty has a mixed record of mediating campus conflict. Mediating bodies are effective if they enjoy a moral authority recognized by all parties to the conflict, if they represent or are the recognized spokesmen for a large group that has an interest in the outcome but has not been consulted about its preferences, if they have not identified with one side so that they can appear to take an impartial and unbiased position, and if they speak with a united voice. Having abdicated all responsibility for moral education and for exercising authority on matters of nonacademic discipline in the past—at least as a body even if not as individuals —the faculty discovers at the moment of crisis that it does not possess a precedent and the institutional means of conflict settlement, that it has no experience in dealing with group conflict, and that student relations in the nonacademic aspects of university life are too important a matter to be left to administrators, trustees, and outside authorities. Nevertheless, in the early moments of the crisis the faculty is in a favorable position to emerge as the spokesmen for the university community as a whole. In the eyes of the large mass of yet uncommitted students, it is invested with a great deal of moral authority. At this point, however, the faculty splits into pro-student and pro-administration factions, which is understandable given the disparities of seniority, political outlook, and prior sympathies that must exist in a large and heterogeneous body. The faculty is not only unable to reach a consensus on how to deal with the crisis, but important faculty groups do not consider majority faculty sentiment binding on their own plans and efforts to negotiate a settlement. Other faculty groups or individuals may even adopt an openly partisan position, while still others use this moment to exact concessions from the administration for greater faculty authority in setting university policy. Thus, the faculty splits into various groups, speaks in confused and contradictory voices; lines of authority become further tangled; the large mass of students remains directionless; the radicals are encouraged to continue in their stance of defiance; the hard-pressed administration expends a great deal of time and energy in placating faculty dissenters on top of other problems. If the faculty manages to come forward decisively with a united voice and is able to adopt a conciliatory and unbiased stance, it will usually assert a considerable influence in the student body and provide both the student radicals and the administration with an opportunity to withdraw their ultimatums and threats without losing face and to gain some credit for yielding to the common good. Should the student protesters be unwilling to compromise at this point, the burden of responsibility for continued disruption and for provoking coercive retaliation shifts upon their shoulders in the eyes of the majority of students. It is upon the silent majority, after all, that the success of the radicals depends since they have to emerge as the victims of the illegitimate and unreasonable use of force.

Chapter *VIII*

CONFRONTATION

POLARIZATION

Few opposition movements start out with the goal of revolution and violent overthrow of the government; neither the leadership and membership nor the goals, ideology, and tactics of a movement are constant over time. These change according to the wider society's reception of the movement and processes internal to the movement (Turner, 1964b: 126). It will be recalled that until 1792 Louis XVI was still called the "Liberator of the French people" and that most revolutions go through a phase when the moderates are in power. In our own time, the early civil rights movement of the 1960s was firmly wedded to the integrationist "I have a dream" philosophy and nonviolent direct-action tactics of confrontation of the Reverend Martin Luther King, Jr., before the more recent stage of urban rioting, black power ideology, and the break-up of the liberal civil rights coalition. Underlying these changes from an evolutionary, reform orientation to a more radical, or even revolutionary, orientation are several processes variously referred to as escalation, polarization, and the split between moderates and radicals. All of them complicate the problem of institutionalized conflict settlement.

The major theorist of the inevitability of revolutionary social change is Marx. His well-known theory of the class struggle is spelled out in the *Communist Manifesto* (1959:1–41) and other writings. As applied to capitalist society, Marx's theory holds that the laws of economics ensure that all social groups and social strata in the society will eventually be absorbed into the two hostile classes of bourgeois-capitalists and proletarian-workers in a gradual process of polarization. The law of the falling rate of profit, of competition, overproduction, and periodic depression, of the pauperization of the masses, will bring about the economic ruin of intermediate layers of the population such as shopkeepers, artisans, small masters, and the like. In time, differences in religious belief, regional traditions, rural and urban life-styles, skills based on craftsmanship and training, even national sentiments, will be erased by the inevitable march of technological and economic change under capitalism. As these differences disappear, the increasingly homogeneous proletariat will become more organized, disciplined, class-conscious, and militant. In time, the revolutionary overthrow of the bourgeois-minority becomes inevitable.

This process of polarization would take time to accomplish, and the class conflict undergoes changes in form corresponding to the different stages of capitalist development. In the first stage there is uncoordinated and localized opposition by wage workers in the same trade or industry against their individual employers, and, thus, no protest yet against the capitalist system as such. Workers who have recently been reduced to wage earners by technological and organizational changes they do not understand engage in machine breaking and other forms of futile protest. Their goal is to recapture their lost freedom as artisans and craftsmen and restore the guild monopolies and precapitalist regulation of wages and prices. They are still oriented to the re-creation of the past social order. In the next stage, wage workers become concentrated in large cities and factory towns. With the spread of machine production, they become reduced to an undifferentiated mass of unskilled laborers so that the earlier divisions among the working class, along craft, occupational, and town and country lines, count for less and less. Workers now organize in larger bodies such as trade unions made possible by the increased size of industries and the workers' concentration in large factories, but mostly for the purpose of raising wages rather than abolishing capitalism. At this stage, the workers of an entire industry face all their employers in large strikes that spread through entire regions. Although the workers generally lose these confrontations, they nevertheless develop leadership and gain organizational experience and class consciousness. In the final stage, as the economic crises of capitalism ruin entire sections of the diminishing ruling classes and the buffer layers of the petty bourgeoisie, polarization proceeds to its full extent. A portion of the intellectuals who recognize the desirability and inevitability of socialism, because capitalism stands in the way of increased production and the satisfaction of human wants, defects to the proletarian side and channels its energies into a constructive political and economic program, the overthrow of the capitalist order, and the establishment of the new socialist society.

Marx intended his analysis of class conflict and revolution as a theoretical model in which the essence of capitalist development was captured in streamlined fashion without the variability of actual sociohistorical contexts. In his analyses and commentaries on the social upheavals in France in 1848–1850 and 1870–1871, he did not minimize existing differences within the ruling and working classes when accounting for the internal dynamics of social conflict. He discussed the role of peasantry and other rural social strata that were excluded from his overall theoretic model altogether. The polarization and class conflict model, as well as the inevitable "laws" of capitalist development that Marx postulated, were mistaken, as we now know from hindsight. Regional, rural-urban, religious, and other differences are still viable forces in advanced industrial countries and still serve as mobilizing foci for a number of political parties and social movements. Nationalism, not international class solidarity, is the dominant ideological expression of our age. The growth of technology and industry created specialization and diversity in the occupational structure in all social classes faster than the leveling and homogenizing effects that Marx foresaw. Later sociologists, notably Durkheim, recognized the integrative forces produced by differentiation based on the complementarity of interests and the increased structural interpenetration in which the socioeconomic gains of some groups would not necessarily occur at the expense of others. The middle class did compromise in country after country on the social question; reform, not revolution, became the dominant trend. Polarization and revolution did occur, but not in advanced capitalist countries. Indeed, it is the greater applicability of the Marxist model to the colonies that made Marxism so attractive to intellectuals in the third world.

In the colonial situation, a dominant foreign cultural and racial minority originally imposed by force and conquest ruled a native majority. This rule was justified by appeals to a racist ideology stressing the biological and intellectual superiority of the whites and, in the most favorable instances, by invoking the paternalist idea that the ruling groups have a duty and right to impose in unilateral and authoritarian fashion certain measures for the welfare of the majority. The natives, like children, were thought to be incapable of knowing and doing what is "good" for themselves; their resistance was punished in the same manner as that of rebellious children. In all phases of life, even in education, the system represented an assault on the dignity and self-respect of the natives. In the economy, it was accompanied by a partial destruction of the agricultural subsistence economy to accommodate the minority interests of planters, mining concerns, large farmers, and trading houses, all of them totally controlled by the ruling white minority. The duality of command

and obey positions permeated all institutions of the society, and the absence of bridges and mobility opportunity rested on legal and informal segregation, a dual standard of life and life-styles, the absence of political rights for the majority. Polarization was particularly severe in the white settler societies of sub-saharan Africa and in Algeria, where, as in South Africa, the history of race relations shows a progressive extension of apartheid even as new social strata resulting from economic change were forming within the African majority. Thus, for example, the limited nonwhite franchise in Cape Province was whittled away after World War II and the earlier English-Afrikaaner split within the dominant group replaced by a pooling of their political forces. If many African colonies did not bear the full weight of the colonial situation, it is because in many of them there were few whites and because some were too poor for economic exploitation. Hence, many people in rural areas were only marginally affected by colonialism.

It is to Marx's credit, despite the shortcomings of the polarization model as applied to capitalist societies, that he analyzed the process of polarization in terms of the structural characteristics of the society and the characteristics of the conflict process itself. Polarization refers to the breaking up of a community, group, or society into two or more internally mobilized and mutually hostile camps or, in Coleman's formulation (1957:13), "the division of the community into two socially and attitudinally separate camps, each convinced it is absolutely right." It now remains to supplement Marx's analysis in the light of more recent contributions, such as Coleman's (1957) on the dynamics of community conflict and Brinton's (1952) on the fall out between moderates and radicals in major revolutions.

In Coleman's analysis, polarization in the community experiencing controversy grows with the formation of new partisan organizations and the emergence of new "extremist" leaders while the existing community leaders and organizations are crosspressured into inaction. At the same time, the issues under dispute have a tendency to change from specific to general, new issues arise, and disagreement gives way to bitter antagonism. In Gamson's (1966) somewhat different terminology, the conflict is likely to shift from conventional to rancorous, a situation during which opponents do not simply regard each other as mistaken or as pursuing different but legitimate goals but engage in tactics considered dirty and vicious and which are in violation of norms generally accepted for waging conflict. Coleman (1957:14) labels the overall process "Gresham's Law of Conflict: the harmful and dangerous elements drive out those which would keep the conflict within bounds." He provides numerous illustrations of it for community controversies in the U.S. of the early 1950s.

Writers on revolutions also have noted increased polarization after the successful overthrow of the *ancien régime* and the initial weeks of rejoicing and hope. In the literature this has usually been discussed as the falling out of the moderates and the radicals (Brinton, 1952). After the collapse of the old regime, power tends to pass to the moderate opposition under the preceding government, who are better organized at this stage than the radicals and enjoy widespread popular support and sympathy for their leadership in the overthrow. Nevertheless, the initial era of goodwill rapidly dissipates as economic crises, the breakdown of administration, the difficulties of administrative reorganization, the requirements of a war economy, and other major problems bring increased hardship to the masses at a time when they expect a turn for the better. Meanwhile, with freedom of association, speech, and political assembly granted to all groups, the radicals organize and recruit discontented elements and in general impede the reestablishment of normality, even while the overthrown conservative forces are regrouping at home and abroad and plotting the reestablishment of the old regime. As the social control of the old order breaks down, competing principles of legitimacy for the future social order are championed by various groups and compromise becomes difficult. The division of moderates and radicals among the revolutionaries occurs over fundamental questions and principles of organization of the new society, such as a monarchy or republican form of government, the status of the church, private property, land reform, foreign investments, alliances with foreign countries or power blocs, and so on, behind which are major differences of material and political interest of the social classes or regions that the country is made up of, and which are expressed in divergent world views, conceptions of social justice, of freedom and equality. The threat of a foreign-based intervention and domestic civil war creates an atmosphere of anticipated violence and actual confrontation in which each group takes coercive measures to protect its gains from the revolution and its future goals.

Concurrent with the processes of social polarization just described occurs attitudinal polarization, its social psychological counterpart, which also makes conflict regulation difficult. Attitudinal polarization is a phenomenon that stems directly from the conflict process itself, and can therefore be analyzed independently of social polarization, though the two interact and reenforce each other. Muzafer Sherif (1966:85; 1956) has demonstrated from field experiments that increases in intergroup hostility, negative stereotypes, and hostile actions occur even in a situation where there are no cultural, class, and observable physical differences between groups if they are cast in a competitive situation where both parties compete for goals only one group could attain. Neither are "personality maladjustment and neurotic tendencies necessary conditions for the appearance of intergroup prejudice and stereotypes."

Rather, attitudinal polarization is explained with reference to processes of group formation under a condition of competition for the same scarce resources and the actions and reactions of the competing parties generated during that competition itself. The analyses of Coleman (1957) and Deutsch (1969) support and complement this perspective. The process itself can be broken down into more elementary social psychological processes having to do with biased perception, distorted communication, and commitment of members to group goals during situations of crisis.

In Deutsch's (1969:17–19) formulation, in a competitive situation, communication between the conflicting parties becomes unreliable and impoverished, and the competitors become more sensitive to differences and threats than to similarities and gestures of good faith. In addition, perceptual distortions arise from the pressures for self-consistency and social conformity. The growth of group identity and solidarity occurs at the expense of hostility and aggression against the competing out-group. There is a tendency for actions to acquire a "moral" connotation: errors of judgement, mistakes based on lack of information, accidental events, are interpreted as part of a pattern of planned measures designed to harm one's opponent and as clear indications of bad faith. In sum, "the usually accepted norms of conduct and morality which govern one's behavior toward others who are similar to oneself" are violated in dealings with the other group. Within each party, there is "increasing pressure for uniformity of opinion and a tendency for leadership and control to be taken away from those elements that are more conciliatory and invested in those who are militantly organized for waging conflict through combat." Once a series of hostile actions and retaliations has taken place, the injuries and outrages perpetrated during the process of intergroup hostility serve as additional stimuli to perpetrate the spiral of escalation, hostile sentiments, and aggressive actions. In time, as has often happened, the origins of the conflict become increasingly irrelevant as the confrontation itself feeds its own further development. In extreme cases, such as rural violence in Colombia in the 1950s, the clashes between the Guelfs and Ghibelines in the Middle Ages, or other instances of feuds such as that between Arab tribes described by T. E. Lawrence, the conflict can persist for years and even decades with the newer generation being recruited to continue the confrontation on both sides. This process has been analyzed most thoroughly in the case of international relations involving competition between power blocs where an arms race, as has happened since World War II, can become institutionalized with powerful vested interests committed to its continuation because of benefits derived from it. Such an arms race then continues independently of the changes in regimes and basic orientation of the nations engaged in it.

The very existence of arms competition becomes the major cause of the continuation of perceived threat, suspicion, fears, and hostile actions, which in turn serve to justify still greater outlays for arms and the search for improved weapons that will allegedly guarantee security. Coleman (1957:11–14) and Boulding (1962: chapter 2) have provided the most detailed account of reciprocal causation and feedback processes that tend to expand an initial controversy into a bitter and destructive conflict in successive escalated steps. It remains to examine what impact the processes of conflict group formation have upon the polarization and escalation of conflict.

All groups engaged in conflict, whether they are threatened and therefore have to organize defensively or whether they initiate a process of confrontation, are faced with the twin problem of mobilizing their members' commitments and resources for the achievement of collective goals against outside resistance and of recruiting new members or otherwise gaining sympathy, support, and outside help from third parties, the uncommitted, and the frequently apathetic public. Many conflict groups are already long-established, cohesive communities. Personal sacrifices for the purpose of enabling the community to wage the conflict will receive group support. Hesitating individuals will be subjected to social pressures for the purpose of contributing to the collective effort. Internal factionalism and dissension in all likelihood will be suspended as the community backs the existing leaders. In the extreme case, recruitment into the conflict group is automatic since by virtue of being a member of the community an individual knows that for better and for worse he will share the collective fate of his fellows. Movements that coalesce from distinct groups and associations have greater problems of recruitment, of member commitment, and of leadership. They cannot use social pressures as easily to build up a support base. They have to put stress on the ultimate benefits to be gained from the goals of the movement, downgrade the risks of participation, and work out a broad appeal with reference to values and principles in order to forge unity of purpose among people of varied backgrounds and beliefs and in order to expand their recruitment base. Outside sympathy and support also have to be mobilized with reference to values and broad principles since the movement, even if successful, may not deliver material benefits to the larger public and sympathizers. However, social control over members will be weak: membership turnover and fluctuations of participation and of the intensity of commitment will be considerable, changing as they do as a result of the repressive policies of the authorities, of the risks of participation, and of the gains realized by partial successes and compromises. When an opposition movement has to rely on mobilizing outside support to pursue its struggle, when its component subunits are diverse, each with somewhat different material goals and needs, when it has few material benefits to distribute to its supporters during the confrontation, in short, when an opposition movement is weak, it will have to make appeals for outside support and increased member commitment based on symbols, ideologies, principles, and values. That, as I have earlier discussed, will tend to make the conflict more difficult to resolve. Of course, there is always the possibility that the rhetoric of appeals and of mobilization will not be carried over into the processes of bargaining and negotiations with the target group.

IDEOLOGICAL ESCALATION

Just as there is an escalation of the means used to carry on a conflict, so it is also possible to speak about an "escalation" of the rhetoric to mobilize support within and outside the movement. Escalation processes occur commonly in all manner of social conflict, not just in the confrontation between protesters and the authorities. As Michels (1959:205ff.) has long ago noted, when trade union leaders are criticized and threatened with ouster because of incompetence, dishonesty, corruption, or failing to pursue the members' interests vigorously enough, they frequently respond by calling into question the loyalty and motivation of their opponents, by insisting that an attack on them personally is a divisive, subversive tactic that will weaken the organization's ability to pursue collective goals. In other words they try to shift the substance of the conflict from their own inadequate performance—an issue on which they are vulnerable—to the principle of disloyalty, of treason, and of undermining the power and unity of the collective effort. This tactic of escalation is also widely used by heads of state and political leaders when the wisdom of their policies, their secretive methods, and their competence are questioned by critics and dissenters. On the other hand, when incumbents attempt to reform the system from within, they will be careful not to undermine the legitimacy of the system. They are more likely to stress the personal shortcomings of individuals responsible for the sad state of affairs and past mistakes rather than question the institutional arrangements that allowed irresponsible and incompetent individuals to perform harmful actions unchecked. When Khrushchev denounced Stalin at the Twentieth Party Congress of the Soviet Communist party in 1956 (Wolf, 1957), he stressed Stalin's suspiciousness, megalomania, psychopathology, and insisted that Stalin violated socialist legality and the principles of Leninist leadership with his cult of personality and terror campaigns. Thus, the basic soundness of the Soviet political system was never questioned by Khrushchev. For critics, the fact that unchecked tyranny was able to have its way represents a fundamental flaw in the institutional structure and cannot be put down to individual shortcomings and the accidents of individual personality. Another historic example of the attempt to escalate and deescalate the issue in a struggle occurred during the Peloponnesian War when the powerful Athenians were trying to persuade the Melians to submit to Athens's rule. The Melians insisted on their right to neutrality and peaceful noninvolvement in the war between Sparta and Athens. The weaker party, the Melians, tried to make appeals based on universal principles of justice and fair play, while the stronger Athenians insisted in arguing their case on grounds of expediency, realpolitik, and mutual self-interest. In the words of the Athenian emissaries (Thucydides, 1960: Book 5),

> we will not make a long and unconvincing speech, full of fine phrases, to prove that our victory over Persia justifies our empire, or that we are attacking you because you have wronged us. . . . You know and we know, as practical men, that the question of justice arises only between parties equal in strength, and that the strong do what they can, and the weak submit.

A not unreasonable hypothesis is that groups that negotiate from a position of strength will tend to deescalate the rhetoric of confrontation, whereas weak groups who must mobilize nonmaterial resources and outside support will base their argument on broad principles and appeals. Also, it is likely that in a contest between two parties of equal strength, neither of whom has an interest in enlisting outside support in its own behalf, escalation on the dimension of values and ideologies will not be resorted to.

The institutional structure of the society will also have a bearing on whether conflict can be expressed specifically in terms of concrete bread-and-butter issues, the application of shared values, and the responsibility of particular incumbents without questioning the legitimacy of the institutions themselves. In a political system where the right of opposition and of criticism is not recognized, it is difficult to voice criticisms and demands against particular individuals and practices since the very act of making demands will be interpreted as an attack upon basic principles. If employees do not have the right to strike, a strike intended only to further the material welfare of the workers will be seen as a challenge to the existing arrangements for waging labor disputes that necessarily raises issues about authority. In such a political system, the strike will be a political act. In colonial Kenya when trade unions in the early postwar years were in their infancy, there was no machinery for negotiation and consultation in labor disputes. According to Tom Mboya (1963:32), "the demands [of the workers for increased wages] could not be put to any particular employer and so they were presented as though they were political demands to the Government." In societies where no one institution and institutional elite dominates other institutions, conflicts in specific areas and over specific issues can be contained easier within one institution, do not spill over into other institutions, and do not become automatically escalated.

The mechanism for institutional escalation of conflict is the judiciary. The lower courts handle the application of accepted principles to issues under dispute. If one of the parties believes that some other more fundamental principle is involved in the dispute and conflict resolution ought to be based on the higher principle, it appeals the decision to a higher court. Thus, in institutionalized conflict, through the courts, there are legitimate and specialized bodies provided for deciding the level at which the issue ought to be dealt with. One of the fundamental differences between institutionalized and other processes of conflict is that escalation is not left for the most part in the hands of the antagonists for use as a tactical device for shifting the focus and the level of the issues and for building support. Unregulated escalation tends to further polarization. In the extreme case where conflict is pursued in the name of the highest principles and noblest causes, compromise will be impossible, and partial successes unsatisfactory.

THE FORMATION OF CONFLICT SECTS

In bitter protracted conflict, there emerge small combat groups, revolutionary sects, guerrillas and partisans, specializing in conflict and dedicated to waging conflict to its ultimate conclusion, whether it be victory or defeat. How can it be that the usual countervailing factors that prevent one's complete involvement in behalf of any particular cause or sphere of activity do not seem to operate in the case of groups for whom conflict on behalf of a cause becomes a way of life (Merton, 1957:269ff.)? Under ordinary circumstances, the necessity of earning a living, the demands of family and of career, the desire for leisure and the enjoyment of life, and hundreds of other obligations and activities that are binding by virtue of one's membership in many different groups and social statuses, check one's total commitment to and involvement in one particular group and one particular cause. Even in revolutions, most of the supporters of the revolutionary movement are but part-time activists. In the U.S. student movement and the civil rights movement, all but a small number of the participants were not involved beyond short-term spurts of activism, while at other times they make financial contributions or try to influence public opinion through daily interactions with their fellow citizens in the normal course of the daily routine of life. Not so, however, for the full-time professional activists who give up family, work, career, leisure, and other social obligations and entanglements as well as the rewards that come with them.

To begin with, as Coser has noted (1956:95–104), these combat groups are usually small and take on the characteristics of sects: there is self-selection within the pool of potential sect members in such a way that only those who already agree with the goals and ideological position of the sect seek entry; further selection is exercised by setting high criteria for membership and by an admissions sequence with several screening points so that only those who are conformist, competent, loyal, and able to put up with discipline make it into the inner circle. During this process of selective recruitment, social interaction with the outside world ceases and social pressures from the outside diminish as outside group memberships are progressively pruned away. Once the candidate or group member has engaged in illegal activity or has been identified by the social control agencies as a sect member, the probability of retracing his steps is much diminished since his chances of getting a job and of pursuing a career free of harassment and of penalties because of his previous activities are slim. Within the sect itself, role and status conflicts become minimized through a process of key status primacy: one key status, that of membership in the sect, becomes the source of rights and obligations to which the competing demands of other roles and statuses are subordinated. If a sect member is married, he or she will be married to another sect member who defines the demands and enjoyment of marital and family life as having a lower priority than the demands of revolutionary activity. The good revolutionary husband or wife will be the one who absents himself or herself from home whenever called upon to do so, who will distribute leaflets and attend meetings, who puts the group's welfare and survival before his or her personal and family welfare, rather than the one who will bring home the paycheck or cook meals. Whereas in ordinary life people maintain a delicate balance between various competing obligations, the sect members redefine their multiple roles so as not to interfere with or even contribute to their revolutionary role. The sect, as a close-knit primary group, sustains these new definitions of role and negatively sanctions those of its members who do not conform to them. Max Weber has described how this process operates for the case of the Puritan sects in his well-known essay "The Religious Rejections of the World and Their Directions" (Weber 1958:323–59). Most religious movements eventually compromise the demands of God and of salvation with the demands of the world. The Puritans, who approximated for Weber the ideal type of the inner-worldly ascetic sect composed of religious virtuosos, were able to overcome in systematic fashion the role conflicts, value conflicts, the conflicts of loyalty that the family, the economic and political order, the erotic and the intellectual spheres of activity presented to them, each of which not only creates daily conflicting demands with the requirements of salvation but offers alternative means of gratification and of attaining meaning and purpose in one's life. The Puritans solved these dilemmas by redefining certain statuses and activities such as work, citizenship, military service. They invested them with religious meaning and enlisted them in the pursuit of salvation, or else they withdrew altogether from certain activities such as artistic pursuits. Thus, work takes on religious meaning and leads to salvation; it does not interfere with religious goals but contributes to them. The New Model Army dutifully imposed God's will upon a wicked and evil world: violence and the use of force did not jeopardize the Puritans' state of grace and salvation chances.

When successful, the religious and political sect can be the agent of a fundamental redefinition of norms and values and its diffusion in a larger population. It becomes the source and active agent of major and rapid social change. A new conception of rights and obligations affecting all roles and institutions is created and can become consolidated before processes of routinization once more chip away gradually at the foundations of the new social order. Every successful revolution for a time carries over into the postrevolutionary social order the ideal of the New Man, the New Family, and the New Commonwealth that bears a strong likeness to the sect's order of status priorities and role obligations. From the point of view of the theory of social conflict, the formation of combat groups of the sect type at the center of social movements represents a polarization of social relations and an escalation of the issues to the level of incompatible world views and fundamental principles of social organization that lead to confrontation with but small chances for compromise and conflict regulation.

THE PREPARATORY PERIOD, PRECIPITATING INCIDENTS, AND THE SPREAD OF DISTURBANCES

Prior to the actual precipitating incidents that are subsequently identified as the start of a continuous period of turmoil, there occurs a preparatory period during which tensions build up and the authorities are provided breathing time for implementing reforms. Confrontation by means of popular disturbances or insurrection does not break out without a preparatory period filled with numerous incidents that signal the existence of widespread grievances. In colonial history, this period is known as a "time of troubles" that precede the full-scale movements for independence: strikes break out, agricultural regulations are evaded and resisted by cultivators, low-key political demands for some political rights and representation in local and national legislative councils and assemblies are voiced. Reforms may be instituted, but are ineffectively implemented or undermined by some groups in the society. The basic conditions giving rise to the grievances are not remedied. In the civil rights movement the phase of continuous direct action in the South started in 1960 with the student sit-in movement and was preceded by the 1954 to 1960 preparatory period during which the 1954 Supreme Court decision was checkmated by legal evasion, economic pressures against blacks, and segregationist violence. Concerning the Northern riots of the 1960s, the National Advisory Commission on Civil Disorders wrote that (U.S. Riot Commission, 1968:111) "disorder did not typically erupt without pre-existing causes, as a result of a single 'triggering' or 'precipitating' incident. Instead, it developed out of an increasingly disturbed social atmosphere, in which typically a series of tension-heightening incidents over a period of weeks or months became linked in the minds of many with a shared network of underlying grievances." Unemployment in Northern ghettos was increasing, the standard of living of low-income black families was actually decreasing while the rest of the nation was making impressive income gains during the Kennedy-Johnson economic boom, and the Civil Rights Act, War on Poverty, and other reform legislation were not improving the condition of life of black slum dwellers.

Many confrontations in fact never take place because the authorities do implement effective reforms during the time of troubles. But often they do not. Many people are not convinced about the need for sweeping reforms in the absence of widespread disturbances; they actually believe that only a minority, stirred up by professional agitators, is seeking changes while the rest of the people are basically contented. The authorities are also frequently reluctant to implement changes under pressure. They do not want to appear weak and subject to manipulation by what is thought to be a minority of troublemakers. In any case, the initial reaction may be to make incremental changes in existing institutions that are simply not sufficient to remedy the underlying conditions giving rise to grievances. At this stage, the authorities may be faced with an institutionalized opposition that is still better organized than the protesters and may be responding to the points of greatest pressure of the moment. The preparatory period allows for organization and leaders to develop among the protesters. As expectations of favorable response to voiced grievances are systematically disappointed and promises are not acted upon, a mood of impatience develops, what historians of revolution have called "cramp." Ordinary citizens are not likely to engage in illegal mass action without this waiting period because they look upon the existing institutions and leaders as legitimate and fear the consequences of direct action. When discontented groups are suppressed by the authorities, they often go underground and continue to mobilize while the legitimacy of opposition in the face of continued hardship gains among the disaffected sectors.

It is within this context of a time of troubles and ineffective reforms that precipitating incidents break out. It is not so much a specific characteristic that identifies a precipitating incident from other similar incidents in the preparatory period; given the underlying conditions and grievances and the increased mobilization of disaffected groups, the probability of incidents occurring that will be seen as symbolic of the unsatisfactory state of affairs, rather than as isolated and accidental events, is high. The precipitating incident is a visible event that becomes interpreted as a typical example of a class of events reflecting unacceptable conditions experienced by many.

Precipitating incidents take the place of prior organization, leadership, and planning in many outbreaks inasmuch as they occur spontaneously and serve to focus attention on a set of conditions defined in terms of justice and injustice, victims and oppressors. However, they must stand in a direct relationship to the underlying grievances shared by many. In the urban riots of the 1960s, according to the National Advisory Commission on Civil Disorders (U.S. Riot Commission, 1968:120, 143, 302–303), for the twenty-four civil disorders surveyed in depth, 40 percent of all incidents in the preparatory periods involved allegedly abusive or discriminatory police action, and in twelve of twenty-four disturbances such incidents were also identified as the final precipitating event. Police incidents were the most frequent kind of event sparking riots. By the same token, police practices were rated by the Commission as the most intense grievance of blacks, including such things as "complaints about physical or verbal abuse of black citizens by police officers, the lack of adequate channels for complaints against police, discriminatory police employment and promotion practices, a general lack of respect for blacks by police officers, and failure of police departments to provide adequate protection for blacks." Widespread belief in police malpractice directed against blacks, the growing spread of the belief in police brutality, and growing open opposition to unchecked police abuses in the slums, all prior to the actual outbreak of rioting, also occurred in the Watts-Los Angeles riot of 1965 (Oberschall, 1968:329–33) and was a typical feature of the preriot situation in the 1960s. Police incidents have a high probability of occurring in public places so long as police and slum dwellers face each other as hostile antagonists, are mutually suspicious of each other's motives and actions, and can count on the support of the police department and fellow officers on the one hand, and residents and neighbors on the other, regardless of the specific circumstances or guilt of the parties in violent police-black encounters.

In the chapter on mobilization, we have already pointed out that precipitating incidents and the initial success of a protest movement at the focal point of a national or international system of orientation, communication, and social control concentrate attention on grievances and expectations of success elsewhere in the system and may lead to a series of uncoordinated, more or less spontaneous, outbreaks of protest. To explain the spread of protest actions one need not invoke theories based on conspiracy, imitation, or contagion. The concept of a system with focal points, the loosening of social control, and the presence of communications networks linking the population groups and the authorities within the system are sufficient to account for the diffusion of protest. In the 1830s and 1840s, radical and reactionary groups everywhere in Europe were taking their cues from Paris, the center of the most liberal and progressive ideas ever since the French Revolution. In January and February of 1848, there were insurrections in Sicily and Tuscany for a constitution; they might have remained isolated events had not the February revolution in Paris led to the ouster of Louis Philippe and the proclamation of a republic in France. This event stimulated a rash of popular demonstrations and civil disturbances in Austria and the German states. Charles Albert of Savoy was forced to promulgate a constitution and called on Lombardy and Venice to aid him in expelling the Austrians from Northern Italy. With the Austrian empire and Germany weakened internally and externally, the non-German peoples in Bohemia and Hungary rose up in revolt to demand independence (Merriman, 1963:209–11). The spread of these disturbances took weeks rather than days and hours to accomplish, because railways and telegraphs at this time did not yet link the European capitals. Only relatively short and internal lines of communication existed. But the newspapers and the movement of people by slower means of communication eventually spread the information within the entire system.

Similarly, the French Revolution of 1789 was followed by a wave of reactions and counterreactions throughout Europe. France had generally been considered the strongest absolute monarchy in Europe. Its weakening created a threat to absolutist and illiberal governments everywhere. Even the English government felt apprehensive, especially after the overthrow of the French monarchy in 1792. In R. R. Palmer's words (1955:360–62),

pro-French and pro-Revolutionary groups appeared immediately in many quarters. The doctrines of French Revolution, as of the American, were highly exportable: they took the form of a universal philosophy, proclaiming the rights of man regardless of time or place, race or nation. . . . In Poland those who were trying to reorganize the country against further partition hailed the French example. The Hungarian landlords pointed to it in their reaction against Joseph II. . . . The hard pressed Silesian weavers were said to hope that "The French would come." Strikes broke out at Hamburg, and peasants rebelled on the island of Rügen. . . . In Belgium, where the privileged elements were already in revolt against the Emperor Joseph, a second revolt broke out inspired by events in France and aimed at the privileged elements. In England the newly developing "radicals," men like Thomas Paine and Dr. Richard Price . . . entered into correspondence with the Assembly in Paris. Businessmen of importance, including Watt and Boulton . . . were likewise pro-French. . . . The Irish too were excited, and presently revolted. Everywhere the young men were aroused, the young Hegel in Germany, or in England the young Wordsworth.

The diffusion of revolt in the manner of 1789 and 1848 has been repeated time and again and can be accounted for in the same way: the Bolshevik outbreaks in 1918 and 1919; strike waves in many countries and on many occasions, e.g., the great railroad strike of 1877 in the U.S.; the sit-in movement in the American South in 1960; the nationalist movements in colonies after World War II; the riots of the 1960s in the U.S.; the student movement and campus upheavals during the same period in this country and abroad; the list can be made much longer. Nowadays the speed of diffusion of social disturbances and countermobilization by the authorities tends to be quicker because of the existence of nearly instantaneous means of worldwide mass communications. In fact, one of the means of social control exercised by authoritarian regimes is to suppress information in the news media about popular disturbances, civil disorders, and strikes, in order that precipitating incidents and protest in an isolated locality will not initiate the process of diffusion. Another method of social control is to suppress the initial outbreak rapidly, ruthlessly, and publicly, in order to deter potential outbreaks elsewhere ahead of the mobilization processes that are expected to be initiated as a result of the original incidents.

Although the mass media can be faulted on many counts in their concentration on the violent and threatening aspects of contemporary social movements in the U.S., they cannot be blamed for the diffusion of protest since, as we have seen, it has frequently occurred before the invention of radio, television, and rapid transportation. Disorders will not spread simply because people who hear about it are infected by some mysterious "social contagion." Disorders do spread if people with dissatisfactions and grievances that have up to that time been ignored decide to initiate direct action when they find out that other groups with similar grievances are already doing so. Where no system of mass communications exists, the news of incidents spreads by word of mouth along lines of travel and transportation and fans out from centers such as marketplaces and small towns, where people periodically gather to transact business or meet for sociable purposes. The agrarian disturbances and the Great Fear of 1789 in France provide an illustration of this process. According to Georges Lefebvre (1957:124–32), France was in the grip of an economic crisis in the spring of 1789. Rural people suffered from food shortages, unemployment, and a business depression that deprived many of them of nonagricultural income in domestic industry and urban employment. Bands of beggars going from farm to farm were a common sight and inspired fear. The convocation of the Estates-General by the crown and the invitation to set forth grievances led people everywhere to believe that their grievances would receive speedy satisfaction. In the context of anticipation and material deprivation rumors spread of an aristocratic plot, of brigands and foreign troops in the pay of the aristocracy intent on undermining the efforts of the "good king" to improve the lot of the people.

The peasants did not wait for Paris to move first. Well before July 14, food riots and social disturbances directed at landlords occurred in many areas. However, the Paris events of July 14 stimulated larger disturbances that fanned out following local disturbances in Normandy, Franche-Comté, Upper-Alsace, and the Mâconais. These disturbances were directed against the aristocracy. The targets of the peasants were the lords' records of payment for manorial dues and the occupation of common lands lost by enclosures. Violence against people was rare. At about the same time the so-called Great Fear originated in local panics and rumors about vagrants, brigands, and troop movements. In the absence of authoritative communications from the central authorities, the local panics

set up numerous currents of which some can be traced for hundreds of miles, and which moreover branched out so as to cover entire provinces. . . . The carriers of the panic were people of all conditions. Fugitives explained their fright by enlarging on each other's stories; postal couriers added to the confusion; then many people sent servants to warn their friends, and village curates, local officials, and gentry put one another on guard. . . . There was no means of verification . . . and unbelievers easily became suspects (Lefebvre, 1957:130).

Although contemporaries subsequently concluded that the panics must have been spread purposely to foster disturbances by various parties bent on causing trouble, the Great Fear of 1789 and the agrarian disturbances can be explained without invoking design and coordinated planning and with reference only to the established communications networks and interactions of thousands of people within the context of economic hardship, of expectations of reform and of aristocratic interference with the reforms, and the old and familiar fear of brigands in the countryside.

In our own day, the spread of social disturbances in a manner similar to the agrarian uprising in eighteenth-century France can still occur in countries that are predominantly rural, where only a minority of rural people are attuned to the mass media of communication, as happened in the Congo in the postindependence wave of unrest and insurgency (Fox et al., 1965–1966; Anderson et al., 1967: chapter 8). The Congo in the early 1960s was the scene of the largest uprising in postcolonial Africa. The first wave of disorders in the Congo took place at the moment of independence: the army mutinied against its Belgian officers, leaving the new state deprived of the only means it had to enforce its authority. Anti-European manifestations in widely scattered parts of the country brought the Belgians back, and subsequently also the United Nations. Large-scale ethnic disorders took place as in Kasai where the Lulua forced the Baluba, a privileged group because of their employment in the modern sector of the economy, to return to their ethnic homeland of Sud-Kasai in a bloody exodus that the central and provincial authorities were neither willing nor able to interfere with; this was followed by the Katanga, Sud-Kasai, and Stanleyville secessions and local countersecessions and disturbances that received the most attention in the press and in the United Nations. However, with the help of the United Nations, and despite the interference and intrigue of foreign powers, after four years the Congo was preserved as a whole and violence had diminished and become localized. No political leadership enjoying legitimacy and effective political power had in the meantime emerged in the capital. The central government's grip on the provinces was tenuous at best.

It is at this stage that widespread rural rebellions, the so-called "Simba" uprising or "second independence" movement, erupted in various parts of the country. By late 1964 the rebels controlled the northeastern and central part of the Congo and almost succeeded in toppling the central government. Other centers of rebellion, notably in Kwilu province, also were established. The movement was fragmented, lacking in central leadership, a common ideology and goals, and a single organizational structure. Despite outside help and foreign interference stressed by the newspapers, it was primarily an internal movement following the time-honored pattern of agrarian uprisings.

The material well-being of the majority of Congolese had declined since 1960 when the country was plunged into chaos, the urban economy declined, and agricultural output decreased. The people had been promised a great deal before independence by the hundreds of political parties and political leaders seeking national and local political offices. Expectations were raised, but only hardship and chaos followed. In much of the Congo lower level civil servants, teachers, clerks, and other employees, had been irregularly paid, if at all, and were angered by the generous salaries and sudden increase in riches and standard of life enjoyed by the politicians and higher civil servants who had reaped the rewards of independence. Thus, amid material hardship for the rural inhabitants, the lower level, educated officials and employees in the government and the modern economic sector also became disenchanted with the high level politicians and administrators in the capital and large urban centers. Many of them joined the rural rebels and became the local leaders and organizers of the movement. Many activists were also drawn from the numerous educated youth who had profited from the rapid expansion of rural primary education but who could no longer be absorbed into the modern sector of the economy in a period of economic chaos and were unable to continue their studies because of the sharply truncated pyramid of the Congolese education system. The bulk of the rebels were cultivators enlisted as a result of material hardship, of local rivalries between chiefs, clans, and tribes, and in reaction to the harsh repression of the army and police, who plundered and threatened life and property indiscriminately in potential rebel areas regardless of the actions of the local population. The rebellion spread from village to village and small town to small town as it moved along the roads following the progress of the rebel "armies" and bands. In each locality new followers were enlisted, the abandoned weapons of the fleeing Congolese army were distributed, and local allies, rival chiefs, and witch doctors joined the rebel ranks and established a skeleton administration. Because of the ethnic heterogeneity and complex rivalries of the Congo, the movement reached certain natural limits that coincided with the districts inhabited by the major ethnic groups that had supported Lumumba and had received short shrift after Lumumba's assassination. The reason that the rebellion was able to extend as far as it did is that in the Belgian Congo, far more so than in the former British colonies where indirect rule left undisturbed a great diversity in local conditions, European rule had deeply penetrated into the Africans' way of life. The highly centralized triple alliance between church, giant corporation, and the colonial administration for the exploitation of the Congo had brought about a uniformity of socioeconomic and administrative conditions that transcended local ethnic and tribal bases. Thus, the economic downturn in the modern sector, political chaos in Leopoldville, and the breakdown of administration at the center had a negative impact felt in thousands of villages and localities throughout the Congo. If a higher proportion of the Congolese people had been in the subsistence economy and if there had been greater administrative and political decentralization, the effect of the political and economic crisis in the capital would have been less and fewer discontented and angry people would have been available to swell the ranks of the rebellion. The Congolese case demonstrates once more that highly centralized polities are far more susceptible to the spread of localized crises and disturbances into nationwide rebellion or revolution than are decentralized polities (B. Moore 1966:459).

THE REACTION TO DISTURBANCES

The manner in which precipitating incidents unfold has a bearing on the subsequent mobilization of discontented people. When peaceful demonstrators seek to present a petition or otherwise wish to have direct access to high officials, the agents of social control may overreact by clubbing, gassing, or shooting them. Such reaction is not accidental inasmuch as an atmosphere of tension has built up during the time of troubles and the authorities and front-line police and troops feel more threatened than a dispassionate analysis of the situation would grant. The victims frequently include women, children, and innocent bystanders. A wave of sympathy sweeps the nonparticipant public and supports continued demonstrations. Repression becomes symbolic of the disregard for human life and brutality of the authorities, their violation of norms of reasonableness and civility and of citizens' right of access to top leaders to have their voices heard. Repression serves as a focal point for mobilizing people. In case of fatalities, the subsequent funeral procession that the authorities are reluctant to ban draws large crowds and proceeds by a circuitous route in populous districts for maximum visibility. The large size of the antigovernment forces is all the more unexpected because of the authorities' prior belief in the small number of disaffected people. They may overreact once more and by their actions feed the process of mobilization. It is crucial for the subsequent unfolding of events that the demonstrators and sympathizers be made up of heterogeneous elements and not be identified in the public mind with a narrow interest group whose demands reflect only the selfish interests of a small group of persons.

When will a public view social disorders as acts of social protest worthy of sympathy and support rather than as deviant behavior—hoodlumism, criminal behavior, illegal acts of disruption designed to benefit particular individuals and groups—that ought to be curtailed and punished? According to the most comprehensive discussion of this topic (Turner, 1969), the protest actions must meet the test of credibility in relation to folk conceptions of social protest and justice, and they must combine a mixture of appeals and threats. To be credible within the framework of the folk conceptions of protest, the protesters must come from a group "whose grievances are already well documented, who are believed to be individually or collectively powerless to correct their grievances, and who show some signs of moral virtue that render them 'deserving'" (Turner, 1969:818). If the protest appears spontaneous and unplanned, if large numbers of people participate in it, if it is known that the discontented groups had repeatedly in the past sought to have their grievances attended to through peaceful means and institutionalized channels, if the protesters show restraint and a willingness to compromise and to cease protesting when their demands are being attended to, then the chances of a favorable and sympathetic public reception of the social disturbances are good. Furthermore, when the threat resulting from protest activity is substantial but not excessive, social disturbances are more likely to be viewed as legitimate protest than if protest is not at all threatening and can therefore be ignored altogether, or if it is excessively threatening. In Turner's view, the chances of continued social disturbances and turmoil being interpreted as protest are rather low: when conciliation is not reciprocated and when protesters do not respond positively to concessions and gains they have obtained, the public will come to see protest activity as deviant acts and power plays for forcing increased benefits from the authorities for unjustified selfish ends.

As Turner points out, the reactions of the authorities and various groups within the public itself are by no means uniform. The authorities, the target groups of the protesters, and influentials and opinion makers may well publicly define the disturbances as protest in an attempt to conciliate the protesters. These groups might decide that concessions through bargaining are a cheaper, more efficient, and less damaging means of handling the disturbances than out-and-out repression. Groups in the population that are advantaged relative to the protesters are more likely to accept the claim of injustice and victimization put forward by the protesters than groups who are not unlike the protesters in socioeconomic standing and citizenship status, groups who are directly threatened by the disturbances such as those who live near the disturbances, own property there, or those who are the agents of social control responsible for containing the disturbances and likely to suffer injuries (Turner, 1969:819–21). All too often, however, the authorities' reaction to social protest is not based on a calm and rational exploration of the most advantageous response, but on faulty information, erroneous views about human nature, misconceptions about crowd behavior, and ignorance of the efficacy of rewards as opposed to punishment.

With the precipitating incidents, confrontation has begun and is carried out in the full light of public opinion. It is the reaction of the authorities, more so than the actions and plans of the opposition, that determines the subsequent course of events, and in particular whether the conflict will remain peaceful or become violent. The common response of the authorities consists of maintaining law and order by searching for and prosecuting ringleaders and alleged incitors behind the popular disturbances. Conciliation and negotiation under duress are ruled out because they are felt to be signs of weakness and a stimulation to further excesses. The authorities put forward a conspiracy theory of the events. The majority of protesters are held to be misled and misguided by a few professional agitators. Hand in hand with the conspiracy view may go the criminal riffraff and under-class theory of popular disturbances (Tilly, 1964b; Oberschall, 1968). The protesters are seen as the lawless, restless, rootless, violence-prone, bottom layer of the population whose "nature" it is to riot on the slightest pretense. These theories receive a certain amount of credibility since neither the authorities nor the public are aware of an alternative, rational, social scientific explanation of how large crowds from a heterogeneous background can congregate and act with some common purpose on short notice without prior collusion, incitement, and preparation.

The authorities' initial views are further conditioned by the biased information they possess. In the absence of direct channels of communication between discontented groups and authorities, the latter may not only underestimate the extent of popular disaffection, but rely on a network of spies, informers, and undercover agents. These men tend to exaggerate the membership strength and influence of conspiratorial groups because their jobs depend on uncovering them and they do not wish to appear negligent in their task. Furthermore, their selective exposure and infiltration of radical groups may well lead them to share the wishful thinking and often unrealistic assessment by these groups of their actual influence, and to mistake vaguely formulated plans and revolutionary rhetoric for full-scale blue prints to insurrection.

Several social psychological mechanisms of social perception also reinforce the authorities' reaction. It has been established that the further away on the ideological left-right spectrum an individual happens to be from a given range on that spectrum, the less likely it is that he can discriminate between various shades of difference in that range. For an extreme right-winger, anybody left of center, whether he be a liberal, socialist, communist, Maoist, Trotskyite, is lumped together under one broad category of "communist" or "revolutionary," whereas a left-winger will tend to see conservatives, Birchites, Goldwaterites, neo-Nazis, racist groups, and so on as "Fascists" pure and simple. Thus, a mental image of the opposition as far more homogeneous, united, and able to act in concert is created. Evidence of disunity, factionalism, rivalries, and the absence of an overarching organization and leadership is conveniently omitted. A similar principle also holds for the perception of social, as well as ideological, differences. Upper-class groups can make fine discriminations about socioeconomic status in the social strata immediately below them, but tend to lump together all groups below the middle class into one undifferentiated stratum of working people. Lower-class people, on the other hand, are keenly aware of important variations within their own ranks but tend to perceive all those above the middle class as the undifferentiated "rich" (Davis et al., 1941). In a similar fashion, the authorities and their agents of social control have a tendency to lump together all potential opponents with whom they are not in communication as the "dangerous and criminal" classes, and thus overreact when faced with a respectable and peaceful group of protesters. This pattern is in fact one key problem of contemporary police-black relations in the U.S. The city police, mostly white and living outside the black community, are unable to discriminate between the hustlers, dope addicts, criminals, and lawbreaking elements of the black slums and the majority of citizens who live there and who are the law-abiding poor and not-so-poor. Arrests, searches, surveillance, harassment are exercised indiscriminately among the entire population, especially the youth who, even when they are gang members, are not all engaged in illegal pursuits as is assumed. In the words of the National Advisory Commission on Civil Disorders (1968:307), "what may arouse hostility is not the fact of aggressive patrol, but its indiscriminate use so that it comes to be regarded not as crime control." Hiring more black police and putting them on the beat in black precincts is not a cure to all the problems between the police and the black community. Just because his skin is black, the black police officer is not going to generate compliance based on sentiments of racial solidarity. But because the black patrolman has grown up or lives in the black neighborhoods and because he is in daily interaction with the people who live there even outside his working hours and because he is accustomed to making complex classifications of these people unlike the stereotypes employed by white police, he will be able to discriminate between lawful and respectable citizens and the criminals and troublemakers and adjust his behavior accordingly.

The evidence accumulated about the generation of popular disturbances and the characteristics of the participants does not support the conspiracy or criminal under-class theories. After sifting all the evidence, the National Advisory Commission on Civil Disorders reported that (U.S. Riot Commission, 1968:202, 111) they "found no evidence that all or any of the disorders or the incidents that led to them were planned or directed by any organization or group, international, national, or local."

A number of studies based on those arrested during riots or self-reported riot participants subsequent to a riot all indicate that in the 1960s the majority of rioters were a representative cross section of the youth and adult males resident in the neighborhoods in which rioting occurred and were not composed of habitual criminals, recent migrants, the unemployed and uneducated under-class (U.S. Riot Commission, 1968:111; Fogelson and Hill, 1968; Oberschall, 1968:326–28). The historical record supports these findings as typical rather than exceptional. The storming of the Bastille on 14 July 1789 in search of gunpowder and arms was not only preceded by extended negotiations between the attackers and the officers in the fortress, but the participants in the assault tended to be men of fixed abode and settled occupations in Paris, predominantly small tradesmen and artisans sprinkled with a minority of wage earners. Many of them were actually enrolled in the newly formed citizens' militia that specifically excluded from its ranks vagrants and the criminal element, as lists of names of survivors of the assault indicate (Rudé, 1967:57–59). Rudé's studies of the social composition of participants in many episodes of collective behavior in France and England during the pre- and early industrial age provide no evidence that slum dwellers and criminal elements were the main participants. On the contrary, small workshop masters, shopkeepers, apprentices, independent craftsmen and laborers, the solid and stable working people of the city population were the most frequent activists (1964: chapter 13). During the Hungarian revolution of 1956, it was the Csepel district of Budapest, the center of steel and heavy manufacturing industry employing the most skilled and best paid workers, that was the first working-class district to organize revolutionary support for the students and intellectuals, was the site of the most determined and longest resistance to Soviet troops, and after the revolution was militarily crushed, held out the longest against the Soviet-backed Kadar government in the general strike led by the Workers' Councils (United Nations, 1957). However, the typical reactions of the authorities in the initial stages of confrontation are not based on the realities so much as on their biased perceptions and state of confusion. Therefore, the probability is rather high that recognition will not be granted and negotiations not entered upon at the opening phase of the confrontation.

DIRECT ACTION

Because recognition is not, or only partially, extended to discontented groups and because they may often lack the civil and political rights of assembly and free speech, direct action in the streets and places of work is a common characteristic of opposition movements. Mass rallies, marches, petitions, demonstrations, sit-ins, sit-downs, boycotts, pickets, strikes, walk-outs, slow downs, squatting, the refusal to pay taxes, resistance to induction into the armed forces, acts of civil disobedience, are all associated with movements of protest, more so even than the more violent actions that take place in riots or insurrections and that receive far more publicity. By the same token, the target group of the protesters, in addition to making use of the police for banning and dispersing rallies, protecting property, keeping production and the normal activity cycle from being disrupted, themselves engage in a variety of direct actions such as lockouts, evictions, blacklisting, arrest of protesters, and other forms of harassment and coercion, legal and illegal. The resort to direct action is no accident. James Q. Wilson has written that (1961:292) the problem of excluded, powerless groups is to create or assemble resources for bargaining. Since these groups lack positive inducements that they can exchange for the demands and reforms they seek, they resort to protest, the use of negative inducements—what Arthur Waskow (1967) has called "creative disorder"—that will inflict damage or injury upon the target groups, though not necessarily physical injury. What excluded groups may lack in individual resources and power they make up in the aggregate through numbers and coordinated effort. Even the poor, if there are thousands of them, can hurt the municipal treasury and business community by boycotting bus lines and stores. More important, visible signs of large-scale popular disaffection can shake the confidence of the general public in the wisdom and ability of their rulers or elected public officials and undermine their position as legitimate leaders.

For movements of protest to be effective, they must show evidence of widespread support—hence, the frequent resort to mass rallies, demonstrations, petitions, and other forms of visible aggregation of the discontented groups and their sympathizers. These can all be called *identification* moves. They are proof that the leaders and demands have large-scale support and should therefore be recognized by the authorities or target group. Discontented groups typically are not provided with the occasion of registering their full strength through elections or by pointing to the number of formally enrolled members in their organizations. Therefore, they resort to identification moves that can be extremely effective weapons for influencing public opinion and one's opponents, as the 1963 March on Washington demonstrated. They are particularly effective if the response is massive and the demonstrators disciplined. During the Algerian war, nothing proved more demoralizing to the French army than the 13 May 1961 massive turnout of demonstrators and green flags of the rebels on every balcony in the Arab quarters of Algiers called for by the FLN at a time when the paratroopers had organized massive indoctrination programs and the colonial administration had sunk a great deal of money into health services, schools, and other improvements for the Arabs (Kraft, 1961:242–46). By the same token, the giant demonstration on 30 May 1969 in support of DeGaulle, following his fighting speech in which he refused to abdicate, marked the turning point of the French "revolution" of 1968. The government and the Gaullists for the first time took the initiative away from the students, workers, and protesters after a period of four weeks of bungling and growing despair (Seale and McConville, 1968:213). Without the massive show of support from a hitherto silent majority that foreshadowed the Gaullist victory at the polls in June, the French government would have been left with no moral resource to supplement the army and police forces in its efforts to stay in power. It is typical of identification moves that the protesters and the authorities publish competing figures to describe the turnout of people in the battle for influencing public opinion. In a similar vein, the authorities have been known to highlight a few atypical outbreaks of undisciplined behavior in an effort to discredit the entire movement, as has happened with antiwar demonstrations in the U.S.

An identification move entails risks, for the turnout may be lower than expected. Poor turnout may strengthen the resolve of the authorities not to extend recognition to the movement since it represents but a minority of special interest groups. Low turnout may be due to poor planning, not just apathy, and to the harassment of the protesters by the authorities. Another danger for the leaders of the movement is the possibility of violent incidents, or even an atmosphere of anticipated violence, before the identification move. Anticipated violence, so often broadcast by the mass media before the event itself and sometimes maliciously spread by the opponents of the demonstration, will tend to keep potential demonstrators away out of fear of physical injury and arrest. The actual outbreak of violence, whether or not provoked by police, can serve to discredit the movement as dangerous and disreputable in the crucial contest for public opinion. That is why leaders seek to exclude from demonstrations certain groups least likely to remain disciplined in advance of the identification move.

Identification moves may be the only means through which the leaders of a movement can demonstrate to their followers and sympathizers their own true strength. Therefore, it is not only a tactic for influencing the target groups. An oppressed and silent majority has no other means of finding out that it is indeed a majority. The stronger the movement, the more likely that it will resort to the tactic of peaceful identification moves. Terrorism, bombings, and assassinations are resorted to by weak groups who already know their lack of mass support and their inability to generate more of it by other means and who therefore have nothing to lose by violence, especially if they have already been discredited in the eyes of the public. Terrorism is based on the conviction that the authorities or target group can be weakened if the citizenry should feel insecure and threatened and should withdraw from active participation in institutionalized activity that alone can ensure the efficient and satisfactory operation of government services, political processes, and public life in the broad sense. Terrorism must be a credible threat if it is to be effective. During the Venezuelan elections of 1962, guerrillas threatened to bomb polling stations to keep people from voting in order to demonstrate the incapacity of the authorities to track them down and to protect the people. As it turned out, the threat was neither carried out nor was it credible, as over 90 percent of the registered voters cast their ballots. Up to this time, guerrillas had been bombing American owned oil refineries, kidnapping U.S.I.A. and U.S. diplomatic staff, or hijacking airliners, but the victims were released unharmed after the publicity benefits of these bold actions were exhausted. If the guerrillas released U.S. officials unharmed, it did not seem credible that they would indiscriminately endanger the lives of innocent Venezuelan citizens.

Systematic use of terrorism and assassinations is an effective and common occurrence, however, in a civil war or internal war situation after a movement with considerable popular support has given up its attempts to achieve recognition by peaceful means and has decided to challenge the existing government by means of protracted violence. It has been noted (Huntington, 1962:25) that in internal war, whether it be the Algerian war, the Cyprus civil war between Greek and Turkish Cypriots, or the Mau-Mau movement in Kenya, many more victims are inflicted upon the uncommitted indigenous population or the "moderate" faction than upon the government forces themselves. The moderates and uncommitted people are the least organized and armed sector of the population and are therefore in a vulnerable position. To the government forces, they are suspect as potential rebel supporters or tools of the rebels, forced to provide shelter and economic resources to the insurgents. To the rebels, the moderates represent a break in the united front of the entire indigenous population against the oppressor and possibly a threat to rebel leadership if the authorities will actively court the moderates or negotiate with them as the true representatives of the population. The moderates are likely to be harassed and victimized from both sides.

While identification moves and terrorism both presuppose considerable leadership and organization within the protest group, spontaneous outbreaks of demonstrations and protest crowds are not unusual in a confrontation. They can occur even under conditions of minimal prior communication between leaders and followers and among a leaderless mass deprived of the freedom of speech and assembly. A sufficient condition for the outbreak of collective behavior is communication, and a shared culture and common orientation among the discontented group. Communication focuses attention on the same incidents, and the shared culture ensures that a similar interpretation of these events will be made. Subsequent similar reaction to the same events is assured by the shared culture, historical precedent, national symbols, flags, holidays, and heroes that all provide clues for the appropriate protest behavior after a number of incidents have built up tensions and raised expectations about great events to follow. Ordinary citizens know that on such occasions crowds will assemble at particular locations in the capital, a central square or avenue, before the Royal Palace, in Parliament Square, before City Hall or some other historically famous landmark where protest crowds have formed in the past, and people are fully aware that other people too will also gather at these focal points and not somewhere else. Such spontaneous assemblies of protest are more likely to occur on national holidays or anniversaries of well-known historic events. Sometimes the authorities themselves provide clues for crowd collection when they broadcast a ban on an anticipated assembly at a certain time and place and thereby reveal to all where and when it will take place. The sight of police cars, lights flashing and sirens screaming, all moving in a certain direction at breakneck speed, is certainly a tip-off to ignorant people that a hostile crowd has formed and where it is likely to be located. The original site of a disturbance becomes the focal point for crowd collection on subsequent days. Other processes of protest can spontaneously develop without prior plans and leaders. The rapid formation of citizens' militia, of workers' councils, the search for arms and ammunition in the face of anticipated repression, procedures for choosing deputations and for electing leaders of assemblies, all proceed rapidly because of historical precedent and shared norms, known and legitimate to all protesters. People in the provinces take their cues from events in the capital, and the villagers from the towns located near them. Thus, protest can spread countrywide without the existence of a conspiracy and by virtue of ordinary processes of communication and a shared culture that has embedded in it guides to action.

Even organizational innovations such as the creation of the St. Petersburg Soviet during the 1905 Russian revolution was not without administrative precedent and situational constraints that helped its creation. The St. Petersburg Soviet, in which Trotsky was to play so important a role, was at first an organization improvised for running the national strike wave that was spreading in Russia in October 1905. Very rapidly it grew into a potential revolutionary assembly exercising political authority and administrative control parallel to the authorities and to the bureaucracy and in competition with them. Had it not been for its failure to control sizable military detachments and for the Witte government's proclamation of the October Manifesto promising civil liberties and constitutional government that split the opposition to the Tsar, it would have eventually grown into an effective diarchy, which is the hallmark of all successful revolutions, notably of the October revolution of 1917. How did the soviets originate?

Up to that time, no independent trade unions controlled and elected by the workers existed in Russia. A system of factory elders modelled after Russian village administration was in effect, but these men were considered to be the stooges of the authorities and of the management. Strikes before 1905 were led by ad hoc factory strike committees with no lasting organizational and leadership continuity in time, and little citywide, industrywide, or nationwide coordination. The revolutionary political parties were illegal; small conspiratorial underground organizations were rent with factionalism and were unsuited for leading several hundred thousand workers into a strike on a moment's notice. A central strike organization therefore had to be created from scratch and had to aggregate somehow the grass roots organizations and strike committees that existed in each industrial establishment (Trotsky, 1923:87). It so happened that the government had some months earlier provided an organizational precedent and model for the strikers to follow in creating a citywide strike leadership: the so-called Sidlovsky commission. This commission was called into being after the "Bloody Sunday" massacre and the ensuing strikes and disturbances in February 1905 in order to investigate the causes of worker unrest and suggest remedies. A citywide election of workers' representatives was undertaken in each factory and industrial establishment to meet with and testify before the commission, with a fixed number of worker representatives per worker in each factory and with smaller establishments conducting pooled elections. Thus, a citywide set of workers' representatives was formed. This procedure was copied with great success by the striking workers of St. Petersburg in October, and the resulting citywide strike committee soon was referred to as the St. Petersburg Soviet (Anweiler, 1958a:43–45; Trotsky, 1923:87–92). The original soviet then served as a model for soviets in other cities and later for the soviets that grew up everywhere in the 1917 Russian revolution.

CONFRONTATION DURING THE HUNGARIAN REVOLUTION

The manner in which a shared culture of nationalist symbols, historical precedent, and patriotic sentiments can serve as the basis of mobilization and organizational structuring in an unplanned and initially leaderless and uncoordinated social movement can perhaps best be illustrated with reference to the Hungarian revolution of 1956. I have already described how, within a context of loosening social control exercised by the Kremlin and the Communist party of Hungary, divisions within the Communist ruling group, the desertion of the intellectuals to the side of the nationalist-reformist intraparty opposition headed by Nagy, the anti-Stalinist mobilization was initiated within the Communist party in the summer of 1956, and how, by virtue of its seizure of some organizations, newspapers, and public forums usually under top party control, this opposition group was beginning to reach the mass of the citizenry in the capital who up to that time had been monopolistically regimented and controlled by the party apparatus, the secret police, and the Communist party-linked associational networks. How could a popular movement under these circumstances overthrow in a matter of days the established government, the totalitarian party, and the entire social control apparatus that had been so effective in curbing dissent and opposition in the previous eight years?

The focal point of the Soviet orbit was at this time, as it still is, the Kremlin and the actions and policies of the top Soviet leaders. The Khrushchev speech denouncing Stalin's crimes and the cult of personality in February 1956 at the Twentieth Party Congress signaled a fundamental change of policy that made the Hungarian Stalinist party leader Rakosi's position vulnerable, since he was personally identified with totalitarian terror and a cult of personality in Hungary that were a faithful replica of Stalin's rule. On top of this, Khrushchev at this time had initiated a policy of easing tensions with Tito and the Yugoslavs, and Rakosi had been the instrument of Stalin's anti-Yugoslav policy in Hungary. Under pressure from the Kremlin, the intellectuals, and reformist groups within the Hungarian party, Rakosi resigned as first secretary of the CP, packed his bags, and left for Moscow and retirement. The new first secretary appointed to replace him was, however, Gerö, another Stalinist closely identified with Rakosi, and not Imre Nagy, the popular prime minister during the new course of the 1953–1955 years when Rakosi had temporarily fallen out of favor with the Kremlin leaders following Stalin's death. Up to that time Rakosi had implemented the forced industrialization, socialization, and Russification of Hungary too fast, too hard, and at too great a cost. Once in power, Gerö initiated a cautious policy of gradual concessions to the reformist elements and intellectuals within the party. The writers previously expelled from the party were readmitted, criticism in the press of Rakosi's abuses was allowed, and promises of liberalization were made. As the political prisoners, many of them Communists, were released from detention, the demand that Rakosi and those in the secret police and the party responsible for totalitarian terror be made accountable for their crimes was voiced ever more openly and frequently. The circulation of the Literary Gazette increased sharply; the writers and intellectuals spoke at meetings of factory workers; yet the people were still suspicious, cautious, and in part apathetic in their response to the attempts of the intraparty opposition to mobilize support. However, social control was loosened (Keckemeti, 1961: chapter 5).

On 6 October, a national holiday of mourning for the patriots of the 1848–1849 national war of independence who had been hanged by the Austrians and Russians, a huge funeral procession—a typical identification move—took place in connection with the reburial of Rajk. The size of the demonstration showed to all that the people of the capital were behind the demands for further reform and that the existing regime was exceedingly unpopular and in a minority position. Rajk had been a Communist leader and potential rival to Rakosi whom Rakosi had purged with many others in 1949 with Stalin's approval for alleged Titoist tendencies. At the time of his resignation, Rakosi had openly admitted that the Rajk purges had been a "miscarriage of justice," but had blamed them conveniently on the head of the secret police, Farkas, who was thereupon arrested. Farkas and his collaborators had however not yet been brought to trial, and the increased demands for Rajk's rehabilitation as well as the initiation of criminal proceedings against both Rakosi and Farkas forced the party leadership to consent to a public reburial of Rajk on 6 October during which the victims of the 1949 purges would be officially rehabilitated. Two hundred thousand people attended this silent, tense, but orderly ceremony in an impressive show of popular strength and explicit criticism of the temporizing Gerö government. At this point disturbances might well have broken out and become the precipitating event for an insurrection against the regime. What was still lacking was a positive program of reform and the hope of success so essential for the initiation of a revolution. These factors were supplied later in the month by the Polish events and the drafting of the students' demands.

Amidst the loosening of social control, several groups in Hungary were trying to establish greater autonomy in hitherto Communist controlled organizations and were trying to press for reforms designed to provide them greater freedom and material benefits. The university students in Budapest were no exception. Considerable dissatisfaction had existed among them with DISZ, the Communist League of Working Youth, to which all students belonged and which "had become an automatic machine of superior organs. It should have been the duty of the DISZ to represent the views of the youth, but it failed to comply with this obligation. Our most important problems have not been attended for years," according to the appeal adopted by a meeting of the Budapest engineering students on 19 October (United Nations, 1957:73–74). The students' initial demands consisted of the abolition of compulsory attendance at lectures, better food, larger allowances, an end to dormitory overcrowding, a reduction in the price for textbooks, greater freedom of travel, a more secure career for engineering students after graduation, and other such narrow demands centering on group benefits. Only the last demand, that Farkas and his secret police associates be brought to trial, had a wider national significance (United Nations, 1957:74). However, as these demands were being formulated by various student groups, the Polish anti-Stalinists under Gomulka managed to consolidate their position in Poland between 19 and 21 October and successfully defended their newly won leadership position against the Kremlin's challenge. The hope and expectation that similar changes in Hungary in the direction of greater national autonomy and equality in Soviet-Hungarian relations would also be feasible if only a new national government under Imre Nagy were to force out the old guard under Gerö now spread within all segments of the population and was clearly reflected in the rapidly changing demands and manifestos of various student groups. From expressing student demands the manifestos changed into formulating national demands. The final manifesto of sixteen points adopted by the engineering students included the immediate withdrawal of all Soviet troops; election of new leaders at all levels within the Hungarian Communist party; a new government under Imre Nagy; the public trial of Rakosi, the head of the secret police, and their accomplices; general elections with universal suffrage, secret ballot, and the participation of several political parties; the reorganization of the entire economic life of the country; public disclosure of all foreign trade agreements and war reparations; reorganization of factory work norms and methods of remuneration; complete freedom of public opinion and of the press and radio; the removal of the Stalin statue, a symbol of "tyranny and oppression"; and restoration of the pre-Communist national flag, coat of arms, army uniforms, and patriotic holidays (United Nations, 1957:69). Moreover, the students called for a public demonstration of solidarity with Poland and with the students' demands on the following afternoon, 23 October. When they were prevented from broadcasting their manifestos, the students reproduced them and distributed them on handbills and placards all over the city. The radio announcement banning the planned demonstration actually publicized the event.

The great demonstration of 23 October was a peaceful manifestation of nationalist and patriotic sentiment during which an initial nucleus of several thousand, composed mainly of students, swelled to a crowd of two to three hundred thousand people by evening in Parliament Square after the march had proceeded from one historic landmark to another by a circuitous route, with patriotic speeches and manifestations taking place at every location. The focal points for speeches were the two public squares in which the statues of Sandor Petöfi and General Bem were located, respectively. Petöfi was the nationally celebrated poet and revolutionary hero of the independence war of 1848. At the foot of his statue, a well-known actor recited Petöfi's revolutionary poem of 1848 that every schoolchild learns by heart and that had initiated and symbolized the 1848 revolution. It starts with the following lines, with the audience expected to recite the last sentence of each stanza:

> To your feet, Magyars,
> The fatherland is calling you!
> Here's the moment, now or never.
> Shall we remain slaves, or shall we be free?
> That is the question—what is your answer?
> In the name of the God of Hungary,
> We swear, we swear
> that we shall remain slaves no longer!

Following the recitation, he read the students' demands to the people. The patriotic manifestation at General Bem's statue had a double historical significance since Bem had been a Polish-born military hero of the 1848–1849 independence war who was subsequently executed by the Russians for his activities in behalf of Hungarian independence. Soldiers, cadets, and factory and office workers returning home after work everywhere swelled the ranks of the demonstrators. Flags were put out on the balconies and windows along the streets. The hammer and sickle were cut out of the Hungarian flag, and other insignia identified with Soviet rule such as the Red Star were ripped off uniforms, flags, and buildings. Later in the evening Stalin's statue was toppled. The demonstrators carried signs reading "Russians Go Home," "Let Hungary Be Independent," "Bring Rakosi to Justice," "We Want New Leaders," "Solidarity with the Polish People," "We trust Imre Nagy" (Meray, 1960; Heller, 1957). The national anthem and other patriotic songs banned in the eight years of Communist rule were repeatedly sung. Everywhere nationalist and patriotic symbols deeply rooted in the history of the Hungarian people and well known to all became the rallying points and foci of solidarity. In the evening, the largest crowd collected in Parliament Square demanding to hear Imre Nagy and hoping for the announcement of his appointment as the new prime minister. When Nagy finally arrived and started his speech with "Comrades," the crowd chanted: "There are no more comrades—we are all Hungarians." At the end of his inconclusive speech, Nagy had to calm the restless and disappointed crowd by singing the national anthem with everybody joining in.

Despite the minimal and hasty prior planning consisting only of the student handbills and despite the absence of prior organized leadership and scheduled events, the shared culture of the demonstrators and of the onlookers provided direction, meaning, and unity of purpose for this historic episode of collective behavior. In fact, one might even argue that it is more difficult to bring about successfully such events when there is a certain amount of prior leadership, planning, and open mobilization within a framework of limited civil liberties and freedom of association and speech. In these circumstances, the possibility of leadership splits, competitive mobilization, and conflicting calls for action are much greater and are likely to result in confusion and a lack of unambiguous signals and cues for action. In a repressive system with no prior mobilization opportunities, masses of people must rely on the cues and direction provided by the common shared culture itself, the internal logic of unfolding events that is interpreted similarly because of a shared outlook and the solidarity sentiments generated by the experience of common oppression and an anticipated common fate.

The people of Budapest and of Hungary did what revolutionary peoples have always done under similar circumstances: they fraternized with the soldiers and the police and successfully brought many of them over to their side, as the crowds in St. Petersburg did in the Russian October of 1917 (Trotsky, 1959:98–99); they raided arms factories, arsenals, shooting ranges, and other known arms and ammunition supply depots to arm themselves against an anticipated attack by Soviet military forces, which came on the following days, as the citizens of Paris did from 11 July to 14 July 1789; they wanted their demands broadcast over the radio, and when they were fired upon, they stormed the radio building; they sacked party offices and bookstores selling propaganda and burned their contents in bonfires in the street; they pulled down the most visible and hated symbols of oppression of foreign rule and restored the old Hungarian street names to the avenues that had been renamed after Russians or obscure Hungarian Communists; when the Soviet tanks entered the city to reestablish their rule, they erected barricades and roadblocks and fought them as best they could; others argued with the Russian soldiers and convinced them that this was not a fascist and counterrevolutionary uprising fomented by the imperialists; they formed a national guard and citizens' militia to coordinate and consolidate the various scattered groups of freedom fighters; they plastered the city with patriotic signs, posters, national flags, and handbills; they freed the political prisoners; they started a general strike as a protest against the

Soviet invasion; they lynched some members of the AVH (secret police) when, despite a general cease-fire, the AVH fired upon a crowd demanding entry into the Communist party headquarters for the purpose of freeing political prisoners thought to be incarcerated in its cellars.

Although many of the revolutionary actions of the people were undertaken under no central direction and without planning, mainly as a reaction to local and neighborhood events, the radio stations in the hands of the revolutionaries did focus attention on the events in the capital where rapid changes in the government were taking place in conjunction with complex negotiations with the Soviet military command and Kremlin leaders who had been flown in to direct the Soviet operations. The presence of the Soviet troops, the military repression of a popular revolution, and the threat of continued Soviet intervention and escalation called forth a reaction of national unity and solidarity making it possible for the diverse social and political groupings composing the revolutionaries to agree on a common strategy in which the Soviet troop withdrawals from Hungarian soil was the foremost nonnegotiable demand. The characteristic trademark of the Hungarian revolution of 1956 was, however, not so much the reemergence of banned political parties after almost a decade nor the shifting composition and activities of top revolutionary committees, but the rapid formation of grass roots revolutionary committees in all parts of the country and among all social classes in the manner of the soviets in the Russia of 1905 and 1917. Everywhere the government bureaucracy and Communist party structure collapsed after the first onslaught, and everywhere revolutionary committees were formed on the spot to seize party offices and the government machinery, to arrest those who hadn't fled, to issue orders, to form groups of resistance fighters, to assure the food supply and as normal a schedule of daily activities as possible, to formulate demands and send delegations to the revolutionary government, to disband collective farms, in short, to run the institutions and organizations that were seized from the Communists. Workers' councils were formed in factories, government offices were run by civil servants' councils, newspapers were issued by their former employees who constituted themselves into revolutionary councils; university faculties, hospitals, the police, the peasants on collective farms, miners, railroad workers, postal employees, small-town residents and villagers, everywhere formed revolutionary councils to seize the means of production and of administration in the name of the people. While the revolution did not last long enough for a full development of the council structure, even in the two weeks of revolutionary freedom there emerged the typical hierarchic centralization of council pyramids proceeding from the local levels through elected delegates to larger territorial, municipal, or industrywide revolutionary councils, which had also been characteristic of the soviets, of the unions, and of the zemtsvos in the Russian revolutions of 1905–1906 and 1917–1918 (Anweiler, 1958a; 1958b).

Though there had been no historical precedent for this in Hungary, this spontaneous phenomenon can be explained with reference to prior discussions and information about councils, to the lack of any other clear-cut alternatives for mobilization, and to the diffusion via the radio of this organizational expression of the revolution once it had emerged in the capital with the first workers' councils. For a decade the people of Hungary had been bombarded with films, public lectures, books, novels, textbooks, expositions, indoctrination sessions, and whatnot describing and glorifying the Russian October revolution of 1917 in which soviets as the spontaneous revolutionary organs of an oppressed proletariat figured repeatedly and prominently. Therefore, this was common and shared knowledge. The factory workers, in particular, had since the summer of 1956 been treated to public discussions in the press and even in factory meetings about the advantages and possibility of establishing industrial worker councils modeled after those in Yugoslavia. Thus the worker-council model was already in the forefront of public attention before the revolution broke out, and it is the Budapest factory workers who initiated the council trend. There were no other clearcut alternatives. The collapse of the Communist party apparatus meant in concrete terms that the managers, high level officials, and administrators previously running factory, office, collective farm, city hall, and so on were not to be found, and in a period of emergency there had to be someone exercising authority in order to continue running the country. Since there were no prior opposition groups with established leaders and organizational networks, some people had to be elected by the local citizenry, villagers, factory workers, office employees, etc., in order to take over the positions vacated by the departed or ousted Communists. These popularly elected bodies were in fact the councils. For a brief few days Hungary was the scene, for the first time perhaps since the Paris Commune and a brief transitional period in the Russian revolution, of a democratically elected and popularly controlled nationwide authority structure not only in the polity but in all the institutions of the society. The council structure, especially the workers' councils, became so deeply entrenched during this short period of time that for over a month after the Soviet reoccupation of Hungary and the cessation of armed resistance, the Kadar government and the Soviet military authorities were forced to keep negotiating with the Central Workers' Council of Greater Budapest concerning the resumption of work in the factories and clashes with Soviet troops, and that the councils were not officially dissolved until a full year after the revolution's defeat (United Nations, 1957:104). No one can tell, of course, whether the revolutionary council structure would have persisted and reshaped the institutions of the society had the revolution been successful.

NONVIOLENT DIRECT ACTION

It remains to consider nonviolent direct action as a means for protesters to advance their cause. Nonviolence is the deliberate abstention from force and from violence. In Miller's words (1966:223), "the one distinct hallmark of nonviolence . . . is the meeting of actual or threatened violence unarmed and purposely . . . without resorting to physical force against the enemy." The two main kinds of nonviolent direct action are noncooperation and civil disobedience. Noncooperation, according to Kuper (1957:73–74) is the reduction or termination of interaction with the target group for the purpose of inducing it to enter negotiations with the protesters. The most common forms of noncooperation are the strike, the boycott, the closing down of businesses, the hunger strike, the resignation of offices and titles, the refusal to serve in the opponent's administration, and surface, minimum compliance with orders and regulations considered illegitimate, such as the icy reception of occupation troops who have to be put up in homes. Civil disobedience is the deliberate and publicly announced refusal to comply with laws considered unjust and illegitimate, together with the symbolic acts of breaking those laws. It includes the refusal to be drafted, to pay taxes, to be registered or to carry mandatory registration and identification cards, the sit-in and all its variations, and so on. Perhaps the most famous examples of nonviolent direct action are the various satyagraha campaigns led by Gandhi in South Africa and in India and the civil rights movement in the United States in the late fifties and early sixties. It is important to note that in neither case was the total confrontation nonviolent since the agents of social control frequently resorted to force and violence to suppress the nonviolent protesters.

The question arises under what circumstances nonviolent direct action is effective as a means of waging conflict. Partly as a result of Gandhi's philosophy and of the frequently religious inspiration of nonviolent campaigns, too much has been made of the impact that unilateral sacrifice and suffering will have on the agents of social control and on the authorities, of the change of policy that might follow from the moral education, change of heart, and moral shaming of one's opponents (Bondurant, 1958). Nonviolence is not likely to be successful unless there exist third parties or an independent public opinion whose support can be mobilized and who in turn will bring pressures to bear on the agents of social control and the government. For this to happen, publicity and access to communication media independent of the authorities are needed. An unpublicized and unnoticed act of civil disobedience can be handled by the authorities as a criminal act, as routine deviance that does not merit special rating. Since nonviolent direct action as a mass movement requires discipline, organization, and a period of learning and moral preparation, it is not likely to occur in circumstances where there is no freedom of association, of assembly, and of speech, in other words, in a totalitarian or repressive system. Even in a free society, it is likely that the "systematic and consistent refusal to use violence . . . would doom every movement of social reform to futility if it were menaced by an intransigent foe whose liberty of action was not bound by the fetish of non-resistance. Even where there is no real intention to use the violence, the threats of violence have won occasional concessions," as Sidney Hook wrote (1937:265). Nonviolence and moral appeal might be effective against an opponent who at least shares many of the humanitarian and religiously inspired values that assign a high positive value to sacrifice and suffering for a collective goal and nonselfish cause. To others it will be a sign of weakness and perhaps even of foolishness. Stalin once replied to a statement of Churchill on the Catholic Church by asking the rhetorical question "How many divisions does the Pope have?" In the case of Gandhi's and Martin Luther King's nonviolent campaigns, it was British home opinion and the parliamentary opposition in one case, and Northern public opinion, Congress, and the Washington administration in the other, that represented the crucial third party in the conflict whose reaction to the repression of peaceful protest campaigns was to swing their support to the side of the protesters.

The success of civil disobedience and noncooperation campaigns depends on the extent of mass participation and is therefore analogous to the identification moves discussed earlier. The more protesters, the more massive the demonstration of noncooperation, the greater the embarrassment of the authorities because their claim to rule based on the consent of the governed is revealed publicly as a fraud. On the other hand a partial walk-out, strike, boycott of government services, or close-down of business establishments has the double effect of realizing gains to those who side with the authorities or remain neutral at the expense of the protesters and of revealing the weakness of the protesters. Since the stakes are high, the temptation for the protest group to enforce compliance in the population with their campaign of noncooperation by force if necessary is high. Therefore, nonviolent noncooperation is more likely in a situation where there is already nearly unanimous opposition to the authorities. An only partially successful boycott in an election will only succeed in having one's opponents or minority candidates of third parties elected, a more undesirable outcome from the point of view of achieving power than if only a certain proportion of the opponents' candidates were elected because of election frauds and intimidation. Election boycotts are notoriously ineffective as noncooperation tactics since they tend to harm the protesters more than they embarrass the target group. Noncooperation is effective if the protesters have an essential service or contribution to make to keep the system operating. A labor strike is a potentially effective tactic, but a student strike is not. Students only hurt themselves, not others, by striking. Therefore, the effectiveness of student strikes must be based entirely on the extent of mass participation and its symbolic interpretation in public opinion; it cannot be based on its potential for stopping the flow of essential goods and services. Boycotts of certain business establishments or government services whose income is based on the transactions of the protesters can be an effective weapon, but embargos and refusals to provide goods, labor, and services to particular establishments or groups when they are going to be provided from alternative sources anyway is going to hurt only the protesters. Another common difficulty with noncooperation campaigns is that the protest group usually has fewer resources than the target group and will therefore experience hardship sooner and more deeply. Strikers will often run out of funds before the employer has to yield as a result of financial weakness; the cost to boycotters of getting goods and services from other sources may be quite high. Time tends to be on the side of the target group. The authorities do not have to take immediate action in response to noncooperation unless vital services are affected.

In civil disobedience campaigns, the symbolic aspect of the confrontation is a more powerful factor than the potential harm to the material interests of the target group; nor is mass participation by the protest group as important for success in influencing public opinion and third parties. A small group, led by a well-known leader whose integrity and sincerity are beyond question, can conduct a civil disobedience campaign, focus public attention on it, and bear the full costs of sanction without in any way diminishing the resources of the larger protest group. In fact, moral resolve, cohesion, and support for leadership within the protest group can be increased at little cost to the protest movement. The authorities cannot afford to ignore acts of civil disobedience in the same way as they might fail to respond to noncooperation, since they are confronted with a public and immediate challenge to their authority that requires response. Kuper (1957:73–74) saw this clearly when he wrote that civil disobedience heightens interaction between the opponents, compels a response by the target group, and provides for an occasion to reconsider relations between the dominant and the subordinate groups. Civil disobedience is a tactic for forcing such a reconsideration of dominance relations in the full light of publicity under circumstances more favorable to the protest group than to the authorities or target group. Civil disobedience is a moral weapon, whereas noncooperation is usually a demonstration of the material and labor contribution that the protest group makes to the authorities and to the system. Civil disobedience is likely to be resorted to when moral persuasion can mobilize powerful third parties on behalf of the goals of the protesters; noncooperation when the protesters must rely on their own collective power primarily against an opponent who can be hurt in the material sense. Both these means of forcing a confrontation are essentially tactics of a weaker, institutionally unrecognized protest group that seeks to enter into negotiations with the more powerful target group. Nonviolent direct action has, however, been the dominant mode of confrontation in only a few of the major episodes of social conflict, since it demands unusual discipline and restraint on both sides, informal agreements and some shared values between the antagonists, and the presence of independent third parties within the context of relatively free political institutions— circumstances not likely to be frequently present in the course of history. Nonviolent conflict comes about through the institutionalization of the conflict process. Nonviolent direct action is one way to advance the process of institutionalization by forcing a redefinition of authority relations and the recognition of the hitherto excluded protest group.

Chapter *IX*

GROUP VIOLENCE

THE BEHAVIOR OF HOSTILE CROWDS

As has been described in the case of the Hungarian revolution of 1956, it is precisely because people in unplanned direct action rely on a shared culture for guidelines and clues that their behavior is far more predictable and follows more established patterns than is commonly thought. Crowd behavior, even in the case of hostile crowds such as in riots, is amenable to sociological analysis without invoking psychopathology, contagion, the herd instinct, suggestion, a common destructive impulse that sways people in a crowd as they suddenly lose their restraints, individuality, and critical faculties acquired through the civilizing process of family and education, and other similar processes popularized by nineteenth-century writers, especially Le Bon. Rudé (1967) has shown that the contagion theories put forward by these investigators rested on erroneous descriptions and accounts and biased and selective choice of facts about crowd behavior during the French Revolution. Even an author as sympathetic as Emile Zola was to the problems of ordinary working people provides distorted and sensationalized descriptions of crowd behavior in *Germinal*. It is only recently that the approaches of several social scientists, notably Ralph Turner's emergent norm theory (1964a) and Roger Brown's use of game theory (1965) applied to crowd behavior, have provided a balanced and scientifically acceptable approach in this area. Turner in particular points out that the alleged anonymity of individuals in the crowd, their uniformity of response, their lack of organization and differentiation, their slavish response to the suggestions of a leader, and their unusual and extreme behavior as compared to their behavior under ordinary circumstances are empirically unsubstantiated and in fact contradicted by reports based on the observations of trained researchers. Turner's critique of the psychological and social psychological mechanisms and processes postulated by contagion theory are equally well taken (1964a:384–87) and, therefore, need not be repeated here.

The newer approach for explaining crowd processes stresses the heterogeneity of composition and response in a crowd, the impact of the actions of the agents of social control upon the behavior of crowds, the fact that the risk and reward structure for a group situation differs from that applicable to individuals, and the emergence of appropriate models and norms of behavior disseminated within a crowd by communications processes. The newer theories stress the continuity between usual group behavior and behavior of individuals in a crowd. Actions and reactions are learned and communicated in the crowd as it collectively defines an acceptable, appropriate, and legitimate response for individuals to make to the situation they are all faced with, and are then supported by group approval and group sanctions. This approach can be illustrated with reference to the urban ghetto riots of the 1960s in the United States.

Hostile crowds do not just collect randomly in time and place within a population that has grievances. They collect after a precipitating event has occurred, when there are eyewitnesses and people standing about and news of the precipitating event is able to diffuse rapidly. On summer evenings in crowded tenements people tend to be out on the sidewalks and doorsteps, and windows are open. Rapid face-to-face communication circulates from bloc to bloc even before the residents are attracted by speeding police cars or announcements of disturbances in the news media. Thus, people are alerted and crowds converge on the location of the original precipitating event. It is obvious that this is more likely to happen in the warmer season than in cold weather, and in fair weather than in rain. Nor are precipitating events arbitrary and unpredictable. Precipitating incidents bear a direct one-to-one relationship with the principal grievances of the potential rioters which they symbolize and typify in a concrete fashion. The National Advisory Commission on Civil Disorders (U.S. Riot Commission, 1968:120–24, 144–49) reported that police practices (i.e., police harassment, brutality, arrests, surveillance, and so on) were the number one grievance of the black urban population and that police action was the final precipitating incident in twelve out of twenty-four disturbances surveyed in depth by the Commission.

Nor is this a novel pattern in the U.S. An investigation of precipitating events in riots that took place between 1919 and 1963 confirms these contemporary findings (Lieberson and Silverman, 1965:889). Moreover, alleged abusive and discriminatory police actions represent also a full 40 percent of the incidents prior to riots that over a period of time poisoned police-community relations. The final precipitating event is first preceded by a series of similar events following which no remedial actions are taken so that the belief in police brutality becomes widespread and part of the folk beliefs and expectations of the population. It then becomes something of a self-fulfilling prophecy. Police about to arrest someone when they expect him to fight back and be abusive are more likely to be jittery and to overuse force than if they expect the arrest to be a routine one. By the same token, a youth in the street is more likely to try to escape or resist arrest if he expects the police to beat him and to haul him off to jail no matter what he did. Under these circumstances police overuse of force, police shootings of suspects who later turn out to be innocent, and forceful resistance to and interference with routine police action by citizens are more likely to occur.

A widespread belief in police brutality is also going to influence the frame of mind of the crowds that collect at precipitating events, the perceptions of the onlookers, and the content of the rumors and messages that circulate in the neighborhood. Few people are going to be able to be impartial eyewitnesses to a police-citizen incident that escalates into a riotous event. Many people do not arrive on the scene until after considerable time has elapsed. Others cannot see what is happening because of the poorly lit streets, because their view is blocked, and because people shift around and the police are pushing them back. As a result, the bits of information, visual and verbal, get selectively pieced together into the previously learned and accepted framework of police brutality. Transmission of rumor studies show that the original message gets shortened, simplified, and modified according to the preconceptions of the transmitters and recipients of the message. Thus, regardless of the actual details and rights and wrongs of the precipitating event, large angry crowds gather in the belief that another unjustifiable violation by police of a strongly held norm has just taken place, such as the police shooting of an innocent youth, an unnecessary arrest, or an unwarranted beating of a suspect.

Very often before the police are assaulted during this process of crowd formation, a phenomenon known as milling occurs: information is passed around to the newcomers, the mood of the angry people is communicated to those who were ignorant or curious or merely uninvolved. The gathering multitude learns from those already present what the proper definition of the situation is and what one's expected reaction to the events should be. Even when a pattern of aggressive behavior against police and property becomes established, not everyone gets involved. Many people are merely curious onlookers; others are willing to encourage rioters without themselves participating; others, the counterrioters, try to calm the angered people and get them to go home. Still others think it a golden opportunity to get themselves consumer goods and liquor at the expense of the alien merchants. The controversy over whether people participate in riots for fun and profit or whether they do so because they are frustrated and angry is a spurious one from the point of view of the present theory, which does not postulate a uniformity of reaction to the same events on the part of the population. It is likely that some people participate and loot for fun and profit while others do so out of outrage because strongly held norms have been violated, while still others condemn the action altogether or withdraw into their houses for security and safety.

Why do people in a crowd situation engage in the kind of behavior that they would not engage in under ordinary circumstances, such as breaking into stores, assaulting police, setting stores and automobiles on fire, beating up motorists, and the like? It is, of course, not strictly true that people individually do not do these things; some people, a minority, in fact do. The point is rather that most of those who do it in the crowd situation would not do it as individuals. Roger Brown (1965: 754–56) has shown in his analysis of hostile crowds the kind of process that is involved. The risk and reward structure for the same actions is quite different when an individual contemplates them himself than when he does so in a crowd.

> For unlawful hostile outbursts there must be enough people to overwhelm the police, enough people so that altogether each one can feel anonymous and therefore secure against legal reprisals. In addition, numbers help to create a temporary belief that the unlawful action is morally right action.

In concrete terms, an individual by himself takes a considerable risk by illegal behavior. His reward is entirely the personal benefit he derives from enjoyment or possession and cannot be publicly shared. In a crowd situation, the risk diminishes considerably, while rewards increase because one gets immediate public approval and social support from the illegal action aside from the private benefit itself. Given that the risk/reward ratio rapidly falls with the increase in the size of the crowd, the theory of participation would predict a corresponding increased probability of hostile behavior. The only mechanism needed for this "payoff matrix" to emerge is the communication of one another's preferences for aggressive behavior within the crowd itself. But that is precisely what happens during milling when group sanctions and support—Turner's emergent norm—for such action are communicated and intentions become crystallized. In similar fashion one can also explain why it is that rain will disperse an angry crowd much more rapidly and effectively than the police. Some crowd members or onlookers, as we have already stressed, are only curious and relatively uninvolved. When it starts raining, they take cover indoors and the size of the crowd diminishes. The risk of apprehension is now increased, and as individuals who have now reached the risk threshold they feel comfortable with depart from the scene, the crowd keeps decreasing further and the risk/reward ratio keeps increasing. Thus, in a short time a large hostile crowd can melt down to a small group, which then becomes amenable to routine social control. Note that throwing tear gas into a crowd does not have the same effect as that of rain. Rain is an "act of God" for which the authorities cannot be blamed. Tear gas may have the opposite effect of angering a lot of uninvolved bystanders and lukewarm crowd members into supporting the activists.

It is true that crowds do often become violent, but even violence is subject to norms embedded in the culture. The preindustrial city and rural people, as the researches of Rudé have shown (1964), rioted predictably as a response to rising food prices and a rising cost of living that tended to coincide with periods of unemployment and crop failure. Food riots were not wild rampages and orgies of destruction. The women and working people who invaded markets and bakeries on such occasions forced the proprietors to hand over their merchandise, but many paid them the "just" preshortage price. These people would invoke the name of the king, the traditional protector of his people, to justify their actions and blame local officials and hoarders who allegedly were not carrying out the king's policies. Nor should it be supposed that lower-class protesters in that age were particularly bloodthirsty and prone to violence. Many large-scale demonstrations were disciplined and nonviolent (Rudé, 1964:239). The overwhelming majority of fatalities during episodes of popular unrest has been attributed to the agents of social control, not the actions of the rioters, although destruction of property occurred with predictable regularity (Rudé, 1964:255–56). Yet, even in those instances where machines, homes, custom posts, or shops were broken into, burned, or destroyed, the members of the crowd showed a remarkable ability to pick those specific targets for destruction that stood in a direct relationship to their grievances and enemies. The ideas and slogans that the crowds expressed during these disturbances had little to do with the rights of man, socialist ideas, or novel revolutionary doctrines; rather, they were drawn from the traditional culture of patriotism, antiforeign sentiments, and conservative antipathy toward the unregulated law of supply and demand in the capitalist marketplace that adversely affected wages and prices.

CONTEMPORARY URBAN RIOTS

As is true for the preindustrial crowd in Europe, so it is also true for the contemporary crowds formed during riots in the America of the 1960s. The goals of the rioters were neither revolutionary nor outside of the mainstream of American values. In the words of the National Advisory Commission on Civil Disorders (U.S. Riot Commission, 1968:6), "what the rioters appeared to be seeking was fuller participation in the social order and the material benefits enjoyed by the majority of American citizens . . . they were anxious to obtain a place for themselves in [the American system]." Granted that many riots saw extensive property damage, yet Watts, Detroit, and Newark were not typical of the civil disorders of the 1960s. Seventy-five percent of the racial disorders reported in the first nine months of 1967 were minor, involving but a small number of people, lasting but one day, requiring no more than local police for control, and inflicting but minor property damage. In more than 60 percent of the 1967 disorders, no deaths and no more than ten injuries were reported. Large property damage was concentrated in a handful of major riots and was grossly exaggerated at the time of the riot, even in the case of Watts, Newark, and Detroit (1968:113–15). Even in major riots one might question whether crowd behavior is essentially an irrational stampede and orgy of destruction and, hence, void of collective social significance and personal meaning. Nothing is gained by defining riot behavior as irrational a priori. There is considerable evidence that the rioters observed certain bounds, that they directed their aggression at specific targets, and that they selected appropriate means for the ends they intended to obtain. Let us examine the facts in the Los Angeles riot of 1965 (Oberschall, 1968:337–40).

The fact that no deaths resulted from the direct action of the rioters is evidence that they observed certain bounds and limits. The first two nights when white motorists were dragged out of their cars and beaten and when newsmen were severely roughed up, none were beaten to death or killed as might easily have happened since the police were unable to offer protection at the time. Furthermore, the sniper fire directed at police and firemen did not result in any fatalities either, despite reports that it was widespread and lasted throughout the riot week and the fact that police and firemen were easy targets. It seems in retrospect that reports of snipers were highly exaggerated and dramatized and that whatever sniping there was, was for obstructing law enforcement and fire fighting and not for killing officials.

The riot crowds gave evidence of being able to pick specific targets for their aggression. Black business establishments, many of them carrying signs such as "Blood Brother" or "Soul Brother" were for the most part spared. Private houses, post offices, churches, schools, libraries, and other public buildings in the riot area were not broken into and burned down, vandalized, or otherwise purposely damaged. Some white-owned stores also were spared. The Los Angeles police, the main target of pre-riot hostility, were also the main target of riot aggression. Only ten National Guardsmen out of a maximum of 13,900 were reported injured, as compared to ninety Los Angeles policemen out of a combined total of 1653 police at the time of maximum deployment. The evidence, meager as it is, supports the view that there was a systematic relationship between the specific targets of aggression and the rioters' grievances.

The destructive and violent behavior of the rioters was confined to specific kinds of behaviors and situations within the riot situation. Eye-witnesses reported that rioters and looters in cars were observing traffic laws in the riot area—stopping for red lights, stopping for pedestrians at crosswalks—even when carrying away stolen goods. Firemen were obstructed in putting out fires set to business establishments, yet one incident is reported where people beseeched firemen to save a house that had caught fire when embers skipped to it from a torched commercial building, and during which firemen were not hindered in any way from carrying out their job. These and similar incidents testify to the ability of riot participants to choose appropriate means for their ends. Though riot behavior cannot be called "rational" in the everyday common meaning of that term, it does contain normative and rational elements and is far more situationally determined than the popular view would have it.

Looting is attractive to people lacking the consumer goods others take for granted. It needs no complex explanation beyond the simple desire to obtain them when the opportunity to do so involves a low risk of apprehension by the police. Such action is facilitated by low commitment to the norms of private property, the fact that others are doing the same thing, and the fact that the stores sacked in this case belonged to "Whitey." These observations can be illustrated by an eyewitness account of one such incident reported in *Time*:

> One booty-laden youth said defiantly: "That don't look like stealing to me. That's just picking up what you need and going." Gesturing at a fashionable hilltop area where many well-to-do Negroes live, he said: "Them living up in View Park don't need it. But we down here, we do need it."

Looting was a predominantly neighborhood activity, often uncoordinated, and carried out in small groups. Between 50 and 65 percent of the minors were arrested less than a mile from their home, and a little over 63 percent were arrested in the company of others, mainly for "burglary," that is, they were apprehended in or near stores broken into. The casual process through which individuals would get involved in looting, and the group and neighborhood aspects of it, are illustrated in the following statement of an arrested minor to a Probation Officer:

> [Minor] states that he was at home when his brother came home and said there was a riot going on in the streets. Minor states that he went out on the streets to watch and met a friend who said that people were going into a store on Broadway and "taking stuff out." Minor states that he and the companion went to observe and after arriving there and seeing everyone taking stuff from the store, he decided that he would take something also. . . . The only reason Minor offers for his behavior is that "everybody else was taking stuff, so I decided to take some too."

While the actions of some looters were described in some accounts as that of a savage mob bent on plunder and fighting each other for the spoils, other descriptions and material, such as a photograph showing two women and one man rolling a fully loaded shopping cart past firemen, suggest a much more relaxed and calm mood.

Looting as well as other riot activity was essentially a group activity during which participants and onlookers experienced a sense of solidarity, pride, and exhilaration. They were bound together by shared emotions, symbols, and experiences that a black man inevitably acquires in white America and that makes him address another one as "Brother." They were also bound together by the common enemy, "Whitey," and struck out against Whitey's representatives in the flesh, the police, the firemen, the merchants, the news reporters, and the motorists, and they felt good about striking out. Bystanders were swept along in this tide of we-feeling.

The rioters did not form an amorphous mass, a collection of individuals acting out private frustrations and hostility. Rioting was a group activity in the course of which strangers were bound together by common sentiments, activities, and goals and supported each other in the manner typical of primary groups. The riot was a collective celebration, a carnival, during which about forty liquor stores were broken into and much liquor consumed. It was also a collective contest similar to that between two high school or college athletic teams, with the supporters cheering and egging on the contestants. One could settle old scores with the police, show them who really controlled the turf, humiliate them, teach them a lesson. Just as a rioting youth was quoted by two black newsmen as saying: "This is what the police wanted—always messin' with niggers. We'll show them. I'm ready to die if I have to." Police Chief Parker mistakenly boasted, "we are on top and they are on the bottom." Both sides in this tragic and deadly contest had a high emotional stake in the outcome.

In assaulting the police and breaking into business establishments, some rioters were not only responding to the long-standing frustrations and humiliations suffered at the hands of the police and the exploitative practices of merchants but were reacting along racial lines that can only be understood in the wider social context of black people in the U.S. Rioters were pelting motorists and firemen with rocks while shouting: "This is for Bogalusa! This is for Selma!" The riot situation became defined in global, dichotomous, we-they terms, where "we" and "they" stood for the two races and the long history of conflict associated with them. While the riot was put down eventually, many blacks saw it as a victory for their side and derived a sense of pride and accomplishment from this public demonstration of their collective power.

Even though the Los Angeles riot was a large-scale riot when measured in terms of number of active participants, the area it covered, the number of law enforcement officers needed to control it, and the total amount of fatalities and property damage, it is not true that every black man in the curfew area was swept along into rioting by an emotional tide of social contagion. In Los Angeles, as in other riots, there were counter-demonstrators urging the people to cool it, and other people took steps to negotiate with the authorities on the best means to restore order and keep the riot from spreading. But in the atmosphere of tension and hostility these efforts came to naught.

VIOLENCE

Violence is but one of several means of conducting conflict. Many conflicts are pursued with a mixture of violent and nonviolent, coercive and noncoercive means, and the amount of violence associated with a single movement and set of issues will fluctuate over time. Although a satisfactory explanation for the incidence of violence must await a theory of social conflict more comprehensive than any so far available, violence is such an important topic that it is worthwhile summarizing in one place a number of insights, generalizations, and partial explanations that have been put forward in the preceding pages and in other works on social conflict and related topics. In the words of Max Weber (1947:133),

> the treatment of conflict involving the use of physical violence as a separate type is justified by the special characteristics of the employment of this means and the corresponding peculiarities of the sociological consequences of its use.

Therefore, we are justified in raising as a distinct question under what conditions conflict will tend to be violent rather than nonviolent and what accounts for the magnitude of violence.

The following discussion on violence is not meant to cover all cases of conflict. It deals primarily with conflict and confrontation taking place between large groups, social strata, and social classes and between these collectivities and the authorities, as manifested in riots and rebellions, in peasant movements and labor wars, nationalist movements and insurrections, in ethnic and regional movements for secession or for integration into the body politic, in revolutions and in wars of national liberation, in student uprisings and other instances of substantial social disturbances and civil disorders. It specifically excludes wars between states, and at the other end, microconflicts such as gang wars, interpersonal conflict, and violence resulting from ordinary crime. The discussion furthermore does not stress the difference between legal and illegal violence because what in particular instances is a legal or illegal, justified or unjustified, use of physical force is a matter that often comes to be a central issue in the conflict, as when the authorities initiate the violence under circumstances where its use is perceived as uncalled for by many people. In many confrontations it is the agents of social control that are responsible for the larger number of injuries, fatalities, and other acts of violent coercion. To limit "civil violence" to "all collective, non-governmental attacks on persons and property, resulting in intentional damage to them," as Gurr does (1967:5), is to exclude a large class of events that occur as an integral part of most confrontations. Violence is the result of interaction between two or more groups during conflict, one of which may be the state or its agents. The same concepts and insights can be employed to shed light on violence perpetrated by all parties locked in conflict.

Collective or group violence has been defined in many different ways, and none has satisfied all the commentators and writers on the topic. Yet, the underlying meaning is clear enough: violence is the use of force with the intent of inflicting damage or injury upon one's opponent in order to coerce him against his will. Group violence in this sense represents a failure to regulate and resolve social conflict through nonviolent and institutionalized channels. It is a common and ubiquitous phenomenon in the contemporary world. Even in relatively peaceful epochs, however, the possibility of violence is never far below the surface, and only utopian philosophies have depicted social systems in which it is altogether absent. On this matter, Durverger (1964:209) wrote appropriately that

> the first object of politics is to eliminate violence, to substitute for bloody conflicts less brutal forms of struggle . . . politics tends to eliminate violence but it never succeeds to do so completely.

It is possible to measure the magnitude of violence by the total number of casualties, fatalities, and injuries that result in a confrontation or series of collective disturbances. A more complex way of measuring it would include the extent of property damage as well, but accurate information on this dimension is more difficult to come by.

Violence as a means of waging conflict is not usually resorted to lightly, without attempts to reach one's objectives through other means. Violence tends to break out after nonviolent means of seeking redress for grievances have failed. Often the discontented groups wait some time for reforms designed to reduce social strain to take effect, and only after the reforms have proved ineffective do they resort to coercive and violent actions. Often, too, the government or ruling groups break a promise or agreement to reform, and thus shut off the more peaceful and institutional channels for bringing about desired changes, before the protest groups initiate coercive and violent actions. For instance, Huntington (1962:25) states that the Huk leaders in the Philippines first attempted to achieve their goals by peaceful means, but when the legislature refused to seat seven elected Huks, their leaders returned to the countryside to spark a revolt. Writing about the Zapata rising in Mexico in 1910–1911, McNeely (1966:155–57) reports that Zapata's native village had a long record of contentions and representations over its land rights, that the new governor paid little attention to the villagers' petitions despite the fact that their legal claims were held up as valid, and that legal action by villagers in Mexico City also failed to produce results. Only after these institutional channels were exhausted did the uprising start. Concerning the Luddite outbreaks in England in 1811, Darvall (1934:47–48, 64) explicitly states that the stockingers and weavers first tried to negotiate their grievances over wages, the rent of frames, the truck system, and other matters, with the hosiers without any positive results. As for the June days in Paris during the 1848 revolution, the working people of Paris did not start erecting barricades until after Louis Blanc's Luxembourg Commission and the national workshops (the two major gains the Paris working people achieved after the overthrow of the July monarchy and the main sources of employment and livelihood for them at a time of economic depression) werè dissolved and the workers given a choice of enlisting in the army, draining marshes, or remaining in Paris without work or pay (Rudé, 1964:172). Examples can be multiplied, and in any case are only meant to be illustrative and suggestive.

Violence is more often initiated by the authorities and the agents of social control than by the protesters, as when peaceful demonstrators, marchers, petitioners, assemblies, and so on are broken up and fired upon. Protesters often initiate actions that are illegal and coercive yet not destructive of life and property, such as squatting on land, cultivating land illegally, refusing to pay taxes, occupying factories and mines, refusing to disperse, and so on, which represent a challenge to the authorities. The authorities on their part do not lightly and randomly initiate violence as a rule. Nevertheless, it is their actions or reactions that start violence, and, when the confrontation is under way, their actions that produce the bulk of the casualties.

For instance the Kerner Report (U.S. Riot Commission, 1968:68–69, 107, 115–16 footnote 20, 164) states that in the 1967 urban riots in the U.S., of the eighty-three persons who died in the seventy-five disorders studied, only about 10 percent were public officials, and that the overwhelming majority of the civilians killed were blacks, and most of these were shot by the police or other agents of social control. In Detroit, rioters were responsible for three deaths at the most, whereas the police and national guard accounted for between twenty-seven and thirty deaths. In summarizing the detailed casualty figures resulting from popular disturbances between 1730 and 1848 in Western Europe, Rudé (1964:225–26) concludes that "destruction of property, then, is a constant feature of the pre-industrial crowd; but not destruction of human lives. . . . From this balance sheet of violence and reprisal, it would appear, then, that it was authority rather than the crowd that was conspicuous for its violence to life and limb." During the Paris Commune of 1871, in contrast to the several hundred troops of the Versailles regiment killed and the sixty-three hostages shot by the Communards, at least twenty thousand Communards were killed, shot as prisoners, or subsequently executed by the authorities, not counting the number of imprisonments and deportations to penal camps (Postgate, 1962:286). In going to standard historical sources, one can produce similar figures for the discrepancy in magnitude of casualties produced by the authorities on the one hand and the insurgents, rebels, protesters, on the other, in confrontations such as the June days of Paris in 1848, the Russian revolution of 1905–1906, the Mau-Mau uprising, the Nyasaland disturbances of 1959, and many others.

As for the authorities initiating or escalating violence, history is filled with such examples. The precipitating event of the February 1848 revolution occurred when between 50 to 100 demonstrators were killed and wounded by troops as they marched in support of the parliamentary opposition after the authorities had banned a large public banquet in Paris (Rudé, 1964:167). The precipitating event in the Russian revolution of 1905 occurred on Bloody Sunday when an immense procession of unarmed workers in their Sunday clothes and chanting church hymns, led by Father Gapon, sought to present a petition to the Tsar and were attacked by the troops and the Cossacks, resulting in a massacre of about a thousand petitioners. Father Gapon had attempted before this event to seek redress for the workers' grievances through bureaucratic channels and had gotten nowhere. In the Hungarian revolution of 1956 (United Nations, 1957:81–83), one of the precipitating events occurred when students, in the evening of 22 October, demanded that the radio station broadcast their resolutions to the Hungarian people and were fired upon by security police inside the radio building after student representatives had already entered the radio building to negotiate with the officials of the radio. In a subsequent aggravating incident on 25 October, a huge crowd of several thousand peaceful people, many of them women and children, were waiting for Prime Minister Nagy to appear when a number of flag-carrying demonstrators appeared in the square and the security police and possibly also Soviet troops opened up on everybody with machine guns, killing anywhere from 300 to 800 people.

The technology of weaponry in a conflict situation seems to be an important and to a large extent independent factor in the magnitude of casualties resulting from confrontations. The matter has so far received little attention in the social science literature. Any steps or means available for crowd control short of the use of firearms will have the effect of lowering the casualty rate. The introduction of tear gas as a means of crowd control and dispersal has probably reduced considerably the magnitude of violence and the number of casualties in confrontations. The availability to police of shields and long batons for protection against rock throwing and physical assault rather than of firearms alone has the same consequence. Access to weapons and the level of weapons technology available to both sides are also important factors in the production of casualties. If one side only has access to modern weapons and the other side possesses merely agricultural tools, spears, arrows and other premodern weapons, casualties tend to be higher than if there is no weapons disparity. This situation frequently occurs when soldiers armed with modern weapons join one hostile group against another and make their weapons available to the side they favor. It also occurs when troops armed with modern weapons face a massed group of opponents armed with only traditional weapons or outdated firearms, as was typical of colonial wars of conquest and the repression of indigenous resistance movements. To be sure, the typical present-day confrontation between troops and police on one side and rioters, protesters, and demonstrators on the other does involve a high degree of weapons disparity, yet casualties tend to be on an altogether lower order of magnitude than in colonial wars and resistance movements. This happens because a number of other factors and variables that stand in a strong causal relationship to the magnitude of violence are also present in these situations and overshadow the effects of weapons disparity. These will be commented upon below.

In the absence of weapons disparity, access to lethal weapons and skill in their use become crucial variables. Modern weapons in and of themselves are not necessarily more productive of casualties than the use of premodern weapons and agricultural implements. If the groups in the confrontation have familiar tools in their homes within reach at a moment's notice and are skilled and accustomed in their use, casualties will tend to be high. Describing the communal riots in India in 1946–1948 that produced close to one million fatalities, Richardson (1960:43) writes that "communal killing was mostly by sticks, small knives, small axes, swords, spears, with only a few shotguns, rifles or automatics."

SOCIAL CONTROL AND VIOLENCE

More important and at the very core of a sociological theory of conflict and of violence is a set of organizational and social control variables. Partiality of the agents of social control in intergroup conflict increases violence and casualties, just as they decrease to the extent that an impartial party intervenes as a buffer or mediator in the conflict. In a common situation, when the confrontation is not directly between the authorities and protesters but between two hostile population groups such as employees and employers or whites and blacks, the casualties tend to be higher if the authorities either openly side with one group against the other or refrain from intervening in the conflict and thus legitimize and facilitate the actions of the aggressor group. In the U.S. during the old-style race riots, police partiality in favor of whites resulted in prolonging the disturbances, inciting the aggressor to increased violence, and in the escalation of weapons used, all productive of numerous victims. This has been documented by Waskow (1967: chapter 10) for the 1919 race riots and by Lee and Humphrey (1943: chapter 4) for the Detroit riot of 1943. It is a common occurrence in communal, tribal, and religious riots producing a very large number of victims that the police or military help and join the aggressor group, as happened during the Ibo massacres in northern Nigeria in 1966 and the anti-Communist massacres in Java in 1965. In all these instances the agents of social control did not play the part of an impartial buffer associated with diminished likelihood of violence. The impartial buffer force is in fact the rationale behind the U.N. peacekeeping force as it was put into operation in Cyprus and elsewhere. In civil disturbances, replacing a hated local police force with other agents of social control not previously linked to repression and partiality tends to have a similar dampening effect upon violence.

Frequently related to impartiality of the authorities, but nevertheless a distinct variable in its own right, is the degree of accountability of the agents of social control. The magnitude of casualties will be greater to the extent that accountability for actions and casualties produced by the agents of social control is low and ineffective. The restraints operating upon the agents of social control to check their usually superior and devastating means of inflicting casualties upon their opponents are more important in keeping violence at a low level than the restraints operating upon the protesters and demonstrators. Officially sanctioned repression, where "everything goes," is perhaps the most extreme form of the absence of accountability and results in the largest massacres. Restraints will also be weak when public opinion favors repression during a period of "red" scare, of nationalism and jingoism, of religious enthusiasm and similar waves of popular fear and hysteria during which members of a certain group have been labeled and targeted as "reds," "traitors," "infidels," and "heretics," to cite but some common examples. In other situations social disturbances may occur in outlying areas, usually rural, with poor communications, so that little information about casualties and the details of the confrontation filters out other than through government controlled sources. It may also happen in situations where the judiciary is subordinate to the executive branch, and the executive in any case not much influenced by an unorganized public opinion. Again, if the protesters belong to a negatively privileged or "pariah" social category, such as a racial or religious minority, peasants, and so on, who have not enjoyed full-citizenship rights and have traditionally been kept in their place by the use of force, casualties will tend to be higher than if the protesters are drawn from more privileged classes and groups, because accountability will be lower, public opnion less concerned, the events themselves less visible and less scrutinized.

Accountability is actually a global concept consisting of a cluster of dimensions and processes. It is useful to respecify and to concretize this notion when applying the above ideas to actual instances of conflict and to specific countries and historical periods. It is probably a truism that accountability will be higher and more effective to the extent that the investigation, prosecution, disciplining, and penalizing of the agents of social control for their actions during confrontations are performed by bodies and organizations located outside of the chain of command of the police or the military rather than left an internal social control matter. It is also more likely to be effective if those responsible for disciplining the agents of social control are drawn from the higher levels of authority rather than from among immediate superiors and representatives of the local community, who tend to enforce the mores rather than the laws and who are closely linked to those who are charged with illegal or excessive use of force. Accountability is made more effective inasmuch as there are clearly spelled out directions and guidelines for the use of force and of procedures for escalating force (reading the riot act or verbal warnings, exhausting the deterrent power of nonlethal weapons, firing warning shots, firing at a single or a few demonstrators to wound but not to kill, shooting to kill only in case of threat to life, and so on), and this is more likely to be the case when the police or military are a highly professional force. Least accountability of social control agents occurs in the case of secret police in a totalitarian regime and the personal "palace guard" in a dictatorial regime, where even high officials within the regime are vulnerable to arbitrary arrest and violence at the whim of the top leaders or dictator. In democratic societies a highly decentralized system of police such as exists in the United States is less suited for a high degree of accountability than the more centralized European systems. In the U.S., the police in many localities are only a partially professional force, and the control of the agents of social control rests in the hands of local officials. In a national, hierarchic police system discipline can be handled at higher levels of authority. The minister responsible for police may be held responsible in the national legislature for the actions of his subordinates and for disciplinary procedures. Accountability becomes a matter in which the opposition parties can directly intervene in routinized, institutional ways and becomes a powerful deterrent to excesses in social control. At the same time a national system of police makes an authoritarian or dictatorial take-over easier than a decentralized police system when a democratic regime totters on the brink of collapse.

Aside from accountability the degree of organization of the conflict groups is a central variable in a theory of violence. A high degree of organization exists when an effective, recognized, stable leadership exercises direction and control over the actions of the rank-and-file participants in the conflict, in contrast to the low degree of organization of people who more or less spontaneously collect as hostile crowds after precipitating incidents, and where at most temporary and local leaders emerge. So far as the degree of organization of the agents of social control is concerned, it is higher to the extent that networks of communication, chain of command, and troop discipline are maintained, and that is more likely to happen if the force is professional and has been trained and is experienced in handling confrontations with protest crowds. The higher the degree of organization of both conflict groups, the lower the likelihood and magnitude of violence. A confrontation likely to be particularly violent is one during which an unorganized, spontaneously assembled hostile crowd faces a disorganized police force or troops, or another unorganized crowd. Moreover, factionalism and leadership rivalries are associated with a lower degree of organization in a conflict group. Thus, if the protest group or the authorities are split into rival camps and factions with competing leaders, the likelihood of violence is greater than if they are internally united. These ideas are intimately linked to the previously described conservative tendencies inherent in large-scale and highly organized opposition movements: to begin with both sides have a stake in conciliation; agreements that are reached are more likely to be enforceable and adhered to; the probability of unplanned incidents resulting from a lack of control over the rank-and-file is lower.

The following historical examples provide a few of many instances in support of the notion that degree of organization varies inversely with the magnitude of violence in confrontations. Compare for instance the February 1917 overthrow of the Tsar with the Bolshevik coup in October 1917. In February, a week long, unorganized, and spontaneous movement, which started as a movement of protest for bread led by women and gradually developed into a general strike, produced 1315 casualties (Pettee, 1938:102; Trotsky, 1959:97–173) at a time when almost all revolutionary leaders were in Siberia or abroad, whereas in October a highly organized and ideological party overthrew the Kerensky government with but a dozen fatalities (Trotsky, 1959:336–436). Consider in addition the Detroit riot of 1967, and the casualties produced by the disorganized police and National Guard, in contrast to the disciplined and well-led paratroopers (U.S. Riot Commission, 1968:99–102). The paratroopers, who followed orders to unload their weapons and remain in evidence on sidewalks and in the street, expended only 201 rounds of ammunition, did not suffer any injuries from gunshot, and inflicted only one fatality. By contrast, the panicked police and National Guard disobeyed orders to unload their weapons, expended thousands of rounds of ammunition, sometimes at each other, hid behind walls and shot out street lights in order not to be visible, and reacted to all conceivable rumors that kept flooding their communications system. Their actions accounted for between twenty-seven and thirty fatalities. Conot (1967:218, 229, 234, 278, 325–26, 329, 339, 367) provides further evidence that in the Los Angeles riot of 1965 many fatalities were produced by police when they became disorganized, panicked, and acted on rumor, no matter how incredible they now appear in retrospect. As a matter of fact, the more violent turn of the black movement in 1964 and later years can be explained with reference to organization. As the black movement shifted from the more organized and better led Southern blacks to the previously unorganized Northern urban lower-class blacks, whom Martin Luther King and other civil rights leaders were unable to mobilize into their organizations, violence increased considerably. In the same vein, the relatively nonviolent summer of 1968 can also be explained partly in organizational terms. By 1968, in urban ghettos, radical and militant blacks had managed to create at least a rudimentary organization network and following, and in addition, many ghetto dwellers themselves had organized into block or neighborhood organizations for pressing their demands or for curbing youth and rioting. It is also possible that the agents of social control were more experienced and organized by the summer of 1968. Thus, unlike theories that focus on magnitude of strain and frustration to explain the lower level of violence in 1968, the present theory emphasizes the changes in degree of organization of both conflict groups between 1968 and earlier years. There is no evidence that strain and frustration were lower in 1968 than in the previous four summers.

So far nothing has been said about some common sociological variables usually linked with social conflict and with violent social conflict in particular. What relationships are there between violence and the number of grievances, the magnitude of strain, the level of frustration experienced by some groups? Is violence more likely when the conflict groups express demands with reference to highly developed ideologies rather than in terms of ordinary folk ideas about justice and injustice, right and wrong? Is violence more likely as polarization increases, as the number of reenforcing, nonoverlapping social cleavages dividing the conflict groups increase, as the past history of mutual injury and hostility dividing them is longer and more intense? These are important questions that at the present stage of knowledge it is difficult to answer. Perhaps the questions themselves are altogether too global and too general, since many processes intervene between the hypothesized causes and the incidence of violent conflict. Many social scientists and historians have noted that it is not the most oppressed groups that rise in revolt, and that overt conflict is not as likely to break out at the height of hardship and the depth of economic depression but rather at a time when conditions are improving. The most oppressed groups are usually the most economically dependent and most vulnerable to negative economic sanctions, and thus unable to risk opposition and to muster the minimum resources needed for mobilization. Their likely reaction is more commonly fear, apathy, and resignation. Coercive social control may be so complete and pervasive that overt protest and opposition likely to lead to a confrontation is impossible. On the other hand, a lesser degree of oppression and of strain under more permissive conditions such as occur when social control is loosened provides opportunities for overt conflict and, hence, also for the occurrence of violence. A theory that omits these and similar intervening variables and processes is apt to be overly simple and misleading. In any case, the variables and processes most likely to predict social conflict may not be the best predictors of violence during conflict.

Certain issues and conflicts are more difficult to compromise and to settle in peaceful fashion, as has already been pointed out in the chapter on the sources of social conflict. Conflicts over material goods and rewards, especially if they are not in short supply, are easier to resolve than conflicts over rights, over authority, and over basic principles such as the legitimacy of the form of government. Whatever the substantive issues, the concrete manner in which the authorities respond to grievances and demands as expressed in their handling of the recognition issue is a particularly important intervening process for understanding the likelihood and magnitude of violence. Recognition means that the authorities recognize the right to protest and to express demands, regardless of what position they may take on the substantive issues and demands, and are willing to listen to, sit down with, talk to, and negotiate in good faith with the leaders, deputies, representatives, spokesmen, and so on of the protesters. Nonrecognition can be inferred from several indicators that signal to the protest group that recognition is not granted or is in the process of being withdrawn: refusal to receive, listen to, debate, discuss and negotiate with one's opponents, arrest of their leaders, harassment of their organizing efforts through arrests, blacklists, curbs on free speech and assembly, and so on. If recognition is granted, the likelihood and magnitude of violence tend to be lower than if recognition is not granted or is being withdrawn. After violence has already broken out, it is likely to diminish as soon as it is extended even in the absence of concessions on substantive issues, or before reforms have taken effect.

Recognition implies that the conflict is on its way to becoming institutionalized and regulated. Recognition itself is a complex process. De facto recognition of an organization claiming to represent a group for purposes of temporary negotiation may be followed by regular consultations with it whenever decisions are taken that affect the welfare of the collectivity. The next step is juridical recognition that obligates the state to protect its integrity against hostile forces, and this in turn may be followed by extensions and specifications of its sphere of authority within the institutional matrix of the society. The further along on the road to full recognition a particular movement or group finds itself, the lower the likelihood of violence when conflict occurs.

Recognition is very much a matter of sharing authority with and extending rights to hitherto negatively privileged groups. At the microlevel, it is the counterpart to the extension of political and civil rights to previously disenfranchised "new" groups and classes, or the achievement of independence by colonial peoples. Recognition is closely linked with several of the variables discussed earlier, organization and accountability. When recognition is gradually extended, the protest group is able to progressively develop a permanent organizational structure and regularize its leadership processes. The consequence is greater control of rank-and-file members by the top leaders and the growth of conservative, moderating tendencies within the opposition group, both of which diminish the chances of violence. On top of that, recognition has a restraining influence on the agents of social control when they are face to face with members of the protest group. With recognition, the claims of hitherto negatively privileged groups to be treated as full citizens, with the same rights of dissent and opposition as others have, is on its way to becoming the norm. Infringement of these emerging norms will be a matter of concern to public opinion; the leaders of the protest group will be in a better position to present their case; visibility of social control will increase. The overall consequence of all these processes is to increase the accountability of the agents of social control when dealing with members of the opposition group, and this has a moderating influence on the use of excessive force and violent coercion. Finally, through their leaders and associations the opposition groups develop regular channels for bringing their grievances to the attention of those in authority without having to resort to mass actions and before their problems become overwhelming. Negotiations can be more readily undertaken as a routinized process, and agreements once reached stand a better chance to be adhered to by all the concerned parties. Thus, the cumulative effects set in motion by recognition, even when partial, reduce the likelihood of violence during conflict.

Perhaps the most promising area to highlight the importance of recognition comes from the comparative study of labor movements. Taft (1966: 127–34) has noted that a leading cause of violence in U.S. labor disputes was the refusal of management to recognize the union. "In cases where the union is recognized, strikes seldom lead to violent encounters. However, in unorganized strikes or in those which have arisen in an effort to gain recognition, the use of violence is more common." A comparison of the labor movements in the U.S. with those of Western Europe supports the view that it is not the magnitude of material strain and frustrations, nor the extremeness of the ideologies used to express opposition, but rather the trio of recognition, organization, and accountability that explain the more violent labor conflict in America. The U.S. labor movement was less ideological, less organized, yet more violent than European labor movements. Taft further writes that "it may appear anomalous that the U.S., a country in which class feeling and class ideology are almost entirely absent, has experienced considerable amounts of violence in labor disputes. . . . With the exception of a small minority, American workers have not been attracted to the various branches of anarchism, communism, socialism, and syndicalism. Yet American history is dotted with clashes between strikers and strikebreakers and police authorities." Another historian of the labor movements, Val Lorwin (1957:37–39), writes in this connection that

> American workers had to fight bloodier industrial battles than the French for the right of unions to exist and to function. Their political history knew nothing like the "June Days" or the Commune. But the rail strikes

of 1877, the pitched battle of Homestead, the Ludlow massacre, were bloodier than Fourmies and Draveil and Villeneuve-Saint Georges. . . . France had nothing like the private armies, factory arsenals, and industrial espionage service exposed by the LaFollette Committee . . . American employers came to recognize the unions only under the multiple pressures of public opinion, administration policy, a reversal of supreme court interpretations, and finally and essentially, worker self-organizations.

An investigation of fifty-four major strikes in the U.S. from the 1870s to the 1930s showed that the occurrence of violence as measured by fatalities was associated positively with the presence of union recognition and union busting as a major issue in the strike (Oberschall, 1970:90).

EPILOGUE

Social conflict, opposition movements, social disturbances, as has been shown repeatedly in these pages, are a result of processes of social change, but they are also one of the usual ways in which change is brought about. Conflict overcomes the basically conservative tendencies in the social order; it prevents the ossification of institutions and builds pressures for responsiveness and innovation. During mobilization and confrontation, new leaders, organizations, ideas, and programs emerge and grow. The opposition leaders and movements of the present frequently become the leaders and political parties that shape the institutions of the future. In a few instances, the changes produced are sharp and total: these are the changes of system referred to by Coser (1967:28–29) that follow the major revolutions when an entire leadership class is replaced, when the distribution of possessions and of authority are reversed, when values, norms, and institutions are transformed. In other instances the movement is suppressed and nothing perhaps is changed save the impossibility of making good the human sacrifices and material resources that have been expended. A movement can be ruthlessly suppressed and yet many of the changes it had sought might still be brought about at a later time, for confrontation is a warning signal to the ruling groups that they had better change course or else face even more explosive upheavals in the future.

More commonly, an opposition movement will be partially successful. The grievances and demands it brings to the surface will receive some attention; the reforms that are drawn up and implemented will go some way in diminishing the underlying causes of discontent. Recognition will be gradually extended to the opposition movement. The discontented groups and the agents of social control will establish relationships of accommodation that replace the earlier relationships of conflict. Certain forms of opposition and protest become accepted as legitimate and come to receive the protection of the law. The groups that most feared and resisted the changes ushered in by the social movement learn to live with them though perhaps not to like them. Those most threatened by the movement will develop a more realistic and balanced assessment of the changes that do occur. As the movement becomes institutionalized, its leaders and organizations take their place with other established elites and organizations in the institutional matrix of society. With more to gain by playing the political game rather than by opposition and with a lot to protect, they will themselves become a component part of the vested interests that are the pillars of social stability and that they had earlier fought. Their primary aim will now be to secure continued benefits to their members and constituents, and they might end up denying the same benefits they fought for to yet newer negatively privileged groups who seek full-citizenship status and a greater share of the national pie. Nevertheless, the situation is not what it was at the start of the movement, because social changes affecting the lives of thousands, if not millions, of people have taken place.

It is rather an academic question whether the same results could have been reached without conflict and confrontation. In an ideal world the answer might be yes, but in the real world resistance to change can only be overcome by considerable expenditures of human sacrifice and material resources. So far in history change has been seldom if ever brought about by implementing a conscious, carefully thought out plan in which the consequences and complex ramifications of social action are correctly spelled out in advance and compensating corrections and modifications are incorporated into the design. Change occurs rather as a response to cumulative pressures and social forces whose result benefits some groups while it creates misery and hardship for others. After a period of social conflict the imbalances are redressed somewhat, but newer processes of change, equally poorly designed, are initiated and call forth yet further conflicts. Elites and opposition leaders can learn from past mistakes, yet the problems they face are never quite the same as those of the past, and the same forces that made for confrontation rather than conflict regulation reappear and exert powerful pressures. So long as planned social change based on a valid social science is a promise rather than a fact—and it is a promise that is still in the distant future—social conflict will be the inevitable companion of social change. Even so, statecraft, reason, civility, and an enlightened self-interest—to which our still imperfect social science can make its modest contribution—can go a long way in reducing the suffering and sacrifices that conflict entails.

REFERENCES

ABEL, THEODORE
  1948/9 "The Operation Called Verstehen," *American Journal of Sociology* 54 (July), 211–18.
ACZEL, TAMAS, and TIBOR MERAY
  1959 *The Revolt of the Mind,* New York: Praeger.
AFRICA REPORT
  1966 Vol. 11 (No. 4) April issue. "Ghana without Nkrumah."
ALLEN, WILLIAM S.
  1965 *The Nazi Seizure of Power,* Chicago: Quadrangle Books.
AMBER, PAUL
  1968 "Nigeria and the Ibo," *Journal of Modern African Studies* 5 (No. 2).
ANDERSON, CHARLES, et al.
  1967 *Issues in Political Development,* Englewood Cliffs, N. J.: Prentice-Hall.
ANGELL, ROBERT C.
  1965 "The Sociology of Human Conflict," in Elton McNeil, ed., *The Nature of Human Conflict,* Englewood Cliffs, N.J.: Prentice-Hall.
ANWEILER, OSKAR
  1958a *Die Rätebewegung in Russland, 1905–1921,* Leiden: Brill.
  1958b "Die Räte in der Ungarischen Revolution 1956," *Osteuropa VIII,* 393–400.

ARON, RAYMOND
    1968   *Main Currents in Sociological Thought,* New York: Doubleday Anchor.

BAILEY, F. G.
    1966   "The Peasant View of the Bad Life," *The Advancement of Science* 23 (No. 114).

BALANDIER, GEORGES
    1955   *Sociologie Acutelle de l'Afrique Noire,* Paris, Presses Universitaires de France.

BANFIELD, EDWARD
    1958   *The Moral Basis of a Backward Society,* Glencoe, Ill.: Free Press.

BANFIELD, EDWARD, and JAMES Q. WILSON
    1966   *City Politics,* New York: Vintage Books.

BARBOUR, FLOYD, ed.
    1968   *The Black Power Revolt,* Toronto: Collier Books.

BARTH, HANS
    1945   *Wahrheit und Ideologie,* Zurich: Manesse.

BELL, WENDELL, RICHARD HILL, and CHARLES WRIGHT
    1961   *Public Leadership,* San Francisco: Chandler.

BELL, WENDELL, ed.
    1967   *The Democratic Revolution in the West Indies,* Cambridge, Mass.: Schenkman.

BENDA, HARRY J.
    1966   "Peasant Movements in Colonial Southeast Asia," *Asian Studies* 3 (No. 3).

BENDIX, REINHARD
    1964   *Nation Building and Citizenship,* New York: Wiley.

BENDIX, REINHARD
    1967   "Tradition and Modernity Reconsidered," *Comparative Studies in Society and History,* 9 (April), 292–346.

BENNETT, LERONE, JR.
    1966   *Confrontation: Black and White,* Baltimore: Penguin Books, Inc.

BERELSON, BERNARD, PAUL F. LAZARSFELD, and WILLIAM N. McPHEE
    1954   *Voting,* Chicago: Chicago University Press.

BIENEN, HENRY
    1967   *Tanzania, Party Transformation and Economic Development,* Princeton: Princeton University Press.

    1968   *Violence and Social Change,* Chicago: University of Chicago Press.

BLASER, COLE
    1967   "Studies in Social Revolution: Origins in Mexico, Bolivia, Cuba," *Latin American Research Review* 2 (No. 3).

BLAU, PETER, and OTIS D. DUNCAN
    1967   *The American Occupational Structure,* New York: Wiley.

BONDURANT, JOAN V.
    1958   *Conquest of Violence: The Gandhian Philosophy of Conflict,* Princeton, N.J.: Princeton University Press.

BOULDING, KENNETH
    1962   *Conflict and Defense,* New York: Harper Torchbooks.
BOULDING, KENNETH
    1966   "Conflict Management as a Learning Process," in Anthony de
            Reuck, ed., *Conflict and Society,* Boston: Little, Brown, and Co.
BRINTON, CRANE
    1930   *The Jacobins,* New York: Macmillan.
    1952   *The Anatomy of Revolution,* New York: Vintage Books.
BROOM, LEONARD, and PHILIP SELZNICK
    1958   *Sociology,* 2d ed., Evanston, Ill.: Row and Peterson.
BROWN, ROGER
    1965   *Social Psychology,* Glencoe, Ill.: Free Press.
BRYSON, GLADYS
    1945   *Man and Society: The Scottish Inquiry of the Eighteenth Cen-
            tury,* Princeton: Princeton University Press.
BUREAU OF LABOR STATISTICS
    1967   Report No. 332, October 1967, *Social and Economic Condition of
            Negroes in the United States.*
BURKE, EDMUND
    1955   *Reflections on the Revolution in France,* New York: Liberal Arts
            Press.
CALVERT, PETER
    1970   *A Study of Revolution,* Oxford: Clarendon Press.
CANTRIL, HADLEY
    1958   *The Politics of Despair,* New York: Basic Books.
CARMICHAEL, STOKELY, and CHARLES V. HAMILTON
    1967   *Black Power,* New York: Vintage Books.
CASSIRER, ERNST
    1951   *The Philosophy of the Enlightenment,* Boston: Beacon Press.
CLARK, TERRY
    1969   "Introduction," in Gabriel Tarde, *On Communication and Social
            Influence,* Chicago: The Chicago University Press.
CLARKE, J. J.
    1961   "Standard Operating Procedures in Tragic Situations," *Phylon* 22,
            318–28.
COLEMAN, JAMES SAMUEL
    1957   *Community Conflict,* New York: Free Press.
    1966   "Foundations for a Theory of Collective Decisions," *American
            Journal of Sociology* 71 (No. 6) (May), 615–27.
    1969   "Race Relations and Social Change," in Irwin Katz and Patricia
            Gurin, eds., *Race and the Social Sciences,* New York: Basic Books.
COLEMAN, JAMES SMOOT
    1954   "Nationalism in Tropical Africa," *American Political Science Re-
            view* 48 (No. 2).
CONDORCET
    1804   *Oeuvres Complètes,* Vol. 21, Paris.
CONOT, ROBERT
    1967   *Rivers of Blood, Years of Darkness,* New York: Bantam Books.

CONVERSE, PHILIP
  1964 "The Nature of Belief Systems in Mass Publics," in David Apter, ed., *Ideology and Discontent,* Glencoe, Ill.: Free Press.

CONVERSE, PHILIP, and GEORGES DUPEUX
  1967 "Politicization of the electorate in France and the United States," *Public Opinion Quarterly* 26, 1–23.

COSER, LEWIS
  1956 *The Functions of Social Conflict,* Glencoe, Ill.: Free Press.
  1957 "Social Conflict and the Theory of Social Change," *British Journal of Sociology* 8, 196–207.
  1961 "The Termination of Conflict," *Journal of Conflict Resolution* 5, 346–57.
  1965 *Men of Ideas,* New York: Free Press of Glencoe.
  1967 *Continuities in the Study of Social Conflict,* New York: Free Press.

COTHRAN, TILMAN, and WILLIAM PHILLIPS, JR.
  1961 "Negro Leadership in a Crisis Situation," *Phylon* 22 (No. 2), 107–18.

COTHRAN, TILMAN
  1965 "The Negro Protest Against Segregation in the South," *The Annals* 357 (Jan. 1965).

CRAIN, ROBERT, et al.
  1969 *The Politics of Community Conflict,* New York: Bobbs-Merrill.

CURRENT POPULATION REPORTS
  1966 Series P-23, No. 17, "Special Census Survey of the South and East Los Angeles Areas, November 1965," U.S. Department of Commerce, Bureau of Labor Statistics, Washington, D.C.

CURRENT POPULATION REPORTS
  1969 Series P-23, No. 29, "Social and Economic Condition of Negroes in the U.S.," U.S. Department of Commerce, Bureau of Labor Statistics, Washington, D.C.

CURRIE, ELLIOTT, and JEROME SKOLNICK
  1970 "A Critical Note on Conceptions of Collective Behavior," *The Annals* 391 (September), 34–45.

DAHRENDORF, RALF
  1958 "Towards a Theory of Conflict," *Journal of Conflict Resolution* 2, 170–83.
  1959 *Class and Class Conflict in Industrial Society,* Stanford, Cal.: Stanford University Press.
  1962 *Gesellschaft und Freiheit,* München: Piper.

DARVALL, FRANK
  1934 *Popular Disturbances and Public Order in Regency England,* London: Oxford University Press.

DAVID, STEPHEN M.
  1968 "Leadership of the Poor in Poverty Programs," in Robert H. Connery, ed., *Urban Riots,* New York: Vintage.

DAVIS, ALLISON, et al.
  1941 *Deep South,* Chicago: University of Chicago Press.

DAVIS, JEROME
    1929   "A Study of 163 outstanding Communist Leaders," in *Publications of the American Sociological Society* 24.

DEMERATH, NICHOLAS J., III, et al.
    1969   *The Dynamics of Idealism: Student Activism and the Black Movement,* unpublished manuscript, University of Wisconsin, Department of Sociology.

DEUTSCH, MORTON
    1969   "Conflicts: Productive and Destructive," *Journal of Social Issues* 25 (No. 1), 7–41.

DIAMOND, STANLEY
    1967   *Nigeria, Model of Colonial Failure,* New York: American Committee on Africa.

DESPRES, LEO
    1969   *Protest and Change in Plural Societies,* Montreal: McGill University, Center for Developing Area Studies, Occasional Paper Series, No. 2.

DILLINGHAM, HARRY C., and DAVID F. SLY
    1966   "The Mechanical Cotton Picker, Negro Migration, and the Integration Movement," *Human Organization* 25 (No. 4), Winter, 344–51.

DOBLIN, ERNEST, and CLAIRE POHLY
    1945/6   "The Social Composition of the Nazi Leadership," *American Journal of Sociology* 51.

DOGAN, MATTEI
    1961   "Political Ascent in a Class Society: French Deputies 1870–1958," in Dwaine Marvick, ed., *Political Decision Makers,* Glencoe, Ill.: Free Press.
    1967   "Political Cleavage and Social Stratification in France and Italy," in Seymour M. Lipset and Stein Rokkan, eds., *Party Systems and Voter Alignment,* New York: Free Press.

DOWNES, BRYAN T.
    1968   "Social Characteristics of Riot Cities," *Social Science Quarterly* 49 (No. 3).

DUBIN, ROBERT
    1960   "A Theory of Conflict and Power in Union-Management Relations," *Industrial and Labor Relations Review* XIII, 501–18.

DUFFY, JAMES
    1963   *Portugal in Africa,* Baltimore: Penguin Books.

DUVERGER, MAURICE
    1964   *Introduction à la Politique,* Paris: Gallimard.

ECKSTEIN, HARRY, ed.
    1964   *Internal* War, New York: Free Press.
    1965   "On the Etiology of Internal War," *History and Theory* 4 (No. 2), 133–63.

EDGEWORTH, F. Y.
    1881   *Mathematical Psychics,* London: C. K. Paul.

EDWARDS, LYFORD
   1927   *The Natural History of Revolution,* Chicago: Chicago University Press.
ELINSON, HOWARD
   1967   *Folk Politics: The Political Mentality of White Working Class Voters,* Ann Arbor, Michigan: University Microfilms.
EMERSON, RUPERT
   1962   *From Empire to Nation,* Boston: Beacon Press.
ETZIONI, AMITAI
   1968a   "Mobilization as a macro-sociological conception," *British Journal of Sociology* 19.
   1968b   "Social Control," *International Encyclopedia of the Social Sciences,* Vol. 14, New York: The Free Press and the Macmillan Co.
FARIS, ROBERT E. L.
   1967   *Chicago Sociology, 1920–1932,* Chicago: Chicago University Press.
FOGELSON, ROBERT, and ROBERT HILL
   1968   "Who Riots? A Study of Participation in the 1967 Riots," in *Supplemental Studies for the National Advisory Commission on Civil Disorders,* U.S. Government Printing Office, Washington, D.C.
FOLTZ, WILLIAM
   1970   "Political Opposition in Single Party States of Tropical Africa," unpublished manuscript, Yale University.
FOSTER, GEORGE
   1965   "Peasant Society and the Image of the Limited Good," *American Anthropologist* 67 (No. 2), April, 293–315.
   1967   *Tzintzuntzan,* Boston: Little, Brown and Co.
FOX RENEE, et al.
   1965/6   "The Second Independence: a case study of the Kwilu Rebellion in the Congo," *Comparative Studies in Society and History* 8.
FRANKLIN, FRAZIER
   1966   *The Negro Church in America,* New York: Schocken Books.
FRIEDRICH, CARL
   1967   *Revolution,* Nomos VIII, New York: Atherton Press.
FREUD, SIGMUND
   1940   *Gesammelte Werke,* Vol. 13, London: Imago.
GAMSON, WILLIAM
   1966   "Rancorous Conflict in Community Politics," *American Sociological Review* 31, 71–81.
   1968   *Power and Discontent,* Homewood, Ill.: Dorsey Press.
GEERTZ, CLIFFORD
   1963   *Peddlers and Princes,* Chicago: Chicago University Press.
GELLNER, ERNEST
   1962   "Patterns of Rural Rebellion in Morocco," *European Journal of Sociology* 3.
GERSCHENKRON, ALEXANDER
   1964   "Reflections on Economic Aspects of Revolutions," in Harry Eckstein, ed., *Internal War,* New York: Free Press.

1966   *Bread and Democracy in Germany,* 2d ed., New York: Fertig.

GERTH, HANS
1940   "The Nazi Party; its Leadership and Composition," *American Journal of Sociology* 45.

GERTH, HANS, and C. WRIGHT MILLS, eds.
1958   *From Max Weber,* New York: Oxford University Press.

GLAZER, NATHAN
1968   "America's Race Paradox," *Encounter* 31 (October 1968), 9–18.

GRAHAM, HUGH D., and TED R. GURR, eds.
1969   *Violence in America,* New York: Signet Books.

GRANGER, G. G.
1956   *La Mathématique Sociale de Condorcet,* Paris: Presses Universitaires de France.

GREER, DONALD
1935   *The Incidence of Terror During the French Revolution,* Cambridge, Mass.: Harvard University Press.

GRIMSHAW, ALLEN
1960   "Urban Racial Violence in the U.S.," *American Journal of Sociology* 66, 109–20.

GURR, TED
1967   *The Conditions of Civil Violence,* Princeton, N.J.: Center of International Studies, Research Monograph No. 28.

GUSFIELD, JOSEPH
1962   "Mass Society and Extremist Politics," *American Sociological Review* 27.
1967   "Tradition and Modernity," *American Journal of Sociology* 72 (No. 4) (January), 351–62.
1968   "The Study of Social Movements," in *The International Encyclopedia of the Social Sciences,* New York: Crowell, Collier and Macmillan.

HAIMSON, LEOPOLD
1964   "The Problem of Social Stability in Urban Russia, 1905–1917," *Slavic Review* 23, December.

HAMILTON, RICHARD
1967   *Affluence and the French Worker,* Princeton, N.J.: Princeton University Press.

HANDLIN, OSCAR
1951   *The Uprooted,* New York: Grosset and Dunlap.

HARCAVE, SIDNEY
1964   *First Blood, the Russian Revolution of 1905,* London: Macmillan.

HARGREAVES, JOHN
1967   *West Africa: The Former French States,* Englewood Cliffs, N.J.: Prentice-Hall.

HAZARD, PAUL
1935   *La Crise de la Conscience Européenne,* Paris: Boivin.

HEACOCK, ROLAND
1965 *Understanding the Negro Revolt,* New York: Pageant Press, Inc.

HEBERLE, RUDOLF
1945 *From Democracy to Nazism,* Baton Rouge, La.: Louisiana State University Press.
1951 *Social Movements,* New York: Appleton, Century, Crofts.

HEGEL, G. W. F.
1953 *The Philosophy of Hegel,* New York: The Modern Library.

HELLER, ANDOR
1957 *No More Comrades,* Chicago: Regnery.

HICKS, JOHN D.
1961 *The Populist Revolt,* Nebraska: University of Nebraska Press.

HINES, RALPH, and JAMES E. PIERCE
1965 "Negro Leadership after the Social Crisis," *Phylon* 26, 162–72.

HOBSBAWM, ERIC J.
1959 *Primitive Rebels,* New York: W. W. Norton & Co.

HODGKIN, THOMAS
1957 *Nationalism in Colonial Africa,* New York: New York University Press.
1961 *African Political Parties,* London: Penguin.

HOFSTADTER, RICHARD
1955 *The Age of Reform,* New York: Vintage Books.

HOMANS, GEORGE C.
1964 "Bringing Men Back In," *American Sociological Review* 29 (No. 6) (December), 809–18.

HOOK, SIDNEY
1937 "Violence," in *Encyclopedia of the Social Sciences,* Vol. 15, New York: Macmillan Co.

HOPKINS, TERRENCE K.
1967 "Politics in Uganda: The Buganda Question," in H. Castanio and J. Butler, eds., *Boston Papers in African Politics,* New York: Praeger.

HUIZER, G.
1969 "The Role of Patronage in the Peasant Political Struggle," *Sociologische Gids* 16 (No. 6), 411–16.

HUNTER, FLOYD
1963 *Community Power Structure,* New York: Anchor Books.

HUNTINGTON, SAMUEL
1962 "Patterns of Violence in World Politics," in Samuel Huntington, ed., *Changing Patterns of Military Politics,* Glencoe, Ill.: Free Press.
1968 *Political Order in Changing Societies,* New Haven: Yale University Press.

JACOBS, PAUL, and SAUL LANDAU
1966 *The New Radicals,* New York: Vintage Books.

JAMES, C. L. R.
1963 *The Black Jacobins,* New York: Vintage Books.

JANOWITZ, MORRIS
  1969   "Patterns of Collective Racial Violence," in H. D. Graham and
         T. R. Gurr, eds., *Violence in America,* New York: Signet Books.
JAYAWARDENA, CHANDRA
  1968   "Ideology and Conflict in Lower Class Communities," *Comparative
         Studies in Society and History* X (No. 4) (July 1968).
JENCKS, CHRISTOPHER, and DAVID RIESMAN
  1968   *The Academic Revolution,* Garden City, N.Y.: Doubleday.
JOHNSON, CHALMERS
  1966   *Revolutionary Change,* Boston: Little, Brown and Co.
KAMENKA, EUGENE
  1967   "The Concept of Political Revolution," in Carl Friedrich, ed.,
         Revolution, Nomos VIII, New York: Atherton Press.
KATZ, ELIHU, and PAUL F. LAZARSFELD
  1955   *Personal Influence,* Clencoe, Ill.: The Free Press.
KECSKEMETI, PAUL
  1961   *The Unexpected Revolution,* Stanford, Cal.: Stanford University
         Press.
KILLIAN, LEWIS
  1965a "Social Movements," in Robert Faris, ed., *Handbook of Modern
         Sociology,* Chicago: Rand McNally, 426–55.
  1965b "Community Structure and the Role of the Negro Leader Agent,"
         Sociological Inquiry 35 (No. 1), 69–79.
KILLIAN, LEWIS, and CHARLES SMITH
  1960   "Negro Protest Leaders in a Southern Community," *Social Forces*
         38 (No. 3), March, 253–58.
KILLINGWORTH, CHARLES, C.
  1969   "Jobs and Incomes for Negroes," in Irwin Katz and Patricia Gurin,
         eds., *Race and the Social Sciences,* New York: Basic Books.
KING, MARTIN LUTHER, JR.
  1964   *Stride Towards Freedom,* New York: Harper and Row.
KOHN, HANS
  1955   *Nationalism,* Princeton, N.J.: D. Van Nostrand Co.
KORNHAUSER, WILLIAM
  1959   *The Politics of Mass Society,* Glencoe, Ill.: Free Press.
  1964   "Rebellion and Political Development," in Harry Eckstein, ed.,
         Internal War, New York: Free Press.
KRAFT, JOSEPH
  1961   *The Struggle for Algeria,* Garden City, N.Y.: Doubleday.
KUPER, LEO
  1957   *Passive Resistance in South Africa,* New Haven: Yale University
         Press.
KUPER, LEO, and M. G. SMITH
  1971   *Pluralism in Africa,* Berkeley: University of California Press.
LABROUSSE, E.
  1949   "Comment Naissent les Révolutions," *Actes du Congres Historique
         du Centenaire de la Révolution de 1848,* Paris: Presses Universi-
         taires de France.

LADD, EVERETT C., JR.
1966   *Negro Political Leadership in the South*, Ithaca, N.Y.: Cornell University Press.

LANE, ROBERT
1962   *Political Ideology*, New York: Free Press.

LANTERNARI, VITTORIO
1968   *The Religions of the Oppressed*, New York: Knopf.

LASSWELL, HAROLD, and DANIEL LERNER
1966   *World Revolutionary Elites*, Cambridge, Mass.: The MIT Press.

LAUE, JAMES
1965   "The Changing Character of Negro Protest," *The Annals* 357 (Jan. 1965).

LAZARSFELD, PAUL F.
1959   "Reflections on Business," *American Journal of Sociology* 65 (July), 1–31.
1961   "Notes on the History of Quantification in Sociology," *ISIS* 52, Part 2 (June), 277–333.

LAZARSFELD, PAUL F., BERNARD BERELSON, AND HAZEL GAUDET
1948   *The People's Choice*, New York: Columbia University Press.

LAZARSFELD, PAUL F., and ANTHONY OBERSCHALL
1965   "Max Weber and Empirical Social Research," *American Sociological Review* 30 (No. 2) (April), 185–99.

LAZARSFELD, PAUL F., and MORRIS ROSENBERG
1955   *The Language of Social Research*, New York: The Free Press.

LE BON, GUSTAVE
1895   *Psychologie des Foules*, Paris: Alcan.
1918   *La Révolution Française et la Psychologie des Révolutions*, Paris.

LECUYER, BERNARD, and ANTHONY OBERSCHALL
1968   "Sociology: The Early History of Social Research," in *International Encyclopedia of the Social Sciences*, New York: Crowell, Collier and Macmillan.

LEE, A. M., and N. D. HUMPHREY
1943   *Race Riot*, New York: Dryden Press.

LEE, MING T.
1968   "The Founders of the Chinese Communist Party," *Civilisations* 18.

LEE, SHU-CHING
1951   "Agrarianism and Social Upheaval in China," *American Journal of Sociology* 56, 511–18.

LEFEBVRE, GEORGES
1957   *The Coming of the French Revolution*, New York: Vintage Books.

LEMARCHAND, RENE
1968   "Revolutionary phenomena in stratified societies: Rwanda and Zanzibar," *Civilisations* 18.

LEPSIUS, REINER
1966   "Parteiensystem und Sozialstruktur," in Wilhelm Abel, ed., *Wirtschaft, Geschichte and Wirtschaftsgeschichte*, Stuttgart: Fischer.

LEVENSTEIN, ADOLF
>1912   *Die Arbeiterfrage*, München: Rheinhardt.

LIEBERSON, STANLEY, and ARNOLD SILVERMAN
>1965   "The Precipitants and Underlying conditions of Race Riots," *American Sociological Review* 30 (No. 6), 887–98.

LINCOLN, C. ERIC
>1961   *The Black Muslims in America*, Boston: Beacon Press.
>1964   "The Negro's Middle Class Dream," *New York Times Magazine*, October 24, 1964.

LIPSET, SEYMOUR M.
>1950   "Leadership and New Social Movements," in Alvin Gouldner, ed., *Studies in Leadership*, New York: Harper and Row.
>1963   *Political Man*, New York: Doubleday Anchor.
>1966   *Agrarian Socialism*, New York: Doubleday Anchor.

LIPSET, SEYMOUR M., and PHILIP ALTBACH
>1966   "Student Politics in Higher Education in the U.S.," *Comparative Education Review* 10 (No. 2), 320–49.

LIPSET, SEYMOUR M., and SHELDON WOLIN
>1965   *The Berkeley Student Revolt*, New York: Doubleday Anchor.

LITTLE, KENNETH
>1965   *West African Urbanization*, New York: Cambridge University Press.

LOMAX, LOUIS
>1963   *The Negro Revolt*, New York: Signet Books.

LOOMIS, CHARLES, and A. BEAGLE
>1946   "The Spread of Nazism in Rural Areas," *American Sociological Review* 11.

LORWIN, VAL
>1957   "Reflections on the History of the French and American Labor Movements," *Journal of Economic History* 17, 25–44.

McCLOSKY, HERBERT
>1964   "Consensus and Ideology in American Politics," *American Political Science Review* 58, 361–82.

McNEELY, JOHN
>1966   "Origins of the Zapata Revolt in Morelos," *The Hispanic-American Historical Review* 46, 153–69.

McNEIL, ELTON, ed.
>1965   *The Nature of Human Conflict*, Englewood Cliffs, N.J.: Prentice-Hall.

MAIR, LUCY
>1963   *New Nations*, Chicago: Chicago University Press.

MANNHEIM, KARL
>1936   *Ideology and Utopia*, New York: Harcourt, Brace & World.

MARSCHAK, JACOB
>1946   "Neumann's and Morgenstern's New Approach to Static Economics," *The Journal of Political Economy* 54 (No. 2) (April), 97–115.

MARSHALL, T. H.
  1965 "Citizenship and Social Class," in *Class, Citizenship and Social Development*, New York: Anchor Books.
MARTIN, JOHN B.
  1957 *The Deep South Says Never*, New York: Ballantine Books, Inc.
MARX, KARL
  1959 "The Class Struggles in France," in Lewis S. Feuer, ed., *Marx and Engels, Basic Writings on Politics and Philosophy*, Garden City, New York: Anchor Books.
MARX, KARL, and FREDERICH ENGELS
  1959 *Basic Writings on Politics and Philosophy*, New York: Anchor Books.
MATTHEWS, DONALD
  1954 *The Social Background of Political Decision Makers*, New York: Random House.
MATTHEWS, DONALD R., and JAMES W. PROTHRO
  1966 *Negroes and the New Southern Politics*, New York: Harcourt, Brace and World.
MBOYA, TOM
  1963 *Freedom and After*, London: Deutsch.
MEIER, AUGUST
  1965 "On the role of Martin Luther King," in *New Politics* 4 (No. 1).
MEIER, AUGUST, and ELLIOTT RUDWICK
  1968 "Negro Protest and Urban Unrest," *Social Science Quarterly* 49 (No. 3).
MERAY, TIBOR
  1960 *Imre Nagy*, Paris: Juillard.
MERRIMAN, ROBERT B.
  1963 *Six Contemporary Revolutions*, Hamden, Conn.: Anchor Books.
MERTON, ROBERT K.
  1957 *Social Theory and Social Structure*, Glencoe, Ill.: Free Press of Glencoe.
MICHELS, ROBERT
  1906 "Die Deutsche Sozialdemocratie," in *Archiv für Sozialwissenschaft und Sozialpolitik* 23.
  1937 "Intellectuals," *Encyclopedia of Social Sciences IV*, New York: The Macmillan Company.
  1959 *Political Parties*, New York: Dover Publications.
MIDDLETON, JOHN
  1969 "Labor Migration and Associations in Africa," *Civilisations* 19 (No. 1).
MILLER, ROBERT
  1966 *Nonviolence*, New York: Schocken Books.
MILLS, C. WRIGHT
  1951 *White Collar*, New York: Oxford University Press.

MONAHAN, THOMAS and ELISABETH
　1956   "Some Characteristics of American Negro Leaders," *American Sociological Review* 21, 580–96.
MOORE, BARRINGTON, JR.
　1966   *Social Origins of Dictatorship and Democracy,* Boston: Beacon Press.
MOORE, WILBERT E.
　1963   *Social Change,* Englewood Cliffs, N.J.: Prentice-Hall.
MORRIS, D. M.
　1960   "The Recruitment of an Industrial Labor Force in India," *Comparative Studies in Society and History* 2 (No. 3), 305–28.
MOYNIHAN, DANIEL P.
　1970   "Memorandum to President Nixon," *New York Times,* Wednesday, March 11, 1970, p. 30.
MURPHY, RAYMOND, and JAMES WATSON
　1967   *The Structure of Discontent,* Los Angeles, Cal.: Institute of Government and Public Affairs, UCLA.
MYRDAL, GUNNAR
　1944   *An American Dilemma,* New York: Harper & Bros.
NASH, MANNING
　1966   *Primitive and Peasant Economic Systems,* San Francisco: Chandler.
NEEDLER, MARTIN
　1966   "Political Development and Military Intervention in Latin America," *American Political Science Review* 60, September.
NEWFIELD, JACK
　1966   *A Prophetic Minority,* New York: Signet Books.
NISBET, ROBERT A.
　1966   *The Sociological Tradition,* New York: Basic Books.
OBERSCHALL, ANTHONY
　1968   "The Los Angeles Riot," *Social Problems* 15, Winter.
　1970   "Group Violence," *Law and Society Review* 5 (No. 1), August.
O'CONNELL, JAMES
　1968   "The Scope of the Tragedy," *Africa Report,* February.
O'LESSKER, KARL
　1969   "Who Voted for Hitler," *American Journal of Sociology* 74.
OLSON, MANCUR, JR.
　1963   "Rapid Economic Growth as a Destabilizing Force," *Journal of Economic History* 23, 529–52.
　1968   *The Logic of Collective Action,* New York: Schocken Books.
OXAAL, IVAR
　1968   *Black Intellectuals Come to Power,* Cambridge: Schenkman.
PALMER, PAUL
　1953   "The Concept of Public Opinion in Political Theory," in Bernard Berelson and Morris Janowitz, eds., *Reader in Public Opinion and Propaganda,* Glencoe, Ill.: The Free Press.

PALMER, R. R.

1955 *A History of the Modern World,* New York: Knopf.

1959 "Sur la composition de la Gauche à la Constituante," *Annales historiques de la Révolution, Française,* 31.

PARETO, VILFREDO

1963 *The Mind and Society,* New York: Dover Publication.

PARSONS, TALCOTT

1949 *The Structure of Social Action,* Glencoe, Ill.: The Free Press.

1951 *The Social System,* Glencoe, Ill.: The Free Press.

1960 *Structure and Process in Modern Societies,* Glencoe, Ill.: Free Press.

PARSONS, TALCOTT, et al.

1961 *Theories of Society,* Vol. I, New York: The Free Press of Glencoe.

PETERSON, RICHARD E.

1968 *The Scope of Organized Student Protest in 1967–68,* Princeton, N.J.: Educational Testing Service.

PETRAS, JAMES

1968 "Revolution and Guerrilla Movements in Latin America: Venezuela, Colombia, Guatemala, and Peru," in James Petras and Maurice Zeitlin, eds., *Latin America, Reform or Revolution,* New York: Fawcett Publications.

PETRAS, JAMES, and MAURICE ZEITLIN

1967 "Miners and Agrarian Radicalism," *American Sociological Review* 32.

1968 "Miners and Agrarian Radicalism in Chile," *British Journal of Sociology* 19.

PETTEE, GEORGE

1938 *The Process of Revolution,* New York: Harper and Bros.

PETTIGREW, THOMAS

1964 *A Profile of the Negro American,* Princeton, N.J.: D. Van Nostrand Co.

PINARD, MAURICE

1968 "Mass Society and Political Movements," *American Journal of Sociology* 73.

PIRENNE, HENRI

1958 *Economic and Social History of Medieval Europe,* New York: Harvest Books.

POSTGATE, R. W.

1962 *Revolution from 1789 to 1906,* New York: Harper Torchbook.

QUETELET, ADOLPHE

1848 *Du Système Social et des Lois qui le Régissent,* Paris.

RADKEY, OLIVER

1950 *The Election to the Russian Constitutent Assembly of 1917,* Cambridge, Mass.: Harvard University Press.

RAPOPORT, ANATOL

1965 "Game Theory and Human Conflict," in Elton McNeil, ed., *The Nature of Human Conflict,* Englewood Cliffs, N.J.: Prentice-Hall.

REED, JOHN
    1967   *Ten Days That Shook the World,* New York: Signet.
REISCHAUER, EDWIN O.
    1965   *Japan, Past and Present,* New York: A. Knopf.
RICHARDSON, LEWIS F.
    1960   *Statistics of Deadly Quarrels,* Chicago: Quadrangle Books.
RINGER, FRITZ
    1969   *The Decline of the German Mandarins,* Cambridge, Mass.: Harvard University Press.
ROBINSON, G. T.
    1967   *Rural Russia Under the Old Regime,* Berkeley: University of California Press.
ROGIN, MICHAEL
    1967   *The Intellectuals and McCarthy,* Cambridge, Mass.: The MIT Press.
ROSBERG, CARL, and JOHN NOTTINGHAM
    1966   *The Myth of Mau Mau,* New York: Praeger.
RUDÉ, GEORGE
    1962   *Wilkes and Liberty,* Oxford: Clarendon Press.
    1964   *The Crowd in History,* New York: Wiley.
    1967   *The Crowd in the French Revolution,* New York: Oxford University Press.
RUDOLPH, L. I., and S. H. RUDOLPH
    1966   "The Political Role of India's Caste Associations," in Immanuel Wallerstein, ed., *Social Change,* New York: John Wiley.
RUSTIN, BAYARD
    1965   "From Protest to Politics: The Future of the Civil Rights Movement," *Commentary* 39 (No. 2).
SCHELLING, THOMAS C.
    1963   *The Strategy of Conflict,* New York: Galaxy Books.
SCHNAIBERG, ALLAN
    1969   "Who Voted for Hitler," *American Journal of Sociology* 74 (No. 6).
SCHNEIDER, RONALD
    1959   *Communists in Guatemala, 1944–1954,* New York: Praeger.
SCHOENBAUM, DAVID
    1966   *Hitler's Social Revolution,* New York: Doubleday.
SCHUMPETER, PETER
    1955   *Imperialism and Social Classes,* New York: Doubleday Anchor Books.
SEALE, PATRICK, and MAUREEN MCCONVILLE
    1968   *Red Flag, Black Flag,* New York: Ballantine Books, Inc.
SEARLES, RUTH, and J. ALLEN WILLIAMS
    1962   "Negro College Students' Participation in Sit-Ins," *Social Forces* 40, March, 215–20.
SHERIF, MUZAFER
    1956   "Experiments in Group Conflict," *Scientific American,* November.

1966 *In Common Predicament: The Social Psychology of Intergroup Conflict and Cooperation,* Boston: Houghton-Mifflin.

SHILS, EDWARD
1961 "The Intellectuals in Indian Political Development," in Dwaine Marvick, ed., *Political Decision Makers,* Glencoe, Ill.: Free Press.

SILBERMAN, CHARLES
1964 *Crisis in Black and White,* New York: Random House.

SKLAR, RICHARD
1963 *Nigerian Political Parties,* Princeton, N.J.: Princeton University Press.

SKLAR, RICHARD, and C. S. WHITAKER, JR.
1964 "Nigeria," chap. 16 in James Coleman and Carl Rosberg, Jr., eds., *Political Parties and National Integration in Tropical Africa,* Berkeley: University of California Press.

1966 "The Federal Republic of Nigeria," in Gwendolyn Carter, ed., *National Unity and Regionalism in Eight African States,* Ithaca, N.Y.: Cornell University Press.

SKOLNICK, JEROME
1969 *The Politics of Protest,* New York: Ballantine Books, Inc.

SMELSER, NEIL J.
1959 *Social Change in the Industrial Revolution,* Chicago: Chicago University Press.

1963 *Theory of Collective Behavior,* New York: Free Press.

1968 *Essays in Sociological Explanation,* Englewood Cliffs, N.J.: Prentice-Hall.

1970 "Two Critics in Search of a Bias," *The Annals* 391 (September), 46–55.

SOROKIN, PITRIM
1927/8 "Leaders of Labor and Radical Movements in the U.S. and Foreign Countries," *American Journal of Sociology* 33.

SOUTHERN REGIONAL COUNCIL
1960 *Intimidation, Reprisal, and Violence in the South's Racial Crisis,* Atlanta, Ga.

1961 "Organizations Supporting the Student Protest Movement," Report L-28, November 30, 1961. Atlanta, Ga., stencil.

1966 *The Continuing Crisis: An Assessment of New Racial Tensions in the South,* Atlanta, Ga.

STAVRIANOS, L. S.
1957 "Antecedents to the Balkan Revolutions of the 19th century," *Journal of Modern History* 29.

STINCHCOMBE, ARTHUR
1965 "Social Structure and Organizations," in James G. March, ed., *Handbook of Organizations,* Chicago: Rand McNally.

1968 *Constructing Social Theories,* New York: Harcourt Brace Jovanovich, Inc.

STONE, LAURENCE
1965 "Theories of Revolution," *World Politics* 18, 159–76.

STOUFFER, SAMUEL
  1966   *Communism, Conformity and Civil Liberties,* New York: Science Editions.
TAFT, PHILIP
  1966   "Violence in American Labor Disputes," *Annals of the American Academy of Social and Political Science,* March 1966.
TALMON, YONINA
  1962   "Pursuit of the Millenium: the relation between religions and social change," *European Journal of Sociology* 3.
TARDE, GABRIEL
  1893   "Foules et Sectes au Point de vue Criminel," *Revue des Deux Mondes* (November 15).
  1969   *On Communication and Social Influence,* Chicago: Phoenix Books.
THUCYDIDES
  1960   *The History of the Peloponnesian War,* Sir Richard Livingstone, ed., New York: Oxford University Press.
TILLY, CHARLES
  1964a   *The Vendée,* Cambridge, Mass.: Harvard University Press.
  1964b   "Reflections on the Revolutions of Paris," *Social Problems* 11.
  1969   "Collective Violence in European Perspective," chapter 1 in Hugh Davis Graham and Ted Robert Gurr, *Violence in America,* New York: Signet Special.
  1970   "From Mobilization to Political Conflict," unpublished paper, University of Michigan.
TILLY, CHARLES, and JAMES RULE
  1965   *Measuring Political Upheaval,* Princeton, N.J.: Princeton Center of International Studies Research Monograph No. 19.
TOBIN, JAMES
  1965   "On Improving the Economic Status of the Negro," *Daedalus* (Fall), 878–98.
TOCQUEVILLE, ALEXIS DE
  1955   *The Old Regime and the French Revolution,* New York: Doubleday Anchor.
TOTTEN, GEORGE
  1960   "Labor and Agrarian Disputes in Japan Following World War I," *Economic Development and Culture Change* 9, No. 1, Part II, 187–212.
TROTTER, WILLIAM
  1916   *Instincts of Herd in Peace and War,* London.
TROTSKY, LEON
  1923   *Die Russische Revolution, 1905,* Berlin: Vereinigung Internationaler Verlagsanstalten.
  1959   *The Russian Revolution,* New York: Doubleday Anchor.
TURNER, RALPH
  1964a   "Collective Behavior," in Robert E. Faris, *Handbook of Modern Sociology,* Chicago: Rand McNally.

1964b "Collective Behavior and Conflict," *Sociological Quarterly* V, 122–32.

1967 "Introduction," in Robert E. Park, *On Social Control and Collective Behavior*, Chicago: Phoenix Books.

1969 "The Public Perception of Protest," *American Sociological Review* 34 (No. 6), 815–31.

TURNER, RALPH, and LEWIS KILLIAN, eds.

1957 *Collective Behavior*, Englewood Cliffs, N.J.: Prentice-Hall, Inc.

UNITED NATIONS

1957 *Report of the Special Committee on the Problem of Hungary*, New York: General Assembly, Eleventh Session, Supplement No. 18 (A3592).

U.S. RIOT COMMISSION

1968 *Report of the National Advisory Commission on Civil Disorders*, New York: Bantam Books.

VENTURE

1966 Vol. 18 (No. 5), June, Ghana issue.

WALLERSTEIN, IMMANUEL

1964 "Voluntary Associations," in James S. Coleman and Carl G. Rosberg, eds., *Political Parties and National Integration in Tropical Africa*, Berkeley: University of California Press.

WASKOW, ARTHUR I.

1967 *From Race Riot to Sit-in, 1919 and the 1960's*, New York: Doubleday Anchor.

WATTERS, PAT

1965 "Encounter with the Future," Southern Regional Council, Atlanta, Ga.: May.

WEBER, MAX

1906 "Russlands Ubergang Zum Scheinkonstitualismus," *Archiv für Sozialwissenshaft und Sozialpolitik* 23.

1909 "Zur Methodik Sozial-psychologischer Engueten und ihrer Bearbeitung," *Archiv für Sozialwissenschaft und Sozialpolitik* 29, 949–58.

1924 *Gesammelte Aufsätze zur Soziologie und Sozialpolitik*, Tübingen: J. C. B. Mohr.

1947 *The Theory of Social and Economic Organization*, Glencoe, Ill.: Free Press.

1958 *From Max Weber, Essays in Sociology*, New York: Oxford University Press.

WILSON, JAMES, Q.

1960 *Negro Politics: the Search for Leadership*, New York: Free Press.

1961 "The Strategy of protest: Problem of Negro civic action," *Journal of Conflict Resolution* 5, 291–303.

WINSTON, SANFORD

1931 "Studies in Negro Leadership," *American Journal of Sociology* 37, 595–602.

WIRTH, LOUIS
    1957   "Types of Minority Movements," in Ralph Turner and Lewis Killian, eds., *Collective Behavior*, New York: Prentice-Hall, pp. 321–26.
WOLF, ERIC
    1955   "Types of Latin American Peasantry," *American Anthropologist* 57 (No. 3).
    1966   *Peasants*, Englewood Cliffs, N.J.: Prentice-Hall, Inc.
    1969   *Peasant Wars of the Twentieth Century*, New York: Harper and Row.
WOLFE, BETRAM
    1957   *Khrushchev and Stalin's Ghost*, New York: Praeger.
WOLFINGER, RAYMOND, et.al.
    1964   "America's Radical Right," in David Apter, ed., *Ideology and Discontent*, Glencoe, Ill.: Free Press.
WOMACK, JOHN, JR.
    1969   *Zapata and the Mexican Revolution*, New York: Knopf.
WRIGHT, CHARLES
    1959   *Mass Communications*, New York: Random House.
YOUNG, M. CRAWFORD
    1966   "The Obote Revolution," *Africa Report* 11, June.
ZINN, HOWARD
    1964   *SNCC, The New Abolitionists*, Boston: Beacon Press.
ZOLBERG, ARISTIDE
    1966   *Creating Political Order*, Chicago: Rand McNally.

INDEX